Unsettling Cather

CATHER STUDIES

CATHER STUDIES 14

Unsettling Cather

Edited by Marilee Lindemann
and Ann Romines

UNIVERSITY OF NEBRASKA PRESS | LINCOLN

The University of Nebraska Press is part of a land-grant institution with campuses and programs on the past, present, and future homelands of the Pawnee, Ponca, Otoe-Missouria, Omaha, Dakota, Lakota, Kaw, Cheyenne, and Arapaho Peoples, as well as those of the relocated Ho-Chunk, Sac and Fox, and Iowa Peoples.

The series Cather Studies is sponsored by the Cather Project at the University of Nebraska–Lincoln.

Library of Congress Cataloging-in-Publication Data
Names: Lindemann, Marilee, editor. | Romines, Ann, 1942– editor.
Title: Unsettling Cather / edited by Marilee Lindemann and
Ann Romines.
Description: Lincoln: University of Nebraska Press, [2025] | Series:
Cather studies; 14 | Includes bibliographical references and index.
Identifiers: LCCN 2024016833
ISBN 9781496241290 (paperback)
ISBN 9781496241825 (epub)
ISBN 9781496241832 (pdf)
Subjects: LCSH: Cather, Willa, 1873–1947—Criticism and interpretation. | American literature—20th century—History and criticism. | American literature—Women authors—History and criticism. | BISAC: LITERARY CRITICISM / Modern / 19th Century | LITERARY CRITICISM / Women Authors
Classification: LCC PS3505.A87 Z885 2025 | DDC 813/.52—dc23/eng/20241010
LC record available at https://lccn.loc.gov/2024016833

Set in Sabon Next LT Pro by A. Shahan.

CONTENTS

ILLUSTRATIONS

Introduction

Unsettling Cather

ANN ROMINES AND MARILEE LINDEMANN

For the Seventeenth International Willa Cather Seminar, held in June 2019, we invited Cather scholars and readers to join us for six days at Shenandoah University, in the Shenandoah Valley of Virginia, the lush and complex site of Willa Cather's birth and first nine years. Here, as an observant daughter of a privileged white family, Cather first encountered differences and dislocations that remained lively, productive, and sometimes deeply troubling sites of tension and energy throughout her writing life, extending to and beyond her last novel, *Sapphira and the Slave Girl*, set in her family's Virginia.

Seminar participants visited many places that were important to young Willa's family—and to other Virginians, both Black and white—as they experienced the persistent powers of enslavement, the French and Indian War (one of Cather's best-known ancestors was a prominent local "Indian fighter" in the eighteenth century), the Revolutionary War, the Civil War, and the Reconstruction era. They also visited the still-new National Museum of African American History and Culture in Washington DC to learn more about how institutionalized enslavement had shaped the world into which Cather was born.

ANN ROMINES AND MARILEE LINDEMANN

Of course the sixty-five papers presented at this seminar, as well as the conversations they sparked, were not rooted solely in Virginia. They covered the whole expanse of Cather's life and work. We hoped that this seminar would unsettle some of our prevailing assumptions about Cather's work and a life that moved from Virginia to Nebraska to Pittsburgh to New York City to New Mexico and farther west, and to Grand Manan Island. Experiences of difference and dislocation, which began for Cather early in her Virginia childhood, continued until her death in 1947 and her New Hampshire burial. We were especially eager to hear from new voices with new perspectives on Cather and the conference theme as we came together in a beautiful Virginia summer week, when the state was observing the four hundredth anniversary of enslavement, begun in the new Virginia colony in 1619, as well as the annual celebration of Emancipation known as Juneteenth.

Seminar participants did not disappoint us. The thirteen essays in this volume of the Cather Studies series are a rich sampling of the fresh and provocative scholarship shared in Virginia in 2019. We welcomed both familiar and new voices, and they introduced us to a variety of compelling ways of seeing and situating Cather's texts—ways that both unsettle and advance Cather scholarship. We have organized the volume in loose groups or clusters of essays that examine a common text or theme. We begin with four essays on *Sapphira and the Slave Girl* that, in different ways, build upon the project begun in Toni Morrison's influential reading, in *Playing in the Dark*, of how race shapes and misshapes the novel. Sarah Clere examines material culture in *Sapphira* and finds that, although that discourse is often oriented toward white characters in positions of power, considering the "historical context and function of objects and household spaces fractures the dominance of the narrative's white perspective and provides insight into the lives of its Black characters." Clere argues that "objects in *Sapphira and the Slave Girl* frequently undermine the idea of a static identity determined by race and social class, pointing instead to the possibility of adaptation and ultimately self-fashioning." Barry Hudek explores biblical allusions in the novel, including some that Cather excised from the typescript, which serves as evidence of the author's awareness of a justice-oriented mode of reading the Bible that would later be termed Black liberation theology. Although Cather rewrote a clearly subversive scene in which the dying Jezebel asks Henry Colbert to read her the story of the Israelites escaping slavery in Egypt, Hudek sees in numerous remaining biblical allusions and in references to songs and hymns a thread of resistance to the imperialist order that produced and justified slavery. *Sapphira and the Slave Girl* contains, Hudek concludes, "clear moments of identification with and, potentially, celebration of Black liberation theology."

Tracyann Williams's reading of *Sapphira* attends not to resistance but to the persistence in the United States of "the unresolved disease of racism and slavery." Williams sees the novel as "a major work, precisely because it is difficult and uncomfortable." Cather's story of the dropsical Sapphira's obsession with the mixed-race young slave woman "offers a window into the American collective cultural and political psyche and the fraught relationship that exists between the races. Much in the way the miller takes in brown wheat and produces white flour, I argue that Cather is refining away the confusion of changing political dynamics, restoring a world in which a mistress with limited mobility can oppress those around her, denying citizenship and agency to those perceived as Other." Speaking of wheat and flour, Steven Shively concludes our *Sapphira* cluster with a chapter that uses the folk song "Weevily Wheat," which explicitly appears in *My Ántonia* and is more cryptically embedded in *Sapphira*, to affirm that traces of Cather's roots in the South are not confined to the single novel she set in Virginia. Drawing widely on music and cultural history, Shively explores the "racial mobility" of "Weevily Wheat," which had connections to the Scots-Irish people of Britain (from whom Cather was descended) and ties to nineteenth-century Black entertainments (e.g., play-parties) as well as to the coded language enslaved people used to convey messages of resistance and protest. Whatever Cather's intentions in engaging with the song in both *My Ántonia* and *Sapphira*, Shively sees it as "a rich example of the ways Cather mixed experience, memory, and her broad cultural life to create art. The song is present as a Black American cultural artifact that adds significant meaning to the novel and to the ways American culture ignores, conceals, and reveals race."

The chapters in our second cluster use sex and/or gender to frame fresh discussions of Cather's literary influences and cultural engagements in the first decade of her career as a novelist. Hannah Wells revisits the question of Walt Whitman's influence not only on *O Pioneers!* but on Cather's fiction more broadly. Wells looks at the divergent ideals of the pioneer articulated in Whitman's poetry and Cather's prose to ground "an ecofeminist reading that explores the negotiation of a right relationship with the land through the intersection of femininity and pioneerism within Whitman's and Cather's schemata of American western expansion." Molly Metherd examines Cather's rendering of a "female national hero" in *The Song of the Lark*'s Thea Kronborg as a reimagining of the American body politic. Metherd explains that "the nation [Cather] imagines into being is not the nation of nativists in the early twentieth century, that is, singular, monolingual, white. Instead, Cather imagines a nation made up of many cultures. Thea is deeply influenced by her experiences in diverse communities in the United States, and the novel situates the aesthetic spirit of these communities as central to both the development of her artistic genius and to the national character. The work reimagines not only the national hero as woman but also a national consciousness as cosmopolitan." In the final essay of this cluster, Geneva M. Gano puts Cather in conversation with anarchist Emma Goldman and places Lena Lingard at the center of *My Ántonia* to ground the claim that the novel offers "Cather's most affirming portrait of free sexual pleasure and desire." Such a reorientation demonstrates that "despite its explicitly nostalgic tone and androcentric perspective, the novel conveys a recognizably radical feminist argument . . . for a woman's right to control her own body and direct her own economic future." That argument aligns Cather to a surprising degree with the more overt sexual radicalism of Goldman's advocacy of free love. Gano concludes, "Cather shows us that Lena's refusal of marriage and childbearing (though, crucially, not love and pleasure) has enabled her alone to emerge unscathed from a brutal frontier capitalism that relentlessly extracts a physical, intellectual, and emotional toll on the young, poor, immigrant women upon whose labor it depends."

Cather's engagements with particular regions as geopolitical, sociolinguistic, and literary sites are the throughline in our third cluster of contributions, which offer fresh comparisons and probing questions into Cather's contexts and shaping environments. Lisbeth Strimple Fuisz, in "Mapping and (Re)mapping the Nebraska Landscape in the Works of Willa Cather and Francis La Flesche," puts *O Pioneers!* and *My Ántonia* in dialogue with La Flesche's memoir *The Middle Five: Indian Boys at School* to consider how the two writers' "representations of place respond to the imperatives of settler colonialism." Drawing on the insights of critical geography, literary, and Indigenous studies, Fuisz finds that Cather's novels "reproduce dominant settler colonial spatial relationships, thereby participating in the naturalization of those forms," while "La Flesche's portrait of the Omaha Nation in *The Middle Five*, in contrast, unsettles depictions of Nebraska as settler space by establishing spatial imaginaries that pre-date and coexist alongside settler spaces." The comparative strategy has significant interpretive value, as Fuisz explains in her conclusion: "Reading Cather, a settler writer, in the context of an Indigenous contemporary like La Flesche denaturalizes her depictions of the landscape, revealing some assumptions about geography and belonging" that are otherwise difficult to see.

For Sallie Ketcham and Andrew P. Wu, Nebraska is a rich repository of experiences that resonated in Cather's life and writing long after she left the state a year after graduating from college. In "Willa Cather and Mari Sandoz: The Muse and the Story Catcher in the Capital City," Ketcham examines the lasting influence the city of Lincoln had on Cather and on Sandoz, who was born a generation later, in 1896. The chapter is a study of parallels and contrasts, as Ketcham explores how "two iconic Nebraska writers pursued higher education, encountered resistance, navigated the town's matriarchal 'blackball' caste system, and began to mold memory, the raw material of their art." She argues that those formative years in Lincoln and at the University of Nebraska "helped determine the trajectory of their careers, launching Cather toward national and international prominence while consigning Sandoz to regional writer status." Her conclusion makes the case for placing the two writers in conversation: "To read the works of Cather and Sandoz side by side, especially *My Ántonia* and *Old Jules*, two books that draw on such similar material, is to engage in a tale of two conflicting and conflicted Nebraskas. Each informs and explicates the other. Together, they provide human dimension and historical context for Cather's and Sandoz's pivotal years as young, evolving writers, for the Lincoln of their past, and for their strangely parallel yet nonintersecting worlds." In "'Blue Sky, Blue Eyes': Unsettling Multilingualism in *My Ántonia*," Wu focuses on the sociolinguistic environment Cather experienced during the period when her closest neighbors included immigrants from a variety of European countries. *My Ántonia* is at the center of his analysis, but Wu notes that "Cather had a keen ear for language diversity and wove it into her fiction in numerous ways" throughout her career. Indeed, the prominence and frequency of moments of multilingualism help situate Cather within the cultural politics of the late nineteenth and early twentieth centuries, as Wu asserts: "Cather implicitly advocates for a cosmopolitan, multicultural America in which multilingualism is commonplace—not a society in which everything becomes 'Americanized.'"

"Regionalism" and "modernism" have often been viewed as antagonistic modes produced by markedly different sensibilities, but that is not how they operate in Jace Gatzemeyer's reading of *Death Comes for the Archbishop*. In "Regionalism Démeublé: Reflective Nostalgia in Cather's *Death Comes for the Archbishop*," Gatzemeyer brings both formalist and historicist concerns to bear on the question of whether Cather was a regionalist or a modernist. The answer, he suggests, is *both*. Gatzemeyer argues that, in *Archbishop*, "Cather had developed a 'modernist regionalism' grounded in a kind of nostalgic longing that would elicit not disengagement with modernity in favor of a prelapsarian place and time but rather a critical awareness of modernity's potentials and pitfalls. Far from the regressive, reactionary nostalgia identified by her critics in the 1930s, the nostalgia evoked by Cather in this novel was a more decidedly 'modern nostalgia.'" This reflective nostalgia "for the imagined past of a particular regional space" is used "to evoke—without moralizing upon—the shortcomings of modernity and to suggest a better way forward."

Our collection ends with a pair of chapters that challenge a critical consensus that has coalesced against Cather's novel of 1935, *Lucy Gayheart*. Joshua Doležal's "The Neuroscience of Epiphany in *Lucy Gayheart*" is a nuanced rereading of a late and often devalued Cather novel. It uses neuroscientific study of cognitive impasses and sudden insights to ground an argument that Lucy's development is not muddled or failed, as has often been claimed, but that it is instead a recursive movement that ultimately leads to genuine epiphany and "existential triumph" in the character's recognition that "Life itself" is "the sweetheart." For Doležal, Lucy's accidental drowning shortly after she has this realization does not undermine the integrity or value of her epiphany. Elizabeth Wells, in "Unsettling Accompaniment: Disability as Critique of Aesthetic Power in Willa Cather's *Lucy Gayheart*," agrees with Doležal that the shift from the triumphant Thea Kronborg in *The Song of the Lark* to Lucy is not necessarily pessimistic, arguing that it may merely indicate Cather's "perspectival shift away from artistic formation and toward artistic production and accompaniment." Wells draws on disability theory, particularly the concept of "narrative prosthesis," which Sharon Snyder and David Mitchell have described as art's unappreciative reliance upon abnormal bodies, since "authors often need disability, as they rely on it to create meaning, [but] they also demand that it be removed in order to cleanse the narrative; having performed the service of artistic prosthesis, characters with disabilities are then let go." The framework obviously applies to the role of the singer Clement Sebastian's accompanist James Mockford, but Wells also uses it to explore the relationship between Henry Gordon and Lucy Gayheart, arguing that Lucy serves as a kind of prosthesis to Harry. Through her, he can experience the pleasures of "trifling things," like art and nature, without sullying his upstanding reputation. Once he marries, however, Lucy can no longer play that role for Harry and so he pushes her away, and his rejection is partly responsible for her drowning. Wells's reading of Lucy's death accords with Doležal's. She doesn't see it as a sign of the character's weakness or an undermining of her epiphany either. She sees it as a critique of "an aesthetic that consumes its accompanists."

Our seminar program included, for the first time, several Black Americans who now live in Willa Cather's birthplace. One of those voices was that of Barbara Davis, a singer who is a minister at a historic Black church in Winchester, Virginia. More than a year after the seminar, she told us that reading *Sapphira and the Slave Girl* for the first time and sitting in on seminar sessions has given her a "fresh perspective" and helped her to "better understand who Willa Cather is. Her legacy can help us to understand the experience of living an entitled life that is entwined with a history of slavery, such as her memories of being a young girl waiting for 'our Nancy' to come 'home.' The seminar gave me hope. Faith in God's people to always seek the truth" (24).

We share Barbara Davis's insight, and hope, in this troubled time of our national and global life, that the truths our authors pursue in this volume—as Willa Cather did in her fiction—will also bring hope to you.

We can't end this introduction without offering sincere thanks to our contributors for their perseverance and patience in working to complete this volume through the massive disruptions and stresses of a global pandemic. We also appreciate the generosity of colleagues who took the time to review essays and the support of the Willa Cather Foundation, the University of Nebraska Press, and the Cather Project at the University of Nebraska–Lincoln. We owe special thanks to John Jacobs of Shenandoah University, host institution for the seminar, for all he did to assure a smooth and rewarding conference and cultural experience.

WORKS CITED

Davis, Barbara, and Ann Romines. "Songs and *Sapphira*: An Interview with Barbara Davis." *Willa Cather Review*, vol. 62, no. 2, 2021, pp. 23–24.

Unsettling Cather

1 Keepsakes and Treasures

Investigating Material Culture in
Sapphira and the Slave Girl

SARAH CLERE

In Willa Cather's last novel, *Sapphira and the Slave Girl*, the circulation of property in various forms and its connection to people of differing statuses indicate an anthropological awareness of culture as a process that is constantly created and enacted rather than a linear progression of achievements. Within the novel, the discourse surrounding material culture orients itself toward white individuals in positions of power; however, examining the historical context and function of objects and household spaces fractures the dominance of the narrative's white perspective and provides insight into the lives of its African American characters. Objects in *Sapphira and the Slave Girl* frequently undermine the idea of a static identity determined by race and social class, pointing instead to the possibility of adaptation and ultimately self-fashioning.

The novel's evocation of place and culture has been noted by a number of reviewers and critics, but its economic underpinning has thus far gone unexamined. Within a capitalist society, material culture is virtually inextricable from the market economy, and the

1

objects within *Sapphira* bristle with economic meaning. The novel's enslaved characters interact with household objects while they are themselves legally owned objects who circulate as possessions within the lives of the novel's white characters. Attending to the culture of *Sapphira and the Slave Girl* without examining the economic factors that undergird it risks flattening the lives of its enslaved characters and ignoring the regional, seemingly isolated locale of Back Creek's connection to larger historical and economic crosscurrents. Both proslavery rhetoric in the late antebellum South in which the novel is set and the Lost Cause–inflected evocations of slavery that still dominated popular American discourse when the novel was written attempted to soften slavery's atrocities and portray it as a system of benevolent care rather than economic exploitation. The ongoing scholarly work of Daina Ramey Berry, Thavolia Glymph, Stephanie E. Jones-Rogers, and Edward Baptist provides new ways of conceptualizing slavery and has been of incalculable influence to my thinking about Cather's last novel.

The beginning of the novel piles up objects and routines that signal Sapphira's gentility and differentiate her from the other white people in the region. Richard Millington's remark that "*Shadows on the Rock* is the reverse of démeublé: it is a book full of things and the practices of everyday life" (para. 10) applies equally to *Sapphira and the Slave Girl*. Sapphira's china is not just good; it is "surprisingly good to find on the table of a country miller in the Virginia backwoods" (7). Her speech and handwriting are "more cultivated than was common in this backcountry district" (19). Her coach with the "Dodderidge crest" ("that mysterious stamp of superiority"), silver coffee urn, English wallpaper, and worn Wilton carpet link her to an older and more stratified culture. These aspects of Sapphira's lifestyle are equated with her English ancestry, distinguishing her from her husband, whose family are termed "immigrants" because they are from continental Europe. The ordinary white people of Back Creek judge Henry for his lack of a southern accent but accept the differences in Sapphira's speech as the prerogative of someone they think of as "an heiress" (9).

As one who inherits objects, property, and people as well, Sapphira's relative prosperity is evident. Her advantages, however, are not initially displayed as emerging from wealth but are explicitly connected to her social class and heredity. The ancestral origin of the luxury objects in Sapphira's household places them outside of an economic framework. The "heavy Wilton carpet, figured with pink and green leaves," has been "'brought over' by Sapphira's mother" from England and contributes to the "settled comfort and stability" of the parlor (43). Sapphira's parlor carpet, however, links her firmly to the decorating trends of the nascent American middle class. As Shirley Wajda points out, "By 1850 the nation's carpet production had tripled, reducing prices, and the American middle class could enjoy in their parlors, dining rooms, and bedrooms a variety of carpets." Wajda also notes that English carpets that had been "imported to the United States as early as 1790" from "carpetmaking centers such as Axminster and Wilton, remained prized possessions" (192). As this information indicates, Sapphira's Wilton carpet might signal her social class, but it is also an example of a luxury object readily obtainable by anyone with sufficient money. The framing of the carpet as an ancestral object connected to Sapphira's genteel background divorces it and the other household objects from nineteenth-century consumer culture. Richard Bushman comments on the symbiosis between luxury goods and the market economy: "Capitalism and gentility should have been enemies. But they were not. Capitalism and gentility were allies in forming the modern economy" (xvii).

At other points in the novel, however, Cather herself destabilizes the association of luxury goods with birth and ancestry. Sapphira's silver coffee urn appears to separate her from the Bethel Church congregation and its "poor plate" just as her good china seemingly signals her family's difference from the poor white Appalachian woman Mandy Ringer, who brings out her "blue chiney cups and plates" when Rachel visits (123). Mandy Ringer's treasured but common china cups and plates (probably, according to Ann Romines's note in the scholarly edition, Staffordshire transferware imported in mass quantities) likewise could be seen as differentiating her from the enslaved people to whose gourd dishes the novel refers (473n123). Cather, however, shows connections with particular domestic objects as economically and socially constructed rather than foreordained and inevitable. Rachel Blake, Sapphira's daughter, displays her own knowledge of silver when she tells Mandy Ringer that the stolen Bethel communion service "aint silver at all. It's plated stuff, and poor plate at that, I can tell you" (127). Rachel might eschew many of the values of the society within which she was raised and spent the first part of her adult life, but she maintains and deploys the knowledge her upbringing and experiences give her.

Mandy Ringer admires the knowledge and experience that allow Rachel to judge the quality of the Bethel communion service but attributes it to Rachel's time in Washington rather than her upbringing in Sapphira's quasi-aristocratic household, telling Rachel, "I wish I could a-had your chance, mam. It's city life that learns you, an' I'd a-loved it!" (128). Mrs. Ringer views Rachel's discernment not as the inevitable product of ancestry but as learned skill derived from urban living, one that a mountain woman like herself could attain if she had the opportunity. Rachel herself learns fine cooking from Sarah, a "free mulatto woman from New Orleans" whom she meets in Washington (139). Sarah's enslaver has freed her, and she supports herself in Washington by cooking food for dinner parties. Till acquires her domestic skills from the English housekeeper Mrs. Matchem, also unhinging vocation from ethnicity and cultural background. Again, we see Cather using a comparative, anthropological model of culture as shared behavior and knowledge.

Within the novel enslaved people are conspicuously absent from the culture of manufactured china and dishware. Cather instead elaborates on enslaved people's use of gourds: "[T]hey were cut into dippers for drinking, and bowls for holding meal, butter, lard, gravy, or any tidbit that might be spirited away from the big kitchen to one of the cabins. Whatever was carried away in a gourd was not questioned. The gourd vessels were invisible to good manners" (24). This passage, which includes a description of the gourd vines twining around slave cabins, contributes to the novel's pastoral tone and reinforces the myth of the plantation as a premodern, self-sufficient space divorced from the larger market economy. Through an examination of local merchants' ledgers and objects unearthed during fieldwork, anthropologist Matthew Greer has uncovered evidence that enslaved people in the northern Shenandoah Valley did in fact participate in the culture of commercial dishware and tea drinking, purchasing tea and using china implements in its preparation and serving: "While enslaved Southerners certainly used these plants to make a variety of household items, the humble gourd was not the only container they owned. Rather, enslaved people purchased and used a wide range of ceramic vessels" ("Cather and Enslaved Life" 4).

The hilly Virginia landscape where the events of the novel play out is itself foregrounded as a possession whose ownership and use shift historically. Cather paradoxically provides readers with more detail about the mechanics of land transfer and ownership in her southern novel than she gives in either *O Pioneers!* or *My Ántonia*, her two frontier novels. Sapphira and Henry's relationship is a cultural and religious fusion, with Henry as the descendant of dissenting working people and Sapphira connected to the landed aristocracy and the Church of England. Their disparate backgrounds come together seemingly harmoniously in the Mill House, built following their marriage in the settlement of Back Creek. The site of Sapphira and Henry's home is a microcosm of European settlement and expansion. Despite the fact that it was ostensibly owned by Thomas, Lord Fairfax and deeded to Sapphira's ancestor Nathaniel Dodderidge around 1647 (28), the land is named and delineated by its Indigenous inhabitants and not deemed safe for European relocation until 1759 (Cather 29). The English settlement of Back Creek begins with a colonial land grant, becomes a type of early frontier narrative, and is then connected to the American Revolution and independence from England. The Revolutionary-era origins of the gristmill that Henry eventually takes over are mentioned twice in the novel. Combined with the history of Sapphira's and Henry's European families and the elderly Jezebel's African birth and experience of the Middle Passage, this brief narrative of the landscape of Back Creek gives the most complete account of origins and migration in any of Cather's novels.

The Revolutionary-era mill becomes an Early Republic home when Sapphira and Henry create the Mill House. Cather notes that, because of its resemblance to Mount Vernon, the Mill House would be familiar to Virginians. Within the novel's context, the explicit connection to Mount Vernon and George Washington presents a mythologized version of American respectability and even refinement. Bushman, however, calls such houses "one of the fixtures of the Southern landscape around 1850" and "the dwelling form most typical of middling farmers in the upland South" (396). He matter-of-factly designates I-houses like the Mill House to be regional "vernacular housing" divorced from the main architectural trends of the more fashionable North. Sapphira's coach with its crest might well have seemed a discordant accompaniment to such a home-spun house. The family portraits—of Sapphira and Henry—that so impress Nancy are also recent; they have been painted by a Cuban painter from Baltimore. Like the architecture of the house, they signify Sapphira and Henry's self-conscious creation of their own American familial line in the Virginia backwoods.

I-houses in the mode of Mount Vernon might not have been the height of fashion throughout America in the nineteenth century, but during the 1930s, when Cather was thinking about her family's past and writing *Sapphira*, such houses had gained a new vogue. Linked to the frequent colonial revivals in American design and no doubt influenced by the 1932 celebration of the bicentennial of George Washington's birth, homes inspired by Mount Vernon appeared in multiple popular contexts. In 1937 *Ladies' Home Journal* published both architectural and interior design plans for a Mount Vernon–inspired house. Catering to Americans of more modest means, both Sears and Aladdin marketed versions of their popular mail-order kit homes in the style of Mount Vernon. The Sears kit home takes a particularly broad view of Revolutionary War–era history by calling its Mount Vernon–inflected home "The Jefferson." The actual Mount

Fig. 1.1. The Mill House in Gore, Virginia. This photo was taken in April 1976 by Willa Cather's niece, Ella Cather Lewis. During the period in which *Sapphira and the Slave Girl* is set, the house was owned by Jacob F. and Ruhamah Seibert, Willa Cather's maternal great-grandparents and the prototypes for Henry and Sapphira. PHO-4-W689-1179. Willa Cather Pioneer Memorial Collection, Willa Cather Foundation Collections and Archives, National Willa Cather Center, Red Cloud, Nebraska.

Vernon was at that time experiencing unprecedented popularity as a tourist attraction. Lydia Mattice Brandt writes that the Mount Vernon Ladies' Association "refused to endorse the widespread commercialization of the house and embarked upon an aggressive preservation and research campaign in an effort to maintain its hold on an 'authentic' vision of Washington's home" (129). Contemporary American readers of *Sapphira and the Slave Girl* would have been nearly as familiar with the style of Mount Vernon and thus the novel's version of the Mill House as nineteenth-century Virginians would have. Cather herself might have read about the extensive improvements being made to the house and its surrounding landscaping in a 1938 *New York Times* article intended to publicize the historic attraction (Brandt 153).

Unlike Till, who is never content in Back Creek, Sapphira does not directly criticize the Mill House or its rustic environment, but the novel offers some evidence that she is aware of her diminished status. When Henry states that he is the first miller who has made a living in Back Creek, she responds, "A poor one at that, we must own" (10). One of the novel's many parenthetical asides reads as follows: "(Loudoun County people were thought to be a little jealous of the older and richer families in Tidewater Virginia)" (160). Frederick County, where Sapphira and Henry live, is of course poorer and more rural than Loudoun County and thus even more marginally placed within the dubious social hierarchy of antebellum Virginia. Sapphira displays her resentment of stereotypes about the supposedly backward upland South when she remarks to Henry's nephew Martin, "Those folks from the Tidewater do hold their heads high, though I've never seen just why they feel called upon" (161).

Sapphira's questioning of the status of Tidewater Virginians might seem like (and probably is) an instance of sour grapes; however, the novel itself constantly disrupts the supposed fixity of social and cultural categories. The person who misses the older and more refined world of Loudoun County most acutely is not Sapphira but Till, who feels entombed in the provincial world of Back Creek, separated from her family and friends at Chestnut Hill, and unable to use her more specialized domestic skills. She misses her old life in a personal way that differs from the stereotypes about enslaved people's supposed loyalty to the master's home. Till's recollection of entering Winchester provides one of the novel's longest and most aesthetically satisfying descriptions: "You drove into town by Water Street, lined on either side with neat mansard houses built of pale grey limestone; grey, but almost blue and not dressed so smooth as to take all the life out of the rugged stone. Such genteel houses they were [. . .] with green window shutters, and brass knockers; a little walled garden and a hydrant behind each house" (76). Focalizing a scene of urban life through the gaze of an enslaved woman is an extraordinary narrative choice for a white author in 1940 and illustrates Till's cosmopolitan orientation.

By the novel's postbellum epilogue, Till's own relationship with household objects has paradoxically become more vexing. In "Nancy's Return," set twenty-five years after the main events of the novel, Till, now sixty-five, still lives in her old cabin and possesses what the child narrator of the epilogue calls "Till's keepsakes and treasures": "She had some of the miller's books, the wooly green shawl he had worn as an overcoat, some of Miss Sapphy's lace caps and fichus, and odd bits of finery such as velvet slippers with buckles. Her chief treasure was a brooch, set in pale gold, and under the crystal was a lock of Mr. Henry's black hair and Miss Sapphy's brown hair at the time of their marriage" (284). Till's possession of these objects has been seen by recent critics as indicative of a nostalgia for the antebellum South. Valerie Rohy depicts Till as a curator intent on preserving material representations of her enslavers: "Caught up in history, Till preserves the artifacts of the Colberts' lives, augmenting memory with metonymic objects that finally supplant the people they are meant to represent.... Preserving these objects, Till makes their past her own" (65). John Jacobs sees the brooch in particular as evidence that "Till keeps alive fond memories of plantation life" and that "her experience and imagination ... never extend beyond the boundaries of the plantation" (para. 7).

The epilogue's narration might push us toward Till's possession of these objects as a sign of nostalgia, but Till's perspective is unrecorded. Till is obviously connected to and probably dependent on the descendants of the Colbert family. Thavolia Glymph says of the WPA interviews of enslaved people conducted in the 1930s, "The continued reliance of many black people on the 'good will' of southern whites did make some black people more cautious about criticizing a time still revered by southern white people" (15). How much more constrained might Till have felt in the late 1870s? Her stories are told while she is providing Sapphira's descendants (presumably free) child care. The family stories and displays of objects entertain the epilogue's narrator, an obviously demanding and probably somewhat spoiled child. Rather than "keepsakes and treasures," these items might be viewed as material goods unconnected to their previous owners. As Greer's research on tea ware illustrates, enslaved people in Webster County participated in mercantile culture and appreciated nonessential goods that beautified their lives and signaled refinement. Apart from Henry's shawl, all of the things Till keeps indicate gentility and luxury. Her appreciation of the "lace caps and fichus" could be a result of their fine workmanship and beauty rather than their association with Sapphira, the woman who attempted to engineer the rape of Till's daughter. Till's dislike of Back Creek and her longing for the relative sophistication of Winchester is made clear earlier in the novel. These objects represent an environment more sophisticated than Back Creek and mean that she can own articles of fine apparel similar to those she cared for when enslaved.

Henry's shawl, the one nonluxury item, is made of "fine Scotch wool" and is warm and practical. The Shenandoah Valley is relatively cool, and elderly people are often sensitive to the cold. In Cather's short story "Old Mrs. Harris" (1932), Mrs. Harris has a "little comforter" that she wraps around her middle when she is chilly at night. This comforter is made from a discarded sweater "of very soft brushed wool" given to her by her neighbor, Mrs. Rosen, whose visiting nephew left it (80). No one reading "Old Mrs. Harris" would assume that Mrs. Harris's cherishing of her "comforter" indicates devotion to Mrs. Rosen or her unnamed nephew. Regarding Till's appreciation for Henry's books, she is literate and in the course of her domestic work would have sometimes had the opportunity to snatch a few minutes to read. It is probable that she has also taught Nancy to read; Nancy's solitary cleaning of the mill room would have given her access to the books Henry kept there. Till could well have wanted Henry's books for the reason most of us want books—to read them.

As Till's possession of his books and shawl illustrates, Henry Colbert is heavily implicated in the domestic world of the novel. Henry's mill room, cared for by Nancy, is "all that was left of the original building which stood there in Revolutionary times. The old chimney was still sound, and the miller used the slate-paved fireplace in cold weather" (49). A remnant of the Revolutionary-era mill, this room is an appropriate setting for Henry, with his convoluted feelings about slavery. The copper pieces in Henry's mill room come from his side of the family and, unlike most of the objects in the novel, are wholly unconnected to Sapphira. To Henry these copper tankards and bowls are both family heirlooms and signifiers of his and Nancy's mutual devotion. When Nancy first puts flowers in the copper tankard, Henry tells her, "I like to see flowers in that stein. My father used to drink his malt out of it" (67). Due to the elements of familial disruption and overlap caused by slavery, these objects can be read in ways that undermine Henry's own understanding of his family. If one of Henry's brothers is indeed Nancy's father, as Sapphira and others hint, then Nancy is Henry's niece and has her own lineal connection to the copper objects from Flanders. Indeed, she is placing flowers in the tankard that belonged to her grandfather.

Domestic objects provide another means of understanding Nancy, who has often been read as a somewhat vague character—Toni Morrison terms her "pure to the point of vapidity" (19). Yet, Nancy is repeatedly able to thwart Martin's attempts to rape her and ultimately proves able to leave all she knows for an unknown future in another country. How much of her seeming passivity is a role that Nancy must assume for her own safety? When Till suggests that Nancy offer a biscuit and eggnog to Sapphira in an attempt to regain her favor, she enjoins her to "smile, an' look happy to serve her" (46). Till knows the control Sapphira has over her child and wants Nancy to regain her enslaver's favor. Crucially, she tells Nancy to dissemble, encouraging her to hide her true feelings and perform the role of an enslaved person happy to serve, hoping that if Nancy plays her role properly, Sapphira will in response resume the part of benevolent mistress. Till's instructions to Nancy underline the opacity of her own thoughts and motivations, hinting at aspects of her character that are not only unavailable to the reader from the novel's narration but that would have been closed off to Cather as a white author.

Nancy's interactions with household objects initially illustrate the demeaning and frightening circumstances of her life within the Colbert household. In an early scene, Nancy is pressing one of Sapphira's caps with a "tiny iron" (20). She tells Rachel Blake that it is a "lil' child's iron" that she "coaxed" from "Miss Sadie Garrett" (20), presumably a local white child. The child-sized iron's presence in the text introduces the world of childhood material culture, nascent in the mid-nineteenth century but omnipresent by the novel's publication in 1940. The image of a young woman, barely out of childhood herself and denied childhood innocence due to enslavement, using a child's toy to do adult work is disturbing. With its transference from a white girl to a Black girl (who must call the younger child "Miss"), the iron as signifier shifts from a toy to a tool. On one level this object represents Nancy's unpaid labor and exploitation, yet her acquisition and skillful use of the small iron also indicate her exercise of agency within the limiting world of slavery.

The wooden hairbrush Sapphira uses to abuse Nancy is another feminine implement that haunts this scene. The ownership of a hairbrush further signals Sapphira's connections to the wider world of fashion. Linda Young notes that "[t]he modern style of hairbrush was an innovation of the early nineteenth century, appearing in growing numbers on richer women's dressing tables from the 1830s; until then, combs had been the standard hairdressing device for all classes" (104–5). Nineteenth-century women washed their hair infrequently, and prolonged brushing was needed to exfoliate the scalp and distribute its oils throughout the hair. Hair brushing was often a communal occupation practiced reciprocally by female relatives and friends and as a chore by servants and enslaved women. While Nancy is ironing, Rachel notices the brush's imprint on her arm, evidence of her mother's recent abuse of the enslaved girl. The hairbrush's shift from grooming tool to implement of punishment seems to transform a tableau of female intimacy into a grotesque spectacle. Read within the historical framework of slavery, however, there is no transformation: intimacy and violence exist in tandem. The hairbrush's use as a weapon merely illuminates the existing power differences between the two women, showing the exploitation at the heart of their relationship.

The reader never sees the actual hairbrush or witnesses the abuse: our perspective comes initially via Rachel, who from behind her mother's closed door hears both Sapphira's chastisement of Nancy for her supposedly clumsy hairdressing and the "smacking sound[s]" of an object repeatedly hitting flesh (16). To Rachel, her mother's hair appears flawless; the novel describes the complexities of Sapphira's hairstyle, indicating Nancy's skill as a hairdresser. The physical results of the punishment are noted later as a parenthetical aside, as Rachel watches Nancy iron and wonders what the young woman thinks about Sapphira's withdrawal of her favor. The text notes that "(the red marks of the hairbrush were still on the girl's right arm)" (22). Cather uses parentheses elsewhere in the novel to provide commentary disguised as seemingly objective, factual observations. Her delineation of the abuses of slavery enters this catalog of historical and contextual details.

The red marks on Nancy's arm gain added significance by their juxtaposition with the iron she is using. Irons can also leave marks—on both fabric and flesh. A red mark on the arm of a person who is ironing brings into the reader's mind a burn with an iron. According to Jacqueline Jones, "When punishing slave women for minor offenses, mistresses were likely to strike with any weapon available—knitting needles, tongs, a fork or butcher knife, an ironing board or a pan of boiling water. In the heat of the moment, white women devised barbaric forms of punishment that resulted in the mutilation or permanent scarring of their female servants" (23). Sapphira could have used the child-sized iron to burn Nancy if Nancy had shown what Sapphira considered clumsiness at that domestic task. Within the system of slavery such violence was viewed by the majority of white people as necessary discipline. Jones partially attributes slave mistresses' cruelty to their own status as victims within the patriarchal slave-ocracy, writing that "white women's anxieties frequently spilled over into acts of violence" (23). Recent work by Glymph and Stephanie E. Jones-Rogers undercuts this perspective by showing the ways in which white women dispassionately used the institution of slavery to secure their own economic independence from their male relatives. Jones-Rogers's research shows slave-owning women's brutal acts of punishment as consciously deployed tactics aimed at labor management rather than Freudian projection. Sapphira's own annoyance at Rachel's disapproval of her "correcting" of Nancy follows Jones-Rogers's thesis. Frustrated with her daughter, Sapphira thinks, "Never having owned any servants herself, Rachel didn't at all know how to deal with them" (18).

Despite her relative narrative passivity, Nancy's role as a subject within the action of the modern novel at times obscures her significance as an object within its historical setting. Before Sapphira turns against her, Nancy's status within the novel is initially very similar to that of Eliza at the beginning of Harriet Beecher Stowe's *Uncle Tom's Cabin*. Stowe describes "that peculiar air of refinement, that softness of voice and manner, which in many cases seems to be a particular gift to the quadroon and mulatto woman" (17). Nancy "had a natural delicacy of feeling," but she also has "Till's good manners—with something warmer and more alive" (45). Eliza displays greater personality and agency than Nancy; however, Cather crucially frames Nancy as an individual, departing from Stowe's classification of Eliza as a representative type of "quadroon" or "mulatto" woman. Initially, Sapphira's preference for Nancy reflects Mrs. Shelby's relationship with Eliza. Sapphira likes her "pretty face" (22) and enjoys having her as a companion. Left unspoken is the fact that possessing such an attractive and valuable slave would have given Sapphira status and indicated her wealth. This partially explains why she "liked to have her in attendance when she had guests or drove abroad" (22) and why, despite her hostility to Nancy, she takes the young woman on her annual visit to Winchester.

Nancy's own consideration of domestic objects within the novel allows her to express herself aesthetically, as she does when she arranges the flowers in Henry's copper tankard, and enables her to imagine herself as connected to the world beyond the Mill House. The portraits of Henry and Sapphira that hang in the parlor hold a particular fascination for her. Nancy's contested parenthood connects her to the family portraits in multiple ways. Meant to signal the Colberts' gentility and the stability of their family, the portraits have a different meaning to Nancy. If, as she hopes, the Cuban painter from Baltimore is her father, then she is the daughter of the artist who painted the portraits and is thus linked by parenthood to a space outside the United States, albeit one where slavery would remain legal until 1886. If one of the Colbert men is her father, then she is linked by genetics to the portrait of Henry and by marriage to the one of Sapphira and is thus as close in kinship to either as Martin is. Her wish that the Cuban painter is her father adds to Nancy's individuality and shows her desire and ability to construct her own identity apart from her role in Sapphira's household, foreshadowing her eventual escape from Back Creek and the new life she forges for herself in Montreal.

The portraits and their origin unsettle Henry as well. Sapphira taunts him about possessing "a kind of family feeling about Nancy," alluding to the possibility that one of his brothers is the young woman's father. Henry emphatically denies it, stating, "You know well enough, Sapphira, it was that painter from Baltimore," to which Sapphira replies, "Perhaps. We got the portraits out of him anyway, and maybe we got a smart yellow girl into the bargain" (12). Nancy, as a light-skinned, straight-haired woman of mixed race, would have had greater value within the antebellum slave economy than an enslaved woman with a darker complexion. Sapphira's designation of her as a "smart yellow girl" shows her awareness of this phenomenon. Biracial or "mulatta" women such as Nancy were highly sought after on the antebellum slave market. Edward Baptist notes, "Starting in the 1830s the term 'fancy girl' or 'maid' began to appear in the interstate slave trade. It meant a young woman, usually light-skinned, sold at a high price explicitly linked to her sexual availability and attractiveness" (240).

Although Nancy's attractiveness is remarked upon early in the novel, she is not initially framed as an object of white male desire. Characters in the world of the novel would, however, have understood, and in Till's case feared, the market value of her beauty. In *Incidents in the Life of a Slave Girl*, Harriet Jacobs writes, "If God has bestowed beauty upon her, it will prove her greatest curse. That which commands admiration in the white woman only hastens the degradation of the female slave" (36). Jacobs's own heroic attempts to guard herself from being raped by her enslaver find a parallel in the stratagems Nancy uses to elude Martin's pursuit. Henry himself explicitly considers Nancy within a marketplace where light-skinned enslaved women are trafficked sexually. When Rachel is asking him for the money to help Nancy escape, he expresses skepticism about Nancy's ability to survive in Montreal: "A pretty girl like her, she'd be enticed into one of them houses like as not" (223).

Were Martin to succeed in his plan to rape Nancy and impregnate her, any children she had would be designated "quadroons" and add value to Sapphira's estate. There is a very real possibility that Sapphira would at least attempt to sell Nancy's children. During the breakfast conversation in which Henry refuses to put his name to Nancy's deed of sale, he tells Sapphira, "You know we never sell our people," and Sapphira replies, "Of course we don't sell our people. [...] Certainly we would never offer any for sale. But to oblige friends is a different matter" (10). Yet Sapphira as a young woman managing her invalid father's estate has certainly sold enslaved people and separated families: "When the increase of the flocks or the stables was to be sold, she attended to it with Henry's aid. When the increase of the slave cabins was larger than needed for field and house service, she sold off some of the younger negroes" (27). Cather with this passage creates a terrible parallel between the offspring or "increase" of sheep and horses and enslaved children. Henry helps Sapphira sell livestock, but she competently sells off enslaved people herself. This fact aligns with Jones-Rogers's research on the active part many white women took within the economic and financial dimensions of slavery. Like Cather's parenthetical asides, the novel's historical commentary provides additional information that sometimes undercuts the rhetorical world the white characters create.

The shifting temporal and regional economics of slavery also affect

Till's market value as both a mother and a worker. Daina Ramey Berry discusses enslaved women's identification in the late eighteenth and early nineteenth centuries as "breeders," demonstrated by having borne a child, as distinct from the forced procreation of the late antebellum period (19–21). In a locale where many laborers were not needed, an enslaved woman's reproduction could be undesirable: "[e]nslaved women in the middle colonies as well as the North were often advertised for sale or exchange due to breeding" (20). Although the birth of children might enrich enslavers, sometimes, as with Till, an enslaved woman's pregnancy and breastfeeding, as well as her attachment to her child, proved to be an inconvenience to her enslavers. Lizzie, the cook, cruelly tells Nancy about her mother's forced marriage to the man she considers her father, who is impotent: "Miss Sapphy didn't want a lady's maid to be 'havin' chillum all over de place,—always a-carryin' or a-nussin' 'em'" (45). To Sapphira, Till's value as a parlor maid who is "presentable and trim of figure" (74) is more important than any reproductive value she possesses. Despite her desire for Till to remain childless, Sapphira's chuckling over "getting a smart yellow girl in the bargain" with the paintings indicates that she thinks of Nancy as an object of intrinsic value, like the portraits. Till herself is a victim of the slave market, forced to leave Chestnut Hill when she is fifteen because "Sapphira Colbert made a trade for her" (73). Again, Sapphira's bargaining for Till underscores Jones-Rogers's assertions about white women's involvement in the slave trade.

Nancy's and Till's respective market values are also strongly connected to their domestic skills. According to Berry, "Enslavers who noted women's skills identified five types of female workers: house servants, field hands, cooks, laundresses, and seamstresses. Only 5 percent of female laborers displayed evidence of work specialization" (18). Nancy exhibits skill in housekeeping, hairdressing, laundry, and needlework, indicating her mastery of a wide range of valuable skills. Ann Romines has written at length about Till's domestic accomplishments and her transference of those skills to Nancy: "later, when Nancy is thrown back on her survival skills as a fugitive in Montreal, her housekeeping accomplishments become a valuable commodity on which she founds her new life as a free woman—thanks, at least partially, to her mother, Till" (217). As Nancy and Rachel prepare to depart Back Creek, Rachel notices that she has brought "one of the old reticules" and says that it will be useful for carrying the letters of support and introduction she will need (227). Indeed, Sapphira has used just such a reticule to carry to Mrs. Bywaters at the post office the note of invitation to Martin. Nancy, however, has brought the reticule for a different purpose entirely; it contains stockings that Sapphira has told her to darn—domestic work left undone that she feels compelled to finish. For Rachel the reticule is indicative of travel, possibility, and legitimacy. For Nancy it means none of those things; it is simply a container that holds work she must do and a symbol of her current life as an enslaved woman obligated to serve Sapphira. Nancy's difficulty in imagining a different life for herself does not foreclose the possibility, as her return as a sophisticated and cosmopolitan woman at the end of the novel illustrates.

Within the world of the novel, Nancy might have taken the reticule inadvertently, but the historical record shows that enslaved people frequently and deliberately absconded with their enslavers' possessions. According to Greer, "An examination of a recent compiling of runaway slave advertisements from twenty-five Mississippi newspapers identified a cohort of 225 individual escapees who equipped themselves with physical objects in order to aid their efforts" ("Bundles" 88). Greer identifies "the display of fine clothing and jewelry to enter into new social networks" as one use of these objects (88). The reticule, like Nancy herself, gains additional meaning and nuance outside the frame of the novel. Rachel herself understands the power of material goods as a form of self-expression and uses them to aid Nancy in her escape. As they flee Back Creek, Rachel gives Nancy her carpetbag and tells her, "From now on we must look spruce, like we was going visiting. I'm glad you've got a feather in your hat. It's real becoming to you" (227). The hat Nancy wears to escape is "an old black turban of Mrs. Colbert's" (227).

When she returns to Back Creek twenty-five years later, Nancy is also wearing a turban (276), but this time it is not the castoff of a white enslaver but part of a carefully considered outfit. The child narrator views Nancy's distinctive fur-lined coat with suspicion: "We had no coats like that on Back Creek" (276). Because it is outside the boundaries of the antebellum South, Nancy's clothing at the end of the novel indicates self-possession and transformation, contrasting with the objects belonging to the Mill House that persist in the novel into the epilogue. The objects in the earlier portion of *Sapphira and the Slave Girl* are more ambiguous, yet they also disrupt the novel's white perspective and turn our attention to the extraordinarily complex and rich lives of the real enslaved people whose indefinable presence shimmers at the edges of the narrative.

WORKS CITED

Baptist, Edward. *The Half Has Never Been Told: Slavery and the Making of American Capitalism*. Basic Books, 2014.

Berry, Daina Ramey. *The Price of Their Pound of Flesh: The Value of the Enslaved, from Womb to Grave, in the Building of a Nation*. Beacon, 2017.

Brandt, Lydia Mattice. *First in the Homes of His Countrymen: George Washington's Mount Vernon in the American Imagination*. U of Virginia P, 2016.

Bushman, Richard L. *The Refinement of America: Persons, Houses, Cities*. Vintage, 1993.

Cather, Willa. "Old Mrs. Harris." *Obscure Destinies*. 1932. Willa Cather Scholarly Edition, historical essay and explanatory notes by Kari A. Ronning, textual essay by Frederick M. Link with Kari A. Ronning and Mark Kamrath, U of Nebraska P, 1998.

———. *Sapphira and the Slave Girl*. 1940. Willa Cather Scholarly Edition, historical essay and explanatory notes by Ann Romines, textual essay and editing by Charles W. Mignon, Kari A. Ronning, and Frederick M. Link, U of Nebraska P, 2009.

Glymph, Thavolia. *Out of the House of Bondage: The Transformation of the Plantation Household*. Cambridge UP, 2008.

Greer, Matthew C. "Bundles, Passes and Stolen Watches: Interpreting the Role of Material Culture in Escape." *Southern Studies: An Interdisciplinary Journal of the South*, vol. 24, no. 1, 2014, pp. 87–96.

———. "Cather and Enslaved Life in the Northern Shenandoah Valley." Seventeenth International Willa Cather Seminar, 17 June 2019, Shenandoah U, Winchester VA.

Jacobs, Harriet. *Incidents in the Life of a Slave Girl*. 1861. Washington Square, 2003.

Jacobs, John. "A [Slave] Girl's Life in Virginia before the War: Willa Cather's Antebellum Nostalgia." *Willa Cather and the Nineteenth Century*, edited by Anne L. Kaufman and Richard H. Millington, Cather Studies 10, U of Nebraska P, 2015, cather.unl.edu/scholarship/catherstudies/10/cs010.jacobs.

Jones, Jacqueline. *Labor of Love, Labor of Sorrow: Black Women, Work, and the Family from Slavery to the Present*. Basic Books, 2009.

Jones-Rogers, Stephanie E. *They Were Her Property: White Women as Slave Owners in the American South*. Yale UP, 2019.

Millington, Richard. "Where Is Cather's Quebec? Anthropological Modernism in *Shadows on the Rock*." *Willa Cather's Canadian and Old World Connections*, edited by Robert Thacker and Michael A. Peterman, Cather Studies 4, U of Nebraska P, 1999, cather.unl.edu/scholarship/catherstudies /4/cs004.millington.

Morrison, Toni. *Playing in the Dark: Whiteness and the Literary Imagination*. Vintage, 1992.

Rohy, Valerie. *Anachronism and Its Others: Sexuality, Race, Temporality*. State U of New York P, 2009.

Romines, Ann. "Willa Cather and the 'Old Story': *Sapphira and the Slave Girl*." *The Cambridge Companion to Willa Cather*, edited by Marilee Lindemann, Cambridge UP, 2005, pp. 205–21.

Stowe, Harriet Beecher. *Uncle Tom's Cabin*. 1852. Random House, 2001.

Wajda, Shirley Teresa. "Floor Coverings." *Material Culture in America: Understanding Everyday Life*, edited by Helen Sheumaker and Shirley Teresa Wajda, ABC-CLIO, 2008, pp. 191–94.

Young, Linda. *Middle-Class Culture in the Nineteenth Century: America, Australia, and Britain*. Palgrave, 2003.

2 Willa Cather's "Black Liberation Theology" in *Sapphira and the Slave Girl*

BARRY HUDEK

Pairing Willa Cather with Black liberation theology might seem strange.[1] After all, she is a white writer predominantly known for her work about pioneer-era Nebraska. Yet, before Cather's exposure to and interest in the variegated immigrant peoples in her second home of Nebraska, she first encountered the dislocated and differentiated peoples of Africa—recently enslaved in the New World—in her native Virginia. This early exposure is not heavily commented upon in Cather scholarship; the bulk of attention has been given to her time spent in Nebraska and the immigrant characters that often inhabit her fiction. What is more, several critics argue that Cather's Black (and other) characters are constructed from racism. Yet her final novel, *Sapphira and the Slave Girl*, returns to her native Virginia. Although this book includes numerous Black characters, it apparently does not disquiet charges of possible racism, despite Cather's calling her Black characters the "most interesting figures" of the novel (qtd. in Romines, Historical essay 365). My exploration of Black liberation theology—a theology itself grounded in

unsettling, differences, and dislocating the white power structures
of the status quo—sheds light on Cather's treatment of race and
racism in her final novel.

Eugene Genovese defines Black liberation theology this way:
"However much Christianity taught submission to slavery, it also
carried a message of foreboding to the master class and of resistance
to the enslaved" (165). Thus, "slaves did not often accept professions
of white [religious] sincerity at face value; on the contrary, they
seized the opportunity to turn even white preaching into a weapon
of their own" (190). Black Americans used Judeo-Christian scrip-
tures to forge "weapons of defense, the most important of which
was a religion that taught them to love and value each other, to take
a critical view of their masters and to reject ideological rationales
for their own enslavement" (6). James Cone, the modern author of
Black liberation theology, adds that it "matters little to the oppressed
who authored scripture; what is important is whether it can serve
as a weapon against oppression" (33). Thus, the meanings of various
biblical stories and characters are contested, not fixed, producing
a tension that plays out among the Black and white characters in
the printed work.

Cather made small but significant changes to her *Sapphira and the
Slave Girl* manuscript that illustrate these complexities.[2] She cut a
reference to the Book of Exodus from an earlier typescript in which
Henry Colbert, not his wife Sapphira, reads the Bible to Jezebel on
her deathbed. In fact, Jezebel requests the reading of slaves escaping
bondage, telling Henry that Till often read from that text to the slaves
on the Colbert property. Such a reference to Exodus and its escaping
enslaved persons would have been a clear and obvious nod to the
idea of Black liberation from white bondage—an allusion Sarah
Clere calls "profoundly subversive" (444).[3] Indeed, a Black African
asking a white enslaver to read Exodus as a comfort before death
could only be read subversively. Seeing themselves as "the modern
counterparts to the Children of Israel," Ira Berlin writes, Black Americans "appropriated the story of Exodus as a parable of their own
deliverance from bondage" (128). Such an inclusion on Cather's part

would have been a clear and obvious signal to, and even a potential affiliation with, the idea of Black agency, resistance, and sympathy for liberation. It was not included in the novel.

Rather, the scene changes from Henry to Sapphira reading to Jezebel, and instead of Henry asking Jezebel what she wants to hear, Sapphira imposes Psalm 23 upon her audience. The reading is intended to "hearten us both" (89), she tells Jezebel. Indeed, Psalm 23, with its well-known verses such as "The Lord is my Shepherd" and "even though I walk through the valley of the shadow of death," is typical Judeo-Christian fare for such an event. However, Sapphira's reading seems ominous, another instance of her attempts to control and subjugate. In reading this ubiquitous biblical classic, Sapphira might be implying that the only escape from slavery is death. Such a reading gives rise to critical claims of, at worst, Cather's racism and, at best, an author representing Black characters without agency.[4] A move to cut a clear and obvious textual marker that works against these charges seems strange, yet Jezebel is not as resigned to death as Sapphira may wish. In a moment of "grim humour," she tells Sapphira that the only thing that might ease her hunger is a "li'l pickaninny's hand" (90). Here is a subtle moment of resistance woven throughout the novel. Jezebel retains her memory of Africa and a hunger for some agency in either being honest about a desire for human flesh or in subversively entertaining Sapphira's preconceived notions about Africa.

Even more, Cather did include potentially subversive biblical allusions in the printed novel. Beyond just Psalm 23, she includes in *Sapphira* references to the Books of Genesis and Daniel, as well as important hymns and spirituals. Much like Exodus, these texts highlight relations between slaves and masters. Indeed, the biblical allusions included in the novel illustrate the differences in reading scripture for the various communities portrayed in the novel. For white Protestants of the historical era within the novel, scripture enforces the status quo in which slaves are expected to obey their masters.[5] For Black readers, however, scripture serves as a means of resistance, a potential for a Black liberation theology—a reading

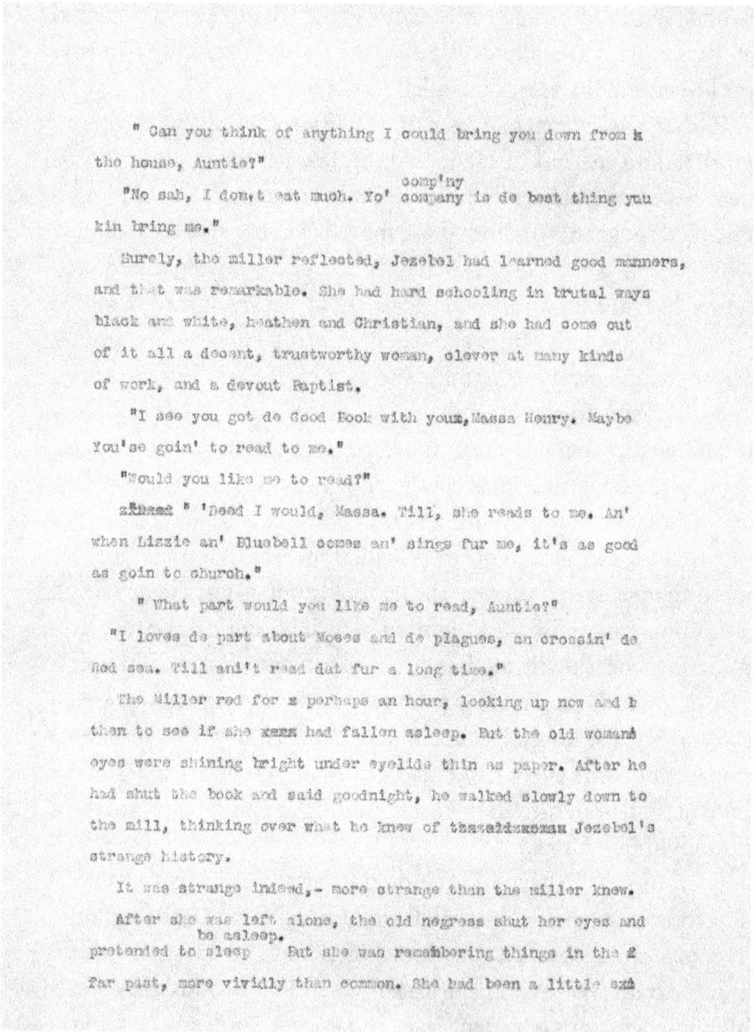

" Can you think of anything I could bring you down from k
the house, Auntie?"

comp'ny
"No sah, I don,t eat much. Yo' company is de best thing yuu
kin bring me."

Surely, the miller reflected, Jezebel had learned good manners,
and that was remarkable. She had hard schooling in brutal ways
black and white, heathen and Christian, and she had come out
of it all a decent, trustworthy woman, clever at many kinds
of work, and a devout Baptist.

"I see you got de Good Book with youm,Massa Henry. Maybe
You'se goin' to read to me."

"Would you like me to read?"

zRhead " 'Deed I would, Massa. Till, she reads to me. An'
when Lizzie an' Bluebell comes an' sings fur me, it's as good
as goin to church."

" What part would you like me to read, Auntie?"

"I loves de part about Moses and de plagues, an crossin' de
Red sea. Till ani't read dat fur a long time."

The Miller red for s perhaps an hour, looking up now and b
then to see if she xemx had fallen asleep. But the old womané
eyes were shining bright under eyelids thin as paper. After he
had shut the book and said goodnight, he walked slowly down to
the mill, thinking over what he knew of thzzoldzwoman Jezebel's
strange history.

It was strange indeed,- more strange than the miller knew.

After she was left alone, the old negress shut her eyes and
be asleep.
pretended to sleep But she was remembering things in the 2
far past, more vividly than common. She had been a little sxå

Fig. 2.1. Cather's typescript for *Sapphira and the Slave Girl* features Jezebel's deathbed request to hear the Book of Exodus read to her once more. Henry obliges her with a long reading of the Hebrews' escape from bondage, which she listens to with rapt attention and personal comfort. Charles E. Cather Collection, Archives and Special Collections, University of Nebraska–Lincoln Libraries.

of the Bible by Black Americans used to fuel hope, survival, and/or strategies of resistance in which slaves upend the imperial narrative by defying their masters.

As such, I argue that Cather's printed allusions contain potential liberatory ethics that Black readers would identify and white readers might miss. Cather's changes to the novel to remove the clear and obvious "subversive" biblical texts of her typescript retain the potential for subversion, given Cather's interest in liberatory texts in earlier drafts. In short, *Sapphira and the Slave Girl* includes Black liberation theology, whether she intended to or not, despite her cutting the reference to Exodus from earlier drafts. This chapter thus highlights Cather's cuts and their meanings, offers some explanation as to why she made them, and also describes why and how the included biblical references of the novel can be seen as liberatory. That is, the potential for subversion was on Cather's mind as she drafted the novel and remains within the printed text despite the deletion of the Exodus material. In all, then, I demonstrate how *Sapphira* can be read as a subversive text.

This chapter builds upon Sarah Clere's work on Cather's earlier typescript by further showing the "possible ways *Sapphira* could have developed" (442). I agree with Clere that "the novel's black characters and how to portray them were very much on Cather's mind when she composed *Sapphira*" (442). In showing these potential ways Cather's novel could have gone, Clere rightly contends that Cather was "attuned to many of the historical realities of the antebellum South" (458). As the typescript shows, Cather clearly was aware of the struggles and issues confronting Black people in the South. In this way, in her early composition of the text, her Black characters exhibit far more agency, awareness, and subversion than in the printed novel. In other words, Cather almost champions a liberatory ethic in her exploration of Jezebel in the typescript. Indeed, Jezebel even has more "power and agency" over her own story, one that "shows her taking calculated action in pursuit of a particular goal" (Clere 445). For instance, in Cather's "Sapphira and the Slave Girl" typescript, the violence Jezebel enacts during her Middle Passage transpires because she is "bewitched and tormented by a thirst to avenge her brothers" (B2F18), whereas in the printed novel the attacks are sporadic and unfocused. In the typescript, she fashions weapons out of the materials given her and chooses her attacks at precise moments based on her watching and assessing the crew's movements—all signs of Jezebel's mental awareness and personal choice. Despite moving away from these instances, Cather may have been more attuned to the realities of African agency and resistance than previously thought.

In fact, I argue that the biblical allusions she did include still frame a conversation about liberatory ethics in the context of a white, Protestant, slaveholding U.S. South and Black Americans oppressed by that religious system. A white author connecting the Book of Exodus to a Black character in the context of slavery is a strong and powerful signal of sympathy for that character and perhaps guilt as well. Cutting those elements certainly seems suspect, given the obvious authorial sympathy with the enslaved African character in the novel. But Cather's texts are not obvious. She shies away from ready-made readings and instead makes interpretation of her work difficult by cloaking her meanings. She is also a writer very much aware of what she is doing. Thus, *Sapphira* still includes biblical allusions that contain the potential for subversion of the slaveholding order, depending on the reader's viewpoint.

It is also possible that Cather came upon these moments of Black liberation quite by accident. Toni Morrison in her book *Playing in the Dark: Whiteness and the Literary Imagination* explores hidden, unexpected, and unintended meaning and consequences of literary texts when white readers write about Black characters or issues. For Morrison, the writer's imagination is a place where all sorts of underlying ideas and tensions can play out in a novel, where they "fight secret wars, limn out all sorts of debates blanketed in their texts" (4). More specifically, Morrison is interested in "the way black people ignite critical moments of discovery or change or emphasis in literature not written by them" (viii) in which the "fabrication of an Africanist persona is reflexive; an extraordinary meditation on the self; a powerful exploration of the fears and desires that reside in the writerly conscious. It is an astonishing revelation of longing, of terror, of perplexity, of shame, of magnanimity" that reveals "the self-evident ways that Americans choose to talk about themselves through and within a sometimes allegorical, sometimes metaphorical, but always choked representation of an Africanist presence" (17). Here, Morrison's analysis shows that Cather, by including biblical and religious materials, may have been teasing such "fears and desires" and that she may not have been fully aware of the impact and meaning upon Black characters. Or, even in teasing out Henry's wrestling with scripture, she may have been wrestling with these ideas herself, or trying to reconstruct a liberatory history that did not exist for her during her Virginia childhood. It is this "choked representation" of the Exodus material that Cather cut from *Sapphira* that I want to explore regardless of why Cather did or did not change the manuscript. Her various biblical allusions, both cut from and still within the novel, reveal these "moments of discovery" white Americans use when thinking about their identity in contrast to a Black other. In fact, differing cultural ways of reading the Bible reveal a similar process about identity and cultural formation in which a biblical passage, such as Psalm 23 or the Exodus material, means one thing to a particular cultural group but something else entirely to another.

BLACK LIBERATION THEOLOGY IN THE NOVEL

Indeed, any encounter with scripture has to contend with the reader's cultural and ideological baggage. A slaveholding white Protestant reading of scripture is different from an enslaved Black American's reading of the Bible. Indeed, there is "no reading [of the Bible] that is not already ideological" (Bible and Culture Collective 4). Thus, when white readers encounter the statement that servants must "obey in all things your masters" (*King James Bible*, Col. 3.22) they could likely read the passage as divine justification for slavery. However, when Black readers encounter texts like Exodus and other moments of triumph by downtrodden characters, they see inspiration for a divine liberation from their oppression.

Further, Black Americans derived hope from individual biblical characters. Seeing them as heroes for the present, many Black Christians found inspiration from stories of triumph by individuals who were mistreated. Lawrence Levine, in his book *Black Culture and Black Consciousness*, articulates such a connection to the Hebrew Bible this way: "For the slaves, then, songs of God and the mythic heroes of their religion were not confined to a specific time or place, but were appropriate to almost every situation" (31). Keith Miller argues that in "identifying with the Hebrews in Egypt and with other Biblical heroes," Black Americans often "leapfrogged geography and chronology," and they "telescoped history, replacing chronological time with a form of sacred time" (20) in which Black Americans "freely mingled their own experiences with those of Daniel, Ezekiel, Jonah, and Moses." These readers "could vividly project Old Testament figures into the present because their universe encompassed both heaven and earth and merged the biblical past with the present." In this way, Black readers were "freeing those models from any constraints imposed by their historical contexts, and entirely ignoring all barriers separating past and present events" (Miller 20–21). In short, scripture is a weapon. Its stories provide oppressed persons with a source of hope and a means of resisting their oppressors. A Black reader of scripture would likely see the liberatory power in the stories Henry references as well as the hymns Cather includes. Black American readers would likely recognize such stories and allusions as a nod toward their liberatory ways of reading the Bible and singing white-authored hymns such as the abolitionist-composed works mentioned in the novel.[6]

CATHER'S CUTS FROM THE TYPESCRIPT

Not only did Cather cut a reference to Exodus, and all that it implies for Black characters in the novel, but Jezebel's specific references to it are moments of triumph over oppressive orders. In one scene that appears in the typescript, Henry cautiously approaches Jezebel, Bible tucked under his arm. "I see you got de Good Book with you massa Henry, meybe you'se goin to read to me," she says as he comes closer. Henry asks if she wants him to, and after hearing that she does, he asks her what she wants him to read. "I love de part about Moses an de plagues, an crossin' de Red Sea. Till aint read dat," she continues, "fur a long time" (B2F18). There can be no question of Cather's choice here. The moments Jezebel celebrates are when Egypt is punished by divine retribution for its oppression of the Hebrews. In refusing to release them from bondage despite various plagues being rained upon the country and then in trying to force the Hebrews to come back after releasing them, Egypt is harmed when trying to assert its control over another group. In both of these Exodus scenes Jezebel mentions, the slave community triumphs in violent ways over the administrative and military control exerted over them. Henry's reading of these particular textual moments seems to animate Jezebel. Instead of the prosaic reading of Psalm 23 Sapphira offers in the published novel, Henry's reading of scripture "for perhaps an hour" (B2F18) seems to offer hope and comfort for Jezebel as she nears death. Jezebel perhaps imagines a future where something like what is described in Exodus happens to the slave-holding U.S. South. It's no wonder that a reading of righteous slaves escaping imprisonment and persecution to then form their own nation would be a comfort to Jezebel, the only character in the novel born in Africa.

Indeed, had the passage been retained in the printed novel, it would have had several impacts. For one, it would have given Jezebel and the Black Americans at Back Creek more community and agency—something Ann Romines in her "Losing and Finding 'Race'" essay argues is largely missing from the printed version. "Cather gives us little sense of the complexity of the slave community" and "how it functioned to facilitate survival and some agency for slaves," she writes (403). The Exodus allusion provides such a glimpse. What is telling is that Jezebel mentions how Till used to read those passages, presumably often, since Jezebel knows them so well. Even though she hasn't read them in a while, they were being read by members of the Black community away from the bounds of institutional (i.e., white-controlled) religious practices as a means of resistance, hope for the future, and survival in the context of the established order. The particular sections Jezebel mentions denote violence against that established order, evoking the plagues brought on Egypt as the pharaoh refused to release the enslaved people of Israel. She further mentions the parting of the Red Sea that, when its divinely divided waters came back together after the slaves' crossing, destroyed the military force sent to bring the Hebrews back into slavery. In sum, when drafting the novel, Cather depicted strategies within the Black American world of *Sapphira* that preserve and enhance Black identity and resistance.

However, Cather's considered inclusion also gives justification to the possibility that a novel by a white author dealing with Black characters might create unintended consequences beyond the writer's control. As Morrison wonders, "What does the inclusion of Africans or African-Americans do to and for the work?" (16). Cather, in her allusion to Exodus, intensifies the idea that Black characters would not care to be where they are in Back Creek or throughout the U.S. South; the Exodus motif thus invalidates the narrative's offering about happy Black Americans seeking their protection from white masters or leaving the only home they have ever known, as several Black characters are represented as having such feelings after Emancipation and manumission. In enacting an exodus, many formerly enslaved people would happily leave for new lands, wherever that journey might lead them, and would do so without a second thought.[7] The action contained within the Exodus narrative—Israel's transition out of Egypt, wandering in the desert, and entering the Promised Land—was not easy. In fact, many Hebrews wondered if they were not better off back in Egypt. Further, the Exodus allusion also implies violence—a violence of carving out a place in the Promised Land by defeating the inhabitants of Canaan. In forming the Hebrew nation into a working group after the impact of slavery, conflict is inevitable.

Lastly, the inclusion of Exodus in the published version of *Sapphira* indicates the need for escape—that Black Americans are in the right for wanting to leave. If Black people in the South are the escaping Hebrews, then white Protestants are Egypt because they have forced Black people to labor for them—a point that Henry makes when musing that Nancy's escape to Canada suggests that "she would go up out of Egypt to a better land." However, in thinking how "Sapphira's darkies were better cared for, better fed and better clothed, than the poor whites in the mountains" (225), Henry immediately undercuts his own beliefs about Black people being more free and better cared for in the South than they would be in the industrial North that lacks the same community context as the U.S. South. Here then is one of Morrison's moments in which the literary imagination shows the "astonishing revelation of terror, of perplexity, of shame, of magnanimity" (17) in a white writer working with Black characters. In connecting to this Black American's need for escape, Cather reveals a certain guilt about the rightness of such claims for the need to escape oppression—for what Black people were experiencing in the antebellum United States is indeed oppression by white Americans. Indeed, white characters in the novel experience guilt in helping the enslaved escape. In the published novel, Rachel—Sapphira's daughter—wonders after she helps Nancy escape if "maybe I ought to have thought and waited" (243). The novel's epilogue, too, seemingly celebrates Nancy's emancipation, the need for it, and her life thereafter. However, the narrator still calls her "our Nancy" in a move that undercuts the complete break from the past. The "our" could be familial and intimate, but certainly also domineering and possessive, since the narrator still seems to view Nancy as family property. In all, keeping the Exodus material in the novel would have made the racial undertones of cutting against the grain of white gentility and beneficent southernness much more evident.

Further, Cather included a scene in the "Sapphira" typescript in which Henry's grandchildren want him to sing a song about the Hebrew children and the fiery furnace, referencing another instance of maintaining one's cultural heritage in the face of imperial pressure to change and one in which simple defiance leads to an upending of the established order. The portion Henry sings for them that "called up pictures to him and to his listeners" asks, "Where, o where are the Hebrew children / Who were cast in a fiery furnace? / Where, o where are the Hebrew children? / Way over in the Promised Land" (BIF25PI3). Here, the song conflates elements from the Books of Daniel and Exodus. In the Daniel story, three Hebrews are cast into a fiery furnace by the Babylonian king Nebuchadnezzar for refusing to bow down and worship the golden statue of himself. They defy the imperial order as it tries to impose its cultural values upon the exiled Hebrews. The three Hebrews refuse, even if it means their death. They are thrown into the fiery furnace but are miraculously saved, unhurt and unscathed upon their release. It is only because they hold to their cultural heritage that they are saved. They are not moved by Babylonian cultural impulses and in fact reject them. In including this biblically based song, Cather's "Sapphira" typescript highlights yet another clear moment of slaves overcoming their circumstances by maintaining their heritage in the face of imperial domination. Such a move also further incriminates Henry's blindness to the plight of the Black people he has enslaved.[8] He does not recognize himself as the imperial master whom his slaves who would identify with the Hebrew children in this drama. In this typescript scene, we see Cather pointing to obvious moments of individual triumph over oppression. So, why did these allusions get cut?

I think Tomas Pollard is correct in asserting that Cather's "characterization requires that the politics of the 1850s surface as background noise for the emotional universe of her characters. Cather's heavy excising of the original text shows her desire to dampen any political heavy-handedness" (40). The Exodus motif would have been clear, obvious, and potentially heavy-handed—it would not take someone versed in biblical theory to read Exodus and see how it might appeal to Africans and Black Americans in bondage. Janis Stout argues that Cather "refused to become directly ideological" and

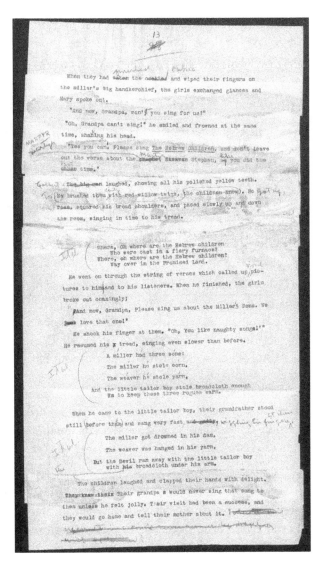

Fig. 2.2. This typescript page for *Sapphira and the Slave Girl* features Henry reading a potentially dangerous song about the enslaved overcoming their imperial masters by holding on to their cultural heritage in defiance of assimilation. Charles E. Cather Collection, Archives and Special Collections, University of Nebraska–Lincoln Libraries.

that her interest was "in writing, in and of itself" (60). In this way, Cather may have cut the Exodus material because it went against her own authorial judgments.

THE PRINTED NOVEL'S LIBERATORY MOMENTS

Even after Sapphira reads Psalm 23 to Jezebel in her attempt to maintain her power over others, the scene still propels Henry to an intense reading of scripture, just as it does in the typescript version (even if Henry's reading of the Bible and his subsequent conclusions about what he finds would have put him into sharp relief against the Exodus material he had just read to Jezebel). In both the printed novel and the typescript, Jezebel's death fosters the following passage:

> Henry Colbert had been reading over certain marked passages in the Book he accepted as a complete guide to human life. He had turned to all the verses marked with a large S. Joseph, Daniel, and the prophets had been slaves in foreign lands, and had brought good out of their captivity. Nowhere in his Bible had he ever been able to find a clear condemnation of slavery. There were injunctions of kindness to slaves, mercy and tolerance. *Remember them in bonds as bound with them.* Yes, but nowhere did his Bible say that there should be no one in bonds, no one at all. (112; B2F18)

As the passage goes on, Henry imagines all people in bonds of some sort and wonders, "Were we not all in bonds? If Lizzie, the cook, was in bonds to Sapphira, was she not almost equally in bonds to Lizzie?" (112; B2F18). For Henry, then, since major positive biblical figures were enslaved, there was no clear condemnation of slavery. Moreover, since people were in bondage to one another anyway, he was bound by southern norms not to condemn or act against the "peculiar institution." He even equates slaves and masters on "almost" equal terms of servitude to one another, certainly a stance that was far from true in the U.S. South.

Further, Henry's "complete guide to human life" seems influenced by Calvinist theology and predestination wherein Jezebel and others are enslaved because of some divine plan enacted before the universe was created. Henry certainly cannot interfere with God's plan. He does imagine a point where the divine plan includes freeing the slaves, and perhaps soon. The Exodus passage itself and Jezebel's own intense interest in these passages undermine Henry's ideas about religion as justification for slavery. Henry does not or cannot see himself as Pharaoh in this drama. He does not connect the violence done against Egypt as something potentially comparable to and possible in the U.S. South, while Jezebel and the Black community seem to make that connection, seeing their own future liberation in these stories. From his limited perspective, Henry's white southern reading of scripture conforms to his cultural surroundings. In his final musings on the above passage, Henry believes that design in nature is clear enough, but he questions how such designs can be accurately seen in human affairs, blaming the "fault in our perceptions" since "we can never see what was behind the next turn of the road" (113). Thus, Henry's own reading should not be taken at face value. His cultural underpinnings and context need to be considered in his interpretation. It should also be considered, then, that Cather included these allusions for this contested tension within the biblical referents evinced in Henry's own grappling with scripture, given the passage's connection to Henry's Quaker friend who "firmly believed" (113)—correctly—that slavery would be abolished in his lifetime.[9] This contrasting theology shows that action is required to bring about emancipation. As Henry wrestles with theological and cultural questions, the Quakers in the novel work toward emancipation, including helping Nancy escape via the Underground Railroad.

Returning to Henry's conclusion that there is "no clear condemnation of slavery" in the Bible, his reading is fraught with white expectations that reading scripture will justify their own stance—that is, Henry sees what he wants to see in the Bible when it comes to maintaining the system of slavery. His reading and subsequent conclusions ring hollow. For instance, Henry cites Joseph and Daniel as major biblical figures who were slaves. In his view, since these major figures were slaves and are regarded as significant figures in Jewish and Christian theology and culture, surely slaves in the United States can be regarded similarly and the institution cannot be morally wrong. What Henry misses, however, is that these slaves upend the intended order—they subvert imperial power from their humble position in bonded service. Henry conveniently forgets or chooses not to see that Babylon's imperial power and excess are the bad actors in the drama. He fails to see that in justifying slavery because of the heroic Daniel's status as a slave, the United States and its systems of racial oppression are on par with Babylon's. What the Daniel text celebrates is how the righteous slave overturns state power and oppression. King Nebuchadnezzar and other Babylonian rulers are each brought low by the humble faith and simple defiance of the slaves in the Daniel text—this is the point of the Book of Daniel, a subversive point that Henry does not want to see, nor is he like those who take action to upend the institutional exploitation of others.

Henry misses similar content in referencing Joseph. The Joseph story in the Book of Genesis contains yet another moment of ascension and triumph for a former slave. Sold into foreign slavery by his jealous brothers, Joseph becomes enmeshed within the Egyptian administrative hierarchy, becoming second only to Pharaoh himself in power and stature. Even though he retains his association with Egypt, Joseph maintains fidelity to his heritage and does not become corrupted by the system around him. Even more, Joseph later comes to have power over his brothers who sold him into slavery in the first place. The tension of the drama, then, concerns how Joseph will use his power over those who betrayed him and sold him into slavery. Joseph reveals his true identity to his brothers, and in their terror at realizing their situation, he has mercy on them. Perceptive readers of Cather's biblical and religious allusions could see how the references might be political after all, depending upon one's viewpoint. Henry, as a typical slave-holding white Protestant, misses the warning of scripture to oppressive regimes featured in the Bible. His own justifications for slavery belie his scriptural underpinning for that system since the slaves depicted within those stories all succeed despite and against their enslavement. In these stories, too, the ones who impose slavery are the villains. As such, Cather ironizes Henry and his acceptance of biblical justifications of slavery. It is difficult to conceive of Cather siding with Henry here or missing the potential political notes of these allusions, given her clear attention to such texts in the typescript. The potentially unsettling biblical allusions she included in the novel still carry the weight of slaves overcoming their circumstances, although they are more subtle.

The songs and hymns referenced in the novel also contain readings against the grain of white Protestant orthodoxy, including covert references to Moses and the Book of Exodus. Prior to Jezebel's death scene, Cather includes the hymn "There Is a Land of Pure Delight."[10] As a church service concludes, Henry joins several of the Colbert slaves, led by the cook Lizzie, who "broke away from Shand," the elderly white male song leader, "and carried the tune along" (80). It is the Black congregants' passionate singing that elevates the experience into a "living worship" that punctuates the service more than any other portion of the day's activities. "Could we but stand where Moses stood," they sing, "And view the landscape o'er / Not Jordan's stream nor death's cold flood / Would fright us from that shore" (81). At the conclusion of their singing, the preacher reacts with "not a smile exactly, but with appreciation. He often felt like thanking" Lizzie (81). The white-authored English hymn is based on the story of how Moses, near death and prohibited from entering the Promised Land for angering God, viewed the Promised Land and knew that, even though he would not enter this new era, the Hebrews he led would. At this moment in Exodus, the Hebrews have finished their wandering in the desert, rid themselves of people still attached to Egypt and its oppressive legacy, and shaped themselves into a nation. They are poised for the next step. That next step—conquering the Promised Land and taking it for their own—is not included in the hymn. Perhaps this is where the preacher has some measure of apprehension, given "those bright promises and dark warnings" sung with "such fervent conviction" by the "Colbert negroes." In fact, for the

Black singers, those "bright promises" and "dark warnings" (80) are moments of Black liberation theology that evoke what is not named in the hymn or the text; the Black singers (and perhaps some of the apprehensive white congregants at the church, too) are seeing the coming freedom from bondage by whatever means necessary. Perhaps, too, the older Black Americans know that, like Moses, they will not live to see this new era, but they know it's coming; they know it's close. Cather certainly has the vantage point of history to know this to be the case. It is also telling that this hymn precedes the section on Jezebel, potentially existing as a precursor to that moment.

Henry, too, reflects upon a hymn that contains more meaning than what he might have intended or known. After Henry's reading of scripture examining the lives of Joseph and Daniel (a reading immediately after Jezebel's death), the interlinking of these themes concludes with Henry singing/praying William Cowper's hymn "God Moves in a Mysterious Way." His night of reading and reflection on the Bible and slavery concludes with him envisioning a time when "a morning would break when all the black slaves would be free" (113). For Henry, this moment is a fait accompli, something God will accomplish at an unknown time in an unknown way. Such a reading dismisses human action and agency in the liberatory drama, something Exodus does not do. Even more, William Cowper, the hymn writer, was a staunch abolitionist. In fact, he wrote "The Negro's Complaint" in 1788.[11] He was also friends with the writer of "Amazing Grace," an important hymn that inspired William Wilberforce in England's abolitionist movement. Henry seems unaware of all of this. Instead, he seems to relegate human action to the background, favoring divine providence without human actors. For Henry, ending slavery is God's business, not his. In capping his Bible reading with Cowper's hymn (later used by Martin Luther King Jr. in the U.S. civil rights movement after *Sapphira*'s publication), Henry ironically cites a prominent figure within abolitionist movements in England that were concurrent to his time, mistakenly using Cowper's hymn to justify staying out of direct action to end Black oppression.

My point here is that Cather would likely have known these

oblique details—her liberatory moments are hidden but still present in the printed novel. This reference could be a sly wink toward abolitionist action by human effort—that political agitation can result in changed circumstances for oppressed people. These references further cloud the idea that slavery itself was beneficial to the enslaved and another moment of divine providence enacted on their behalf. Although he frees the Colbert slaves after Sapphira's death, Henry never risks anything to do so. His freeing of the enslaved is not a dramatic upending of the antebellum social order, nor is it an economic risk for his property or standing in the community. He *does* find gainful employment for the formerly enslaved, taking time to ensure they have community and employment, but this poses no challenge to slavery writ large; his actions do not subvert the social order within his family or community life. He does not risk rebuke or challenge from Sapphira, as he would have done if she were still living, and he does not seem to be hurt economically in freeing the enslaved. In fact, to keep the contentious Lizzie and Bluebell from returning, he tells them they are "needed at the mill place no more" (281). Henry might be saying whatever is needed to keep them from coming back, but the emphasis on need is telling— had they, and others, still been needed, would he have freed them? Nevertheless, Henry clearly sees the humanity in Black people and is commended for the trouble he takes in getting "good places fur his people" (281), as Till reports. But he never risks his own standing or person to work on their behalf, as many of those he cites, seeks counsel from, or reads about did. Here, Henry is again ironized by his limited perspective and choice that he cannot (or chooses not to) see. For Cather's readers—readers with the gift of historical perspective—the irony would not be lost.

Cather's intertexts matter. What she chooses to include is significant, even if those inclusions were derived from a subconscious reflexivity of a white writer crafting Black characters. The intertexts that remain in the printed version of *Sapphira* reveal a differing ethics and way of reading scripture between oppressor and oppressed and/or reference figures in abolitionist movements, even if they are not immediately recognized by white readers. Read from the perspective of Black Americans, in fact, Cather's biblical allusions reveal heroes who triumphed over imperialist actors. These heroes persevered and triumphed by remaining true to their beliefs and heritage. Daniel and Joseph were not made better by slavery but succeeded because they maintained their Hebrew heritage in the face of obliteration and acculturation by the imperial order. When those orders tried to impose their will upon the two men, these humble slaves upended the imperialist order in their fidelity to their traditions and refusal to capitulate. In including these seemingly oblique biblical allusions in the printed novel, Cather maintains a thread of resistance throughout *Sapphira and the Slave Girl* that, although not so direct for her characters as it was in the unpublished manuscript, is one that contemporary Black readers would likely recognize.

Simply put, the printed novel is loaded with liberatory allusions. It may very well be that Cather was "willing to sacrifice the realism and verisimilitude of the individual characters and relationships in favor of the larger dramatic and aesthetic demands of her novel," where the "realism and personhood of various characters must be subordinate to the narrative itself," as Clere maintains (458). Or it may be that Cather felt the novel was more reflective of reality by omitting overt references to liberation. Cather's biblical allusions illustrate a writer contending with the issues of Black liberation from slavery; she certainly thought about these moves and how best to represent that struggle throughout the composition of *Sapphira*. She seems also to have chosen the way Black Americans read scripture: against the grain, in ways hidden from white readers and interpreters of scripture, and toward oppressive aims. I wonder if Cather—an astute reader of the Bible—figured this out for herself, hit upon this approach by accident, from guilt, or perhaps gleaned such views from her acquaintance with Harlem Renaissance artists while she lived in New York City. In assessing Cather's relation to Black American characters or contemporary issues, her biblical allusions in *Sapphira* should not be overlooked. Whether she intended to include them or not, *Sapphira and the Slave Girl* contains clear moments of identification with and, potentially, celebration of Black liberation theology.

NOTES

1. As a historical term, Black liberation theology did not exist in Cather's era. James Cone created the term in the 1970s. Using biblical texts to fuel resistance against oppression certainly occurred during and before Cather's writing of the text and within the historical context of the novel. See also Henry Louis Gates Jr.'s *The Signifying Monkey*, especially the idea of the "talking book," also known as the "ur-trope of the Anglo-African tradition" (131), where Black readers and writers "seize upon topoi and tropes to revise their own texts" (128).

2. I reference the manuscript given to the University of Nebraska–Lincoln Archives and Special Collections by Charles Cather in 2011, which seems to precede other prepublication manuscripts (Clere 442).

3. I want to thank Sarah Clere for inspiring my work here. She was the first to study the *Sapphira* typescript, and she pointed me in the direction of the Exodus material for further study. Also, the James Woodress Research Grant allowed me to complete some work on this essay. I am indebted to both.

4. For those critical claims, see especially the works by Morrison, Urgo, and Camacho.

5. I use the term "white Protestant" throughout while recognizing that it does not fully capture the denominational diversity of the era and of the novel. My point is to highlight the contrast between the Black liberationist reading of theology with the impulses of the white characters.

6. For a contemporary Black reading of some of the songs included within the novel, see the Barbara Davis interview by Ann Romines. In fact, Jezebel's story resonated with Davis, a minister of a historic Black church near Cather's Virginia birthplace, when she read *Sapphira*. In Jezebel's story, Davis told Romines, she was "reminded of the Prophet Daniel and the three Hebrew Boys that had their Judean names changed to Babylonian names by their Babylonian captors. It did not break their spirit or change who they were. That is the feeling I get with Jezebel" (24).

7. I don't want to take the exodus metaphor too far, as many Black Americans exercised the right to stay in the areas they knew as their homes.

42

This plays out in the novel with the characters Sampson and Tansy Dave. Sampson—Henry's head mill hand—breaks down at the prospect of being freed by Henry, stating that Back Creek is his home and he wants to be among people he knows. Tansy Dave remains attached to the area even after leaving to live in the mountains. Although he occasionally returns, he is still regarded as a Colbert "property loss" (242). Dave's loss is taken lightly by Sapphira, since familial and cultural ties bind them to the place. For such enslaved characters, Exodus does not have to mean leaving but may suggest freedom from oppression and a threat of violent oppression for daring to leave.

8. The Sacred Harp songbook series credits Peter Cartwright for this song. Cartwright is white, but he left Kentucky for Illinois, per his autobiography, to "get entirely clear of the evil of slavery" (140). It is thus another hymn written by an antislavery advocate who was white.

9. I focus primarily on Henry and not Sapphira because of Henry's religious influences and his relationship to the Bible. He is identified as having been raised Lutheran and married to an Episcopalian, but he attends a Baptist church and is influenced by an elderly Quaker. He eagerly joins in singing with those in bondage and identifies their worship as authentic, even more so than the worship of white congregants. Henry's many Christian influences might seem to indicate all Christianity here—that this is an issue with which all forms of Christianity must engage. Further, Henry is a reader of scripture who studies the text for himself, as opposed to Sapphira, whose Episcopalian upbringing would have led to more of a focus on liturgy rather than scripture study. In the printed novel, Sapphira moves to use scripture to dominate Jezebel (which Jezebel resists), as she has no qualms about dominance and hierarchy. Henry's personal reading of scripture might come from his Lutheran background, or very possibly his Baptist influences, or it may reflect the personal reading culture prominent in the United States at the time. In short, Henry, influenced by many U.S. versions of Christianity, wonders if he too is complicit in slavery—all potentially reflective of Cather's and a white reader's own wrestling with these issues.

10. Isaac Watts, known as the "Father of English hymnody," composed "There Is a Land of Pure Delight" in 1709. Watts broke with German and Calvinist traditions in writing hymns with lyrics in contemporary language styled on New Testament rhythm and language rather than metrical psalms. Further, Watts was a Nonconformist like his father and refused scholarships to Oxford and Cambridge, instead attending the Nonconformist Dissenting Academy and later becoming a Lutheran minister. Watts could be

seen as a figure of principled rebellion against established religion and religious norms who sided with regular Christians rather than established leadership—something Henry seems to want to be, although he is not quite ready to buck tradition at the beginning of *Sapphira*.

11. William Cowper's "The Negro's Complaint" (1788) works against some of Henry's notions about the beneficent nature of slavery upon the enslaved. Cowper writes, "Forced from home and all its pleasures / -Afric's coast I left forlorn [...] Men from England bought and sold me / -Minds are never to be sold" (365). Cowper shows, then, an enslaved person who has a mind and agency that cannot be bowed by the institution; that person was better off before and only served to "increase a stranger's gold" when enslaved. In fact, Cather's typescript, as Clere argues, shows a more willful, strong agent in Jezebel than the printed novel does. All these moves undercut Henry's resignation and fatalism about his own role in manumitting his slaves and working against slavery in the U.S. South.

WORKS CITED

Berlin, Ira. *The Making of African America: The Four Great Migrations*. Viking-Penguin, 2010.

The Bible. King James Version, kingjamesbibleonline.org/. Accessed 8 April 2024.

Bible and Culture Collective. *The Postmodern Bible*. Yale UP, 1997.

Camacho, Roseanne. "Whites Playing in the Dark: Southern Conversation in Willa Cather's *Sapphira and the Slave Girl*." Romines, *Willa Cather's Southern Connections*, pp. 65–74.

Cartwright, Peter. *The Backwoods Preacher: An Autobiography of Peter Cartwright*. Applewood Books, 2009.

Cather, Willa. *Sapphira and the Slave Girl*. 1940. Willa Cather Scholarly Edition, historical essay and explanatory notes by Ann Romines, textual essay and editing by Charles M. Mignon, Kari A. Ronning, and Frederick M. Link, U of Nebraska P, 2009.

———. "Sapphira and the Slave Girl." Typescript. N.d. Box 18, Folder 2, and Box 1, Folder 25, Series 2: Manuscript and Publication Materials. Charles E. Cather Collection (MS 0350). Archives and Special Collections, U of Nebraska–Lincoln Libraries.

Clere, Sarah. "Cather's Editorial Shaping of *Sapphira and the Slave Girl*." *Studies in the Novel*, vol. 45, no. 3, Fall 2013, pp. 442–59.

Cone, James H. *A Black Theology of Liberation: Fortieth Anniversary Edition.* Orbis Books, 2012.

Cowper, William. "The Negro's Complaint," 1788. *The Poems of William Cowper,* C. Wells, 1835, Internet Archive, archive.org/details /poemsofwilliamco00cowp/page/364/mode/2up?q="Negro's+Complaint". Accessed 29 June 2024.

Davis, Barbara, and Ann Romines. "Songs and *Sapphira*: An Interview with Barbara Davis." *Willa Cather Review,* vol. 62, no. 2, Winter 2021, pp. 23–24.

Gates, Henry Louis, Jr. *The Signifying Monkey: A Theory of African-American Literary Criticism.* Oxford UP, 1988.

Genovese, Eugene. *Roll Jordan, Roll: The World the Slaves Made.* Pantheon Books, 1974.

Levine, Lawrence W. *Black Culture and Black Consciousness: Afro-American Folk Thought from Slavery to Freedom.* 1978. Oxford UP, 2007.

Miller, Keith. *Voice of Deliverance: The Language of Martin Luther King, Jr., and Its Sources.* U of Georgia P, 1992.

Morrison, Toni. *Playing in the Dark: Whiteness and the Literary Imagination.* Vintage-Random, 1993.

Pollard, Tomas. "Political Silence and Hist'ry in *Sapphira and the Slave Girl*." Romines, *Willa Cather's Southern Connections,* pp. 38–53.

Romines, Ann. Historical essay. Cather, *Sapphira and the Slave Girl.*

———. "Losing and Finding 'Race': Old Jezebel's African Story." *Willa Cather: A Writer's Worlds,* edited by John J. Murphy, Françoise Palleau-Papin, and Robert Thacker, Cather Studies 8, U of Nebraska P, 2010, pp. 396–411.

———, editor. *Willa Cather's Southern Connections: New Essays on Cather and the South.* UP of Virginia, 2000.

Stout, Janis P. *Cather among the Moderns.* U of Alabama P, 2019.

Urgo, Joseph. "'Dock Burs in Yo' Pants': Reading Cather through *Sapphira and the Slave Girl*." Romines, *Willa Cather's Southern Connections,* pp. 24–37.

3 Willa Cather's State of the Union
Sapphira and the Slave Girl

TRACYANN F. WILLIAMS

A portrait of the mixed-race woman (or "mulatta") as a key to modernist culture's fixation on race may be obtained through examination of *Sapphira and the Slave Girl*, Willa Cather's last novel. I explore the author's presentation of slavery and the mixed-race woman, a crucial figure in a melodramatic plot of abuse. In addition, I trouble the mixed-race woman's relationship to and confrontation with the construction of white womanhood in Cather's novel. This tension is usually absent from fiction, as it is typically not central to the plot. However, it is in this tension that I examine discussions of American national identity, power, and oppression, particularly of a nation built on enslaved labor during ante- and postbellum America.

Although published in 1940, *Sapphira and the Slave Girl* takes place in the nineteenth century, mainly in 1856, with the epilogue set in 1881. A complex text with slavery at its center, the novel focuses on Sapphira Dodderidge Colbert, a wealthy heiress, and her relationship to those around her. Despite deteriorating health and confinement to a wheelchair, Sapphira powerfully controls the operations of the family's Back Creek farm. But there are greater implications pre-

45

sented by Cather's novel. The marked, incapacitated white woman symbolizes the United States, swollen with the unresolved disease of racism and slavery. These issues erupt in Back Creek—and continue to stagnate throughout the United States. It is no wonder then that Sapphira is busily arranging the rape of Nancy, the "slave girl" of the title, finding sexual violence to be the one significant way to continue controlling Black bodies. To this end, I argue that Back Creek is a metaphor for the United States, a cultural and political "backwater" obsessed with (but unable to come to terms with) the ramifications of race and slavery.

Cather's Sapphira is the possessor of power and privilege in the novel, due to her family lineage and financial holdings in Back Creek. Although she has resided there for more than thirty years, she is not native to the area, having come from east of the Blue Ridge Mountains. As a wealthy heiress and landowner with slaves, Sapphira sees the white people native to Back Creek as simple, "very poor" people. More plainly, her favorite slave, Till, describes the people of Back Creek as "poor farmers and backwoods people," among whom Till's finer domestic service skills "had little chance" (70–71). Because of the Colberts' status within the community, Back Creek residents seem to be wary of their wealth and influence. At the same time, these people view their own whiteness as the only leveling agent in their poverty.[1] David Fairhead, the preacher at Rachel Blake's and Henry Colbert's church, observes that some of the poorer "mountain boys" resort to stealing and petty crime rather than work alongside Black laborers because they believe that their white skin grants them a certain degree of privilege: "It's the one thing they've got to feel important about—that they're white" (83). The residents of Back Creek cling to their whiteness as a marker of their privilege, much as Sapphira exercises her white and class privilege to be a propertied slaveholder and arranges her household as she sees fit. In Back Creek, tensions are on display in the relationships between the slaveholders and other white-presenting people. Back Creek folks are also painfully aware of the gradations of whiteness. It is noted that Henry Colbert, Sapphira's husband, "had grown up in a neighbourhood of English settlers [and had adopted their speech patterns]. [...] This was not, on Back Creek, a friendly way of talking" (9). However, his wife is allowed to speak as she likes because "a woman and an heiress had a right to" (9). The Back Creek residents seem to tolerate Sapphira Colbert. They don't have to like her, however. Cather's portrait of the United States (as represented by Back Creek) illustrates that wealth and privilege may be held by a limited few, in this case, one wealthy white woman who uses a wheelchair.

It is important for me to further deconstruct the subtleties within whiteness presented in the novel. The residents of Back Creek may think Sapphira and Henry an odd pairing, but Sapphira also sees herself very differently from the other members of her immediate family and is a beneficiary of the gradations of whiteness. As cultural historian Maurice Berger says in his book *White Lies*, "Whiteness is not a univalent category. The strengths and limitations of one's own whiteness depend on many factors; its power and privileges are not awarded evenly or evenhandedly" (166). Sapphira is of English heritage.[2] Her ancestors had come from the British Isles, whereas Henry Colbert and his family are considered "immigrants" because their grandfather came from Flanders (part of modern-day Belgium). The people of Back Creek "never forgot that he was not one of themselves" (9), implying that, like Sapphira, they too were of English ancestry.[3] In addition, Henry is Lutheran, not of the Church of England like his wife. This fact seems to be of note since the reader is informed that there were "disadvantage[s] of having been raised a Lutheran" (110). The difference in religion suggests a kind of character defect, as we understand that Henry's ambivalence about slaveholding (though he supports it, in essence, by not exercising his own ability as a man to free the slaves until after his wife dies) is related to his upbringing and religious background. In fact, the newlyweds' relocation to Back Creek allows Sapphira to avoid questions about Henry's "vague ancestry, even his Lutheran connections, [which] would have made her social position rather awkward" (25). I see a critical point here about gradations of whiteness and privilege, one that can be demonstrated through John Hartigan Jr.'s "Locating

White Detroit." Hartigan astutely explains that, in the United States, people are attempting a discussion of "an irregular terrain in which some whites always sit insecurely in the larger body of whiteness.... [T]he gap between whiteness and whites opens distinct horizons of social and political contexts" (204). This statement underscores the need for incisive analyses of class, which certainly plays a significant role in discussions of whiteness. In Cather's novel, Sapphira is living in a white community and yet is among strangers, foreigners even. The reader, then, can problematize the socioeconomic privilege of Cather's title character and how that white privilege still goes unchallenged.

On its surface, it may appear that Sapphira's privilege is a consequence of her marriage, adhering as it does to the typical strictures of nineteenth-century marriage contracts. Historian Elizabeth Fox-Genovese's work on gender in the plantation South is useful in demonstrating that Sapphira's world is an anomaly. "[T]he lady, like other women," Fox-Genovese writes, "remained bound by a broad vision of appropriate gender relations.... In a world dominated by male strength, women could not aspire to be the head of a household" (203). In contrast, the novel takes pains to describe how the heiress feels about her property. As a child, she inherits a rather sizable Back Creek property from her uncle.[4] This place is part of an area described as "nameless except for [its] unpronounceable Indian [name]" (29). That Sapphira inherited the Back Creek property as a child aligns with historian Stephanie E. Jones-Rogers's research into the activities of slaveholding women in her study *They Were Her Property: White Women as Slave Owners in the American South*. Through numerous examples, Jones-Rogers illustrates how southern women actively managed their plantations because "[t]hey had an immense economic stake in the continued enslavement of African Americans" (150). Similarly, the fictional Sapphira is a formidable presence in the novel, controlling the day-to-day operations, including the lives of her enslaved property. She finds in Henry, four years her junior, a serendipitous match. Henry had been serving as a business advisor to Captain Dodderidge after the older gentleman became incapacitated by a riding injury. Perhaps even more conveniently, Henry, as well as his father before him, is a miller. (The land, which included a water mill, had been rented for fifty years by various tenants.) Henry provides something invaluable to his wife: he offers her the ability as a female to dictate much of the day-to-day course of her life, including their move to Back Creek. Henry's "vague ancestry" and convenient ambivalence about slavery further contribute to his perceived powerlessness. As Judith Fetterley notes in her essay "Willa Cather and the Question of Sympathy: An Unofficial Story," "[Sapphira] married a man willing to let her be the master" (19).

As a master, Sapphira has the power or right to make decisions about her property, including her slaves. Many theorists have written about the underlying motivations for Sapphira's problematic plan for Nancy, ranging from an inability to act on her own lesbian desires to an attempt to enact her power, literally using Martin Colbert, her nephew by marriage, as a phallic substitute.[5] Part of the horror of Sapphira's aging and physically declining body rests in her inability to be sexually intimate with another human being or to be procreative. Sapphira's husband, Henry, rebuffs her expressions of longing for physical company or contact a number of times. For example, after Jezebel's funeral, Sapphira says, "'Surely you don't mean to go back to the mill tonight, Henry, with your good clothes on,'" but her husband explains he has business to tend to and leaves her in the house. Therefore, it is possible that the violence of the sexual act that Sapphira arranges for Nancy is a manifestation of Sapphira's frustrations with her own sexual life. It is also possible that she remained unmarried as long as she did because she is unable to act upon same-sex desire. In addition, though Sapphira was then a vital young woman, she could also have been asexual. There is also the possibility that Sapphira is tiring of the proscriptions of "white ladyhood" and, in the case of Nancy, having to obtain her husband's permission to take action. However laced with sexual tension or the need to demonstrate power her decision may be, the novel provides evidence that Sapphira's motivation lies in the Back Creek world she has constructed for herself.

50

TRACYANN F. WILLIAMS

Very early in the text, Sapphira offers, "I ought to be allowed to arrange Nancy's future" (12). And why shouldn't she control Nancy's body? In the groundbreaking book of literary criticism *Playing in the Dark: Whiteness and the Literary Imagination*, Toni Morrison contemplates this question in her analysis of *Sapphira and the Slave Girl*: "It is after all *hers*, this slave woman's body, in a way that her own invalid flesh is not" (23). In a violent text, articulating white female autonomy in tension with slavery's continuance in a U.S. backwater, Sapphira is trying to make unsettling "arrangements" for Nancy. With this knowledge, Till's loyalty to Sapphira can come across as a romanticized notion of Black female loyalty to their slaveholders— even to the detriment of her relationship with her own daughter. But Till's behavior can be better explained as a consequence of how slavery distorts interpersonal and particularly family relations. Due to the nature of female enslavement and the difficult circumstances under which enslaved women were required to accommodate the sexual advances of white males, it is not clear that Till's liaison with Nancy's father was consensual. However, it is interesting to contemplate that Nancy's father could be the Cuban painter who had visited Back Creek some years earlier to paint the portraits of the Colberts that hang in the parlor.[6] The novel reports conspiratorially, "He was a long while doing them" (74). One wonders if this line is about the Cuban painter's portraits or his sexual liaisons with enslaved females. Whatever significance can be derived from the line, a possible union between Till and the portrait painter can be imagined as the only agency or defiance Till might have exercised after her arranged marriage to Jefferson. And, regardless, Nancy's paternity is not known, this "in spite of her resemblance to the portrait painter from Cuba" (68). The identity of her father continues to be the subject of wide speculation on Back Creek, again due to certain presumptions about the nature of slavery. To imagine a consensual union between two people of color destabilizes the social and legal prescriptions of slavery in the United States. The preferred narrative (because it is the more commonly "accepted" one under slavery) is that one of Henry's brothers is Nancy's father: "The Colbert men had a bad reputation where women were concerned. [. . .] Nancy was often counted as one of the Colbert bastards" (68). Nancy's paternity is more likely connected to the Cuban painter, yet time and again the characters assert that the young slave girl is a Colbert. Certainly Till, as Sapphira's property, is subject to her mistress's will, a familiar American narrative that Cather's novel reinforces. I assert, however, that for all the gossip about the male Colberts' inability to control themselves sexually, an "inter-American" paternity narrative that displaces the Colberts, including Sapphira, is quite compelling. Their potential lack of masculine potency in relation to Till and control over the American narrative is unsettling. With Jacob Colbert as Nancy's alleged father, Cather writes a paternity story that cleaves more to the United States' narrative of miscegenous activity between Black enslaved females and white men.[7]

The other issue that these speculations raise concerns the ways that white enslavers are able to control the narrative and the circumstances of Black family construction. For example, Sapphira "married [Till] off to Jefferson," who was many years her senior. In fact, he is chosen for Till by Sapphira because he is a "capon man," or sterile. He is also described as having certain "incapacities [that] were well known among the darkies" (74). At a time when enslaved persons were not permitted to marry each other (or, for that matter, anyone of their choosing), it is interesting that Sapphira chooses a sterile man for her prized parlor maid once Till presumably is sexually viable. The underlying tension in fact is that a sexually active Till might be distracted from her focused attention toward her mistress. On the other hand, Nancy has fallen out of favor with Sapphira, having been "treated [. . .] like an untrustworthy stranger" for some time (47). Sapphira could be trying to find some utility for Nancy by simultaneously manipulating the "slave girl's" possible fertility, with the added benefit of increasing her own wealth. Jones-Rogers's research about white women's involvement in slavery supports this reading. She observes that white women "personally orchestrated acts of sexual violence against enslaved women and men in hopes that the women would produce children who would increase their wealth" (149). In this way, one can imagine a possible, though incredibly troubling, rationale for Sapphira's plan for Nancy. Because she is unable to sell Nancy without her husband's permission, Sapphira decides to tie the slave girl to the Back Creek farm through procreative and profit-based means, which amounts to something very different from the fate she envisioned for her devoted housemaid Till. Cather shows not only how slavery distorts human relationships but also that female enslaved persons are part of an economy that permits open access to their sexuality.

It is also necessary to note that Cather neglects to imagine Till's feelings of having to live with Jefferson (or even the previous sadness of having to leave the intimacy of her relationship with the Devonshire housekeeper Mrs. Matchem, who served as Till's mentor in the art of domestic service). The reader is informed that "Till accepted this arrangement with perfect dignity" (74). Closer analysis reveals that Till, through her sexual relations, might have been retaliating in the only way she could. The Cuban painter is commissioned "[s]ome years after [Till] had moved her belongings from her attic chamber in the big house over to Jeff's cabin" (74), and she is pregnant soon after. Till's decision to have a liaison with the Cuban painter, if she did indeed do so, would be her only known act of rebellion against Sapphira's efforts to control the people and action around her. Sapphira suffers from what I would call an "entitled impotence," asserting herself in the only arena she can control. The potential circumstances of Sapphira's plan to "couple" Nancy with Martin provide additional evidence of Sapphira's desperation to assert power and authority.

Sapphira has betrayed Till twice, having separated the young woman from Matchem and then set out to arrange her sexual future. And yet, Till remains exceedingly loyal to her mistress. Till has a congenial relationship with Sapphira, very different from Nancy's. Till counsels Nancy on how best to placate Sapphira's recent bad humor with her. Yet, their conversation reinforces the master-slave relation because their relationship is predicated on Sapphira's needs and Till tending to them. For example, Till suggests to Sapphira that she will "wear the kid shoes around the house a few days more an' break 'em in for you," so that the new shoes will not pinch her mistress's swollen feet (34). Sapphira is even described in one of her direct addresses to Till as having "joked" with her slave. Throughout the novel, their interactions do come across as "pleasant," in the sense that they do not evoke the "contemptuous indulgence" she exercises with some of the other enslaved persons (138). Still, for all the apparent good humor, there is a self-preservation bordering on an utter selflessness within Till with respect to her relationship to Sapphira.[8] "Anything that made trouble between her and the Mistress would wreck the order of the household" (217). Such was the training that Till took to heart under the tutelage of the Devonshire housekeeper, Matchem, that "there was all the difference in the world between doing things exactly right and doing them somehow-or-other" (72–73). Ultimately, though, Till's service props up her mistress's white ladyhood, making it possible for Sapphira to effect her plan for Nancy's sexual life. As Morrison suggests in *Playing in the Dark*, "That condition could only prevail in a slave society where the mistress can count on (and an author can believe the reader does not object to) the complicity of a mother in the seduction and rape of her own daughter" (21). How does Cather come up with such an inexplicably violent text?

In the midst of this disturbing plot line, the novel explores how slavery might be troubling the balance of Sapphira's marriage. One of the key events in the novel is the illness and death of Jezebel, an older slave on the Back Creek farm. After Jezebel's funeral, Henry has a moral wrestling with himself about slavery. He reminds himself that he has the "legal right" to free all of Sapphira's slaves, but it is not a serious thought. Practical questions like "Where would they go? How would they live?" (110) allow Henry to trade the slaves' individual liberty for his wife's good humor. He eventually comes to the conclusion that "[n]owhere in his Bible had he ever been able to find a clear condemnation of slavery [. . .] nowhere did his Bible say that there should be no one in bonds, no one at all" (112). That Cather has Henry Colbert ruminating on slavery for several pages, examining the moral and religious underpinnings of the institution, is curious. It results in problematic analyses like literary theorist Mary Ryder's observation that Henry may be "the most enslaved character of the book" though he is a propertied white male, albeit through marriage.[9] Henry evokes sympathetic feelings because he is recognizable, simultaneously wrestling with white supremacy and benefiting from its trappings. However, Henry's perceived oppression in a text where enslaved people have no freedom of movement, much less the ability to exercise their own personhood, is suggestive of the continued potency of white supremacy, even at the end of the twentieth century (when Ryder's analysis appears).

Sapphira's husband, Henry, is described many times in the novel as being different, almost foreign, in comparison to his wife. He is even in opposition to his blood relatives with respect to their views of how to treat Black people: "She had married the only Colbert who had a conscience, and she sometimes wished he hadn't quite so much" (110). Henry's ruminations, though, do little to affect race relations in Back Creek. Henry settles upon an observation he has made, seemingly over many years, that the Bible seems to justify the slave system. As Ryder notes, "What he seeks is mercy, God's forgiveness for his involvement in a system that he instinctually feels is wrong but with which he will not interfere because of his commitment to his wife" (134). He is hopeful that slavery will soon end, thus putting an end to his interminable conflict.[10] He further comforts himself by recalling a recent interaction with Sampson, a "mulatto" slave. When Henry offers his head mill hand an opportunity to work as a free man in the Pennsylvania Quaker mills, Sampson begs beseechingly to stay a slave, citing his wife and children as the reasons he wishes to remain enslaved. In this way, the reader might misinterpret Sampson's comfort with slavery, particularly by his wanting to keep his family together (though there was certainly no guarantee that the Colberts would honor a commitment to them). However, Sampson further reveals "he'd a'most sooner leave the chillun than leave the mill" (111), suggesting that his loyalty is actually more to the mill and Henry Colbert than to his love for and commitment to his family. There are real material and interpersonal concerns revealed through the characters of Henry Colbert and his slave Sampson. Yet, Sampson's statement makes plain Cather's connection to other nostalgic treatments of slavery and enslaved persons, like those in Margaret Mitchell's *Gone with the Wind* (1936), and contradicts accounts contained within nineteenth-century narratives of enslavement. Authors of such narratives, Mary Prince among them, articulate how freedom—even that which is granted in foreign places with the clear knowledge that there will be no reunion with family in this lifetime—is the only reasonable end to the barbaric institution of slavery. Prince states more than once, "To be free is very sweet" (94). Sampson, however, cannot imagine freedom within the world of the novel. In the end, Sampson's unwillingness to be freed assures Henry of the rightness of slavery—and its continuance in Back Creek. In an intimate exchange with his wife, Henry decides, "There are different ways of being good to folks. [...] Sometimes keeping people in their place is being good to them" (264). We learn in the epilogue that Henry frees all the slaves upon Sapphira's death, going to "a wonderful lot a' trouble gittin' good places for his people" (281). Still, the cumulative effect of Henry's early comments and actions reveals a willful blindness to his social responsibility, not unlike other white people who avoid examining their indirect role in the oppression and violence against Black people.

In fact, Henry's intermittent conversations with his wife about slavery, specifically regarding what to do with Nancy, begin in the first scene of the novel and lay the groundwork for Sapphira's eventual drastic action. Further, because Sapphira is unable to imagine any kindnesses being bestowed upon her slaves, except within the narrowly prescribed guidelines of her own mind, she begins to have suspicions about Henry's late-night musings and goings-on at the mill. After Jezebel's funeral, Sapphira observes a "deep conversation" between Henry and Nancy in which Henry is described as "speaking very earnestly, with affectionate solicitude" in his interaction with the grieving young woman (105). Cather writes that Henry had "forgotten himself" because "he was not speaking as master to servant. [...] It was personal" (105–6). Has he exceeded the prescribed nature of master-slave relations? The thing is, there are no legitimate rules in a practice as despicable as slavery. The preoccupation with adultery allows these characters to refocus attention away from issues that are more uncomfortable. Were Sapphira to truly believe that her slave was having an affair with her husband, she could sell Nancy away from the familiarity of her surroundings and make a profit. But Henry has made it quite clear that he will not give his permission for the sale. Before she hatches the rape plot, Sapphira devises an elaborate scheme to take Nancy on her annual spring visit to Sapphira's sister through the Easter holidays because "[i]t would smarten [Nancy] up, to see how people do things" (53). One can assume that Nancy would see how other enslaved females behave with their mistresses and follow suit. The trip does not provide the desired lessons, evidently, so more drastic means are necessary. More tellingly, Nancy is a threat to Sapphira because of her youth, beauty, and mixed-race status, symbolic of a new America. The novel informs the reader that "Nancy came into the world by accident," indicating that the circumstances of her birth were unusual (suggesting her likely Cuban paternity). Although unable to pass for white, Nancy has greater proximity to whiteness than the other slaves on Back Creek, hence her potentially increased mobility (something Sapphira is literally lacking).[11] Slavery, we are told, "was their natural place in the world" (217), and yet Nancy's existence communicates otherwise. Bluebell, another slave, suggests that the very mixture of Black and white (if you believe the popular narrative of Nancy's origins as a Colbert) makes Nancy dangerous: "she's stuck up, havin' white blood [. . .] dat set all de culled folks agin her" (184). Individuals standing at the crossroads of Black and white can be read as symbolic of a new America. Furthermore, Sapphira's nephew, Martin, observes, "The niggers here don't know their place, not one of 'em" (181), after his interactions with Sampson and Nancy, both mixed-race persons who do not behave according to their prescribed roles. These racially mixed persons are part of the new or evolving United States, but that country is unrecognizable to most white people. Valerie Babb has noted that "filling cultural

institutions with representations only of whites . . . all generate
a spontaneous, if subconscious, recognition of the supremacy of
whiteness and sanction the perception that whites intrinsically have
more right to what is American than do other groups in the United
States" (42). Cather's use of the "mulatta" character ultimately offers
a window into the American collective cultural and political psyche
and the fraught relationship that exists between the races. Much in
the way the miller takes in brown wheat and produces white flour, I
argue that Cather is refining away the confusion of changing political dynamics, restoring a world in which a mistress with limited
mobility can still oppress those around her, denying citizenship and
agency to those perceived as Other.

While there is no excuse for Sapphira's despicable plans to "arrange
Nancy's future," I would locate her declining health as one moti-
vating factor for her actions. The first descriptions of Sapphira's
appearance place her in direct contrast to Nancy. Sapphira's hands
are plump compared to Nancy's "slender, nimble hands" (21). Further descriptions of Sapphira's body indicate that she is not well:
"The Mistress had dropsy and was unable to walk [. . .] all the more
cruel in that she had been a very active woman" (13–14). In these
lines, the reader can understand how devastated Sapphira might
feel about her failing health and deformed lower limbs. Dropsy,
more commonly known today as edema, is a pooling of fluid in
certain areas of the body (frequently in the limbs) and suggests the
presence of other medical issues. Her condition literally has her
housebound and dependent on others, which in some ways may
intensify her frustration. Sapphira was previously able to be mobile
or to manipulate modes of mobility; her current level of despair
might also be amplified by the realization that she has become—
like many nineteenth-century women—tied to the home. The evidence of her physical deterioration, which is masked to the public
with "dresses [that] touched the floor," also signals Sapphira's mortality. Is Cather giving a portrait of the 1850s (or her own time of
the 1930s)? I argue that Sapphira's incapacitation and swollen legs
are indicative of the state of the Union. At a time when nations are

immersed in discussions of personhood and citizenship, she is what is left over, an incapacitated white female body unable to reproduce. Almost a century after the novel's publication, the United States is arguably still a backwater, unable to fully live up to the promises of its founding principles.

It may be useful to read some vulnerability into the characterization of Sapphira. Early in the novel, she reflects on illness, divulging her feelings about her father's debilitating illness in relation to her current physical condition. "In those days she had not known the meaning of illness. To be crippled and incapacitated, not to come and go at will, to be left out of things as if one were in one's dotage" (107). I would posit that perhaps the father and daughter's shared illness, one passed down in families, is racism and white privilege. Sapphira never characterizes herself as "crippled and incapacitated" until after she witnesses Nancy and Henry in conversation after Jezebel's funeral. Once Henry rebuffs Sapphira's request that he stay in the house that evening, she is taken to her room by Washington, another slave, and Till prepares her for bed. If nothing else, these pages depict Sapphira's lack of mobility. What have been historically perceived as masculine tendencies (mobility, willingness to explore, trying to create one's own destiny, etc.) become thwarted by incapacitation in Sapphira, similar to the state of Captain Dodderidge in his final days.

However, Sapphira's deteriorating physical condition provides additional information for the reader. Cather's Back Creek is a white southern utopia that reveals what is safely hidden in the American imagination about race—and the desire for the continued oppression of Black people. These meditations are arguably central to the text, causing the kind of violence and hysteria evident in Sapphira's plan for Nancy. There is an extended, bucolic description of Back Creek making reference to white flowers and trees, particularly the dogwoods with "their singular whiteness" (117). These are lasting memories shared by "[e]very Virginian" and subtly evoking the shared experiences of whiteness as it relates to slavery and the subjugation of Black people.[12] Literary scholar Patricia Yaeger observes that this whiteness "becomes a haunting *signifier of what cannot be thought* or organized either in the nineteenth-century historyscape of the novel or in the landscape of the 1930s from which Cather herself is writing" (147). Further illustrating the lasting impression of whiteness and slavery is the appearance of Cather herself as the five-year-old narrator in book IX who refers to "our Nancy" (274). Although the narrative in that section takes place some twenty-five years after the main events of the novel, the child is intimately acquainted with Rachel, Till, and Nancy. She has been hearing about "our Nancy" her entire life, the possessive indicating a certain investment or participation in Black subjugation. The use of the first person in this section also suggests the immediacy of the child's connection to slavery and the Civil War.

Before Nancy's return, Cather cannot imagine any intimacy between mother and daughter. There is a void of feeling or emotion through much of the text. In Till and Nancy's first scene together, Cather has them cleaning in a flurry of activity in the service of Sapphira. There is no conversation of a personal nature between them, since Cather does not consistently imagine relationships among her slaves that are not adversarial. One might argue that most (if not all) of the novel's relationships involve various complex expressions of oppression and power. For example, Rachel's marriage depicts affection, but she too operates in service to her husband, and the reader learns of their relationship in oblique summary: "self-abnegation which [...] took the form of untiring service to a man's pleasure and of almost idolatrous love for her [male] first-born" (142). Rachel has two older sisters that Sapphira has "married very well" (133). Yet, Sapphira takes to her room to deal with the shock that Michael wants to marry sixteen-year-old Rachel. She cannot imagine that she was not the architect of Rachel's life prospects, which she had decided would be rather limited. The novel informs the reader that "even from an invalid's chair she was still able to keep her servants well in hand" (56). Given that Till thwarted Sapphira's plan (when she was impregnated by the Cuban painter *or* Jacob Colbert) and Rachel frustrated her marriage plot (by wedding Michael Blake), Sapphira must turn her attention to Nancy. One wonders if Sapphira's motives do not also relate to complicated feelings of jealousy surrounding Nancy's looks and beauty. Regardless, this tension speaks very clearly to the lack of sisterhood among the women in Sapphira's household and Nancy's incredible vulnerability. Toni Morrison notes that "[t]he absence of camaraderie between Nancy and the other slave women turns on the device of color fetish. . . . The character [Cather] creates is . . . a fugitive within the household" (23). To further the point, we can turn to Cather's published correspondence; in a 14 October 1940 letter to Dorothy Canfield Fisher, she revealed that the real-life "meeting between Nancy and Aunt Till . . . was one of the most moving things that ever happened to me when I was little" (*Selected Letters* 592). Although we have access to the child's recollection of their meeting, the reader has not had access to the interiority of these Black women's lives. Cather is perhaps unable to imagine or commit to exploration of that interiority because this is *her* book, certainly not that of the nameless slave girl in the novel's title—or her enslaved mother. Any camaraderie exists between Cather and her titular character.

Because Sapphira has made so much of the Colbert men's curse of being womanizers, one wonders if Henry Colbert is suppressing his desire for Nancy. The novel explains that he had inherited the Colbert curse (191) but that he has gotten a handle on it since being married. The knowledge of his nephew's sexual plans for Nancy threatens to undo Henry; he is described as not being able to look at Nancy for a while because she suddenly becomes a woman to him. Then, he seems to be proving his virility and reclaiming his Colbert masculinity and viability as a man, while mowing the wheat fields (207–8); right after this action he begins obsessing about Martin's designs and how his own relationship with Nancy is not the same. In fact, I argue that the novel portrays him as seeing Nancy *for the first time* through Colbert eyes because Martin has awakened something dormant within Henry. Perhaps the change in how Henry sees Nancy is why he contributes to her escape. Henry is involved but cannot face the reality of his action: "Hush, Rachel, not another word! You and me can't talk about such things. It ain't right. [. . .] I can't be a party to make away with your mother's property" (223–24). But he does make "a way" for Nancy to escape by financing the journey. Yet, simultaneously, Henry admonishes his daughter with the following statement: "[N]othing must pass between you and me on this matter; neither words nor aught else" (224). In order to maintain the fragile reality on Back Creek, there can be no record of their transaction.[13] In other words, it is best for all involved that Rachel and Henry forget the betrayal of their contract with whiteness.

Although Nancy escapes with Henry and Rachel's support, she remains ensnared in the memories of Back Creek's residents. The first-person child-narrator of the epilogue shares that her lullaby evoked memories of Nancy: "*Down by de cane-brake, close by de mill / Dar lived a yaller gal, her name was Nancy Till*" (274). Just over one hundred pages earlier, Martin Colbert sings these lines in one of his first attempts to overpower Nancy. As he says, "There never was a finer morning for picking cherries or anything else" (177). That the child-narrator finds soothing words that originate in the violence of owning Black bodies is not surprising due to the disconnect in the American psyche that cannot reconcile its past. It is also evidence of the extent to which slavery and white privilege are part of the fabric of the United States.[14] For her own part, the child already has prejudices about Black people. Although the child has no lived memory of slavery, she cannot embrace a fully realized Black person. She admits that she expected the actual Nancy to be "the picture I had carried in my mind," that of the pejoratively rendered "yaller gal" (277). Nancy's words, then, are described as "too precise," causing the child to be "repelled" (284). For example, Nancy enunciates the syllables of the word *history*, which the child says she "didn't like. [. . .] Even my father said 'hist'ry'" (284). Nancy's speech pattern is described as not being "friendly" in the novel. In Back Creek, as in the recesses of the American mind, there are behaviors particular to Black people, behaviors that aren't legible in a stereotypically racialized American narrative. There is a connective thread to earlier points in the novel about Black women's position, such as the big fuss made over Jezebel's illness and death. Yet, the entire section of the novel devoted to the old slave's passing is bursting with descriptions of Black men and women as various creatures. The beloved slave is depicted as looking like a "lean old grey monkey" with a "cold grey claw" (88, 91). Most tellingly, Jezebel is descended from "a fierce cannibal people" (93). It's as if Cather thinks her readers may have missed that the only thing "Auntie" Jezebel craves in her last days is a "li'l pickaninny's hand" (90). Jezebel's deathbed revelation of cannibalism further underscores the common perception that slavery is needed to control Black people's behavior. There are erotic connotations to the old Black woman desiring the child's hand, which are disturbing.[15] And yet, Jezebel has been intimately tied to Sapphira for so long that she could be channeling her troubled mistress's thoughts, which are too horrible to place on the white female. Jezebel's desire takes the place of Sapphira's suppressed longing to consume and control the flesh of her slave girl. As Morrison concludes, "[T]he author employs [Black characters] in behalf of her own desire for a *safe* participation in loss, in love, in chaos, in justice" (28). With all of this in mind, how do we place this work?

Sapphira and the Slave Girl deserves to be part of the conversation about Cather's oeuvre, because she is writing about what people need to read.[16] Given the recent work of scholars like Jones-Rogers, Cather's work about a white female slaveowner becomes that much more relevant. As Jones-Rogers notes about women enslavers, the "products of these women's economic investment . . . were fundamental to the nation's economic growth and to American capitalism" (xiii). White women's slaveholding and ensuing wealth were an integral piece in the positioning of the United States as a superpower. She also notes there was an additional gain for these women: "slavery was [white women's] freedom. They created freedom for themselves by actively engaging and investing in the economy of slavery, and keeping African Americans in captivity" (xvii). The white slaveholding female, like the fictional Sapphira, traded on the horrors of slavery for their own gain, disrupting our understanding of female-to-female interactions, as well as notions about frailty and helplessness. In the end, as Morrison notes, authors have a particular responsibility to the characters they create: "[a]n author is not personally accountable for the acts of his fictive creatures, although he is responsible for them" (86). Cather's novel demands a nuanced textual exploration that allows readers to reconcile its contents with her position as an iconic American author.

Critics are often disquieted by Cather's arguably racist articulation of Black characters in *Sapphira and the Slave Girl*, which played a role in the lack of attention to the novel until recent years. Part of the discomfort derives from the American belief that the absence of formal, legal discrimination necessarily means the absence of any further complicated or troubling issues surrounding race. There is also the belief that no one should make pointed assertions on race in polite company and certainly not a celebrated novelist like Cather. As Toni Morrison notes in *Playing in the Dark*, "The contemplation of this black presence is central to any understanding of our national literature and should not be permitted to hover at the margins of the literary imagination" (5). Any illusions about Cather's intentions throughout the text should be quelled by the author literally entering the text. Cather offers a signed postscript following the epilogue, indicating that her parents relayed stories of "acquaintances whom they had met" on their visits to Virginia, though they were "unknown" to her (288). She simply had a "lively fascination" for their names. Cather dispels the fiction of the story in her 14 October 1940 letter about the novel to close friend Dorothy Canfield Fisher, which reveals that this story and "darkey speech ... was deep down in my mind exactly like phonograph records" (*Selected Letters* 592). Further, Cather's 9 November 1940 letter to American editor and author Viola Roseboro indicates the immediacy of the material: "not very much of it is actually fiction. . . . I scarcely know where my own contribution to it begins" (*Complete Letters* #1502). Cather also shares both the challenge of the material and rendering it accurately. She sent Roseboro one of two advance copies of the novel, admitting, "The stage trappings of such a narrative are so easily come by, but there is something else which eludes and eludes—I mean the

64

Terrible" (*Complete Letters* #1502). These views signal *Sapphira and the Slave Girl* as a major work, precisely because it is difficult and uncomfortable. No such discussions will call into question Cather's skill as an author. In the end, *Sapphira and the Slave Girl* shows the American white woman knowing and writing the disease of racism, leaving bare the gaps and omissions in a collective history yet to be fully addressed.

NOTES

1. The field of whiteness studies has extensively unpacked how individuals view the currency afforded by white skin privilege, as well as how that privilege shifts and changes depending on time and circumstance. For representative works, see especially those of Lipsitz, Frankenberg, and Babb.

2. Note that Sapphira's given name has various associations that may provide more context for the character's motivations (Romines, Historical essay 413–14).

3. According to Ann Romines, residents who inhabited the Back Creek area were typically of English, German, and Irish extraction (Historical essay 303).

4. The provenance of the Back Creek property also connects to larger issues of whiteness and privilege. One Nathaniel Dodderidge was deeded a tract from the "original" owner, Thomas, Lord Fairfax, in 1747. Fairfax's actual landholdings were some "five million acres of forest and mountain." The only reason he releases some parcels to "desirable settlers" (Cather, *Sapphira* 28–29) is to placate dissatisfaction in Virginia's legislative body over individuals holding such a large estate. The Native Americans who previously occupied the land are deemed unimportant and an afterthought. Until Sapphira moves to Back Creek, no Dodderidges live on the farm, vacant for some hundred years. It is important to note that, according to Ann Romines, Cather herself was born in Back Creek Valley, Virginia, on family property deeded by Lord Fairfax around 1750 (*Cather's Southern Connections* 2).

5. For discussions of sexuality and homoeroticism in Cather's work, see the chapter "'Dangerous Crossing': Willa Cather's Masculine Names" in Judith Butler's *Bodies That Matter*, as well as Eve Kosofsky Sedgwick's essay "Across Gender, Across Sexuality." Marilee Lindemann, in *Willa Cather: Queering America*, also presents a helpful argument against readings that focus solely on homoerotic desire. And noting "the Sapphic pun in the name of Cather's

heroine," Lisa Marcus offers a smart reading that considers the implications of race, gender, and sexuality in her essay "'The Pull of Race and Blood and Kindred': Willa Cather's Southern Inheritance."

6. The character of the "Cuban painter" is a provocative, ghost-like presence in the novel. He is possibly another "mulatto" figure, passing through Back Creek and the issues of race presented therein. Regardless, he paints white people—and perhaps beds Black people. The fact that he is unnamed is intriguing as well, given that the text names various tangential characters.

7. If that is the case, then, Sapphira is arranging to have Nancy raped by her half-brother, Martin, further reinforcing narratives about liaisons involving white men and enslaved Black women.

8. Till and Sapphira's relationship resonates with what may be seen between two characters in the movie *Imitation of Life* (1934). The nature of the interracial relationship is different (master-slave in the novel versus business "partners" in the film). However, one can read the difference in perception between male, white, and external production (Miss B) versus female, Black, and internal pursuits (Delilah). Both *Sapphira and the Slave Girl* and *Imitation of Life* construct a mixed-race daughter (Nancy and Peola, respectively) who disrupts the natural course of this primary relationship.

9. The book is set in the 1850s South, but Cather is writing the book in ⟨1930s⟩ the late 1930s, well after the Civil War and the Emancipation Proclamation, while the horrors that World War II will inflict are becoming more apparent. As Ann Romines has noted, "Willa Cather's Virginia had not yet been shattered by death, removal, or loss. . . . Returning to *Sapphira* was also a way of forgetting the daily horrors of the war news after World War II had begun" (Historical essay 362). Cather may be questioning what transpired in the tensions of the pre–Civil War period, as well as the outcome of the war. It is also likely that the author is considering the perceived simplicity of the earlier time, through the lens of whiteness, a somewhat safer pursuit than a late 1930s world being ravaged by fascist aggressions.

10. Cather presages the liberal, well-intentioned white person's conundrum, brought into stark reality by reaction to numerous instances of police brutality and murder in 2020. Initially, people participated in rallies and contributed millions of dollars to organizations like Black Lives Matter but soon moved into complacency and suspicion about antiracist activism when discussions moved to advocate actively toward defunding the police.

11. Historically, some lighter-skinned Black people have experienced treatment that is more favorable or have had access to greater social mobility due to their visual and actual proximity to whiteness. Cather explores this

dynamic briefly in her discussion of the free mixed-race woman, Sarah, who helps Rachel Blake prepare and serve food at the Washington dinner parties she hosted for her husband (139).

12. See also James Baldwin's 1965 short story "Going to Meet the Man," which explores intraracial bonding through the communal experience of lynching.

13. In the end, Rachel also wrestles with the decision she has made to assist Nancy. She is described as knowing the deep hurt she has exacted upon her mother, by humiliating the older woman whose health is rapidly declining. Rachel wonders aloud, "Maybe I ought to have thought and waited" (243). These ruminations, similar to her father's earlier in the novel, suggest how disposable slavery's horrors are.

14. In her documentary *Traces of the Trade: A Story from the Deep North* (2008), filmmaker Katrina Browne reveals that her New England ancestors were the largest slaveholding family in the United States. She also reveals the enduring effects of slavery on the psyche. As children, she and other relatives hummed a nursery rhyme taught to them presumably by older generations. She discovers that the subjects of the seemingly innocuous tune, Adjua and Palidor, were slaves owned by her family.

15. Interestingly enough, journalist Nicholas Wade has reported that archeologists discovered evidence of cannibalism among English settlers at the Jamestown Colony site in Virginia.

16. I would argue that the silences around slavery and white supremacy undergird the motivations for the violence visited upon the U.S. Capitol and members of Congress on 6 January 2021. The very symbol of a traitorous and failed insurrection, the Confederate battle flag, was unfurled in the Capitol rotunda.

WORKS CITED

Babb, Valerie. *Whiteness Visible: The Meaning of Whiteness*. NYU Press, 1998.
Baldwin, James. "Going to Meet the Man." *Early Novels and Stories*. Library of America, 1998.
Berger, Maurice. *White Lies: Race and the Myths of Whiteness*. Farrar, Straus and Giroux, 1999.
Butler, Judith. *Bodies That Matter: On the Discursive Matters of "Sex."* Routledge, 2011.
Cather, Willa. *The Complete Letters of Willa Cather*, edited by the Willa

Cather Archive team, *Willa Cather Archive*, cather.unl.edu/writings/letters. Accessed 3 September 2021.

———. *Sapphira and the Slave Girl*. 1940. Historical essay and explanatory notes by Ann Romines, textual essay and editing by Charles W. Mignon, Kari A. Ronning, and Frederick M. Link, U of Nebraska P, 2009.

———. *The Selected Letters of Willa Cather*, edited by Andrew Jewell and Janis Stout, Knopf, 2013.

Fetterley, Judith. "Willa Cather and the Question of Sympathy: An Unofficial Story." Romines, *Willa Cather's Southern Connections*, pp. 10–21.

Fox-Genovese, Elizabeth. *Within the Plantation Household: Black and White Women of the Old South*. U of North Carolina P, 1988.

Frankenberg, Ruth, editor. *Displacing Whiteness: Essays in Social and Cultural Criticism*. Duke UP, 1997.

Hartigan, John, Jr. "Locating White Detroit." Frankenberg, *Displacing Whiteness*, pp. 180–213.

Imitation of Life. Directed by John M. Stahl, performances by Claudette Colbert, Louise Beavers, and Fredi Washington, Universal, 1934.

Jones-Rogers, Stephanie E. *They Were Her Property: White Women as Slave Owners in the American South*. Yale UP, 2019.

Lindemann, Marilee. *Willa Cather: Queering America*. Columbia UP, 1999.

Lipsitz, George. *The Possessive Investment in Whiteness: How White People Profit from Identity Politics*. Temple UP, 1998.

Marcus, Lisa. "'The Pull of Race and Blood and Kindred': Willa Cather's Southern Inheritance." Romines, *Willa Cather's Southern Connections*, pp. 98–119.

Mitchell, Margaret. *Gone with the Wind*. Macmillan, 1936.

Morrison, Toni. *Playing in the Dark: Whiteness and the Literary Imagination*. Vintage, 1992.

Prince, Mary. *The History of Mary Prince: A West Indian Slave, Related by Herself*. 1831. U of Michigan P, 1997.

Romines, Ann. Historical essay and explanatory notes. Cather, *Sapphira and the Slave Girl*.

———, editor. *Willa Cather's Southern Connections: New Essays on Cather and the South*. UP of Virginia, 2000.

Ryder, Mary. "Henry Colbert, Gentleman: Bound by the Code." Romines, *Willa Cather's Southern Connections*, pp. 130–37.

Sedgwick, Eve Kosofsky. "Across Gender, Across Sexuality: Willa Cather and Others." *Displacing Homophobia: Gay Male Perspectives in Literature and*

Culture, edited by Ronald R. Butters, John M. Clum, and Michael Moon, Duke UP, 1989, pp. 53–72.

Traces of the Trade: A Story from the Deep North. Directed by Katrina Browne, Alla Kovgan, and Jude Ray, California Newsreel, 2008.

Wade, Nicholas. "Girl's Bones Bear Signs of Cannibalism by Starving Virginia Colonists." *New York Times*, 1 May 2013, nytimes.com/2013/05/02/science /evidence-of-cannibalism-found-at-jamestown-site.html. Accessed 3 May 2013.

Yaeger, Patricia. "White Dirt: The Surreal Racial Landscapes of Willa Cather's South." Romines, *Willa Cather's Southern Connections*, pp. 138–55.

4 Back to Virginia

"Weevily Wheat," *My Ántonia*, and
Sapphira and the Slave Girl

STEVEN B. SHIVELY

Willa Cather makes it easy for readers (and scholars) to give little attention to the song "Weevily Wheat" in *My Ántonia*. Cather places the verse in the pleasant kitchen of the Harling house; here daily life is filled with laughter, cleanliness, playful children, music, and good food. A happy Ántonia mixes a cake as the children, Jim Burden and the young Harlings, "were singing rhymes to tease Ántonia":

> I won't have none of your weevily wheat,
> And I won't have none of your barley,
> But I'll take a measure of fine white flour,
> To bake a cake for Charley. (154)[1]

The "Weevily Wheat" moment contains multiple unspoken, sometimes concealed, connections to Virginia, particularly and surprisingly to Black American culture. The song—overlooked, nondescript, seemingly innocent—exemplifies the depths of Cather's Virginia heritage and the cultural cross-pollinations prevalent in her work.

Bernice Slote notes that in *Sapphira and the Slave Girl* "a life-time load of unwritten, cancelled Virginias, comes back across the prairies to both beginnings, the life and the art" (112). Slote's statement still resonates, but two International Willa Cather Seminars in Virginia and over two dozen South-centric essays later we have become increasingly aware that many of Cather's Virginia memories were written as much as they were "cancelled," and they appear, sometimes clearly but often clouded, in much of her writing before *Sapphira*. Ann Romines notes the "complicated legacy of Virginia memories" while arguing "that much of Cather's best fiction *before* her specifically Southern novel of 1940 [*Sapphira*] is, on some level, engaged with the problem of how to remember and to render the South" ("Admiring" 279). In particular, Romines points out that "the South surfaces in *My Ántonia* through Jim Burden's early memories and the Virginia landscape of his dreams and in the troubling inset story of Blind d'Arnault, an African American artist who was born a slave" (279). I argue here that "Weevily Wheat" carries compelling messages about Cather's conflicted relationship with the South and the ways she wrote about Black Americans.

My analysis seeks to provide an affirmative answer to the question posed by Anne Goodwyn Jones in "Displacing Dixie: The Southern Subtext in *My Ántonia*": "Can we ... find traces of the South troubling the Midwestern terrain of *My Ántonia*?" (89). Jones locates such traces in the d'Arnault episode of course but also in Jim's relationships with the Shimerdas, his ideas of male heroism, and his ongoing tensions with white southern masculinity. Elizabeth Ammons, in "*My Ántonia* and African American Art," concludes that "[Cather's] novel is deeply indebted to and shaped by African American music" (59). Ammons concentrates her perceptive analysis on Blind d'Arnault, the most significant presentation of a Black American musician in the Cather canon. While d'Arnault represents the most intentional and self-aware (though neither fully intentional nor fully aware) such portrait outside Virginia, ghosts of a Black American musical presence in the novel are also significant.[2] "Weevily Wheat" represents such a ghost, a moment whose Blackness has been unknown, ignored, and concealed. Furthermore, the reality of weevil-infected wheat and the associated metaphorical, signifying meanings communicate important aspects of the slave experience in the United States, expressing both the inherent unfairness of slavery and the strength of enslaved people.

The lyrics Cather includes are the chorus to a longer song, popular in the nineteenth century and with wide geographic and ethnic distribution. (Some of the many variants change the "Weevily Wheat" chorus to a verse; others, under titles like "Charley over the Water" or "Charley, He's a Dandy," eliminate it and emphasize Charley as a ladies' man.) The lyrics vary considerably depending on such factors as geography, culture, and occasion. Found in collections of slave songs and Appalachian backcountry music but also in compilations of Irish and Scottish American folksongs, Wyoming ranch songs, pioneer songs of Minnesota, Indiana play-party songs, and more, the song's popularity continued in the twentieth century, when it appears in the writings of iconic folk music collectors John and Alan Lomax, in musical scores by Peggy Seeger, in twenty-six entries in the *Checklist of Recorded Songs in the English Language in the Library of Congress*, in over a dozen tapes and records in the Library of Congress, and in perhaps the best-known collection of American folk music, Carl Sandburg's *The American Songbag*. Hamlin Garland drew on its popularity in his short story "The Sociable at Dudley's: Dancing the 'Weevily Wheat'" from *Prairie Folks*, and Laura Ingalls Wilder memorably captured its power in *On the Banks of Plum Creek* when Pa Ingalls sings and plays "Weevily Wheat" on his fiddle in a climactic Christmas Eve moment joyfully celebrating his safe return after being lost in a blizzard. YouTube videos and online curriculum guides teach contemporary students to sing and dance "Weevily Wheat." The song's popularity suggests an influential cultural artifact grounded in family, neighborhood fun, and the midwestern pioneer experience. And so it appears in *My Ántonia*. Cather's song choice, however, carries and conceals meanings that are often at odds with these assumptions.

There is nothing obvious, neither textually nor contextually, in the "Weevily Wheat" incident in *My Ántonia* to connect it to Virginia or to anything involving Black Americans. The song and its coded language were nevertheless important to nineteenth-century Black Americans in terms of entertainment, metaphorical meanings, and suggestions of protest. The song's obvious characteristics—its subject of wheat and its genre of folk singing and dancing—provide a starting point for establishing a link to slave life. Wheat was an important crop in nineteenth-century Virginia, and it was subject to pests such as weevils. Before Cather knew the wheat fields of the Midwest, she knew the cycle of planting and reaping in Virginia, and she knew wheat as the source of grain for mills, including those her family had operated. Wheat was the largest crop in Frederick County, Virginia, home of the Cather family and the primary setting of *Sapphira* (Romines, explanatory notes 407–8, 432–33, 456, 500). As in the novel, Black Americans worked with wheat in the fields, the mills, and the kitchens, and wheat was a common subject of popular songs. Singing and dancing are of course universal to virtually all groups, including enslaved Black Americans. Lawrence W. Levine notes the widespread presence of music and dance among slaves (15), a fact Cather acknowledges in *Sapphira*, even given the relatively small population of slaves at the Mill Farm and in the Back Creek region. In that last Cather novel, the singing of Lizzie and Bluebell is much admired, and Tansy Dave "used to play for the darkies to dance on the hard-packed earth in the backyard" (204). Romines documents that "[d]ances on Saturday nights and special occasions were common on plantations throughout the South" (Explanatory notes 497). The musicality of Black Americans is also present in *My Ántonia* through visiting "negro minstrel troupes" (153) and Blind d'Arnault's capacity to perceive the hired girls dancing in the kitchen as well as his ability to "draw the dance music out of [the piano]" (185).

In particular, versions of "Weevily Wheat" are prevalent in compilations of the music of Virginia and the rest of the South, and it is common in accounts of Black American music. Even though folk music was rarely written down, as early as 1868 "Weevily Wheat" was documented by John Mason Brown in "Songs of the Slave": "who could hear, without a responsive tapping of the foot and unbending of the wrinkled brow, 'I won't have none of your weevily wheat / I won't have none of your barley'?" (619). In his important collection *Negro Folk Rhymes: Wise and Otherwise*, Thomas Talley includes a common "Weevily Wheat" variant that discards the negative weevils and includes several fun verses emphasizing the dandy Charley and his appeals to women. The Virginia Folklore Index in the Archive of Folk Song at the Library of Congress includes eleven listings of recordings (index in Folder 13; recordings in Folders 6, 7, 10). The Gordon Manuscripts of the American Folk-Song Collection include two versions of "Weevily Wheat" (item 2603, vol. 9; item 3387, vol. 11) contributed by B. Clay Middleton, who notably collected folk material from Loudoun County, Virginia, an important place in *Sapphira* and well known to the Cather family. (While this archival material was recorded in the twentieth century, notations make clear that the song is part of a long-standing folk tradition.) "Weevily Wheat" was also popular in more mountainous regions of Virginia, places like Timber Ridge in *Sapphira*. Sandburg counts "Weevily Wheat" among the songs of pioneers who "left their homes to take up life in the Alleghenies and to spread westward" (161). John and Alan Lomax note that "'Weevily Wheat' has been enjoyed at play parties in backwoods districts in every part of the country" (xxxvi). Considerable cultural exchange occurred between Black workers and their white masters and fellow workers, a point affirmed by Levine: "black slaves engaged in widespread musical exchanges and cross-culturation with whites among whom they lived" (6). Cather includes such musical amalgamation in *Sapphira* when Black and white congregants and mourners experience music together at church and at Jezebel's funeral. It also occurs in *My Ántonia*, most notably when Sally Harling plays on the piano "the plantation melodies that negro minstrel troupes brought to town" (153).

Scholars and collectors often classify "Weevily Wheat" as a play-party song and game closely related to a dance but without the physical contact or movements that made dancing objectionable to some. Dena Epstein confirms the entertainment's slave origins when she defines "play party" as "a celebration for children and young adults which originated during slavery and features games, singing, and dancing" (43). "Weevily Wheat" is part of a lively account of play-party fun enjoyed by Black Americans, as told by Alice Wilkins, born a slave in 1855; her narrative was transcribed by an employee of a Work Projects Administration (WPA) effort to record the memories of former slaves:

> Wen I wuz raisin' my chilluns, dey had dey play-parties an' some of de games dey played wuz "Weevily Wheat," de boys stood in a line an' de gals in 'nuther line facin' de boys, dey sing as de boys swing dey partners an' den dey promenade up an' down de line an' swing each one of de boys an' gals, dey sing, as dey promenade an' dance to de music of de Jews harp.

> "Oh, I won't have none of your weevily wheat,
> I won't have none of your barley,
> It'll take some flour an' half an' hour,
> To bake a cake for Charley."

> Wen de parties over dey com's home a tired an' a happy chillun's to dey old mammy an' pappy, an' to dey dreams. (S. Brown)[3]

Black Americans' fun sometimes carried serious messages as well, revealing hardship and protest to those who could see through the disguises. Music (and stories and other aspects of life) popular with children often had metaphorical meanings for adults; words and phrases expressed covert messages. Oppressed people, whose talk was often overheard and whose every circumstance could be observed by overseers and owners, spoke coded language with meanings known only among themselves—language replete with metaphor, pun, and irony. As Eileen Southern, a Black musicologist, has written, "We know, of course, from the testimony of ex-slaves that the religious songs ... often had double meanings and were used as code songs" (200). Southern extends her claim to the "satirical song," noting that often "the slaves slipped a derisive verse or two about white listeners into songs they were improvising thus following in a hallowed

African tradition for satire" (173). Zora Neale Hurston includes in *Mules and Men*, her treasury of Black folklore, a discussion about "by-words"; one man says, "There's a whole heap of them kinda by-words. [...] They all got a hidden meanin'" (125). With language they created and controlled, Black Americans became artists with a subversive message.

Weevil-infested wheat, the circumstance prompting the song "Weevily Wheat," is a prominent example of coded language. In a prefatory note to *Weevils in the Wheat: Interviews with Virginia Ex-Slaves*, the editors explain the book's title:

> Weevils in the wheat (often simply "bugs in the wheat") was an expression used by slaves to communicate to one another that their plans for a secret meeting or dance had been discovered and that the gathering was called off. The "weevils" were either members of the patrols that were organized to discourage movement of the slaves off the plantation at night or fellow slaves who, as part of a loosely organized spy system, were willing to turn informer for small favors granted them by slaveowners. The use of such a secret code was only one of numerous adaptive strategies developed by the slaves that enabled them to lead relatively full lives—in spite of "weevils in the wheat." (Perdue, Barden, and Phillips n.p.)

The location in Virginia of the slaves whose recollections constitute the book *Weevils in the Wheat* is particularly significant due to Cather's own family heritage and her fiction set in Virginia, especially *Sapphira*. The phrase "weevils in the wheat" turns the tables on a common expression in white culture, "slave in the woodpile" (typically using a more racist word for "slave"), to describe people in a place where they do not belong, where they can cause trouble. Now, however, the misplaced people, the potential troublemakers, are white, and it is the Black Americans who identify them, warn others, and prevent harm. The slaves are not naïve and innocently trusting; rather, they are savvy. To sing "I won't have none of your weevily wheat" or, as in many versions, "I don't want none of your weevily

STEVEN B. SHIVELY

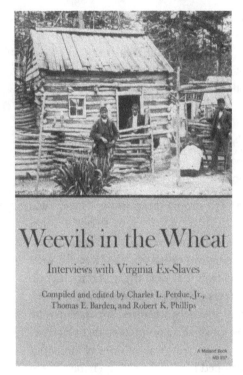

Fig. 4.1. The cover of a collection of slave narratives from Virginia. Charles L. Perdue Jr., Thomas E. Barden, and Robert K. Phillips, editors, *Weevils in the Wheat: Interviews with Virginia Ex-Slaves* (Indiana UP, 1980). Reprint of 1976 edition published by the UP of Virginia.

wheat" makes a literal complaint, but it also expresses an attitude, a desire to get rid of a broad range of "bugs," of outsiders, of troubles.

An aspect of Black life particularly fraught with double meanings and coded language was sex. Sex was a nearly inescapable source of trauma and anxiety and a tool white people used to control and dominate Black Americans during and after slavery. Sex can also be characterized as fun; it is often a source for jokes and other comic forms. Consequently, sexual double entendres were (and remain) common. "Weevily Wheat" probably carries such language. In 1927 Guy B. Johnson wrote about "the presence of double meanings of a sex nature in the blues" and other "Negro songs" (12, 13). Johnson points out common terms for female sex organs, including "bread," "cookie," "cake," and "short'nin' bread" (14). If, as Johnson argues, "[m]y baby loves short'nin' bread" is sexual innuendo, then "make a cake for Charley" likely had a sexual double meaning. At least one of Talley's "Weevily Wheat" variants carries sexual overtones:

> Charlie's up an' Charlie's down.
> Charlie's fine an' dandy.
> Ev'ry time he goes to town,
> He gets dem gals stick candy. (84)

The potentially risqué vocabulary (up an' down, fine an' dandy, stick candy), the targeting of "dem gals," and the offer of sweets for presumed favors insinuate sexual meanings, both pleasurable and threatening. Cather uses this paradoxical connotation of sweetness when she recounts the history of Old Jezebel in *Sapphira*. When the young Jezebel was inspected by a doctor for a prospective buyer, the doctor offered her a square of maple sugar, apparently to test her disposition. Cather writes, "She crunched it, grinned, and stuck out her tongue for more" (97). This moment captures Jezebel's spirit but also contains sinister implications of a sexual nature.

An earlier and more politically charged use of "weevily wheat" occurred when Sojourner Truth spoke the words. Margaret Washington, in her biography of Truth, provides context and an example: "Sojourner Truth ... especially loved speaking in parables, using fables, metaphors, and humorous anecdotes to unravel or reduce complexities to simple yet serious understanding. Her 'weevil in the wheat' was a master parable that contextualized a major issue and revealed her signifying technique" (282–83). In response to the Supreme Court's *Dred Scott* decision that Black Americans were not protected under the Constitution, Sojourner Truth spoke a comparison to the weevil-in-the-wheat as a way to criticize the decision. Washington records the account of Truth's Quaker friend Joseph Dugdale:

> "Children, I talks to God and God talks to me," she said. "Dis morning I was walking out, and I got over de fence. I saw de

wheat a holding up its head, looking very big." Her powerful deep voice rose as she emphasized VERY BIG, drew up to full height, and pretending to grab a stalk of wheat, she discovered "dere was *no* wheat dare!" She asked God, "What *is* de matter wid *dis* wheat?" And he says to me, "Sojourner, dere is a little weasel [*sic*] in it." Likewise, hearing all about the Constitution and rights of man, she said, "I comes up and I takes hold of dis Constitution." It also looks "*mighty big*, and I feels for my rights, but der ain't any dare." She again queried God, "What *ails* dis Constitution?" The Constitution, like the infested wheat, was rotten, and God declared, "Sojourner dere is a little *weasel* [*sic*] in it." (283)

Sojourner Truth emphasizes the infectious, destructive nature of the weevil, and she powerfully casts her talk in religious terms with God pointing out the cause of the evil. To sing "I won't have none of your weevily wheat" affirms the ability to perceive rottenness and the courage to reject it.

"Weevily Wheat"—in terms of song, language, ideas—was significant to Black Americans as entertainment but also as a commentary on slavery and discrimination. The words Cather includes in *My Ántonia* certainly make more sense coming from enslaved and mistreated people than from children. Furthermore, Cather extends the gendered nature of resistance from the household slaves of *Sapphira* to the "hired girls" of *My Ántonia*. "Resistance was woven into the fabric of slave women's lives and identities," argues Elizabeth Fox-Genovese while locating this resistance in daily life: "The ubiquity of their resistance ensured that its most common forms would be those that followed the patterns of everyday life" (329). When "Weevily Wheat" is removed from the dance floor and the mouths of children and examined in the context of slavery or other oppressed peoples, especially women, its participation in the language of resistance becomes apparent. The words carry a burden (making do with weevily wheat) yet speak resistance (I don't want). Viewed in this way, the speaker or voice is transformed from a teasing child to a strong female resistor of injustice demanding something better:

Fig. 4.2. Sojourner Truth, circa 1864. Mathew Brady Studio. National Portrait Gallery, Smithsonian Institution.

I won't have none of your weevily wheat,
And I won't have none of your barley,
But I'll take a measure of fine white flour [...]. (*My Ántonia* 154)

Here is awareness of unfair treatment of workers: the usual ration for slaves and servants was lousy wheat and rough grains. Refined flour was reserved for masters and the wealthy. Cather knew the unfairness if not the particulars, both from her knowledge of culture and literature and from observation; she had written of the harsh reality of Ántonia's family eating frozen, rotten potatoes they got from the postmaster's garbage (72). Among cultural figures who expressed sympathy for workers is Frederick Douglass, who recorded a widely known slave song in his autobiography *My Bondage and My Freedom*:

We raise de wheat,
Dey gib us de corn;
We bake de bread,
Dey gib us de cruss;
We sif de meal,
Dey gib us de huss;
We peel de meat,
Dey gib us de skin,
And dat's de way
Dey takes us in. (202)

The injustice for those who did the work is obvious even though slaveholders often tried to argue that their slaves were cared for and happy. The people who planted the wheat, cultivated and harvested it, kept the flour mill going, then baked and served the bread usually received only bits and pieces of secondhand rations. And they knew it.

The preference in "Weevily Wheat" for "fine white flour" over barley and rough wheat acknowledges a historical reality. Harold McGee, in *On Food and Cooking: The Science and Lore of the Kitchen*, points out the historic nature of negative feelings about barley: "The historian Polybius (2nd century BC) reports that reluctant soldiers were punished by confinement and barley rations, and Pliny said that 'barley bread [. . .] has now fallen into universal disrepute.' In the Middle Ages, and especially in northern Europe, barley and rye breads were the staple food of the peasantry, while wheat was reserved for the upper classes" (235). The desire for quality wheat is present in most versions of "Weevily Wheat," but of the more than thirty American versions I have seen, only Cather includes the word *white*, a word that goes beyond description to carry racial undertones, especially in the context of Virginia rather than Nebraska. Usually the lyric reads "I want some flour and half an hour," although Dale Cockrell, who has written about Laura Ingalls Wilder's use of the song, once represents the line as "I'll take the very best of wheat" (*Music* 48) and another time as "I want fine flour in half an hour" (*Ingalls Wilder Family* 17). With her choice (or memory) of "white," Cather evokes a Black folk tradition satirizing white food. The exuberance of Paul Laurence Dunbar's "The Party," for example, celebrates that "[w]e had wheat bread white ez cotton an' a egg pone jes' like gol'" (85). Langston Hughes and Arna Bontemps cite tales in which food has racialized implications, including, "In a Pittsburgh hash-house one day a Negro customer said to another one at the counter, 'here you are up North ordering *white* bean soup. Man, I know you are really free, now'" (503). Occurring before the Blind d'Arnault episode, the word *white* in "Weevily Wheat" seems to mean little in *My Ántonia*, probably nothing beyond description, but in racially mixed settings like Virginia it would have been a meaningful code word.

In *Sapphira and the Slave Girl* Cather repeatedly demonstrates her awareness of the distinction between refined wheat flour and flour made from other grains. Her precise mentions of light bread and white flour indicate Cather understood the complex economic, social, and racial meanings of such labels. The first example occurs when Sapphira gives instructions to the kitchen slave Lizzie about preparation of food for watchers during Jezebel's wake: "Mrs. Blake will tell you how many loaves of light bread to bake" (101). Calling attention to the significance of "light bread," Cather includes a rare footnote explaining that "'[l]ight' bread meant bread of wheat flour, in distinction from corn bread." Light bread is a mark of Sapphira's generosity and her desire that Jezebel be paid respect, but it is also a mark of Sapphira's concern for appearances. Bread made from good wheat flour is a clear example of noblesse oblige, of Sapphira doing her perceived duty to take good care of her slaves and to sustain her reputation.

White flour is a point of pride at the Colbert mill. When Henry Colbert presents to Sampson, his head mill hand and slave, a plan for securing Sampson's freedom and a job in Philadelphia, Sampson objects because at the Colbert mill they are able to "bolt finer white flour than you could buy in town" (111). When it comes to flour—and by code word, much more—being "fine" and "white" is a mark of achievement, at the top of a hierarchy of accomplishment. The words "finer white flour" are a near echo of the lyric Cather uses in "Weevily Wheat"—"fine white flour," words that are not usually part of the song.

The next *Sapphira* occurrence of fine wheat bread comes when Rachel prepares a gift basket she will take to Mrs. Ringer, who is white, at her backcountry home: "she had also a fruit jar full of fresh-ground coffee, half a baking of sugar cakes, and a loaf of 'light' bread. The poor folks on the Ridge esteemed coffee and wheat bread great delicacies" (119). This passage reinforces the idea that light bread is a treat brought to people of lower socioeconomic status, both white and Black, by generous rich people.

Cather's final mention of light bread in *Sapphira* comes in the novel's closing section, after the Civil War and after the deaths of Sapphira and Henry Colbert. Till, now a servant instead of a slave, tells the story of Sampson, now a successful worker at an automated roller mill in Pennsylvania. When Sampson visits the Mill Farm, he comes to Till's cabin "every day he was here, to eat my light bread" (282). Due to the kindness of the new miller, Till still lives in her old cabin, but now she bakes light bread for herself and her guests. Sampson says, "Just give me greens an' a little fat pork, an' plenty of your light bread. I ain't had no real bread since I went away." Circumstances are different from previous instances with light bread: no longer is white bread only bestowed on economically poor people like slaves and backcountry folks by their economic superiors. Till, who still lives in much the same economic and social circumstances as when she was a slave, now has regular access to the former delicacy. Sampson, while racially united with Till, has achieved comparative economic success in "a wonderful good place" where he has "done well." His presumed progress, however, has occurred in a large, mechanized Philadelphia mill where the machinery "burns all the taste out-a the flour" (282). Light bread is a marker of Cather's observation that "[t]he war had done away with many of the old distinctions" (271) even as it affirms the racial, cultural, and socioeconomic importance of refined wheat bread.

Sapphira repeatedly acknowledges the significance of white bread atop the foodstuff pecking order as it portrays destructive social injustices in Sapphira's household. Nevertheless, the novel lacks a strong voice of resistance, especially in domestic activity. Objections to slavery are expressed privately and in broad strokes and by only a few white characters. The novel's recognition of the sexual threats and harms that accompanied slavery is important, as is the help of a free Black minister in guiding Nancy to the Underground Railroad's promise of safety, but acknowledgment of the social injustice of the privileged class controlling the products of the laboring class is understated. A few occasions of largesse seem to satisfy the characters. The closest example of voiced resistance comes from Old Jezebel, who replies to Sapphira's inquiry about what she might need: "The old woman gave a sly chuckle; one paper eyelid winked, and her eyes gave out a flash of grim humour. 'No'm, I cain't think of nothin' I could relish, lessen maybe it was a li'l pickaninny's hand'" (90). Even near death, Jezebel refuses to play the part of the grateful slave and declines to show proper appreciation for her mistress's visit. Jezebel's rejection could be cast as an echo of the verse from "Weevily Wheat": "I won't have none of your fake manners / I won't have none of your food / But give me a dark baby's hand to eat / And that's enough for me." Such a verse does not exist, but Jezebel's brush-off of Sapphira's offer captures the anger in the song's defiant refusal of weevily wheat.

Sapphira contains only veiled suggestions of unfairness, nothing like that voiced in the protest song from Frederick Douglass's autobiography: "We raise de wheat, / Dey gib us de corn." This note of anger and resistance, missing in *Sapphira*, was, however, often present in popular Black American music. The words of "Weevily Wheat," placed in the plantation culture of the South instead of the Harling family kitchen, suddenly resound with social protest: "I won't have none of your weevily wheat [...] but give me a measure of fine white flour." The voice is assertive, firm, demanding. Structurally and rhetorically, Cather's verse resonates with a verse of "Mule on de Mount," from Hurston's *Mules and Men*:

> I don't want no cold corn bread and molasses,
> I don't want no cold corn bread and molasses,
> Gimme some beans, Lawd, Lawd, gimme beans. (269)

A similar but even stronger message of resistance presents itself in the folk song commonly known as "No More Auction Block." The subtle move from "I don't want" to "No more" powerfully opposes economic injustice. One verse in particular speaks to agriculture:

> No mo' peck of meal for me,
> No mo', no mo',
> No mo' peck of meal for me,
> Many thousands gone. (Work 456)

Other common verses lead with the lines "no more driver's lash for me," "no more pint o' salt for me," "no more mistress' call for me," "no more children stole from me," and "no more slavery chains for me." Cornmeal and salt were usual slave rations. Including them in a litany of complaints that includes the whip, chains, and children taken from their mothers indicates that the singers knew the full range of persecution inherent to slavery. The routine distribution of a stingy allotment of poor food was a mark of white authority and control that ultimately called for a response of "no more" and "I don't want." Not including overt protest in *Sapphira* does not mean that Cather was unaware of protest in the songs and stories of Black

Americans. Her artistic purposes lay elsewhere. Just as *My Ántonia* contains ghosts of plantation Virginia, *Sapphira* contains ghosts or shadows of Black Americans' protest and resistance.

Given the prevalence of "Weevily Wheat" in the South and its racialized, symbolic meanings, it may seem odd that Cather included it in *My Ántonia* rather than in *Sapphira*, but I believe she probably did embed an allusion to the song in *Sapphira*. When Martin Colbert comes upon Nancy in the cherry tree, his purposes are sexual, and he greets her with the words, "Cherries are ripe, eh? Do you know that song?" (178). The explanatory notes to the scholarly edition suggest "'Cherries Ripe,' an anonymous old children's song," and "'There Is a Garden in Her Face,' a song by Thomas Campion," as possible sources (Romines 493). A more likely source for Martin's allusion is a verse included in many versions of "Weevily Wheat." Sandburg renders it as:

> The higher up the cherry tree
> The riper grow the cherries;
> The more you hug and kiss the girls
> The sooner they will marry. (161)

An intriguing version rendered in Black American dialect that substitutes "Sweet-uh" for "riper" appears as part of "Squirl, He Tote a Bushy Tail" in *Eight Negro Songs*, collected by Francis H. Abbot (Abbot notes that he collected the songs in Bedford County, Virginia):

> High-uh up de cherry tree,
> Sweet-uh grow de cherry,
> Soon-uh yuh go cote dat gal,
> Soon-uh she will marry. (21)

This verse from a song popular among both white and Black southerners would have been familiar to people like Martin Colbert and Nancy Till, and Cather has them say both "ripe" and "sweet" in the frightening scene (177–80). The specific detail of a cherry tree; the sexual undertones of ripe, sweet fruit, particularly cherries; and the

overt mention of hugging and kissing reinforce the sinister implications of the scene in *Sapphira*.[4] Recognizing "Weevily Wheat" as
a likely point of connection between *My Ántonia* and *Sapphira and
the Slave Girl* suggests other commonalities between the two novels:
both feature strong women from upper and lower socioeconomic
groups, both include troubling scenes with stereotyped Black characters, and both recognize the threat of sexual assault for slave women
and hired girls.

If Cather carried "Weevily Wheat" in her memory bank as she
moved from Virginia to Nebraska, she enacted a migratory process
common to folk music, including "Weevily Wheat." Many scholars believe it originated among the Scots-Irish people of Britain,
the region from which Cather's ancestors emigrated. Russell Ames
writes that "'Weevily Wheat' is ancient, derived perhaps from an old
Scottish play" (69). *The Nursery Rhymes of England* includes a version
that substitutes "nasty beef" for "weevily wheat":

> Over the water, and over the sea,
> And over the water to Charley.
> I'll have none of your nasty beef,
> Nor I'll have none of your barley;
> But I'll have some of your very best flour;
> To make a white cake for my Charley. (Halliwell 8)

In *On the Trail of Negro Folk-Songs*, Dorothy Scarborough establishes
the racial mobility of songs like "Weevily Wheat": "One of the most
fascinating discoveries to be made in a study of southern folk-lore is
that Negroes have preserved orally and for generations, independent
of the whites, some of the familiar English and Scotch songs and
ballads, and have their own distinct versions of them" (33).

According to most scholars, the "Charley" of "Weevily Wheat"
commemorates Bonnie Prince Charlie. As early as 1904 Emma Bell
Miles posited, "It is not improbable that the Charley of these songs
is the Prince Charlie of Jacobite ballads, for a large proportion of the
mountain people are descended from Scotch highlanders who left
their homes on account of the persecutions which harassed them

during Prince Charlie's time, and began life anew in the wilderness of the Alleghenies" (121). The line "Charley over the water" also suggests this view. Cather herself reinforced a relationship between Charley Harling and Prince Charlie when she wrote, "[Ántonia] seemed to think him a sort of prince" (151).[5] Understanding the Charley of the song as Prince Charlie underscores the message of economic and social disparity and the satirical method of "Weevily Wheat"; an enslaved cook in a plantation kitchen baking a cake for a prince calls for sarcasm: "Sure, just give me some good flour and I'll bake a cake for the prince himself." A more culturally relevant association is possible when "Charlie" is understood as a common, usually pejorative, label often used by slaves for the master, the owner of the plantation, no matter his real name: the *Random House Historical Dictionary of American Slang* defines Charlie as "white men regarded as oppressors of blacks—used contemptuously. Also Mr. Charlie, Boss Charlie." In each of its cultural iterations, "Weevily Wheat" communicated economic and social disparity: yeoman farmers and serfs set against Bonnie Prince Charlie, house slaves set against plantation mistresses and Boss Charlie, and immigrant hired girls set against the merchant class.

Never a uniquely Black American cultural expression, "Weevily Wheat" lost its visible ties to Black culture as it spread across the Midwest and West. This process was not unusual, especially once the forced interactions endemic to slavery were replaced with the forced segregation of Jim Crow. In addition, more Black Americans stayed in the South or migrated to cities than left for the rural Midwest, where the song remained popular. It is likely that some cultural purging also occurred, a harmful process noted by Perry A. Hall in "The Appropriation of Music and Musical Forms": "[A]s musical forms are absorbed, they eventually become reshaped and redefined, subtly and otherwise, in ways that minimize their association with 'Blackness'" (32).

"Weevily Wheat," like Willa Cather, landed in Red Cloud, Nebraska. Rachel Crown documents that her mother sang a version of the song (without the adjective "white") in Red Cloud in the 1880s (45). The

88

STEVEN B. SHIVELY

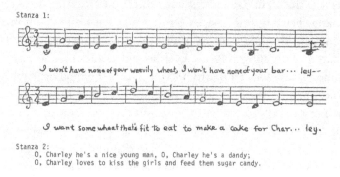

Fig. 4.3. A version of "Weevily Wheat" reported by Rachel Crown to have been sung in Red Cloud by her mother and grandmother in the 1870s or 1880s. *Willa Cather Review*, vol. 31, no. 4, Fall 1987, p. 45. Willa Cather Foundation, Red Cloud, Nebraska.

song and the girl both carried complex and intertwined influences, including Black American culture. We cannot know where or when Cather became aware of "Weevily Wheat," whether in Virginia or Nebraska, whether first from connections to Black people or from family or friends, but it seems probable that she first encountered it in Virginia, where Black life touched her childhood in significant ways. In any case, it is a rich example of the ways Cather mixed experience, memory, and her broad cultural life to create art. The song is present as a Black American cultural artifact that adds significant meaning to the novel and to the ways American culture ignores, conceals, and reveals race.

Surely Cather knew many folk songs she could have used in this moment of her novel. A study of her purposes in selecting "Weevily Wheat" is beyond the scope of this chapter, but the scene is structurally and thematically significant. It provides a transition between the harsh winter on the prairie and the increasingly troubled life of the town, and it anticipates the scene in Ántonia's parlor near the end of the novel. The moment informs several themes: agency and voice for women who are outsiders, the importance of childhood, music and dance as counters to stifling aspects of small-town life, economic and social disparity, and more. Whether or not Cather intended a Black cultural component to this part of her novel, whether or not she knowingly or unknowingly participated in the erasure of a Black presence, the song as a cultural artifact still carries racial meanings. Cather's lived experience of Virginia and the pieces of its culture she carried with her were diverse; they should not remain shadows or ghosts but should be examined for rich and profound meanings and for insights into Cather's creative process.

NOTES

1. Some versions of the lyrics use "Charley" and some use "Charlie." I use "Charley" in my commentary as the form Cather used, but I quote other texts as published.

2. I borrow the label "ghost" from Ammons (75–79), who gets it from Toni Morrison. Morrison calls for "the examination and re-interpretation of the American canon . . . for the 'unspeakable things unspoken'; for the ways in which the presence of Afro-Americans has shaped the choices, the language, the structure—the meanings of so much American literature. A search, in other words, for the ghost in the machine" (11). Morrison's "unspeakable things unspoken" resonates with Cather's "the thing not named" in "The Novel Démeublé" (50).

3. I came across Wilkins's narrative on a brittle carbon copy of a typed manuscript in Sterling Brown's papers at Howard University. At the time of my visit, organizing of the papers was incomplete; the artifact was in a folder labeled "WPA Ex-slave narratives" in Box 52, WPA items, although the librarian told me numbers and labels would likely change. The papers are currently closed to researchers. Brown worked on the WPA Federal Writers' Project that collected the narratives of former slaves. Janis P. Stout's essay "'Down by de Canebrake': Willa Cather, Sterling A. Brown, and the Racialized Vernacular," while focused almost exclusively on *Sapphira* and the ballad "Nancy Till," has prompted me to consider Black American vernacular representations of "Weevily Wheat" even as Cather ignored (or concealed) them.

4. See Stout's essay "'Poor Caliban'" for a discussion of ways that "[r]ace, music, and sexuality are . . . linked" in Cather's letters and fiction (31).

5. Cather may have chosen the name Charley in part because the prototype for Charley Harling was Charles Hugh Miner. Charles was also a common Cather family name; Willa Cather's father bore that name.

WORKS CITED

Abbot, Francis H., collector. *Eight Negro Songs*, edited by Alfred J. Swan,
Enoch and Sons, 1923.

Ames, Russell. *The Story of American Folk Song*. Grosset & Dunlap, 1955.

Ammons, Elizabeth. "*My Ántonia* and African American Art." *New Essays on
My Ántonia*, edited by Sharon O'Brien, Cambridge UP, 1999, pp. 57–83.

Archive of Folk Song. AFC 1978/005, Virginia Folklore Index 1932–1977.
American Folklife Center, Library of Congress, Washington DC.

Brown, John Mason. "Songs of the Slave." *Lippincott's Magazine*, vol. 2,
December 1868, pp. 617–23.

Brown, Sterling. WPA items, Ex-slave Narratives, 1941. Box 52, Sterling Brown
Papers. Moorland-Spingarn Research Center, Howard U, Washington DC.

Cather, Willa. *My Ántonia*. 1918. Willa Cather Scholarly Edition, edited by
Charles Mignon with Kari Ronning, historical essay and explanatory
notes by James Woodress with Kari Ronning, Kathleen Danker, and Emily
Levine, U of Nebraska P, 1994.

———. "The Novel Démeublé." 1922. *Not under Forty*, Knopf, 1936, pp. 43–51.

———. *Sapphira and the Slave Girl*. 1940. Willa Cather Scholarly Edition,
historical essay and explanatory notes by Ann Romines, textual essay
and editing by Charles W. Mignon, Kari A. Ronning, and Frederick M.
Link, U of Nebraska P, 2009.

"Charlie." *Random House Historical Dictionary of American Slang*. 1994.

Cockrell, Dale, editor. *The Ingalls Wilder Family Songbook*. A-R Editions, 2011.

———, editor. *Music from* On the Banks of Plum Creek. A-R Editions, 2012.

Crown, Rachel. "Folk Song for the 1988 Year of *My Ántonia*." *Willa Cather
Pioneer Memorial Newsletter*, vol. 31, no. 4, Fall 1987, p. 45.

Douglass, Frederick. *My Bondage and My Freedom*. 1855. Yale UP, 2014.

Dunbar, Paul Laurence. *The Complete Poems of Paul Laurence Dunbar*. Dodd,
Mead, 1922.

Epstein, Dena J., with Rosita M. Sands. "Secular Folk Music." *African American
Music*, edited by Mellonee V. Burnim and Portia K. Maultsby, Routledge,
2006, pp. 35–50.

Fox-Genovese, Elizabeth. *Within the Plantation Household: Black and White Women of the Old South.* U of North Carolina P, 1988.

Gordon, Robert W. Manuscripts. American Folk-Song Collection, volumes 9 and II, 1921–30. Library of Congress, Washington DC.

Hall, Perry A. "The Appropriation of Music and Musical Forms." *Borrowed Power: Essays on Cultural Appropriation*, edited by Bruce Ziff and Pratima V. Rao, Rutgers UP, 1997, pp. 31–51.

Halliwell, James Orchard, collector. *The Nursery Rhymes of England.* 5th ed., London, 1886.

Hughes, Langston, and Arna Bontemps, editors. *The Book of Negro Folklore.* Dodd, Mead, 1958.

Hurston, Zora Neale. *Mules and Men.* 1935. Harper Perennial, 2008.

Johnson, Guy B. "Double Meaning in the Popular Negro Blues." *Journal of Abnormal and Social Psychology*, vol. 22, no. 1, 1927, pp. 12–20.

Jones, Anne Goodwyn. "Displacing Dixie: The Southern Subtext in *My Ántonia.*" *New Essays on* My Ántonia, edited by Sharon O'Brien, Cambridge UP, 1999, pp. 85–109.

Levine, Lawrence W. *Black Culture and Black Consciousness: Afro-American Folk Thought from Slavery to Freedom.* 1977. Oxford UP, 2007.

Lomax, John A., and Alan Lomax, collectors and compilers. *American Ballads and Folk Songs.* Macmillan, 1934.

McGee, Harold. *On Food and Cooking: The Science and Lore of the Kitchen.* Scribner's, 1984.

Miles, Emma Bell. "Some Real American Music." *Harper's Monthly Magazine*, vol. 109, July 1904, pp. 118–23.

Morrison, Toni. "Unspeakable Things Unspoken: The Afro-American Presence in American Literature." *Michigan Quarterly Review*, vol. 28, no. 1, 1989, pp. 1–34.

Perdue, Charles L., Thomas E. Barden, and Robert K. Phillips, editors. *Weevils in the Wheat: Interviews with Virginia Ex-Slaves.* UP of Virginia, 1976.

Romines, Ann. "Admiring and Remembering: The Problem of Virginia." *Willa Cather's Ecological Imagination*, edited by Guy J. Reynolds, Cather Studies 5, U of Nebraska P, 2003, pp. 273–90.

———. Explanatory notes. Cather, *Sapphira and the Slave Girl*, pp. 405–540.

Sandburg, Carl. *The American Songbag.* Harcourt, 1927.

Scarborough, Dorothy. *On the Trail of Negro Folk-Songs.* Harvard UP, 1925.

Slote, Bernice. *The Kingdom of Art: Willa Cather's First Principles and Critical Statements, 1893–1896.* U of Nebraska P, 1966.

Southern, Eileen. *The Music of Black Americans: A History*. 1971. Norton, 1997.

Stout, Janis P. "'Down by de Canebrake': Willa Cather, Sterling A. Brown, and the Racialized Vernacular." *Willa Cather and the Arts*, edited by Guy J. Reynolds, Cather Studies 12, U of Nebraska P, 2020, pp. 21–43.

———. "'Poor Caliban': Willa Cather and the Song of the Racial Other." *Willa Cather Newsletter and Review*, vol. 47, no. 2, Fall 2003, pp. 29–32, 42.

Talley, Thomas W. *Negro Folk Rhymes: Wise and Otherwise*. Macmillan, 1922.

Washington, Margaret. *Sojourner Truth's America*. U of Illinois P, 2009.

Work, John W. "Negro Folk Song." 1923. *The New Negro: 1892–1938*, edited by Henry Louis Gates Jr. and Gene Andrew Jarrett, Princeton UP, 2007, pp. 453–57.

5 "Keen Senses Do Not Make a Poet"

Cather's Respectful Rebellion
against Whitman in *O Pioneers!*

HANNAH J. D. WELLS

> O you daughters of the West!
> O you young and elder daughters! O you mothers
>   and you wives!
> Never must you be divided, in our ranks you are
>   united,
>   Pioneers! O Pioneers!
>
> —Walt Whitman, "Pioneers! O Pioneers!"

Literary tradition, and common sense, dictate that when
an author borrows material, especially a title, from a literary ancestor, the move signals an endorsement of the earlier message. This
tradition constitutes the most straightforward explanation of Willa
Cather's use of a poem from *Leaves of Grass* for the title of her 1913
novel *O Pioneers!* Yet even a cursory glance at Walt Whitman's "Pioneers! O Pioneers!" from 1865 reveals the deep differences between
Cather's portrait of nineteenth-century pioneerism in the American

Midwest and that of her poetic predecessor. When juxtaposed with the pioneer characters of Cather's novel, the characters of Whitman's poem reveal—along with their admirable grit and gumption— shallow, conventional relationships with their fellow pioneers, the land they traverse, and the ancestral heritages they leave behind. By contrast, each of these realms of pioneer life is questioned and nuanced in Cather's narrative. Why, in the face of their differences, would Cather choose Whitman's poem for her own title, and what does her choice tell us about her overarching pioneer vision for the American Midwest?

Cather's complete endorsement of Whitman can be ruled out without much difficulty; on the other hand, the possibility of her complete rebellion against him is somewhat more plausible. Especially at a time when disenfranchising the white male canon is *le dernier cri*, critics must be vigilant against constructing anachronistic allies. In the case of Cather, it is surely true, as Hermione Lee argues, that by appropriating Whitman's title the novelist hopes to "transcend, imaginatively, expected sexual roles" and "interven[e] in a masculine language of epic pastoral" (5). Yet several shades of nuance exist on both sides of such a transcendence and intervention. For example, Whitman, too, scorned traditional gender roles in a number of ways.[1] Moreover, I would argue that Cather's appropriation of Whitman's title is far from signaling a latent hope to decanonize the poet. Sharon O'Brien correctly, if somewhat vaguely, identifies the middle path by which a conclusion about Cather and Whitman can be traced: "Cather was being *rebellious as well as respectful* in alluding to Whitman. Her novel radically revises the vision of pioneering and settlement Whitman advances" in his poem (440, emphasis added). Even within the bounds O'Brien sets, opinions on Cather's view of Whitman still vary widely (when they are mentioned at all). I intend to complete a reoriented reading of *O Pioneers!*, informed by the poem from which it draws its title and, more broadly, by Cather's explicit response to Whitman and the male literary tradition he represents. As Maire Mullins stipulates, "Whitman's imprint on Cather's work needs further consideration, not only because Whitman was an important influence on [*O Pioneers!*] and on the subsequent direction of Cather's fiction, but also because this relationship raises an important question about the dynamic that is created when a female writer looks back to male precursors for models" (123). In extending Mullins's and O'Brien's work here, I offer an ecofeminist reading that explores the negotiation of a right relationship with the land through the intersection of femininity and pioneerism within Whitman's and Cather's schemata of American western expansion. First, I consider the place of Whitman's poem "Pioneers! O Pioneers!" within American political and literary history. I then contrast Whitman's work with Cather's divergent ideal of the American pioneer character in "Nebraska: The End of the First Cycle" and look briefly at her opinionated stance toward Whitman as a basis for understanding the differences between their visions. Lastly, I offer my reading of *O Pioneers!* in light of these differences and their manifestations in the novel, especially in the characters of Alexandra, Cather's successful pioneer heroine, and Emil, her tragic portrait of a classic pioneer hero. Exploring Cather's balance of respect for and rebellion against a mainstay of the American literary canon, I argue, allows today's readers to examine that balance in their own approach to canonical works and cultivate a more fruitful and flourishing tradition.

"WE TAKE UP THE TASK ETERNAL": WHITMAN AS CATHER'S LITERARY ANCESTOR

The poem that lends *O Pioneers!* its title has a deep history in itself. First published in *Drum-Taps*, Whitman's 1865 collection of poetry of the American Civil War, "Pioneers! O Pioneers!" later appeared in *Leaves of Grass* (1871) under the heading "Marches Now the War Is Over."[2] Whitman never understated the influence of the Civil War on his poetry, famously declaring "my book and the war are one" (6). This bare assertion downplays Whitman's initial detachment from the war and his subsequent personal transformation during its later years, when he served as a nurse in front-line hospitals. *Drum-Taps* and the surrounding war poems document a parallel poetic transformation, from belligerent recruitment poetry to more subdued, reflective battlefield poetry, concluding with hopeful reconciliation poetry. "Pioneers! O Pioneers!" occupies a unique space in this saga, pairing the martial tone and rhythm of the earlier recruitment marches with Whitman's rekindled hope for the future of his country after the war. The most marchlike of his "Marches Now the War Is Over," it is also the most overtly political. Whitman underpins the poem with his hope for postbellum reconciliation efforts: "All the hands of comrades clasping, all the Southern, all the Northern, / Pioneers! O pioneers!" (lines 35–36). The militant language and martial rhythm seem to be designed to rouse the ranks of war-weary soldiers to this "newer, mightier" cause (line 19). In one respect, Sharon O'Brien correctly describes the poem as a "jingoistic hymn to progress, manifest destiny, and the Westward Movement," but on the other hand, the past Whitman hopes to leave behind has been stained by the blood of the Civil War: the pioneers' goal is a type of peace (440). From his view, it would have been more jingoistic not to hope for progress.

Hardworking youths, finally leaving the battlefield, still hold on to their weapons and tools in the first stanza of Whitman's pioneer portrait. The un-Whitmanesque regularity and heavy trochees give the piece a constant martial motion; the pioneers are always moving forward. Their militant tirelessness is the first of several traits Whitman's pioneers possess that we will see countered in Cather. Whitman's fifth stanza introduces another: his youths are urged to leave behind "all the past" and to detach themselves from the old world "beyond the seas" (lines 14, 16). Nothing good is left in dying Europe; all promise of a better life lies to the west and must be created anew. Unlike the poem's structure, this message is stock-in-trade Whitman. In one stanza, he reflects on the new task of the distinctly American poet or artist:

> Minstrels latent on the prairies!
> (Shrouded bards of other lands, you may rest, you have done
> your work,)

Soon I hear you coming warbling, soon you rise and tramp
amid us,
　　Pioneers! O pioneers! (lines 85 88)

The termination of the non-American poet's task parallels the pioneer's duty to forget the "old world," which, for Whitman, signifies
not only European ancestry but also much of antebellum America.
To this sentiment, Cather proves "rebellious as well as respectful"
once again. Her choice of epigraph, a line from Adam Mickiewicz's
Pan Tadeusz, regarded by some as Europe's last great epic, handily
rejects Whitman's attempt to silence the "bards of other lands." Yet
Mickiewicz's description of "[t]hose fields, colored by various grain,"
conjures up for Cather images of the Nebraska prairie rather than
the Lithuanian countryside. Thus, her pioneers must hold sacred
some memories from the old world, though not without the ability
to adapt them to their new surroundings.

　　Whitman next urges his pioneers to conquer the new world for
its rich resources:

　　We primeval forests felling,
　We the rivers stemming, vexing we and piercing deep the
　　mines within,
　We the surface broad surveying, we the virgin soil upheaving,
　　Pioneers! O pioneers! (lines 25–27)

These westward advancers resemble an army without a (human)
enemy; rather than the nation's divided forces of the Civil War, the
ranks are made up of reconciled Americans all. And unlike a Civil
War battalion, the pioneers make no exclusions based on gender:
daughters, wives, and mothers are invited to join as well (lines 81–
84; see chapter epigraph above). In their mission of progress, these
men and women show no care for their homeland in Europe nor
for the gendered, sexualized land they traverse. America becomes
their prisoner of war; their weapons are raised against the land itself.
These more violent traits fuel the fire of Cather's rebellion against
her poetic forebear, as is evident in her own portrait of the westward
advancers of the American prairie.

added unique culture
as entity plus [handwritten margin notes]

"Westward the course of empire takes its way" was the poetic text of the first telegraph message sent across the Missouri River into Nebraska, as Willa Cather reports in her 1923 essay "Nebraska: The End of the First Cycle."[3] Writing a decade after publishing *O Pioneers!*, Cather takes the opportunity to praise the pioneering immigrants who had once inhabited her home state. She describes a realistic lifestyle quite different from Whitman's imagined ideal. First, she highlights the diverse European backgrounds of many early Nebraskans: "On Sunday we could drive to a Norwegian church and listen to a sermon in that language, or to a Danish or a Swedish church. We could go to the French Catholic settlement in the next county and hear a sermon in French, or into the Bohemian township and hear one in Czech, or we could go to church with the German Lutherans" ("Nebraska" 237). Unlike Whitman, who paints the "elder races" of Europe as a single category—drooping, jaded, and near extinction— Cather recognizes, both here and in *O Pioneers!*, the importance of varied backgrounds to the early Americans of the Midwest and West. In one reading of her epigraph from Mickiewicz, the fields "colored by various grain" represent the various heritages of the people who inhabit them (*O Pioneers!* title page). This distinction from Whitman deepens when she writes of European immigrants who inhabited Nebraska: "They brought with them something that this neutral new world needed even more than the immigrants needed land" ("Nebraska" 237). Cather's description of the land as "neutral" and her admission that immigrants brought something with them from the old world, especially something good and vital, pits her firmly against Whitman on the right role of an American pioneer. He would have every inhabitant of the United States be American and leave behind remnants of another identity, whereas Cather castigates American lawmakers for their "Americanization" of immigrants, including their conviction that "a boy can be a better American if he speaks only one language than if he speaks two" (237).

Cather also admits, as Whitman does not, that the days of the pioneer are numbered. In fact, she claims the pioneer's story is over until a "new story worthy to take its place" has begun: "The gener-

ation that subdued the wild land and broke up the virgin prairie is
passing.... They can look out over these broad stretches of fertility
and say: 'We made this, with our backs and hands'" ("Nebraska" 238).
Here, stronger parallels with Whitman's poem emerge as Cather
describes the gendered land being controlled by human power and
prosperity; Cather's virgin prairie is broken up, while Whitman's
virgin soil is upheaved. Indeed, the most evident similarity between
the two writers is their blatant disregard of the Indigenous inhabitants of the land, for whom the "virgin prairie" was an established
home. Nevertheless, Cather's description of the passing of the pioneer generation leaves her in a fundamentally different position
from Whitman, who imagined American westering and pioneerism
to be interminable. The differences between them stretch from the
pioneers' relationship with the past in Europe to their relationship
with the future in the American West. In the face of these differences, what merit did Cather see in her poetic American forebear?

This question only increases in complexity against Cather's stated
opinion of Whitman. One of her numerous critical statements on
literature from her college era, published in the *Nebraska State Journal* in 1896, devotes three snarky paragraphs to a discussion of the
people's "good, gray poet," about whom she reflects, "Just why the
adjective good is always applied to Whitman is difficult to discover,
probably because people who could not understand him at all took
it for granted that he meant well" (*Kingdom of Art* 351). Cather goes on
to critique Whitman's work as essentially unpoetic, lacking "the finer
discriminations" of good poetry and filled with "the unreasoning
enthusiasm of a boy," or—hilariously—a "joyous elephant" (352). "The
poet's task is usually to select the poetic," she writes; "Whitman never
bothers to do that" (352). Only begrudgingly does she admit that he
possesses a "primitive elemental force" and an "undeniable charm"
(352). His charm is simplistic, and the modern world is far too complex for it, in her eyes. Cather's final 1896 word on Whitman claims
Leaves of Grass as the prime evidence that "keen senses do not make
a poet" (353). Nor, she would argue, do they make a pioneer. Whitman's pioneers resemble him, according to Cather's portrait: they

have keen senses that allow them to survive in the wilderness and are full of enthusiasm and elemental force throughout their journey. For Whitman, as for Cather, the pioneer and the artist of the American Midwest do not have dissimilar tasks. Cather's critique of Whitman's unpoetic senses thus reflects back on her own work: for both the characters in her novel and herself, even a strong and careful attentiveness to nature is not enough. In addition, she calls for a sense of moderation, discernment, and a positively poetic discrimination to govern the actions of the true pioneer, whether debouching upon the wide prairies of the Midwest or the wide horizons of American literature.

Cather's critique of Whitman was penned almost two decades before the publication of *O Pioneers!*, and her opinion may have shifted in that time. James Woodress goes so far as to "charge these wrong-headed comments on Whitman to the author's own youth and immaturity" (326). Nevertheless, the evidence suggests that Whitman did not, contrary to the claim of Maire Mullins, "early on serve as Cather's implicit muse and model" (123). While Mullins's argument is comprehensive and thoughtful as a whole, other critical work often assumes the truth of this part of her thesis implicitly, without further exploration. Such an assumption can lead to a reading of *O Pioneers!* as an encomium to Whitman, with her pioneers constituting an "epic response being reinforced by the Whitman title of the book with its rhetorical challenge to conquer the wild country" (Stouck, "Epic Imagination" 31). Any reading that subordinates Cather's work to Whitman's misses her clear indication that she understood the dangers of his pioneerism too well to merely perpetuate his beliefs. Unlike the average reader she indicts, Cather did not take it for granted that Whitman "meant well"; she subjects his words and intentions to her own more discriminating poetic judgment.

"RAISE THE MIGHTY MOTHER MISTRESS": ALEXANDRA'S PIONEER VISION

The moments of elevated style in *O Pioneers!*, found, among other places, in the introductory poem, were probably influenced by Whitman's style and syntax. That this early novel is the only one Cather prefaced with original poetry suggests a direct response to Whitman within her writing style.[4] The *O Pioneers!* proem, "Prairie Spring," mimics his work in its irregular line lengths and its catalog of elements within the scene it describes. Woodress avers that this work is Cather's "only really first-rate poem," contrasting it with her more formal, metrical verse in *April Twilights*, and he credits Whitman as her inspiration (329). Certainly both writers "sound the epic theme" in their works and "celebrate the dynamic growth of the American democracy as experienced by the immigrant settlers of the pioneer west," as David Stouck writes (Historical essay 294). Despite the stylistic and formulaic similarities between these celebrations, however, Cather's rebellion against Whitman is as clear in "Prairie Spring" as anywhere in the novel. Although she uses a recognizably similar syntax, she undermines the driving unity of much of Whitman's poetry, especially "Pioneers! O Pioneers!" Halfway through her poem, after a description of the silent landscape, she cuts in with a dichotomous second perspective: "Against all this, Youth." This shift juxtaposes youth's "insupportable sweetness [. . .] fierce necessity [. . .] sharp desire" with the stolid character of the ancient land. Whitman would have the land pliantly surrender to pioneers armed with pistols, axes, and plows, but here Cather's land is "full of strength and harshness," indeed no virgin soil to be upheaved by young, fierce intruders.

There is in Whitman's poem a tacit assent to the work of mastering nature in order to force it to bend to the human will. The roots of this project are often said to lie in the scientific revolution of the seventeenth century, spearheaded by men like Francis Bacon and René Descartes, although its origins could really be traced as far back as Genesis, when the inhabitants of Shinar said to one another, "Come, let us build ourselves a city and a tower with its top in the heavens, and let us make a name for ourselves" (*English Standard Version Bible*, Gen. 11.4). For Descartes, global renown was not the goal but rather the practical aim of making human beings the "masters and possessors of nature" in order to "enjoy, without any pain, the fruits of the earth and all the goods to be found there" (Descartes 49). This is not to say that the process of conquering nature will not be painful; to bear the brunt of the difficulty is the task of pioneers, whether they are breaking ground in seventeenth-century European science or nineteenth-century American expansion. Whitman's pioneers are made aware of their sacrifice by the speaker. Their lot is "not the cushion and the slipper [. . .] / Not the riches safe and palling" but rather the "diet hard, and the blanket on the ground," with the hope that their followers will someday be able to enjoy the pleasures they must forgo (lines 90–91, 95). This objective raises many questions—technological, political, and moral—but the one to which Cather attends in her novel is discerning which way of life is more choice-worthy: the painful but noble sacrifice of the pioneers, the pleasant leisure of the next generations, or another way, which shuns the role of conqueror of nature's forces and that of enjoyer of nature's goods and seeks a more reciprocal relationship with the natural world.

Cather explores these alternatives within her wider inquiry into the proper place of humans on the prairie and the proper status for the prairie in the minds of its inhabitants. Since it is presented with an agency of its own, the land in *O Pioneers!* resists categorization as a passive substance to be molded and manipulated to the purposes of active human intellect. Cather's opening scene, a flashback to Hanover "thirty years ago," captures the land's unfriendliness to the products of human artifice, for "the dwelling-houses were set about haphazard on the tough prairie sod. [. . .] None of them had any appearance of permanence, and the howling wind blew under them as well as over them" (11). Reactions to this apparent malevolence of nature vary: for Whitman's brand of pioneer, it might be viewed as a challenge—an environment where the conquest of nature must of necessity advance in order to quell the natural threats to human life. This reaction is responsible for the change in the landscape at the start of "Part II: Neighboring Fields," where the technological advancements of "telephone wires," "gilded weather-vanes," and "light steel windmills" have helped the human population of the prairie to thrive. Others, like the young Carl, may instead look for a chance to escape the land's harshness, whether that be a city, where the conquest of nature has been more thoroughly achieved, or a place more generously endowed with natural resources, like a gold mine. Against both responses, the correct perspective, Cather makes clear, is Alexandra's understanding of the prairie's natural harshness as a sign of its strength and resilience, which allows her to set her "human face [...] toward it with love and yearning"; in return, the "Genius of the Divide [...] must have bent lower than it ever bent to a human will before" (64). Far from a conquest, this reciprocity between land and human (we are, after all, another part of "nature") pervades *O Pioneers!*, while it is utterly lacking in Whitman's pioneer poem.

Whitman's gendering of the land as female and virginal points to another tension between Cather and her literary ancestry. Since Cather's primary pioneer figure is a woman, how does Alexandra's relationship with the land reinvent the sexualized conquering that Whitman so enthusiastically promotes? Stouck writes that borrowing a title from Whitman implicitly entails borrowing "its rhetorical challenge to conquer the wild country," putting Alexandra in the role of conqueror ("Epic Imagination" 31). But this is exactly what Alexandra knows *not* to do; she "defines herself in relation to—instead of against—the natural world" (O'Brien 434). This relationship, which may simply be defined as a mutually beneficial friendship, is realized in Cather's elevated prose at the end of "Part I: The Great Divide": "It fortified her to reflect upon the great operations of nature, and when she thought of the law that lay behind them, she felt a sense of personal security. That night she had a new consciousness of the country, felt almost a new relation to it. [...] She had never known before how much the country meant to her" (68–69). Alexandra's familial revelation precedes the most erotic agricultural imagery in *O Pioneers!*, appearing in the first three paragraphs of "Part II: Neighboring Fields." For the established farmers of the Divide, the land "yields itself eagerly to the plow [...] with a soft, deep sigh of happiness," marking a consensual palliation of the traditional rape of the virgin soil (74). With these lines, Cather acknowledges the presence of the vital young pioneer men Whitman invokes, but their mastery pales alongside Alexandra's understanding of the true nature of the land as revealed in the next paragraph, where it is made clear that the land's erotic allure was not meant for humankind after all. Rather, the land "gives itself ungrudgingly to the moods of the season, holding nothing back" (74). Into this complex, cyclical love affair between land and atmosphere the pioneer's agricultural practices intruded, while Alexandra instead stands back and encourages the rightful lovers with her platonic friendship.

Whitman's own infamous complexity regarding gender has generated as much speculation as Cather's and is a prominent theme in his published works. For this reason, I find it insufficient to say, as Hermione Lee does in her introduction to *Willa Cather: Double Lives*, that Cather's only or primary motivation in crafting Alexandra's story is to recast Whitman's male-dominated pioneer narrative with a female lead. Lee is largely correct that "the western frontier was a man's world," although there were many single woman homesteaders like Alexandra, but nevertheless Whitman's poem does not "erotically apotheosize" the "penetration of the West . . . as an all-male Olympiad" (Lee 5). I concede that "Pioneers! O Pioneers!" is one of Whitman's more conventional portraits of masculinity, but it is by no means exclusive. In the second stanza, the speaker calls to the "Western youths" who are "full of manly pride and friendship," but this description could apply to a woman with unconventional qualities, such as Alexandra (lines 9–10). A later stanza calls to "you daughters of the West!" and bids the women to join the "united" ranks of pioneers (lines 81–82), not to follow "along behind with the pack-horses," as Lee suggests (5). Whitman would, we sense, be as exuberant about a woman upheaving the virgin soil as he would a man. Thus, I propose recasting Cather's primary subversion of the poem not as one of gender but as one of discerning the right relationship to the land. Alexandra's success depends on the "spiritual perceptions" Cather claims Whitman lacks, which enable an artist to "select the beautiful from the gross" (*Kingdom of Art* 352). The gross, for Alexandra, are those people around her who view the land as spoils of conquest. The beautiful are those sympathetic characters, including men such as Carl and Ivar, who treat it as a resolute old friend.

Lifelong friends, even nonhuman ones, are not given up easily, and Whitman's chant of "moving yet and never stopping" (the poem contains no fewer than thirty-six gerunds) marks a final significant distinction between his prototype of the pioneer and Cather's. Whitman's poem ends at daybreak with a reveille calling the pioneers to their places in the ranks. In his imagination, colored as it was by the broken realities of the eastern states, American westering was a ceaseless process. The task of the pioneer was never finished; it was the "elder races" who had "halted" and the pioneers who must press on in youthful vigor (line 13). An attachment to the land in any place would be impossible to form, as would a relationship with any settled person. By contrast, Cather's novel ends at sunset with Alexandra inside her home. This pioneer heroine forms a deep attachment to the land and a stable relationship with her partner by the novel's end. The "great peace" she feels at home and her concern that Carl might ask her to "go away for good" seem to preclude any remnants of traditional pioneerism in middle-aged Alexandra (271–72). She and Carl, two old friends with little left of passion, finally concede to staying "safe" (273), a concept scorned by Whitman's pioneers: "Not the cushion and the slipper, not the peaceful and the studious, / Not the riches safe and palling, not for us the tame enjoyment" (lines 90–91). The final image of Alexandra signals a natural completion of the pioneer task in Cather's conception that simply cannot exist for Whitman. Even this last distinction is blurred in the final, Whitmanesque sentence of the novel: "Fortunate country, that is one day to receive hearts like Alexandra's into its bosom, to give them out again in the yellow wheat, in the rustling corn, in the shining eyes of youth!" (274). Although Alexandra decides that it is not "fittest" for her to die "upon the march," as Whitman's pioneers claim for themselves (line 55), her eventual death will enter into a natural cycle that flourishes with youthfulness. The final word of the novel recalls the poetic message of "Prairie Spring," so Whitman ought not be far from the reader's mind in either passage. The primacy of youth is a constant refrain in "Pioneers! O Pioneers!" even from the first line, where the speaker calls to his "tan-faced children" to ready their weapons and march. His pioneers continue their passionate "advancing on" until the very hour of their imminent death. This prominent trait of youthful abandon informs my understanding of Emil as Cather's subversive depiction of a classic Whitman pioneer.

"ALL THE HAPLESS SILENT LOVERS": EMIL'S PIONEER TRAGEDY

The seventeenth stanza of "Pioneers! O Pioneers!" is often cited as the clearest parallel to Cather's plot and cast of characters.[5] It reads,

> All the hapless silent lovers,
> All the prisoners in the prisons, all the righteous and the
>   wicked,
> All the joyous, all the sorrowing, all the living, all the dying,
>   Pioneers! O pioneers! (lines 65–69)

This stanza shifts its focus away from the pioneer, leading Bernice Slote to suggest that the novel's Whitman connection "is less with the pioneer movement as such than with the concept of the great and varied scope of ongoing life in America" (12). It is true that the secondary characters of *O Pioneers!* whom this stanza evokes are removed from the pioneer movement, but the narrative arc of the poem clarifies that every aspect of the "great and varied scope" of life is of import to the true pioneer. This stanza appears as Whitman's speaker attempts to persuade pioneers to take up or continue their task. Think of all those people, he says in effect, who are relying on us to succeed; "all the pulses of the world [...] beat for us" (line 57). In other words, those listed in this stanza are *not* pioneers, including the silent lovers Emil and Marie, the prisoner Frank, the righteous Ivar, and the ordinary person working to thrive on the Nebraska prairie. Part of each pioneer's task is to care and provide for these people. Without a doubt, Alexandra manages to do this more tenderly than Whitman's militant ranks of young men might have. But Emil, Alexandra's particular favorite, reacts uncomfortably to her attempts at care. He proves not to be the "hapless silent lover" he appears. Rather, at the decisive points in his life, he acts with all the heedless, ceaseless passion of the Whitman pioneer.

Recalling Cather's "Prairie Spring" proem, Emil emerges as the personification of "Youth," with its "insupportable sweetness [...] fierce necessity [...] sharp desire." Part II of the novel begins with a portrait of Emil armed, like Whitman's opening image, with a scythe, effectively attacking the earth in an attempt at mastery. Alexandra admits to building her home, and tending her land, in hopes of Emil taking it over. She believes that Emil's potential as an American pioneer justified her family's move: "I'm sure it was to have sons like Emil, and to give them a chance, that father left the old country. It's curious, too; on the outside Emil is just like an American boy" (108). In light of Whitman's vision of a new American race unhindered by European constraints, Emil first appears to fit perfectly into the poet's model. But Alexandra finishes by indicating that "underneath he is more Swedish than all of us," pointing out the reality that emigrants do not leave their past identities behind when they move (108). Although Emil does display conventionally Swedish traits, his nature also expresses the restlessness of a western frontiersman, telling Marie, "'I must go somewhere, mustn't I? [...] What do I want to hang around here for? Alexandra can run the farm all right, without me. I don't want to stand around and look on. I want to be doing something on my own account" (140–41). Emil is shown to have the urge for wandering and surveying that Whitman's pioneers possess. In this respect, he models a potential for pioneerism, but his plans for ceaseless exploration are soon thwarted.

Cather's decision to model a character after Whitman's pioneers necessitates her depiction of the consequences she believes that lifestyle to have, which culminates in Emil's tragic demise. Emil's epiphany in church, his last wild ride to Marie, and their death scene all include ironic echoes of Whitman's poetic style in keeping with Cather's critique of his work. The nearest equivalent in the novel

108

to Whitman's ranks of pioneers is the scene after Amédée's death, when Emil and other young men let "their youth [get] the better of them" by forming a cavalry swept over with "a wave of zeal and fiery enthusiasm" (226). Emil rides an internal wave of similar power at the confirmation service, during which "he felt as if a clear light broke upon his mind, and with it a conviction that good was, after all, stronger than evil, and that good was possible to men. He seemed to discover that there was a kind of rapture in which he could love forever without faltering and without sin" (228). Reminiscent of Whitman's poetic speaker, who cries, "O beloved race in all! O my breast aches with tender love for all! / O I mourn and yet exult, I am rapt with love for all" (lines 38–39), Emil's epiphany of universal love reminds us that Cather condemned Whitman's failure to discriminate; in his poetry she finds "the name of everything in creation set down with great reverence but without any particular connection" (352). Emil's close echo of Whitman in this scene also explains the narrator's sarcastic judgments upon his thoughts: "And it did not occur to Emil that any one had ever reasoned thus before, that music had ever before given a man this equivocal revelation" (229). Given the importance that music, especially opera, held for both Cather and Whitman, and the thematic parallels in these passages, I would argue that one man on Cather's mind who had been given "this equivocal revelation" was that good, gray poet.

In the unfolding of Emil's ecstasy and death, Cather shows the unsustainability of life for a pioneer who fails to discern and connect. Emil's Whitmanesque perceptions continue as he leaves the church, feeling drawn to the beauty of the hole where Amédée would be buried: "The heart, when it is too much alive, aches for that brown earth, and ecstasy has no fear of death. It is the old and the poor and the maimed who shrink from that brown hole; its wooers are found among the young, the passionate, the gallant-hearted" (230). Such heedless wooers of death are found throughout Whitman's poetry, and they are always sensuously attracted to the natural world, just as Emil is on his ride to Marie. Marilee Lindemann identifies this outlook as the "'corporeal utopianism' Michael Moon has described as the heart" of Whitman's poetic corpus and contrasts it with a "corporeal dystopianism" found in Alexandra, for example, as she harshly scrubs her body after a semierotic dream (qtd. in Lindemann 39). The same dichotomy pervades the hyperphysical description of Emil and Marie's death scene. In the initial description from Frank's perspective, the scene is full of motion, with a heavy-handed sprinkling of gerunds (eleven in a single paragraph; 236). In the later description from Ivar's perspective, the story of the death is told by the traces of blood through the scene. This hematological tragedy emphasizes the "problems in the oft conjoined strategies of reading the world as if it were a body and reading the body as if it were a world," two acts that make up Whitman's central legacy in American literature (Lindemann 39). Cather's continuing critique of Whitman's physicality points to the transcendent spiritual vision she finds necessary for true pioneers, like true artists, to maintain. The concession that the bloodstains "told only half the story" (241) confirms this vision, since "above Marie and Emil, two white butterflies [...] were fluttering in and out among the interlacing shadows" (241), symbolizing the two lovers' souls; in Greek, the word *psyche* refers to the butterfly and to the souls of the dead. This vignette adds a hint of eternity to the scene that is absent from the deaths in Whitman's poem. While the gaps left by the dead in the ranks of the living pioneers are quickly filled, Whitman makes no mention of the bodies nor the souls of the deceased.

Emil and Marie die at sunset, but events of the section titled "The White Mulberry Tree" end the next day at dawn, just as "Pioneers! O Pioneers!" does. The new day represents both the freshness of youth and the indifference of the natural world to human affairs. If you are one of Whitman's pioneers, you are up with the sun or you are left behind. The tragedy of "The White Mulberry Tree," far from undermining the satisfying ending of the section titled "Alexandra," offers the same message in negation. When Alexandra completes her pioneering task, she settles and finds safety and comfort. Emil finds no fruitful outlet for his restlessness and no lawful one for his passion. The only "hapless silent lover" in Emil is in his corpse; up

until his abrupt end he was "conquering, holding, daring, ventur-
ing," or at least attempting to, right along with the foremost pioneers
of Whitman's poem (line 23). Cather's main critique of Whitman
is his lack of discernment, which Maire Mullins counts as Alexandra's "most important talent" (129). Emil, as Cather's answer to the
Whitman prototype of the pioneer, also lacks this ability to pursue
a right relationship with the people and the land around him, one
that turns on the virtues of moderation, delayed gratification, and
reciprocal fulfillment of the potential of both parties: a relationship
of cooperation rather than conquest. This failure is his undoing, and
it signals the undoing of the entire vision of American expansion
as Whitman would have it.

Ultimately, Alexandra Bergson's success where others failed
relies on the kind of unity with the land and its spirit experienced
by Whitman's ideal poet, as described in "As I Sat Alone by Blue
Ontario's Shore," the poem that precedes "Pioneers! O Pioneers!"
in the 1871 edition of *Leaves of Grass*: "The proof of a poet shall be
sternly deferr'd, till his country absorbs him as affectionately as he
has absorb'd it" (line 219). Cather's success writing the prairie in *O
Pioneers!*, especially after her disenchantment with her 1912 novel
Alexander's Bridge, might well be described in these terms. Despite
its borrowed title, *O Pioneers!* represents Willa Cather's own pioneering work as an unprecedented novelist of the American Midwest.
By 1913 this region had already been irreversibly imprinted by the
hands of the "first cycle" of immigrants and transplants from the
East. Whitman attempted to document the efforts of those early
generations of American midwesterners in the postbellum era, while
Cather picked up the work where he left off by documenting the
efforts of their biological and metaphorical descendants. As a literary descendant of Whitman, Cather fittingly pays homage to the
poetic heritage he established while revealing a bold revision of his
pioneer ideal. Cather's tribute to Whitman is all the more poignant
due to her courage in breaking from the canonical mold he had
cast of the pioneer experience in the Midwest. Her criticism of his
poetic sensibilities makes her resemble all the more the poet who

had turned away from the withering canon of his American literary ancestors. Within the novel, Alexandra Bergson mirrors her creator with a bold vision that looks backward with respect for her heritage and forward with rebellion against its vices to establish a flourishing farm through a more positive tradition. Adopting the bold vision of these female pioneers, Alexandra and Willa, may enable today's readers to find the same fruitful balance of respect and rebellion.

NOTES

I extend my gratitude to the editors and reviewers for their valuable feedback on this chapter, as well as to readers of my earlier drafts, especially Joshua Doležal, steadfast mentor.

1. See Amy Parsons's excellent work for a recent discussion of Whitman's sexuality as it impacted his view of the Civil War.

2. In the 1881 edition of *Leaves of Grass*, the section "Marches Now the War Is Over" was removed from the manuscript and its poems recategorized or omitted (Whitman 192n4). Later editions, including the widely published 1891–92 deathbed edition, include "Pioneers! O Pioneers!" in the "Birds of Passage" section, a placement that emphasizes the poem's imaginative westward movement rather than the East Coast reality its speaker hopes to leave behind.

3. The line comes from "On the Prospect of Planting Arts and Learning in America," penned by Irish philosopher Bishop George Berkeley (1685–1753), the choice of which would have been much to Whitman's chagrin, I imagine, had he known.

4. Cather did write poetic verses to preface some of her early short stories, such as "A Son of the Celestial" (1893), "The Way of the World" (1898), and "The Conversion of Sum Loo" (1900). Like her poetry in *April Twilights*, these verses utilize traditional rhythm, rhyme, and meter and as such are probably inspired by European or "Europeanized" models (Woodress 324). Robert Thacker places the shift in Cather's poetic style around the turn of the twentieth century, after which "she did not altogether abandon European scenes as inspiration, but overall, . . . she had turned her face West, to the stuff of her own experience in her own home place" (16).

5. For instance, David Stouck, following Bernice Slote, cites this stanza and the preceding one as lines that "anticipate scenes in the novel" (Historical

essay 293; Slote 12), and Maire Mullins notes that they are "directly related to the characterization and themes of Cather's novel" (128).

WORKS CITED

The Bible. English Standard Version, Crossway, 2001.

Cather, Willa. The Kingdom of Art: Willa Cather's First Principles and Critical Statements, 1893–1896, edited by Bernice Slote, U of Nebraska P, 1967.

———. "Nebraska: The End of the First Cycle." The Nation, 5 September 1923, pp. 236–38, Willa Cather Archive, cather.unl.edu/writings/nonfiction/nf066. Accessed 11 January 2020.

———. O Pioneers! 1913. Willa Cather Scholarly Edition, edited by Susan J. Rosowski and Charles W. Mignon with Kathleen Danker, historical essay and explanatory notes by David Stouck, U of Nebraska P, 1992.

Descartes, René. Discourse on Method, translated by Richard Kennington, edited by Pamela Kraus and Frank Hunt, Focus Philosophical Library, 2007.

Lee, Hermione. Willa Cather: Double Lives. Pantheon Books, 1989.

Lindemann, Marilee. Willa Cather: Queering America. Columbia UP, 1999.

Moon, Michael. Introduction. Leaves of Grass and Other Writings, by Walt Whitman, edited by Michael Moon, Norton, 2002.

Mullins, Maire. "'I Bequeath Myself to the Dirt to Grow from the Grass I Love': The Whitman-Cather Connection in O Pioneers!" Tulsa Studies in Women's Literature, vol. 20, no. 1, 2001, pp. 123–36.

O'Brien, Sharon. Willa Cather: The Emerging Voice. Oxford UP, 1987.

Parsons, Amy. "Desire, Forgetting, and the Future: Walt Whitman's Civil War." Arizona Quarterly: A Journal of American Literature, Culture, and Theory, vol. 71, no. 3, 2015, pp. 85–109.

Slote, Bernice. "Willa Cather: The Secret Web." Five Essays on Willa Cather: The Merrimack Symposium, edited by John J. Murphy, Merrimack College, 1974, pp. 1–19.

Stouck, David. Historical essay. Cather, O Pioneers!, pp. 283–303.

———. "O Pioneers! Willa Cather and the Epic Imagination." Prairie Schooner, vol. 46, no. 1, 1972, pp. 23–34.

Thacker, Robert. Foreword. April Twilights and Other Poems, by Willa Cather, 1923, Everyman's Library, 2013, pp. 11–22.

Whitman, Walt. Leaves of Grass and Other Writings, edited by Michael Moon, Norton, 2002.

Woodress, James. "Whitman and Cather." Études Anglaises, vol. 45, no. 3, July 1992, pp. 324–32.

6 Americans' Coming of Age

Willa Cather's Female National Hero in *The Song of the Lark*

MOLLY METHERD

In the summer of 1913, when Willa Cather sat down at her desk in Greenwich Village to begin work on her third novel, *The Song of the Lark* (1915), the United States was a rapidly changing nation. Advances in transportation and communication were altering the space of the American landscape, and decades of unprecedented immigration and urbanization were changing the shape of the American city. The dynamic changes propelling the United States into modernity left many feeling dislocated and anxious to define the unique character of the United States, either to fix it in place or to reimagine it to reflect the realities of the new century. Cather not only lived during these monumental social and technological shifts, she experienced them firsthand as she moved from the home of her teenage years in the prairie town of Red Cloud, Nebraska, to her life as a professional author and editor of *McClure's Magazine* in New York City.

Critics have noted the many autobiographical elements in *The Song of the Lark* as the novel follows the development of Thea Kronborg

MOLLY METHERD

from her childhood in the West to her success as an artist in New York and explores a female protagonist coming to terms with her artistic vocation. The narrative is structured as a bildungsroman, a genre of youth and mobility (Moretti), which tells the story of a young protagonist developing, through education and experience, into a fully realized adult. It is also more specifically a *Künstlerroman*, or novel of artistic development. It opens in the 1880s with Thea Kronborg as a young girl living in the small town of Moonstone, Colorado, yearning to be a great musician but facing Victorian-era gender expectations and codes of behavior, and it follows her thirty-year "intellectual and spiritual development" (*Song of the Lark* 479) through her musical training in Chicago and ultimately to her triumph as an independent woman and an opera diva on the New York stage.

While the term *bildungsroman* is often used loosely to mean a coming-of-age story, theorists of the genre, including Mikhail Bakhtin, Franco Moretti, Fredric Jameson, and Jed Esty, stress that in a bildungsroman the protagonist matures alongside a developing nation. It typically opens in an amorphous setting, a time of imminent change with a protagonist "on the cusp of two epics," and it offers a sequential account of personal and societal events as they unfold in time (Bakhtin 23). The nation takes shape as the hero moves toward maturity, and by the conclusion a fully formed national character has been revealed in poetic form. In writing a bildungsroman, Cather enters into the contemporary debates to define the form and character of the American nation.

This genre of nation-building, however, does not typically have a female protagonist. In fact, as feminist scholars have demonstrated, the female bildungsroman usually fails to reach closure because the protagonist lacks the agency to subvert the rules of her patriarchal society, a necessary step toward identity formation and nation-building.[1] There is ultimately no place for a female hero as a fully realized subject in the preconceived and idealized form of the nation. Despite these generic and gendered obstacles, Cather wrote a female bildungsroman that transgresses traditional form to achieve success and closure. Susan Rosowski has shown how Cather's novel pushes against

the traditional form of the bildungsroman by upending gendered stereotypes and writing a female character who "clearly follows the conventionally male narrative patterns" ("Writing" 69). Thea is the hero
on an artistic quest while the men take on secondary, supporting roles
as nurturers and witnesses to her journey. Marilee Lindemann agrees
that *The Song of the Lark* offers an alternative to heteronormativity (56).
She argues that Cather subverts the order of the realist novel through
what she terms the queerness of the work, its excesses and blurred
boundaries represented most significantly by Thea's realization of
her female body as a locus of pleasure and power. Both Rosowski
and Lindemann recognize how *The Song of the Lark* upends narrative
conventions just as Thea subverts the social conventions to find her
own identity as a woman and an artist. Lindemann further finds that
it is Thea's "utopian corporeality" that affords Thea the agency to follow her artistic goals, to earn the highest recognition in her field and
fulfill her narrative desire. In Thea, Lindemann argues, Cather offers
a new model for success and creates "the grounds for reimagining the
relations between politics and the body in the U.S." (54).

While Cather reimagines politics and the body in *The Song of the*
Lark, she also reimagines the nation's body politic. The nation she
imagines into being is not the nation of nativists in the early twentieth century, that is, singular, monolingual, white. Instead, Cather
imagines a nation made up of many cultures. Thea is deeply influenced by her experiences in diverse communities in the United
States, and the novel situates the aesthetic spirit of these communities as central to both the development of her artistic genius and
the national character. The work reimagines not only the national
hero as woman but also a national consciousness as cosmopolitan.

CULTURE AND COSMOPOLITANISM: BROOKS AND BOURNE'S VISION FOR A NEW AMERICA

While Cather was writing *The Song of the Lark*, a group of
writers, social critics, and social scientists were debating ideas about
nation, self, art, and culture in salons in Greenwich Village and on

the pages of the small magazines, including *The Dial*, the *Atlantic Monthly*, and *The Nation*. The vision of the nation that Cather puts forward in the novel engages with many of these contemporary debates. As Susan Hegeman and Eric Aronoff have demonstrated, an interdisciplinary group of thinkers known collectively as the Young Americans, including Van Wyck Brooks, Lewis Mumford, Edward Sapir, Randolph Bourne, Ruth Benedict, and Waldo Frank, rejected the nineteenth-century notions of culture as a singular entity evolving toward the perfection of Western civilization and instead were thinking about cultures that are plural, synchronic, spatially bounded, and meaningful unto themselves. Two influential works, Van Wyck Brooks's *America's Coming-of-Age* (1915) and Randolph Bourne's "Trans-national America" (1916), were published within a year of *The Song of the Lark* and share similar ideas about the role of the artist, the importance of friendship in community, and the diverse and cosmopolitan nature of the United States. Cather certainly knew of the Young Americans and would have been familiar with their writing. As Janis Stout demonstrates, Cather and Bourne had mutual friends, including the feminist anthropologist Elsie Clews Parsons and the writer Elizabeth Shepley Sergeant ("Modernist"). Brooks was a prominent voice in intellectual circles and was also "well acquainted" with Parsons (Aronoff 27). Bourne reviewed both *The Song of the Lark* and *My Ántonia*, and Cather, in a letter to her brother Roscoe on 5 January 1919, lamented the untimely death of "poor Bourne," whom she lauded as "the ablest of our critics" (*Complete Letters* #2085).

In their respective *America's Coming-of-Age* and "Trans-national America," Brooks and Bourne critiqued the United States for its Victorian gentility, its self-interested devotion to moneymaking, its conformity and xenophobia. They depicted the United States as rootless and without a cultural center. Americans, they believed, were losing their connection to place and to ethnic traditions and melting into an aimless society of mass consumers without a usable past or native artistic tradition to define them. Brooks compared the nation to a "vast Sargasso sea—a prodigious welter of unconscious

As We Need to do

2025
1915
90

life, swept by ground-swells of half-conscious emotion" (164), and Bourne saw "detached fragments of peoples . . . with leering cheapness, falseness of taste and spiritual outlook." They lamented the divisions in American life, the separation between what Brooks called the "Highbrow," or transcendent ideals disconnected with daily life, and the "Lowbrow," or the "catchpenny realities" of practicality and self-interested moneymaking (7). Americans, they argued, should embark on a cultural renaissance. It must reject the social norms and competitive individualism that suffocate the spirit and separate the individual from the body, men from women, work from pleasure.

To do this, Brooks and Bourne believed that Americans should "delve more deeply into the very heart of their country's traditions, retrieving and renewing those aspects of the national heritage that nourished the intuitive values of the soul rather than the cold calculation of commerce" (Blake 74). They argued that when Americans immerse themselves in the experience of everyday life and form friendships grounded in shared experience, common aesthetic appreciation, and vigorous intellectual exchange, they would root their consciousness and cultivate their personalities. They would then "breathe a larger air" and feel a "pleasurable sense of liberation from the stale and familiar attitudes" (Bourne, "Trans-national"). At times romantic and utopian, they employed the ideals of organic communities and mystical wholeness as well as essentialist notions of native cultures as remedies to the crisis of modernity. Yet, their views were characterized by what Casey Nelson Blake terms "aestheticist pragmatism" (6). For the Young Americans, such feeling and experience in community would not mystically transform the divided individual into a whole being but rather would cultivate the individual personality and confer the agency necessary for democratic participation and social action for the common good (Blake).

Experience, friendship, culture, community, personality, art— these are the building blocks for individual and national renewal. Although Brooks and Bourne, along with the Young Americans cohort of writers, have been critiqued as cultural nationalists, as Casey Nelson Blake and Susan Hegeman argue, their work, along with their publication *The Seven Arts*, was deeply committed to a broad, cosmopolitan vision of America (Blake 2; Hegeman 105). Brooks and Bourne in their works *America's Coming-of-Age* and "Trans-national America" used these shared ideas to further develop their own arguments. In *America's Coming-of-Age*, Brooks critiqued American culture through his analysis of the failings of American literature. He called for a new American writer who could throw off imitation and supposed refinement, integrate the "Highbrow" and "Lowbrow," and make a new literature out of engagement with American life in an epic expression of the American spirit (44–105). In "Trans-national America" Bourne laid out his vision of the nation as a trans-nation, or a federation of cultures with distinctive languages, religions, and traditions living side by side in a "common American background" with a unique creative energy and a new cosmopolitan outlook.

The bildungsroman is an appropriate genre for a fictional engagement with the ideas of the Young Americans at this moment of national soul searching and rapid social change, not only because Brooks uses a metaphor of human development in the very title of his work, *America's Coming-of-Age*, but also because the genre can have a performative element, helping to give form to the collective experience of the nation not yet fully imagined (Boes 41–42). However, the Young Americans would never have considered a woman as the hero of their American cultural renaissance. To these writers, women were teachers of genteel Victorian culture, caretakers of the private realm, and sentimental consumers—all forces they rebelled against. Instead, in their early works they favored an American art characterized by a rugged manliness and called for a male writer who would act with virility, "impressionability," and "gusto" (Brooks 93). Through the power of personality and a robust artistic expression, they imagined this strong, masculine writer would overcome divisions in order to construct a usable past and define the new American spirit.[2]

Thus, Brooks and Bourne develop a radical critique of the alienation of modern American society, its conservative piety, and its nativist views and suggest a path for cultural renewal through a new artistic voice (Brooks) and a cosmopolitan union of ethnic cultures (Bourne). In *The Song of the Lark*, Cather takes up similar ideas, yet, perhaps even more radically, she imagines a woman, Thea Kronborg, as the artist of epic proportions. In the novel, Thea achieves the independent identity and narrative closure that has eluded other female protagonists, and she does so through her individual will to defy social norms and doggedly pursue her art and also through her friendships and experiences with otherness in plural communities of the American West. Thea matures into a woman of personality alongside a cosmopolitan nation and is able to embody the spirit of the nation through her artistic expression. *The Song of the Lark* is both Cather's genre-bending depiction of a woman's artistic development and an assertion of her own performative vision of the American nation at this contested moment of national identity.

EMPLOTTING A NATION

The Song of the Lark traces Thea's personal journey, from her adolescence and artistic awakening in Colorado, to her early professional training as a young woman in Chicago, and finally to her success as an opera diva in New York, a journey that mirrors the developing nation. The first third of novel depicts Thea's childhood in Moonstone, Colorado, a small town that, like Thea herself, is still taking shape. Life in Moonstone moves at a slow pace. The town is unfinished, newly delineating itself from the surrounding high desert sand dunes where Thea prefers to roam. The long street between the town and the train depot, for example, cuts through a "considerable stretch of rough open country staked out in lots not built up at all" (41). Most of Moonstone's Euro-American residents have no linguistic or cultural connections to the countries of origin of the ancestors. Instead, they fashion themselves as assimilated, middle-class Americans. Thea never feels that she fully fits in among Moonstone residents, most of whom are defined by their social hierarchies and lack of aesthetic appreciation.

MOLLY METHERD

most of her characters in this time free issue period

At seventeen, Thea leaves behind the languid days of her childhood and moves to Chicago to begin her training in earnest. The
settings shift from country roads and family homes to city streets and
apartment buildings, and the pace of the novel quickens to match
the pace of this "big, rich, appetent Western city" (215). Thea moves to
Chicago in the 1890s, when the city was newly rebuilt and modern-
ized after the great fire of 1873 and was maturing into civic existence.
Thea too begins to mature. She leaves behind her "queer country
clothes" and gets "used to living in the body of a young woman"
(284). As Michelle Moore notes, Chicago at the time was beginning
to attend to the "higher life" of art, yet the city's understanding of art
was "overwhelmingly utilitarian" (95). Thea initiates her professional
training here and broadens her artistic education at the symphony
and the Art Institute. Yet she mostly encounters people without aesthetic appreciation, concerned with the utilitarian goals of "[m]oney
and office and success" (294) rather than art and ideas.

1890s

The third and final site of development in the novel is New York
City immediately before Thea leaves to study in Germany and then
ten years later, when she returns to the city as an opera diva in
full possession of her artistic greatness. The New York sections are
mainly set in grand hotels and fashionable restaurants, in Thea's
house, which was "as impersonal as the Waldorf, and quite as large"
(450), and in the Metropolitan Opera House. Thea has reached the
pinnacle of her career: she is a great American artist living among
the grand buildings and public spaces of a city with a fully refined
aesthetic appreciation. Thus, Thea's journey to become a mature
artist parallels the industrial, civic, and aesthetic development of
the modern, urban nation.

Thea's development, however, is at odds with the familiar story of
mobility and American progress moving from east to west. In *The
Song of the Lark*, traditions, ideas, and modes of artistic expression
begin in the American West.[3] Thea moves eastward, carrying with
her the accumulation of her experiences in western landscapes and
communities that she then synthesizes into her uniquely American
artistic expression. People and ideas also move along south/north

routes in the novel. Thea's friend Juan Tellamantez migrated north from Mexico and often heads south, disappearing for months at a time. Another friend, Ray, "had drifted, a homeless boy, over the border" (57), and midway through the novel Thea too travels south through Mexico. In fact, the Colorado region seems much more connected to Mexico than to the eastern United States in the novel. The landscape is depicted using words like *arroyo* and *piñón*, offering signs that the region was a part of Mexico just four decades before the novel opens.[4] At one point Dr. Archie receives a letter from Thea at his house in Denver, and he "sat with astonishment" (382) at the New York postmark. Dr. Archie "had known that Thea was in Mexico, travelling with some Chicago people, but New York, to a Denver man, seems much farther away than Mexico City" (382). In this novel of national becoming, Cather re-maps the nation to depict multidirectional poles of influence and highways of work and travel beyond the more commonly imagined, unidirectional movement of people and ideas from the eastern center to the western periphery.

FROM DIVISION TOWARD WHOLENESS

While these three sites of increasing maturity—Moonstone, Chicago, and New York—mirror Thea's personal development, it is not in and through these spaces that Thea grows into an artist and a woman. In fact, these settings are more frequently obstacles to Thea's development. Much as Brooks and Bourne do in their writings, the novel depicts urban sites as materialistic, impersonal, and emotionally draining. According to these writers, the city accentuates the divisions in American life: between pioneer acquisitiveness and puritan strictures, as well as between urban and wild, men and women, popular culture and high art. Thea too feels divided and unfulfilled in these spaces. Yet in the natural spaces and plural cultures of the West, she finds other ways of being in the world. As a young girl in Moonstone, Thea often steps off the sidewalk and ventures outside the socially ordered town center. She enters into the high desert landscape that to her feels "young and fresh and kindly" (243). Thea finds inspiration in the beauty of the natural world, for the "absence of natural boundaries gave the spirit a wider range" (243). On the edge of town, Thea encounters communities of Germans and Mexicans who feel deep social prejudices in town but who, she romantically imagines, are "given another chance" in this landscape (243). She finds what Bourne would call a "federation of cultures" speaking their own languages and practicing their own traditions ("Trans-national").

Tobias Boes, in his study of the history of the bildungsroman, argues that in the genre "the life of the protagonist will always resist fulfillment in institutional structures" (7) as well as "nationalism's expectation for closure" (3). According to Boes, this resistance appears in anachronistic moments in the text when the narrative leaves "behind a merely sequential model of history and forge[s] links between the vernacular realities of different peoples—their 'thick sense of time' with all its contradictory rituals and practices" (34). Boes calls these moments "cosmopolitan remainders" (3). In Cather's bildungsroman, there are many such asynchronous moments in which Thea forges links with vernacular rituals and practices. In fact, in *The Song of the Lark* these interruptions to the forward-moving structure occur so frequently and have such an impact on the narrative development that it is difficult to view them simply as remainders. Thea is profoundly influenced by her experiences in liminal communities outside of the urban settings where aesthetic appreciation and artistic production is a part of everyday life. Here, Thea develops her artistic genius in ways that would not otherwise have been possible amid the gendered norms and expectations in urban America.

FRIENDS FROM CHILDHOOD

From an early age, Thea knows she is different from everyone around her. She feels this difference as an amorphous and undefined twoness that must be guarded and kept secret. She has a greater aesthetic sensibility, an openness to new people and ideas, and an eye toward greatness incomprehensible to the people of her small town. Yet her twoness seems also more foundational, more central to her identity. Critics have compellingly argued that it is a coded reference to her sexual or gender identity that must be kept hidden from the strictly heterosexual norms of Moonstone. Her art, then, becomes a means to express her full identity. Thea does not spend time with girls her age and instead befriends four men who are at least ten years older: Dr. Archie, Wunsch, Spanish Johnny, and Ray.[5] The first section of the novel, "Friends from Childhood," is named for these men, who are all progressives, idealists, and freethinkers. They are also misfits and outsiders. They see in Thea someone striving to be different, someone who reflects their own strivings. They offer her not only camaraderie and acceptance that she does not find among her peers but also the guidance and encouragement to follow a path to overcome divisions and achieve full self-expression.

Dr. Archie, the town physician, is an atheist, a romantic, and an intellectual in a town of small-minded people, and he has the "uneasy manner of a man who is not among his own kind" (94). Thea's music teacher, Wunsch, is a German immigrant and talented musician who struggles with alcoholism and is treated with disdain by the teetotaling townspeople. Juan Tellamantez, called Spanish Johnny, is a Mexican painter, a decorator, and a mandolin player who teaches Thea songs with Spanish lyrics. Spanish Johnny is an outsider not only because he is Mexican but also because he has a tendency to get drunk and disappear for months at a time. Ray Kennedy is an "aggressive idealist, a freethinker, and, like most railroad men, deeply sentimental" (51). His difference comes from leaving home as a young man and traveling through the West and Mexico. What Thea likes the most about Ray is his "love for Mexico and the Mexicans" (57). Ray can "speak Spanish fluently, and the sunny warmth of that tongue kept him from being quite as hard as his chin, or as narrow as his popular science" (57). This unlikely quartet become the foundational figures in Thea's early life. Thea, for her part, is never disconcerted by their varying degrees of outsider status in Moonstone. In fact, it seems also to be what draws her to them. The fifth friend is Fred

Ottenburg, the son of an established and wealthy German-American family in the beer-brewing industry that maintains its linguistic and cultural connections to Germany, who introduces Thea to patrons and supporters in Chicago and saves her from the city by inviting her to his ranch in Arizona. Fred becomes her friend and lover, her financier, and, in the epilogue, her husband. As she grows into a great artist, these men become supporting characters to her central narrative.

Thea's friends help her to understand her twoness. They introduce her to art, ideas, and ideologies that she otherwise would not have encountered in her small town. Wunsch teaches her about beauty and truthfulness in art, something he calls desire, and he plants the seed for her to train in Germany. Dr. Archie introduces her to books and ideas, Spanish Johnny teaches her new types of music, and Ray and Fred show her the world beyond Moonstone and Chicago. This group of men offer her a community of shared aesthetic values and an exchange of ideas that help buoy her in her development into an independent woman and an artist. In fact, her childhood friendships in plural communities anticipate an idea that Bourne will explore in his essay "Trans-national America" the following year, that is, the "good life of personality lived in the environment of the Beloved Community" (97).

Thea engages most meaningfully with these friends and mentors who shape her aesthetic education and support her artistic journey in settings outside of town: in the natural landscape or in small communities of Germans and Mexicans. Her early musical training with Herr Wunsch takes place in the home of the Kohlers, German immigrants who keep to themselves and are looked down upon by the townspeople. Thea is one of only a few outsiders who has ever walked through Mrs. Kohler's extensive garden, a verdant oasis of fruit trees and exotic flowers, and into their home. Thea finds another refuge from the town life in the Mexican community, which has "neat little yards with tamarisk hedges and flowers and walks bordered with shells or white washed stones" (46). Thea seeks out the Mexicans as she does the Kohlers. Although the townspeople feel "a grave social discrimination against the Mexicans" (167), Thea likes to sing with them because they are "kind to their families and have good manners" (262) and because she believes "[t]hey're a talented people" (264). These communities, with their unfamiliar gardens and architectural styles, not only look and feel different, they also sound different. German and Spanish words, phrases, song titles, and lyrics are left untranslated, and the narrative stresses the heavily accented English of several characters. Wunsch, for example, insists that "it is necessary to know well the German language" (83). And Spanish Johnny tells Thea that as a young girl "you take the air and you sing it just-a beauti-ful" (252). Cather transcribes the unconventional word order and uses dashes to highlight the accented pronunciations in order to emphasize the characters' difference.

Cather's novel thus depicts the American West as a region defined by immigrant communities that defy the notion of the American melting pot and assume differing attitudes toward assimilation. By walking beyond the edge of the town and immersing herself in these different languages and immigrant cultures, Thea learns about forms of music, art, and community that she would have never experienced within the geographic and social boundaries of her small town, and she begins to translate herself in the world in new ways. Thea learns some German from her teacher Wunsch, and she "knows enough Spanish for" singing (251) from her time spent in the Mexican community. She also comes to appreciate her own foreignness. She says, "I used to be ashamed of being a Swede, but I'm not any more. Swedes are kind of common, but I think it's better to be something" (93). Thea too rejects assimilation and begins to develop her own identity.

In fact, the two most significant moments in the narrative of Thea's artistic development occur not in the music studios or performance halls of Moonstone, Chicago, or New York but during a *danza* in the Mexican town outside Moonstone and among the ruins of the cliff-dwelling peoples in Panther Canyon, Arizona.[6] These sites are not, as some critics have suggested, just quaint backdrops for a novel set in the Southwest or convenient locations to add local color but instead are two mirrored, asynchronous moments that are nonetheless catalysts in the narrative of individual and national becoming. In these two settings, Thea engages with an idealized and, to different degrees, imagined community and encounters new models of ethics and artistic production that inspire her. In these sites, she further overcomes her sense of twoness. She experiences an embodiment that allows her to craft a unified personality as an artist and a woman.

WHOLENESS IN COMMUNITY: THE MEXICAN *DANZA*

After her first year of study in Chicago, Thea returns to Moonstone for the summer and accepts an invitation from Spanish Johnny to a dance in the Mexican town. When Thea steps off the Moonstone sidewalk and onto the sandy path to go to the dance, time slows down. The descriptions lengthen and become more vivid. It was a "soft, rosy evening. The sand hills were lavender. The sun had gone down a glowing copper disk, and the fleecy clouds in the east were a burning rose-colour, flecked with gold" (254). The velvety lavender, copper, rose, and gold colors of the landscape contrast with the muted and highly ordered town she leaves behind. When she arrives, she finds the dance to be unlike those she is used to attending at the Firemen's Hall in Moonstone, where the country auctioneer called out the square dances and the "boys played rough jokes and thought it smart to be clumsy and to run into each other on the floor." Instead, the "Mexican dance was soft and quiet," and there was an "atmosphere of ease and friendly pleasure in the low, dimly lit room" (255). The "men were graceful and courteous" (255), and the girls wore dresses and had flowers in their hair. There is a "kind of natural harmony about their movements, their greetings, their low conversations, their smiles" (255–56). Sarah Clere finds Cather's depiction of the Mexican town to be "anachronistic and quaint" (157). While the romantic depiction of the Mexican community is asynchronous, that is, out of time with the forward-moving pace of the narration, it is not inconsequential in the narrative development. It is not a glimpse of the past frozen in time but rather a present-day, alternate social order clearly juxtaposed to the normative life in Moonstone. It is a community that offers artistic inspiration and one possible model through which to reimagine the developing American nation.

As a privileged outsider, Thea finds a place where she can explore her artistic desire outside of the social constraints and gender norms of both cultures. Young girls from Moonstone do not go alone to the Mexican town, and even though the "Mexican women of the poorer class do not sing like the men" (260), Thea sings with the men in Spanish late into the night. Her difference, which Janis Stout demonstrates is marked by frequent references to her whiteness ("Brown and White"), allows her to disregard social norms. Through her art, however, Thea experiences connection. She "had never before sung for a really musical people, and this was the first time she had ever felt the response that such a people can give" (258). They recognize her artistry, applaud her skill, and encourage her to perform in Mexico City. When she sings, she feels the audience "turned themselves and all they had over to her. For the moment, they cared about nothing in the world but what she was doing. Their faces confronted her—open, eager, unprotected. She felt as if all these warm-blooded people had debouched into her" (258). They debouched into her, that is, flowed through narrow straits into something wide, like rivers into the sea. She embodies her audience, and they become one. To twenty-first-century readers this certainly sounds like an odd "appropriation of Mexican music and of otherness, a figurative acquisition of their very selves" (Clere 158). Yet Thea does not take something from Mexican culture—a rhythm, a song, a stylistic technique—and pass it off as her own. Instead, Cather describes a moment of aesthetic connection and transcendence between artist and audience. Thea opens herself to them and reveals her secret artistic desire, and they in turn offer her something she has never had before: communal approval, encouragement, and aesthetic appreciation.

What Thea does take from this experience is a sense of herself as an artist and of her own agency and determination. When she returns from the *danza*, the dream-like quality of the narration ends. Her family is furious. Her sister tells Thea that "[e]verybody at Sunday-

128

MOLLY METHERD

School was talking about you going over there and singing with
the Mexicans all night, when you won't sing for the church" (264).
Thea defends her choices. She says, "I like to sing over there. [. . .]
I'll sing for them any time they ask me to. They know something
about what I'm doing" (264). This experience allows her to see again
with fresh eyes her own difference from the town and from her own
family. It becomes a threshold moment in Thea's development, for
in this moment she decides to leave her childhood home, determined never to return.

PHYSICALITY AND PERSONALITY
IN PANTHER CANYON

After another year of study in Chicago, Thea again feels
discouraged, riddled with self-doubt, and overwrought with the fast
pace of the city. Frayed and frustrated, she spends the summer on an
Arizona ranch owned by her friend and love interest from Chicago,
Fred Ottenburg. The property includes centuries-old cliff dwellings
of the Sinagua, a part of the Pueblo nation. This section stands out
for its unique setting and also for the quality of the narration and the
impact it has on Thea's future. Just as in the journey to the Mexican
danza, the forward movement of the novel is interrupted as Thea
enters into the canyon that is out of place and time from her life in
Chicago. The tone is hushed and mythical; the descriptions of the
landscape are detailed and drawn out. With this dramatic shift in
setting and change in narrative texture, it is of little surprise that this
section has received significant critical attention as the mystical and
modernist center of the novel. Like Thea's experience at the dance,
her time in Panther Canyon is a threshold moment in the text where
Thea makes decisions that change the direction of her life.

Released from the social expectations and norms of behavior of
the big city and the pressures of training, Thea feels as though the
"personality of which she was so tired seemed to let go of her" and
she is "getting back to the earliest sources of gladness that she could
remember" (326). The landscape moves her. She again opens her-

self to the physical experience of this place with its deep, womb-like canyons and nurturing spaces that Ellen Moers calls the "most thoroughly elaborated female landscape in literature" (258). Here Thea attunes herself to her own body and becomes a receptacle for everything around her—the heat, the stones, and the sounds of the cicadas (330). Alone on the mesa, she imagines herself in communion with the Sinagua women of the past, a community of women unlike any she has known, for her life has been shaped by male friendships. She begins to embody the spirits of the women through the landscape (332–33), and a sort of imagined conversation develops: "[C]ertain feelings were transmitted to her, suggestions that were simple, insistent, and monotonous, like the beating of Indian drums. They were not expressible in words, but seemed rather to translate themselves into attitudes of the body" (333). Critics have noted that she begins to "play Indian" as she imagines the women who traveled the worn paths before her and finds herself trying to walk as they did with "the weight of an Indian baby hanging to her back as she climbed" (332). In the shards of women's pottery that she finds, Thea recognizes their artistic expression (336) and equates their art to her own voice. She realizes that, in "singing, one made a vessel of one's throat and nostrils and held it on one's breath" (335), and this helps her to see connection between her voice and her body (338). In Panther Canyon, Thea experiences creativity as embodiment rather than as rote training, emulation, or forceful self-assertion (Conrad 292). She also comes to see how, despite the "inevitable hardness of human life" (509), the Indigenous women were still able to realize their artistic desire and create something beautiful and enduring. This model of resolve and perseverance is what Thea has been lacking and what she achieves by seeing herself as part of a tradition of women artists.

vessel as
pottery =
holding
Note

Even as she imagines herself embodying the spirits of the Sinaguan women, Thea takes on more stereotypically masculine qualities. She is athletic, playful, and "unceasingly active" (353), hiking, exploring new sites, wrestling and competing with Fred in stone-throwing contests, and embracing the dangers of a lightning storm. She takes on a "muscular energy and audacity,—a kind of brilliancy of motion" (353) and "became freer and stronger under impulses" (360). Like Brooks and Bourne, Cather imagines that Thea's experiences in beloved communities can free her from the social, sexual, and gender divisions of modern American culture. In communion with a community of spiritual and aesthetic richness, she can achieve agency to unify dualities, the feminine and the masculine, and to cultivate her personality. Away from social restrictions and prying eyes, she feels free to share a new intimacy with Fred and embraces her sexuality. This transformative experience allows her to reject moral guilt and gendered rules of sexual behavior and becomes another step in her process of artistic liberation. Fred notices that she has come in to her personality "that carried across big spaces and expanded among big things" (353). "Personality" is a term of particular import to the Young Americans at the turn of the century; they use it to mean something akin to character developed through self-reflection and engagement with others. Thea becomes more confident, more at home in her body, more feminist. She is less apologetic, and her voice acquires a richness and depth. Fred says that "[n]ow she has let herself be beautiful" (392).

Through these experiences, Thea is able to further unify the twoness, to unite her body and spirit and accept herself fully as an artist with full agency over her own life. She believes that "cliff dwellers had lengthened her past. She had older and higher obligations" (339). This realization helps her to accept the social consequences and make her artistic desire public. She decides she will not return to Chicago: "Thea at last made up her mind what she was going to try to do in the world, and that she was going to Germany to study without further loss of time" (338–39).

FEELING CULTURE: ENCOUNTERS AS EMBODIMENT

A common critique of *The Song of the Lark* is that Cather sees the cliff dwellers in Panther Canyon as a noble civilization worthy of emulation but focuses only on past cultures and ignores the real, living Indigenous peoples. There is no doubt that the novel overlooks the colonial history that devastated the Pueblo people as well as the contemporary Indigenous cultures around Panther Canyon. Reading these two mirrored sequences together, however, reveals that it is not only the fixed ruins of the Sinagua people that give Thea artistic inspiration; it is also the living people of the Mexican community. It is not only the long past but also the very real present that inspires her and renews her artistic vision in a way that life in an American city can never do. It is therefore not simply nostalgia for an ancient culture or a lost way of life but rather contact and connection with otherness in its many forms that produces these effects.

Reading the depictions of idealized communities in the context of the larger progressive intellectual debates of the early twentieth century reveals the ways in which "the great, good places of Cather's fiction emerge as part of a larger cultural pattern, namely the Utopian idealism of progressive America and its reforming drive to recreate the nation as an earthly Eden" (Reynolds 15). In both scenes, Thea enacts the modernist desire to escape from the pressures of civilization into what she experiences as more authentic or organic communities and become whole. In these mirrored sequences, Thea feels exhausted by her training, weighed down by expectations, and fed up with the people around her. She goes alone into nature to encounter another culture, one that is spatially set apart from modern, urban life. In stark contrast to her own communities in Moonstone and Chicago, she finds communities she views as dignified and graceful, living in harmony with nature and integrating aesthetics into everyday life. Narrative time slows down and becomes thick, and the landscape feels imbued with symbolic meaning. In these communities, she feels freed from the judgments and restraints of her own culture. She finds that she is able to "breathe a larger air" (Bourne, "Trans-national"). Her experiences are physical, spiritual, and intellectual and prompt her to a new sense of herself in the world.

As these two narrative sequences are untethered from narrative time, they exist outside of the teleology of individual and national development characteristic of the bildungsroman. Yet they are central to her development as an artist. At both the Mexican *danza* and in Panther Canyon, Thea finds not just an imagined mystical wholeness in community. More practically, she finds new models of artistic expression that show her a feasible way forward as an artist and lead her to make crucial decisions about her future. At the *danza*, she finds the appreciation and encouragement that she often lacks in the petty social world of Moonstone or the competitive environment of her training in Chicago. The women and men alike admire her artistry and encourage her to sing in Mexico City. In Panther Canyon, she marvels at the women artists who endure in their effort to craft beautiful pottery despite such difficult conditions. In both instances, it is not that she finds cultures that assign different, more liberal, roles to women; it is that she finds people who, despite their own obstacles, remain committed to their artistic expression. She is relieved of her self-doubt and learns that to succeed as an artist she must "demand things for herself" (511), lessons she could not have otherwise learned in the patriarchal, American city. What is more, she not only learns from these cultures, she embodies them in what Lindemann calls a "corporeal utopianism" as a part of broader artistic tradition (39). This physical experience of embodiment fills her up, makes her whole. Encounter becomes embodiment, experience integrates with aesthetics, and a new model for artistic life is revealed.

Both sequences are also threshold moments, or points of no return, in the narrative. Once Thea goes to the *danza*, she refuses to live in the town of her childhood. She rejects the town's desire for homogeneity, the townspeople's racist attitudes, and their restrictions on female behavior. Once she goes to Panther Canyon, she refuses to return to Chicago with its restrictive sexual norms and assumptions that women must sacrifice themselves for others. What emerges from these threshold moments is a feminist narrative approach to the bildungsroman that resists the nationalist desire for fixed definitions, completeness, and closure and, as Deborah Lindsay Williams argues, instead introduces a "flexible, nuanced worldview that is not threatened by difference but is instead challenged by it, altered because of it: a cosmopolitan perspective" (160). More than just "remainders" here, these encounters with other cultures enable Thea to succeed in the bildungsroman where so many other female characters have not. *The Song of the Lark* subverts the conventional narrative logic of the bildungsroman, the novel of nation formation, by positioning the plural cultures of the American West, including Indigenous cultures decimated by colonialism, as central to Thea's development and therefore to American artistic expression. In so doing, these sections reveal a more complex and inclusive understanding of national identity.

AMERICAN ART AND A COSMOPOLITAN VISION

For a female artist at the turn of the twentieth century, overcoming alienation from the modern world and finding a mystical wholeness are not enough to unleash artistic greatness. She not only needs to overcome her own twoness; she faces more practical obstacles. She cannot advance her goals in Moonstone, Chicago, and New York along with the nation because there are no structures in mainstream American cities to support the progressive development and ultimate success of a female artist. Thea must look outside the normative spaces of the nation for inspiration and representation. After her time in Arizona, Thea must leave the country. She has come to terms with her twoness by learning to express her artistic desire and locate it within a tradition of women's art, and she also has come into her own body, its female and male gender expressions and sexual desire. Yet in the United States she cannot fulfill her desire. In her social views and her artistic vision, she has evolved faster than the nation itself. She needs first to go to Mexico, where she can be "exceptionally free" (363) from gossip and judgment to be with her lover outside of marriage. Then, she must travel to Germany for advanced training in opera that she cannot find in the United States. As a woman and an artist, Thea needs what the nation, still caught in relative adolescence, cannot offer her.

Yet as a bildungsroman, or the genre of nation-building, the narrative cannot go outside the nation. Cather recognized this when she removed the section she initially wrote about Thea in Germany, believing that the novel should stay focused on Moonstone.[7] So, two-thirds of the way through, the novel is left without a protagonist. In an awkward move, the narrative shifts to focus instead on two of Thea's friends, Fred Ottenburg and Dr. Archie, in Denver and New York. They speculate about Thea and talk of Moonstone, filling in the gaps of her absence. Narrative space and time become untethered from the life of the protagonist, and the structure of the bildungsroman unravels temporarily. In his unsigned review of the novel in the *New Republic*, titled "Diminuendo," Randolph Bourne puts forward a critique echoed by many subsequent readers and reviewers who feel unsatisfied by this narrative shift, finding that the section focused on Dr. Archie and Fred Ottenburg drags on too long and lacks the emotional power of the first two-thirds of the novel. Bourne, in fact, thought the novel should have ended when Thea leaves for Mexico. In her preface to the 1932 edition, Cather agreed that she should have "disregarded conventional design" (617–18) and finished the novel before Thea becomes successful.

While the section titled "Dr. Archie's Venture" wanders away from the central premise of the novel, Thea's travels abroad do align with the novel's privileging of the cosmopolitan over the national. Randolph Bourne in "Trans-national America" argues that the cultures that make up America create points of access to the world beyond the nation. Similarly, in *The Song of the Lark* Thea's experiences with German and Mexican immigrant communities that welcomed her, taught her about art and language, and gave her a broader world view create access points for her travels in Mexico and Germany. As Dr. Archie insists toward the end of the novel, Thea "was born a cosmopolitan, and I expect she learned a good deal from Johnny when she used to run away and go to Mexican Town" (408). Cather demonstrates how the many cultures in the United States create a broader transnational perspective and allow Americans to turn outward from small-town provincialism and to look beyond national borders toward an "intellectual internation-alism" (Bourne, "Trans-national").

FROM THEA TO "KRONBORG":
PERSONAL AND NATIONAL TRIUMPH

In the final book of the novel, titled "Kronborg," Thea has returned to New York as a successful opera star performing at the Metropolitan Opera House. *The Song of the Lark* ends in a scene of triumph. Thea gives a virtuoso performance in Wagner's *Die Walküre* with all of her living "friends of childhood" in the audience. In this final scene, Thea becomes fully visible, seen, and appreciated for all her talents. In full possession of her voice and her body, she reaches the height of artistic achievement. She claims her right to self-expression, her position as a female artist, and her place in the world. Cather's bildungsroman rewrites "our national myth and placed female creativity at its center" (Rosowski, "Writing" 68).

Even in Thea's moment of personal triumph on a national stage, the last book of the novel repeatedly stresses that it was her child-hood in the West that allowed her to achieve such great heights. While her training in Germany offered her a "new understanding," Thea's friend Fred Ottenburg believes that it was her childhood in Moonstone that kept her from "getting off the track" (406) and that it gives her voice a unique quality, like "inherited memory, like folk-music" (494). Thea also believes it was her "rich, romantic past" (506), her contact with the landscape and with the different cultures of her Colorado childhood that shape her artistic vision. She says "the light, the color, the feeling" of Moonstone are in everything she does (506). Thea is able to translate the cosmopolitan experiences of her childhood in the West into a uniquely American artistic expression. Thea thus becomes what Van Wyck Brooks insists has been missing from American literature: an artist "with a certain density, weight and richness" and a "deep, moving, shaking impact of personality" who can synthesize "every admirable characteristic of a people" and create artistic expression that defines and expresses American life (39).

MOLLY METHERD

BEYOND THE PERSONAL TO THE NATIONAL

Thea's individual narrative desire is fulfilled in her triumphant performance at the close of the novel. Yet as a bildungsroman, the narrative still has some loose ends. It takes a curious epilogue to fully produce generic closure. The epilogue jumps in time and space to Moonstone in 1909. No longer the small prairie town Thea left two decades before, Moonstone has matured as well. The streets are "harder and firmer than they were twenty-five years ago" and "cultivation has modified the soil and the climate, as it modifies human life" (531). The people "are much smarter" and the children "all look like city children" (531–32). Thea has married Fred and is at the height of her career, living a cosmopolitan life. She travels the world with the Metropolitan Opera Company, earning a thousand dollars a night. Through her art, she "has given much noble pleasure to a world that needs all it can get" (534).[8] Yet with an odd storybook tone, the epilogue focuses not on Thea herself but on her impact. She has become a legendary figure in Moonstone. Her aunt Tillie, the last Kronborg in town, is consumed with Thea's success. She is always telling stories about Thea and "lives in her niece's triumphs" (534). The people in town also follow Thea's accomplishments and share their memories of her. Her life takes on a mythic quality that brings them "real refreshment" (536). Her story has become their own.

The epilogue, then, becomes insurance that the novel will be read not only as a fictional account of one woman's artistic achievement but also as the mythic tale of a national hero. Through the course of the novel, her life becomes a collective national story that mirrors the nation coming into being. At the novel's opening, in 1881, the United States was a young nation whose borders, citizenry, and place in the world order were still up for debate. Thea moves from the "vague, easy-going world" (528) of the provincial West with its young, fresh landscape to her first real professional training as a young adult at seventeen in the "crush and scramble" of a big "western" city, Chicago, and finally to a "life of disciplined endeavor" (528) and the peak of aesthetic achievement at the opera house in metropolitan New York right around 1900, just as the nation is becoming industrialized and masses of people are moving from the farms into cities. In the epilogue, set in Moonstone in 1909, Tillie reads about Thea's successes in the New York newspapers she has delivered to her Colorado home and keeps photographs of Thea and a phonograph recording of her performance. These are all technologies that have shaped the modern nation in the span of Thea's life. Thea's story becomes a performance of the nation revealing its shape in space and time.

As literary history shows, the female bildungsroman typically cannot achieve closure. There are too many obstacles that prohibit the protagonist from developing her full identity and expectations that impede her from expressing herself with agency. In *The Song of the Lark*, Cather takes what Boes identifies as small moments of resistance to nationalism's drive toward closure in the modern European bildungsroman, what he calls "cosmopolitan remainders," and instead situates the cosmopolitan at the center of the novel (3). If Thea's individual development as an artist is a metaphor for national formation, then contact with otherness, the plural cultures of the West, including the German immigrants, the living Mexican culture, and the more distant Indigenous past play an important part in the shaping of the nation. Cather's bildungsroman demonstrates that it is not in a singular national narrative but rather through a transnational one, operating in and through many different cultures, that a female protagonist can develop independence and agency.

Cather thus writes a successful female bildungsroman, an idealized yet nonetheless audacious act of writing a woman as the heroine and focal center of a cosmopolitan American nation. From her childhood in the West, Thea cultivates a rich personality and finds "a new song in that blue air that had never been sung in the world before" (243). Through friendships and experiences in diverse western communities and through courage, determination, and tireless training at home and abroad, she shapes this natural song into an aesthetic expression of the American nation. Through her body and the organ of her art, her physical voice, she synthesizes the rural and the urban, the West and the East, the "Highbrow" and the "Lowbrow," the female and male, tradition and modernity into a fully realized aesthetic expression of American identity. Thea becomes the unifying force who creates an "underlying coherence" (Brooks 120) and an "epic expression" (Bourne, "Trans-national") of the nation in the years just before the United States enters World War I, when such coherence still seemed possible.

NOTES

1. For more on the female bildungsroman, see the work of Abel, Hirsch, and Langland, of Lazzaro-Weis, and of Maier.

2. In fact, as critics from Paul Lauter and Nina Baym to Guy Reynolds have demonstrated, Brooks's notion of a "usable past" and the Young Americans' call for a vigorous and manly spirit of American literature influenced literary critics in the 1930s and 1940s to favor grand narratives of struggle and perseverance written by men over domestic narratives they deemed too feminine and therefore not serious literature. They assembled the American literary canon based on such an evaluative matrix, a canon that continued to largely exclude women writers for the next half century.

3. In 1923 Cather expressed a similar idea of the American West as a place of youth and talent that can offer an antidote to American art and society. "It is in that great cosmopolitan country known as the Middle West that we may hope to see the hard molds of American provincialism broken up; that we may hope to find young talent which will challenge the pale properties, the insincere, conventional optimism of our art and thought" ("Nebraska").

4. Cather herself imagined that she felt this Mexican influence on her childhood. In a letter to Sarah Orne Jewett dated 24 October 1908, Cather writes about the "Latin influence" in the West. She writes, "We had so many Spanish words, just as you had words left over from Chaucer. Even the cowboy saddle, you know, is an old Spanish model. There was something heady in the wind that blew up from Mexico" (*Complete Letters* #0140).

5. Most critics overlook Spanish Johnny as one of the "friends from childhood," although he clearly plays a role in Thea's early life. Thea mentions him later in a list of her Moonstone friends (240), and he appears with the other living friends at her final performance at the end of the novel.

6. Much critical attention has been dedicated to Thea's time in Panther Canyon; however, apart from Janis Stout's essay "Brown and White at the Dance" and Sarah Clere's "Locating Mexicans in *The Song of the Lark*," there

has been only passing reference to Thea's encounters with Mexican cultures and little analysis of the role these interactions play in her development as an artist.

7. In a 15 March 1916 letter to Dorothy Canfield Fisher, Cather explains that she wrote the chapters set in Germany but then edited them out, believing that this would have hurt the unity of the novel and that the focus should stay on Moonstone (*Complete Letters* #0351).

8. As Eric Aronoff demonstrates in *Composing Cultures*, Cather walks a line between two competing notions of culture in the early twentieth century: an evolutionary progressivism and the notion of multiple cultures as plural and coherent unto themselves.

WORKS CITED

Abel, Elizabeth, Marianne Hirsch, and Elizabeth Langland. *The Voyage In: Fictions of Female Development*. UP of New England, 1983.

Aronoff, Eric. *Composing Cultures: Modernism, American Literary Studies, and the Problem of Culture*. U of Virginia P, 2013.

Bakhtin, Mikhail. "The Bildungsroman and Its Significance in the History of Realism (Toward a Historical Typology of the Novel)." *Speech Genres and Other Late Essays*, U of Texas P, 1986.

Baym, Nina L. "Melodramas of Beset Manhood: How Theories of American Fiction Exclude Women Authors." *American Quarterly*, vol. 33, no. 2, 1981, pp. 123–39.

Blake, Casey Nelson. *Beloved Community: The Cultural Criticism of Randolph Bourne, Van Wyck Brooks, Waldo Frank, and Lewis Mumford*. U of North Carolina P, 1990.

Boes, Tobias. *Formative Fictions: Nationalism, Cosmopolitanism and the Bildungsroman*. Cornell UP, 2012.

Bourne, Randolph. "Diminuendo." *New Republic*, 11 December 1915, pp. 153–54.

———. "Trans-national America." *Atlantic Monthly*, July 1916, theatlantic.com/magazine/archive/1916/07/trans-national-america/304838/.

Brooks, Van Wyck. *America's Coming-of-Age*. B. W. Huebsch, 1915.

Cather, Willa. *The Complete Letters of Willa Cather*, edited by the Willa Cather Archive team, *Willa Cather Archive*, cather.unl.edu/writings/letters. Accessed 11 January 2021.

———. "Nebraska: The End of the First Cycle." *The Nation*, 5 September 1923, pp. 236–38, *Willa Cather Archive*, cather.unl.edu/writings/nonfiction/nf066. Accessed 5 January 2021.

————. *The Song of the Lark*. 1915. Willa Cather Scholarly Edition, historical essay and explanatory notes by Ann Moseley, textual essay and editing by Kari A. Ronning, U of Nebraska P, 2012.

Clere, Sarah. "Locating Mexicans in *The Song of the Lark*." *Willa Cather's The Song of the Lark*, edited by Debra L. Cumberland, Editions Rodopi, 2010, pp. 149–64.

Conrad, Angela. "Women and Vessels in *The Song of the Lark* and *Shadows on the Rock*." *Willa Cather at the Modernist Crux*, edited by Ann Moseley, John J. Murphy, and Robert Thacker, Cather Studies 11, U of Nebraska P, 2017, pp. 289–302, jstor.org/stable/j.ctt1qv5psc. Accessed 13 January 2021.

Hegeman, Susan. *Patterns for America: Modernism and the Concept of Culture*. Princeton UP, 1999.

Jameson, Fredric. *The Political Unconscious: Narrative as a Socially Symbolic Act*. Cornell UP, 1981.

Lazzaro-Weis, Carol. "The Female 'Bildungsroman': Calling It into Question." *NWSA Journal* vol. 2, no. 1, 1990, pp. 16–34.

Lindemann, Marilee. *Willa Cather: Queering America*. Columbia UP, 1999.

Maier, Sarah E. "Portraits of the Girl-Child: Female Bildungsroman in Victorian Fiction." *Literature Compass*, vol. 4, no. 1, 2007, pp. 317–35.

Moers, Ellen. *Literary Women*. 1976. Oxford UP, 1987.

Moore, Michelle E. *Chicago and the Making of American Modernism: Cather, Hemingway, Faulkner, and Fitzgerald in Conflict*. Bloomsbury Academic, 2019.

Moretti, Franco. *The Way of the World: The Bildungsroman in European Culture*. New ed., Verso, 2000.

Reynolds, Guy. *Willa Cather in Context: Progress, Race, Empire*. St. Martin's Press, 1996.

Rosowski, Susan J. *The Voyage Perilous: Willa Cather's Romanticism*. U of Nebraska P, 1986.

————. "Writing against Silences: Female Adolescent Development in the Novels of Willa Cather." *Studies in the Novel*, vol. 21, no. 1, Spring 1989, pp. 60–77.

Stout, Janis P. "Brown and White at the Dance." *Willa Cather Newsletter and Review*, vol. 49, no. 2, 2005, pp. 37+.

————. "Modernist by Association: Willa Cather's New York/New Mexico Circle." *American Literary Realism*, vol. 47, no. 2, Winter 2015, pp. 117–35.

Williams, Deborah Lindsay. "'Fragments of Their Desire': Willa Cather and the Alternative Aesthetic Tradition of Native American Women." *Willa Cather and Material Culture: Real World Writing, Writing the Real World*, edited by Janis Stout, U of Alabama P, 2005, pp. 156–70.

7 "As Dangerous as High Explosives," or, The Sexual Lives of Hired Girls

Sex Radicalism in *My Ántonia*

GENEVA M. GANO

In 1971 feminist literary scholar Blanche H. Gelfant became one of the first of Willa Cather's critics to identify sex and sexuality as the objects of the author's many "deflect[ions]," "negations[,] and evasions": those crucial elements of fiction not specifically named on the page yet so palpably present in the text (62, 82). It is to Gelfant's groundbreaking essay, "The Forgotten Reaping-Hook: Sex in *My Ántonia*," that the subtitle of this chapter refers, and its writing would be unthinkable without Gelfant's direct intervention into readings of the novel that have persistently mischaracterized it as a young man's sentimental coming-of-age narrative set in the late nineteenth-century Nebraska frontier. Following Freudian lines of thought, Gelfant diagnoses Jim Burden, the novel's narrator, as being motivated by intense sexual fears that produce an "insistent need ... to turn away from the very [sexual] material he presents" (81). Indicating that these fears are shared by the author, Gelfant argues that they result in a "disingenuous" or unreliable narrative of sexual development, and she places them squarely at the center of the novel's concerns (60).

Gelfant's analysis has provoked an extensive and ongoing scholarly discussion of sex and sexuality in Cather's work, much of which accords with her claim that "Cather consistently invalidates" and "bar[s]" the possibility of happy, healthy sexual experience—what Gelfant calls "normal sex"—"from her fictional world," showing instead that "physical passion [is] disastrous" (61, 62). This chapter considers My Ántonia as being both exemplary and exceptional in relation to this model. In this novel, the reader witnesses not only some of the most devastating consequences of toxic, socially sanctioned (i.e., "normal" in Gelfant's terms) heterosexual acts but also Cather's most affirming portrait of free sexual pleasure and desire. The evidence of this is not hidden but consists of the explicitly named (though almost always overlooked) source of a great deal of the novel's interest: the sex lives of Black Hawk's memorable "foreign" contingent of "hired girls."[1] In Jim's narrative, these young, poor, immigrant women stand out as being simultaneously in danger—especially vulnerable to sexual predation—and "dangerous" figures of unregulated sex and sexuality. Among these, one—not Jim's Ántonia but her own woman, Lena Lingard—emerges quite literally as the novel's central subject, freely and openly "g[iving] her heart away when she felt like it," all the while enjoying undeniable successes in her professional, family, and personal life (Cather 290). Artist and lover, but never muse or mother, Lena Lingard emerges as an exemplary female artist and modern career woman, one who achieves fabulous success without compromises or regrets.

If Lena Lingard is resituated at the center of My Ántonia, Ántonia Shimerda's role as the text's nominal heroine and primary device through which the reader may be exposed to the workings of Jim Burden's consciousness must be reevaluated. Instead, she takes her place beside Lena, Tiny, and the novel's other poor, immigrant young women who navigate the economic landscapes of the late nineteenth-century American West. Together, their stories reveal the overdetermined relationship between women's sexual conduct and their relative subjugation or freedom within the U.S. capitalist economy, a position integrally linked to gender, class, and race. Ultimately, perceiving Lena's centrality to *My Ántonia* permits us to see that, despite its explicitly nostalgic tone and androcentric perspective, the novel conveys a recognizably radical feminist argument—one that here aligns Cather, surprisingly, with anarchist Emma Goldman—for a woman's right to control her own body and direct her own economic future.

RADICAL SEX AND POLITICS IN PROGRESSIVE ERA GREENWICH VILLAGE

Willa Cather and Emma Goldman admittedly make an unlikely couple; individually, they inhabit virtually opposite roles in both the popular and the critical imaginary. Recent scholarly interventions have scarcely loosened a long-held perception of Cather as a somewhat reclusive traditionalist with aristocratic leanings, while Goldman has been remembered as a dangerously passionate revolutionary and outspoken partisan of the immigrant working classes. Both of these characterizations merit a degree of reconsideration, however, particularly in the years in which these women's lives most closely overlapped, between 1906 and 1918. As readers of this volume are likely aware, Cather claimed allegiance with a cultural elite that addressed itself to the transcendent art of the novel rather than the turmoil of popular politics, a move that distanced her from the muckraking journalism that had initially brought her to New York City. At the same time, in interviews and published comments about her work, she frequently projected an image of herself as accessible, down-to-earth, and sincerely interested in the imaginative and material lives of hardworking farmers and small-town folk—people around whom she was raised and with whom she claimed to be familiar (Bohlke).

Emma Goldman, perhaps less well known to Cather's readers, was a self-proclaimed "firebrand" and radical anarchist who founded and published *Mother Earth*—officially a "monthly magazine devoted to Social Science and Literature" but better known as the nation's most widely circulating anarchist magazine between 1906 and 1917. The

144

anarchism it promoted emphasized personal liberation and voluntary association as well as active, collective struggle to abolish capitalism and overthrow church and state (Cornell; Hsu). More idealist than insurrectionary, Goldman's *Mother Earth* was established with an inclusionary vision of anarchism, one that explicitly "aim[ed] for unity between revolutionary effort and artistic expression" (qtd. in Cornell 39). Like many of Cather's most memorable characters, Goldman was an immigrant to the United States from eastern Europe; in the United States, she became immersed in the growing radical, foreign-led anarchist movement in the late nineteenth century and eventually became one of its most recognizable leaders worldwide. Over the course of her life she was imprisoned, beaten, and physically, legally, and financially threatened for her activism; she was deported under the Alien Act of 1918 for her anarchist views, but she continued to espouse them in Russia, Europe, and Canada until her death in 1940. Although she cultivated a public image as a radical activist, Goldman in fact spent much of her time fundraising, which involved hobnobbing with New York City's wealthy, cultured, leftist elite, with whom she spoke not only about wage slavery but also about modern art and literature, free speech, and free love.

While archival evidence has not shown that Cather and Goldman knew each other personally, it would be almost inconceivable that the two powerful female writer-editors, almost exact contemporaries, were not aware of each other. They both lived and worked in New York City's intimate but bustling Greenwich Village from 1906, when Cather moved there from Pittsburgh, until Goldman's deportation at the close of World War I. This was a critical period in each of their careers, as they were both expanding their national and international profiles. The year that Cather arrived, Goldman began publishing *Mother Earth* in Greenwich Village. In addition to writing for and publishing the journal, Goldman circulated continuously throughout the city, region, and nation, giving widely publicized lectures to promote the anarchist cause. Willa Cather was based in Greenwich Village while she conceived, wrote, and revised her first novels, including *My Ántonia*. Her friend Elizabeth Shepley Sergeant recalled that she was a vital participant in social life during this period, though she avoided exclusive "circles" (140). With her partner, Edith Lewis, Willa Cather regularly hosted musicians and artists for tea in her home at 5 Bank Street, dined at the Hotel Brevoort, and attended the theater (Jewell), a passion she shared not only with Goldman, who lectured nationally on the subject and published a book about it in 1914, but with virtually all of the Village's movers and shakers in the 1910s, including members of the Greenwich Village–based Washington Square Players, the Provincetown Players, and organizers of the Paterson Strike Pageant (Falk).

During the period in which these women lived in Greenwich Village, the neighborhood became known around the world as ground zero for a "lyrical Left" of socially engaged writers, artists, and arts workers (Abrahams, Stansell). According to Christine Stansell, this hotbed of radical bohemianism was anchored by a core group of feminists that included militant suffragists, birth control advocates, and free love proponents—those on the radical end of a broad spectrum of Progressive Era feminisms that also included middle-class clubwomen, maternalists, civic reformers, and wealthy philanthropists (Muncy). Many of these women were connected through their membership in Heterodoxy, a Greenwich Village–based feminist women's group and social club that ran from 1912 through the 1940s. The club's members met bimonthly for lunch, hosted presentations by guests, and offered one another mutual support. Although Goldman and Cather both had friends, relations, and associates who were involved in the group, neither was a member. Both held themselves apart from the feminist organizations and clubs that proliferated in the Village, such as Heterodoxy, the New York Women's Trade Union League, and the New York Equal Suffrage League. Elizabeth Shepley Sergeant reported that Cather detested the very thought of joining such a group (127), while Goldman railed against them publicly as wrongheaded institutions that would not lead to women's true liberation—something she considered impossible within a state-defined and male-led capitalist democracy—because they were wrongly focused on what she called the "fetich" [*sic*] of women's suffrage (*Anarchism* 201). At issue for each of the women seems to have been a general and sweeping opposition to what Cather referred to as "deadly conformity" and a vision of individual freedom, regardless of gender, that they held in common; both were convinced that personal liberation for women would not come about through their participation in reformist social clubs (qtd. in Jewell 60).

Emma Goldman's views on the subject were particularly well known. Although she was one of the most prominent female political activists in the nation, she publicly decried "the narrowness of the existing conception of women's independence and emancipation" as espoused by mainstream women's suffrage groups (*Anarchism* 223). In her widely reprinted 1906 essay for *Mother Earth*, "The Tragedy of Women's Emancipation," she expressed her belief that winning equality with men—an equality defined primarily by the right to vote and work alongside them within a capitalist system—would fail to liberate either sex. In speeches and in widely disseminated published essays such as this one, she described the pursuit of "equality" under capitalism as a profoundly diminished vision of women's emancipation that failed to promote the ideals of freedom espoused by Mary Wollstonecraft and other feminist forebears.

Goldman further argued that, in order to win even a "partial" equality with men (as female voters in the Far West had done by gaining the right to vote and own property), modern feminists promoted a "narrow puritanical vision" of feminine morality and manners that did not liberate women but instead established new fetters (*Anarchism* 225). She believed that in the push toward suffrage, women had willingly bound themselves to crippling ethical and social conventions, many of which were reinforced by a punishing array of vice laws. According to Goldman, the tactical straitening of the expanded feminist vision within a rigid, moralizing paradigm at the end of the nineteenth century had exacted a heavy sacrifice from women. Instead of advancing on the path toward liberation, this narrowed vision of feminism further constrained women's daily practices and diminished the pleasures of their "inner li[ves]" (*Anarchism* 226). For Goldman—and, I would argue, for Cather—the freedom to express their "inner lives" was of the utmost importance, surpassing the attainment of legal rights to vote, work, or hold property.

For Goldman, the ultimate expressions of women's emancipation involved asserting her rights to her own body in the form of free love and free motherhood (Hemmings; Lumsden; Marso). As Clare Hemmings has argued, "Goldman consistently situate[d] sexuality in a broad political context of the sexual division of labour, the institutions of marriage and church, consumerism, patriotism and productive (as well as reproductive) labour" (43). She framed "sexual freedom as both the basis of new relationships between men and women and as a model for a new political future" (44). In her essay "Marriage and Love," Goldman argued that sexual freedom—free love and free motherhood—was impinged upon most directly by the convention and institution of marriage. "Marriage and love," she declared, "have nothing in common" (*Anarchism* 233). For Goldman, love, expressed emotionally and physically regardless of gender, was central to human liberation: all humans had the right to "acknowledge" and "satisfy" what she characterized as the "demands" of "wild" physical desire freely and without moral censure or legal coercion (228). Marriage, on the other hand, was a "travesty on human character," a "snare," and a "prison" (241). It fundamentally corrupted love. It caused "sorrow, misery, humiliation . . . tears and curses . . . agony and suffering" by requiring a "slavish acquiescence to man's superiority" and by compelling a wife's submission to her husband legally, financially, socially, and sexually (236). Compulsory sex within marriage, she argued, was worse than prostitution, in which a woman's underpaid sexual labor at least received some direct monetary compensation, she retained her legal rights to her own person, and her work was circumscribed to sex and not nannying, cooking, cleaning, and more.

While Goldman frequently affirmed dominant views of motherhood as women's most "glorious" right (but not what Teddy Roosevelt called their "first and greatest duty"), she insisted that women have free choice about when and if to bear children, becoming an early and uncompromising proponent and practitioner of "fam-

GENEVA M. GANO

ily limitation" in the 1910s, a cause for which she was imprisoned in Portland, Oregon, and New York City (Hsu 247, 261). At a time when Comstock laws made disseminating information about birth control illegal but a husband's conjugal rights were being upheld in the courts, Goldman railed against compulsory motherhood as a perverse institution that transformed the "glory" of motherhood into a "duty" and a "nightmare" ("Social Aspects" 136). Like fellow Greenwich Villager Margaret Sanger, with whom she was closely allied in the 1910s, Goldman had worked as a nurse and midwife among poor, immigrant women in New York's Lower East Side. As she testified in the pages of *Mother Earth*, this experience demonstrated to her the "terrible yoke and bondage of enforced pregnancy," which forced women to risk their health and sacrifice their youth while becoming a "mere machine" for babymaking and babyrearing in the service of the church, the race, the state, and the capitalist system that entwined them all (*Anarchism* 243).

As I experienced in Nashville at clinic

This undeniably devastating account of marriage and childbearing as it appeared to Goldman and other radical feminists in the Progressive Era—that is, those whose liberal feminism was aligned with a distinctly anticapitalist critique—must seem a far cry from what we can ascribe to Cather, who has regularly been characterized as politically conservative and uninterested in feminism.[2] This is especially the case if we believe Cather's views were aligned with Jim's romantic vision of Ántonia Cuzak at the end of the novel, when she is finally married off to a decent man of her own race and class and appears as a sacrificial earth mother of a dizzying brood of "ten or eleven" children (Cather 319). However, if we consider Ántonia as something of an outlier among Cather's unmarried pioneer heroines Alexandra Bergson and Thea Kronborg and instead see Lena Lingard as the third of that trinity, we can see the author quietly building an argument not necessarily against heterosexuality per se but rather for a woman's right to resist or refuse marriage and childbearing in the pursuit of a future of her own choosing—a view that exactly aligns with the radical feminism articulated by Goldman.[3] In this context, *My Ántonia*'s "hired girls" collectively represent a class of especially vulnerable women who struggle, under significant pressures, to gain and keep control of their economic and sexual lives outside of motherhood and marriage.

"DANGEROUS AS HIGH EXPLOSIVES": THE HIRED GIRLS TAKE BLACK HAWK

"The Hired Girls" provide the title and focus of the second (and second-longest) book in *My Ántonia*. It is a crucial book for many reasons, including that it is the first of three (with "Lena Lingard" and "The Pioneer Woman's Story") whose titles call explicit attention to women; the novel's first and last books, "The Shimerdas" and "Cuzak's Boys," refer to the farm families' patriarchs. The book is also important for its expansion of the novel's social world. Here, individual stories are brought together for consideration; they add up to something more than an assemblage of personal anecdotes. From this point onward, Ántonia's life story can be seen alongside those of a number of others who face similar challenges as poor, young, immigrant women from farming families, including the three Bohemian Marys, the Danish laundry girls, Norwegian Anna, Lena Lingard, and Tiny Soderball. All of these young women, regardless of their wishes for their own futures, "had no alternative but to go into service" in *service* order to "pay for ploughs and reapers, brood-sows, or steers to fatten" and "clear the homestead from debt" (Cather 194, 193).

For a man of his class and background, Jim Burden does a generally laudable job of bearing their stories and acknowledging the strain that these women are under. Nonetheless, as Gelfant has commented, Jim "knows of but does not experience the suffering and violence inherent in his story" and tends to romanticize and sexualize their servitude (Gelfant 79). "Physically they were almost a race apart," Jim recalls wistfully, noting their "positive carriage" and "freedom of movement," which he ascribes to the hard, out-of-doors work that the country girls did before being entering service in town (Cather 192). By contrast, the daughters of the town's well-to-do families seemed "cut off below the shoulders," and he complains that "when one danced with them their bodies never moved inside their clothes" (192). In Jim's view—and apparently the view of other young men in the town—the physicality of the hired girls, required by their jobs, significantly enhanced their sexual appeal; it made them seem inherently less repressed and more accessible. Jim casually notes, without comment, the regularity with which a young man busy at his business in town might be distracted by a glimpse of Lena Lingard's "slow, undulating walk, or Tiny Soderball, tripping by in her short skirt and striped stockings," while another might be tempted by the sight of "Tiny, arching her shoulders at him like a kitten" at the hotel where she worked or "the four Danish girls, smiling up from their ironing-boards, with their white throats and their pink cheeks" (195–96). Although Jim often sympathizes with the hired girls, he also participates in their sexual objectification: his stolen kiss from his friend Ántonia serves as a case in point (217).

Although the town boys and the country girls "came together on neutral ground" at the Vannis dancing tent (197), it was not there but in the workplace that the girls were most attractive to the men who knew themselves to belong to a class above. For instance, the four Danish girls (who never are named in Jim's recollections) "never looked so pretty at the dances as they did standing by the ironing-board, washing the fine pieces, their white arms and throats bare, their cheeks bright as the brightest wild roses, their gold hair moist with the steam or the heat and curling in little damp spirals about their ears" (215). In observations such as these, we see that the sexual attention and—as the novel details—vulnerability that these hired girls experience in Black Hawk is absolutely imbricated with their status as young, working-class, immigrant women.

The adolescent Jim is outraged that the "American" town boys dally with the hired girls at the dances but have no serious intentions to legally, financially, and socially bond themselves to them in marriage. Yet he himself sneaks out of his grandparents' home every weekend to attend the dances and boldly kisses Lena Lingard and Ántonia with no serious intentions of his own and no thought as to the repercussions his sexual attentions could have for them. Indeed, it is because of an unwanted kiss from a town boy (not Jim, but it easily could have been) that the hardworking Ántonia, who is personally beloved by the Harling family, is abruptly dismissed from her position and forbidden to return to the house. That the dances (and kisses) occur off the clock makes no difference to the Harlings, who see Ántonia as their property to feed, clothe, shelter, and work as they see fit, an arrangement that far exceeds most modern worker-employer relationships. She is the Harlings' Tony, just as the other hired girls are known around town as the Gardners' Tiny and the Marshalls' Anna (Cather 198). After all, this is the arrangement they had brokered with Ántonia's male guardian, her older brother Ambrosch, who begrudgingly permits her to have shoes but directly receives the bulk of her wages. The Harlings, who have a strict view of middle-class propriety and seem to obsessively gossip about the sexual lives of their neighbors' hired girls, largely keep Ántonia confined to the house. Lena, who tracks Ántonia down at the Harlings' not long after her arrival in Black Hawk, is on to something when, at the conclusion of her first visit, she asks "in a guarded whisper," "You can do what you please when you go out, can't you?" (159). The unanswered question lingers throughout the book, until Ántonia finally asserts her right to freely conduct herself *freedom* as she wishes and without the permission of her male overseers—to "have [her] fling" if she so chooses—by announcing, "Mr. Harling ain't my boss outside my work" (202, 200).

Among the hired girls, Ántonia is one of the last to claim her personal time as her own, cowed as she has been on the isolated farm by a domineering mother and bullying older brother, and then guarded jealously by the large, busy Harling family, who take advantage of her innocence and good nature by asking her to make taffy and entertain the family late into the evening, long after her work as the family's cook has been concluded for the day. Ántonia knows that the Harlings "don't like to have [her] run much" or "go gadding about" with the other hired girls (Cather 158), whose gender, race, class, age, and marital status make them vulnerable to the predations of the town's ostensibly respectable and reputedly dissolute men alike. Wick Cutter's intended rape of Ántonia—all of the townspeople know that this is not his first assault on a young woman in his employ—is the novel's most explicit example of this, but hardly the only one.[4] Although they were "such good cooks and such admirable housekeepers," the "three Marys were considered as dangerous as high explosives to have about the kitchen" because of how men responded to their presence; two of the three young women, Jim Burden relates, had been "embarrassed" and "forced to retire from the world for a short time," presumably to abort unwanted fetuses or bear and give away babies because their male employers found them sexually irresistible (196). Indeed, Jim confirms that all of the "country girls were considered a menace to the social order" of the town (195), and boys like himself who consorted with them were likely to get a reputation for being "sly" (209). To the "respectable," native-born class of townspeople, the "explosive" nature of the "menace" that the sexually free young women represent is no less threatening than the bombs associated with anarchy itself.

Although the hired girls are not revolutionaries, the independent lives they build in Black Hawk offer them a crucial degree of distance from a dehumanizing frontier capitalism that depends on women's undervalued, reproductive labor (Moore). For a while, Ántonia envies and attempts to emulate the freedom that the others claim. However, she is not like Lena Lingard or Tiny Soderball, who each take meaningful and decisive steps to forward their careers by avoiding what Judith Fetterley has described as the "developmentally dangerous" notions of romantic love, marriage, or children ("Fiction of Female Development" 227). This careful avoidance, despite the fact that the novel strongly intimates that both are sexually active with men, thus leaves the reader to imagine what forms of family limitation they employ in order to preserve their freedom. In contrast, Jim's "good" Ántonia remains largely in thrall to a sexual morality that is inseparable from a patriarchal economic system in which her labor is and should be sacrificed so as to forward the economic prospects of the male head of the household (Cather 305).

Jim Burden loses contact with Ántonia, Tiny, Anna, and most of the hired girls when he leaves Black Hawk behind to go to college, but he hears about them from time to time by way of town gossips. When Ántonia finds herself pregnant and unhappily unwed, he is told that she works for her brother even harder than before, apparently in penance for her stumble. When Jim meets her again, after a twenty-year lapse, he finds her safely married in what he seems to believe is the best possible ending for her, given her options. She is out from under her hard-driving brother Ambrosch, but the marriage also works her very hard, as she bears and tends her many children as well as the farm where she and her husband live. The evidence of the physical and intellectual wear of her labors is shocking to Jim; she is physically unrecognizable—her hair is grizzled, her chest is flat, her skin is hardened, she is almost toothless—and she has lost most of her hard-won English as well. Ántonia's companionate marriage, marked by an "easy friendliness" between husband and wife, seems to lack sexual and romantic desire (Cather 347); this also marks a change in Ántonia, as Jim had counted her strong passions as being among her core characteristics.[5] At the story's conclusion, Jim praises her—her body, anyway—as a "rich mine" from which "Cuzak's boys" have emerged and through which he can access memories of his own childhood (342). Cather's metaphor, admittedly more organic than the "mere machine" that Goldman utilized in her contraception speeches, nonetheless reveals the physical toll that babymaking and babyrearing has had on the once vital woman; the reader can perhaps feel relieved that Cather's fallen woman manages to come out "battered, but not diminished" (321). However, if a heroine can be imagined as something other than a fertile vessel for producing boys, the final outcome for the good, naïve Ántonia must be reckoned ambivalent at best, and the novel's highly colored, deeply sentimentalized ending must ring hollow.

154

GENEVA M. GANO

"IT'S ALL BEING UNDER SOMEBODY'S THUMB": LENA'S CRITIQUE OF MARRIAGE AND MOTHERHOOD

An attentive reader will recall—against Jim's illusory, concluding pronouncements—that it was not "the road of Destiny" (Cather 244) that finally reunites Jim and Ántonia but rather their constant, mutual friend Lena Lingard, who had prompted Jim to make the effort to reconnect (360); Lena, we learn casually, has continued to maintain contact with them both over the years. Although she has received little critical attention, Lena Lingard is not an inconsequential pastime but literally a central figure in Jim's life story; the novel's third and central book is explicitly named for and devoted to her—the only book in the novel that has such a focus—while after the second book, Ántonia recedes as a primary speaker and actor and shifts to the novel's background, where she appears primarily through the recollections of others. The third book directs the reader's attention to Lena's intimate relationship with Jim, which persisted beyond their juvenile kisses in Black Hawk to lazy Sunday mornings together in her apartment in Lincoln, where, he meaningfully recalls, "Lena was at least a woman, and I was a man" (267). We already know that Lena—not Ántonia—is the one who appears routinely in Jim's erotic dreams; in the novel's central book, we learn that she returns his feeling, frankly confessing that she has "always been a little foolish about [him]" (284). We can't really fathom what Lena sees in the rather unremarkable Jim, but the novel provides ample reason for his interest in her. Lena's ethereal beauty attracts admirers of all kinds, but this is not her only attractive quality. Her talent for her art—dressmaking—is undeniable, her placid good nature in the face of vicious "talk" and violent threats is almost unbelievable, she is serenely free from jealousy (unlike Ántonia—or Crazy Mary), and she is generous to and thoughtful of others, especially her mother. Even though *My Ántonia* begins and ends with children and purports to tell a chastely romantic tale of two childhood friends, its narrative arc traces Jim's first, young amour—one that is truly romantic and quite explicitly sexual in nature, with a woman he can never possess. Although she may not be recognizable as a modern "sex radical" according to the model of bohemian Greenwich Village, she loves freely, deliberately eschews marriage and motherhood, and pursues her personal passion and talent for beautiful creation as a dressmaker.

The pressures Lena faces as a young, poor, immigrant woman are similar to those faced by the novel's other hired girls. Like them, Lena was raised on a farm but moves to Black Hawk in order to help support her family with her wages, although this also means that her father will have to find someone else to do the labor of the farm chores and her mother will lose her assistance with the baby handling and bottling. At the same time, she keenly understands that distance from the family's daily demands on her time will give her the opportunity to become independent and develop her talents. She takes it seriously: when she appears at the Harlings' doorstep at the beginning of book II, she is "brushed and smoothed and dressed like a town girl," perfectly composed, and exceptionally well-spoken (Cather 155). She informs Ántonia's employers, the Harlings, that she has "come to town to work," and although they make inquiries about her sexual life—they want to know if she will marry a young man with whom she has reputedly been involved—she refocuses the conversation on her intention to work as a dressmaker (157). Her comments reveal that her own passion is focused not on "Nick or any other man"—or indeed, as she declares matter-of-factly, marriage at all—but rather on the dresses she will create and the materials that she will be working with, the mere thought of which elicits her sighs of approval (157). While this exchange marks the reader's first encounter with Lena, her stance on marriage is made clear; she will affirm it repeatedly throughout the novel to those like Jim who don't believe that such a beautiful young woman will follow through with her intention to remain single.

Lena's career mirrors to a large degree those of the other major female protagonists in Cather's early novels: Alexandra Bergson and

Thea Kronborg. Like Thea and, arguably, Willa Cather herself, Lena is a truly gifted artist whose successes may seem to have come to her easily but were in fact advanced over the course of long years of determined apprenticeship and the steady development of both her craft and her clientele.[6] Although we see relatively little of Lena before she comes to town, the scene of her knitting socks for her siblings while also tending cattle on the prairie is sufficient to indicate her juvenile attempts at creation with the rough tools and time at hand. W. T. Benda's illustration of this scene, one of eight commissioned by the author for the novel, is the only one that shows a single character's identifiable, personal features.[7] In this significant illustration, Lena is deeply absorbed in her art, equally heedless of the cattle that her father assigned her to watch and of her own personal appearance: her thin, tattered clothes literally fall from her body (revealing a pert nipple) as the fruits of her labor are subsumed by the pressing needs of her father's large family.

Lena's talent and dedicated work in Black Hawk pay off, and she is aided rather than derailed by her female employer, Mrs. Thomas, who allows Lena "a room of [her] own" and a measure of freedom that is withheld from the other hired girls (Cather 158); she is never the Thomases' Lena. Within a few years she is able to move to the capital city of Lincoln and open her own dress shop in a fashionable part of town; she does so well that by the time Jim enters college there she has begun to furnish and build a home for her mother "before she is too old to enjoy it": this is perhaps the novel's clearest indication of her right character and arguably her crowning achievement, even if Black Hawk's gossips whisper otherwise (191). Jim is "puzzled" by Lena's successes, although he accepts that "she had great natural aptitude" for dressmaking and observes that the great satisfaction she gets from it allows her to work tirelessly into the evenings (270). He notes that she does not seem to "push" in order to get ahead, as most people who are successful in business seem to do, nor does she drive herself so hard as to exclude other pleasures (270). When she wants to, she treats herself to dinners out, the theater, flowers, and candy.

Fig. 7.1. W. T. Benda's original illustration of Lena Lingard. Willa Cather, *My Ántonia*.

at the good life that Lena creates for herself is predicated on .eliberate rejection of marriage and childbearing is imperceptible to Jim, who has it in his head that "[e]very handsome girl like you marries, of course" (Cather 282). Lena, however, has maintained an essentially Goldmanian view of marriage since she first got away from home; she reasserts it at length at the end of book III, in the last exchange she has with Jim before he leaves her to continue his studies at Harvard. When Jim presses her as to why she won't marry, she gives a number of reasons. A modern careerwoman might propose that a husband and children would disrupt a woman's professional path, but this practical consideration for rejecting marriage is not one that Lena (or Goldman) identifies. "Mainly," Lena tells Jim, "it's because I don't want a husband" (282). She concedes that "men are all right for friends," but a husband will inevitably assert his will, to which he expects his wife to submit. While Goldman would argue that marriage requires a wife's "slavish acquiescence" to a man, Lena, who prizes her independence, puts the anarchist argument even more plainly: she prefers to "be accountable to nobody" (282). Secondly, she cherishes having a "minute to myself" and a bed—and home—of her own: "she remembered home as a place where there were always too many children, a cross man, and work piling up around a sick woman" (283). As the oldest daughter, Lena "couldn't remember a time when she was so little that she wasn't lugging a heavy baby about, helping to wash for babies, trying to keep their little chapped hands and faces clean" in the effort to help her overworked mother with the endless nannying, cooking, and cleaning (283). Lena's own resolution never to marry comes directly from her own firsthand experience of what Goldman had referred to as the "duty" and "nightmare" of marriage that had literally driven her beloved mother to her sickbed. "You can't tell me anything about family life," Lena testifies. "I've had plenty to last me" (283). When Jim protests that it isn't all like that, she replies with finality, "Near enough. It's all being under somebody's thumb" (283). Judith Fetterley has argued that *My Ántonia*'s "hostility to marriage would be hard to exceed"; more than any other character in the novel, Lena

Lingard articulates this hostility directly and adamantly, albeit in her typically easygoing way (Fetterley, "Dilemma" 48).

Lena's rejection of marriage does not mean, however, that she has rejected love; it would seem that she is in total agreement with Goldman that the two "have nothing in common." As many of those who gossip about Lena's affairs imply, she puts into active practice the Goldmanian principle of "free love" by acknowledging and satisfying her physical desires and "giv[ing] her heart away when she felt like it" (Cather 290). We know from Jim that Lena "lets [him] kiss her" without any strings attached (217), and she confesses to pursuing him to his rented room in Lincoln, where she boldly "beg[an] it" (284) by proposing that he "come and see me sometime when you're lonesome" (261). Nor is Jim her only lover; the reader gets the strong feeling that *My Ántonia*'s documentation of Lena's sexual and romantic escapades is suggestive rather than exhaustive or explicit. Just as Goldman openly advocated, physical love is simply a pleasure for Lena; by giving it away, untethered to either legal and social contracts and obligations or the capitalist system where everything is supposed to have a price, Lena makes sex and desire into defiant, radical acts of anarchist joy (Hemmings).

In the final book of the novel, we learn that Lena has achieved the American dream, going from literal rags to ample comfort, if not riches. Although the ambitious adventure seeker Tiny Soderball "achieves the most solid worldly success" of all of the boys and girls who grew up together in Black Hawk, Tiny's singular pursuit of money has taken its toll on her, body and soul: she has sacrificed an important part of herself along the way—three toes on her once-dainty foot, a symbol of her sexuality—and has become exhausted, embittered, and disinterested in life (Cather 291). Lena, by contrast, seems to have found the key to eternal youth: she still "enjoys things" and "never gets any older" (294). With Tiny, she has moved to San Francisco, an even larger field for her talents as a dressmaker, and has continued to reap the rewards that her talent and skill have brought to her and that marriage and motherhood would have forced her to renounce.

Lena's path toward personal autonomy and fulfillment—through free love and freedom from motherhood—is of course anathema in Black Hawk. The Widow Steavens's comments on the subject make this clear when she laments that the morally conventional— that is, "good"—Ántonia had "come home disgraced" while loose Lena "turned out well" (Cather 305). Even though Lena serves as the novel's model of generosity, kindness, tolerance, filial duty, and loyal friendship (not to mention artistic genius), the Widow Steavens sweepingly condemns her in a lengthy tirade, declaring that she "was always a bad one, say what you will" (305). Emphasizing the "great difference in the principles of those two girls"—she is clearly speaking specifically to Lena's sexual practices—the Widow Steavens gnashes her teeth at having to "give credit where credit is due" by acknowledging the indisputable good that Lena has done for her mother and siblings (305). Lena's flagrant flouting of the community's moral codes of right sexual conduct cannot be forgiven or forgotten.

The Widow Steavens's disapproval notwithstanding, Cather never assigns Lena her comeuppance: no "babies come along pretty fast" for Lena, as they do for the married couple Ántonia and Cuzak, and her story does not adhere to the predictable, tragic path of the fallen woman. Even if the Widow Steavens cannot accept it, Cather shows us that Lena's refusal of marriage and childbearing (though, crucially, not love and pleasure) has enabled her alone to emerge unscathed from a brutal frontier capitalism that relentlessly exacts a physical, intellectual, and emotional toll on the young, poor, immigrant women on whose labor it depends. While these issues surface in other well-known Cather novels, it is through her collective portrait of the hired girls in *My Ántonia* that she makes her radical feminist critique of this brutal form of capitalism most explicit. Her hired girls not only expose the close relationship between women's sexual practices and their relative subjugation or freedom within the U.S. capitalist economy, but it is one of them who comes to stand as Cather's positive example of a poor, immigrant woman who has fully, successfully, unqualifiedly made good.

NOTES

1. Daryl Palmer's treatment of Cather's construction of the town life in *My Ántonia*'s book II, "The Hired Girls," is extensive but deals minimally with the girls themselves.

2. Marilee Lindemann connects Cather's "Woman Artist Stories" to "the heady feminism of the New Woman," which she says seems politically "uncharacteristic" of Cather (194–95); Keiko Arai extends this suggestion by focusing particularly on Lena Lingard's relationship to the New Woman. Judith Fetterley puts Thea Kronborg's rejection of marriage, home, and family in a more radical context in "Willa Cather and the Fiction of Female Development." More recently, Lisa Mendelman follows Fetterley in an extended discussion of Cather's revision of the marriage plot in *The Song of the Lark*, focusing on Thea's apparently free and unencumbered sexual activity.

3. Lindemann identifies many failed women artists in Cather's oeuvre and argues that they serve as "cautionary tales" about the necessity of avoiding the "social machinery of heterosexuality" (200).

4. Donna Devlin's investigation into a bastardy suit filed by Annie Sadilek (the acknowledged prototype for Ántonia Shimerda) reveals the historical grounds for Cather's fictional treatment of sexual predation of the hired girls in Red Cloud, Nebraska.

5. For different perspectives on marriage in *My Ántonia*, see articles by David Stouck, Blanche Gelfant, and Judith Fetterley.

6. Paula Woolley argues that Ántonia is a storyteller and therefore an artist, but unlike the majority of Cather's other serious artists, her art is uncultivated and untrained. See also discussions in articles by Marilee Lindemann and Amy Ahearn.

7. Jean Schwind has argued that Cather's close involvement in commissioning and selecting the illustrations for the book indicate that they reflect Cather's intentions and serve as the novel's essential visual supplements. Keiko Arai points out that Benda's suggestive illustration of Lena portrays her as the peasant artist who hears Jules Breton's "Song of the Lark" (256); this suggests that Lena is here portrayed as already having, at a young age, a natural (primitive) feel for art.

162

WORKS CITED

Abrahams, Edward. *The Lyrical Left: Randolph Bourne, Alfred Stieglitz, and the Origins of Cultural Radicalism in America*. UP of Virginia, 1986.

Ahearn, Amy. "Full-Blooded Writing and Journalistic Fictions: Naturalism, the Female Artist and Willa Cather's *Song of the Lark*." *American Literary Realism*, vol. 33, no. 2, Winter 2001, pp. 143–56.

Arai, Keiko. "A Portrait of a Self-Made Woman: Lena Lingard in *My Ántonia*." *Something Complete and Great: A Centennial Study of* My Ántonia, edited by Holly Blackford, Rowman and Littlefield, 2018, pp. 247–69.

Bohlke, L. Brent, editor. *Willa Cather in Person: Interviews, Speeches, and Letters*. U of Nebraska P, 1986.

Cather, Willa. *My Ántonia*. 1918. Willa Cather Scholarly Edition, edited by Charles Mignon and Kari Ronning, historical essay and explanatory notes by James Woodress, assistance with explanatory notes by Kari Ronning, Kathleen Danker, and Carrie Levine, U of Nebraska P, 1994.

Cornell, Andrew. *Unruly Equality: U.S. Anarchism in the Twentieth Century*. U of California P, 2016.

Devlin, Donna. "A Pioneering Tale of a Different Sort: Annie Sadilek Pavelka and Sexual Assault." *Willa Cather Review*, vol. 61, no. 3, Winter 2020, pp. 13–19.

Falk, Candace. "Emma Goldman: Passion, Politics, and the Theatrics of Free Expression." *Women's History Review*, vol. 11, no. 1, 2002, pp. 11–26.

Fetterley, Judith. "*My Ántonia*, Jim Burden, and the Dilemma of the Lesbian Writer." *Lesbian Texts and Contexts: Radical Revisions*, edited by Karla Jay and Joanne Glasgow, NYU Press, 1990, pp. 145–63.

———. "Willa Cather and the Fiction of Female Development." *Anxious Power: Reading, Writing, and Ambivalence in Narrative by Women*, edited by Carol J. Stingley and Susan Elizabeth Sweeney, State U of New York P, 1993, pp. 221–34.

Gelfant, Blanche H. "The Forgotten Reaping-Hook: Sex in *My Ántonia*." *American Literature*, vol. 43, no. 1, March 1971, pp. 60–82.

Goldman, Emma. *Anarchism and Other Essays*. Mother Earth, 1910.

———. "Marriage." *Firebrand*, 18 July 1897, pp. 269–73.

———. "The Social Aspects of Birth Control." 1916. *Anarchy! An Anthology of Emma Goldman's Mother Earth*, edited by Peter Glassgold, Counterpoint, 2001, pp. 134–40.

Hemmings, Clare. "Sexual Freedom and the Promise of Revolution: Emma Goldman's Passion." *Feminist Review*, vol. 106, no. 1, February 2014, pp. 43–59.

Hsu, Rachel Hui-Chi. "Beyond Progressive America: *Mother Earth* and Its Anarchist World (1906–1918)." 2016. Johns Hopkins U, PhD dissertation.

Jewell, Andrew. "Willa Cather's Greenwich Village: New Contexts for 'Coming, Aphrodite!'" Faculty Publications, U of Nebraska–Lincoln Libraries, 2004, pp. 59–80.

Lindemann, Marilee. "Cather's 'Elastigirls': Reckoning with Sex/Gender Violence in the Woman Artist Stories." *Violence, the Arts, and Willa Cather*, edited by Joseph R. Urgo and Merrill Maguire Skaggs, Fairleigh Dickinson UP, 2007, pp. 191–203.

Lumsden, Linda L. "Anarchy Meets Feminism: A Gender Analysis of Emma Goldman's *Mother Earth*, 1906–1917." *American Journalism*, vol. 24, no. 3, 2000, pp. 31–54.

Marso, Lori Jo. "A Feminist Search for Love: Emma Goldman on the Politics of Marriage, Love, Sexuality, and the Feminine." *Feminist Theory*, vol. 4, no. 3, December 2003, pp. 305–20.

Mendelman, Lisa. *Modern Sentimentalism: Affect, Irony, and Female Authorship in Interwar America*. Oxford UP, 2019.

Moore, Jason W. *Capitalism and the Web of Life*. Verso, 2015.

Muncy, Robyn. *Creating a Female Dominion in American Reform, 1890–1935*. Oxford UP, 1994.

Palmer, Daryl W. "Recomposing Nineteenth-Century Nebraska: Red Cloud Newspapers and Cather's 'Hired Girls' in *My Ántonia*." *Willa Cather Newsletter and Review*, Summer 2012, pp. 2–9.

Schwind, Jean. "The Benda Illustrations to *My Ántonia*: Cather's 'Silent' Supplement to Jim Burden's Narrative." *PMLA*, vol. 100, no. 1, January 1985, pp. 51–67.

Sergeant, Elizabeth Shepley. *Willa Cather: A Memoir*. 1953. Ohio UP, 1992.

Stansell, Christine. *American Moderns: Bohemian New York and the Creation of a New Century*. Verso, 1996.

Stouck, David. "Marriage and Friendship in *My Ántonia*." *Great Plains Quarterly*, vol. 2, no. 4, Fall 1982, pp. 224–31.

Woolley, Paula. "Fire and Wit: Storytelling and the American Artist in Cather's *My Ántonia*." *Cather Studies, Volume 3*, edited by Susan J. Rosowski, U of Nebraska P, 1996, pp. 149–81.

8 Mapping and (Re)mapping the Nebraska Landscape in the Works of Willa Cather and Francis La Flesche

LISBETH STRIMPLE FUISZ

Scholar Tol Foster (Anglo-Creek) argues for the importance of what he calls "relational regionalism," which examines historically situated writers alongside each other (268). Regional frames, explains Foster, acknowledge tensions, complexities, and multiple perspectives. As he notes, "Native and settler histories and culture are not capable of being separated" (268). However, American literary studies, which began by centering the works of settler writers and which historically mobilized texts for U.S. nation-building purposes, must broaden its frame of reference, urges Foster, to engage with Indigenous authors on their own tribally specific terms to consider ways in which they have worked within and against settler literary traditions (267–68).

Following Foster's approach, I put the geographical imaginings of Willa Cather (1873–1947) in dialogue with those of a contemporary regional writer, Francis La Flesche (1857–1932) of the Omaha

Nation. Specifically, I examine the landscapes of *O Pioneers!* (1913) and *My Ántonia* (1918) in relation to those portrayed in La Flesche's memoir *The Middle Five: Indian Boys at School*, published in 1900.[1] Different ways of viewing the land and people's relationships to it emerge through this comparison. Building on insights from critical geography, literary, and Indigenous studies, I examine how these writers' representations of place respond to the imperatives of settler colonialism. Cather's novels, I argue, reproduce dominant settler colonial spatial relationships, thereby participating in the naturalization of those forms. La Flesche's portrait of the Omaha Nation in *The Middle Five*, in contrast, unsettles depictions of Nebraska as settler space by establishing spatial imaginaries that pre-date and coexist alongside settler spaces.

The regional frame engenders some interesting similarities and contrasts between Cather and La Flesche. In biographical terms, both spent their childhoods in the West and their adulthoods on the East Coast. A settler, Cather came to Nebraska with her family in 1883 and left it in 1896 after graduating from the University of Nebraska. La Flesche was born on the Omaha Reservation in 1857, the son of one of the last principal chiefs of the Omaha people, and spent much of his adult life after 1881 living and working in Washington DC, first for the Office of Indian Affairs and later for the Bureau of American Ethnology of the Smithsonian Institution. He received an honorary degree from the University of Nebraska in 1926, nine years after Cather received her degree.[2] As writers, both draw on their childhood experiences in crafting their narratives, and their work connects them to the place now called Nebraska. Cather's early novels cemented her reputation as a writer of the plains and a dominant literary voice of Nebraska. La Flesche wrote or coauthored important monographs on the Omahas, the only tribal nation in that area to retain its pre-Nebraska homelands, and he has been recognized as "the first professional American Indian anthropologist" (Liberty 51). In *The Middle Five*, La Flesche returns to this homeland as the setting for his memoir. Read alongside each other, *O Pioneers!*, *My Ántonia*, and *The Middle Five* reveal competing raphies. Depictions of the landscape in Cather's novels establish ......r belonging and legitimate the land claims of key characters. In a similar fashion, but with different aims, La Flesche's narrative asserts Omaha land rights through his depiction of the landscape and his characters' relationships to it.

My analysis rests on several key assumptions about geography. A place such as the region that Cather and La Flesche represent is productively understood as being both a literal geographic site and a social construct. Places acquire meaning through human actions. A given place may have multiple, contradictory meanings attached to it. In *Native Space: Geographic Strategies to Unsettle Settler Colonialism* (2017), Native American studies scholar Natchee Blu Barnd uses the term *spatiality* to convey the sense that "space is a product of our social imaginings and actions, which coalesce into coherence as well as material form.... In this way, spatiality signals the individual and collective processes we engage in to produce space and the ways that we are also produced by spaces" (13). Artifacts such as maps are not objective recordings of place but cultural texts that reveal the worldview of the mapmaker even as they suggest how others will view and experience this place. Cather and La Flesche as mapmakers then have their own spatialities that reflect their historical and sociocultural locations. I will follow Barnd's usage of the concepts of Indigenous spatiality and settler spatiality to mark differences around conceptualizations of land and human relationships to it. Barnd reminds readers that "these different spatialities are rooted in the historic and racialized experiences of peoples who experienced colonialism as either colonized or colonizer" (14).

My analysis therefore relies on historical explanations of settler colonialism. Settler colonialism is at its core a geographic project. As historians Mary-Ellen Kelm and Keith D. Smith declare, "settlers come to stay," and that requires land (2). As part of the process of acquiring land and asserting dominance, a settler colonial state like the United States constructs new geographical entities that, as Barnd describes, displace preexisting Indigenous spatialities. But, as Barnd also shows, this displacement is often partial, with geographi-

Fig. 8.1. Francis La Flesche, n.d. #00688600. National Anthropological Archives, Smithsonian Institution.

cal imaginings existing in overlapping tension. Thus, because settler colonialism is a spatial project, it can be contested on spatial grounds.

In addition to Barnd's work, I draw on Seneca scholar Mishuana Goeman's theory of "(re)mapping" to explain how settler geographies can be contested by Indigenous writers. In her study of late nineteenth- and twentieth-century Indigenous writers, *Mark My Words: Native Women Mapping Our Nations* (2013), Goeman theorizes "(re)mapping" as a discursive act that "refute[s] colonial organizing of land, bodies, and social and political landscapes" in order to "generate new possibilities" for Indigenous peoples (3). For Goeman, (re)mapping involves two moves: exposing dominant conceptualizations of space that fundamentally reordered Native existence and presenting alternative, sovereign spatialities "literally grounded in ... relationships among land, community, and writing" (13). Although she acknowledges that these sovereign geographies may not dislodge dominant settler ones, they can denaturalize them and call into question the control exercised through spatial arrangements (15). Native peoples, notes Goeman, have historically recognized the role of literature and cartography in legitimizing settler land claims and thus the value of asserting their own spatialities to counter territorial expansion (25–26). In this way, (re)mapping recognizes the power of the representation of place to reinforce or to critique social formations. Using Goeman's and Barnd's theories allows me to consider how the works of Cather and La Flesche produce divergent spatialities, clarifying the assumptions about place that animate their depictions of the landscape.

Integral to the process of producing settler space in what is now the United States are the survey and the grid, two spatializations that bear on both Cather's and La Flesche's geographical imaginings. In a chapter titled "(Not) in Place: The Grid, or, Cultural Techniques of Ruling Spaces," Bernhard Siegert explains that, within South and North American settler colonial systems, the cartographic grid represents and orders space to facilitate the control of people, land, and other nonhuman beings (103). Siegert charts how this technique functioned in the United States beginning with the Land

Ordinance of 1785, which used a grid-shaped survey to partition the Northwest Territory, an area west of the Allegheny Mountains. The federal government wanted to sell the land to pay off debt incurred during the Revolutionary War. Siegert stresses the importance of this survey technique: "Although the rectangular survey prescribed by the Land Ordinance of 1785 only concerned territories between the Appalachians and the Mississippi, it became the model for the subsequent appropriation and colonization of the entire continent" (112). The survey marked the land with a grid pattern based on longitude and latitude, creating units of geography called townships that were then divided into parcels measuring 640 acres (112). The manner in which these townships and lots were sold created the checkerboard pattern often seen on cadastral maps. In this process of surveying and selling, observes Siegert, "[g]rid patterns, colonization, and real estate speculation coincided" (112–14). The grid survey ultimately covered 69 percent of what has become the continental United States (115). Siegert concludes, "Nothing was left untouched [by the survey]: The rectangular system guaranteed that no shred of land remained masterless. . . . [T]he uniform system of rectangular townships and sections assigned to everything—wilderness, plains, forest, or swamp—its own place. Nothing was allowed to fall off the grid" (115). This manner of portioning the land enabled the conceptualization of land as a commodity, an abstract space, seemingly removed from social and political forces (Blomley 127).

Such settler colonial systems of spatial production inform the depiction of the Nebraska landscapes in Cather's *O Pioneers!* and *My Ántonia*. I argue that a view of land as abstract space is integral to these narratives and contributes to their construction of Nebraska as settler space. At first glance, the concept of land as abstract space may not seem relevant to the work of Willa Cather. Previous scholarship has demonstrated the centrality of place in all its particulars to Cather's imagination.[3] I suggest that images of abstract space work alongside images of particular places in Cather's fiction to map settler geographies and define settler belonging. Both *O Pioneers!* and *My Ántonia* offer scenes in which the reader is given sweeping panoramas of the landscape and scenes that offer close-up views of that landscape (and sometimes both). I trace the relationship between these two ways of looking at the landscape, arguing that close-up views signal the main characters' affinity for place, while sweeping views reveal the economic control characters exercise over the landscape.

My discussion augments scholarship that has established Cather's sense of place as fundamental to her artistic production. Susan J. Rosowski's 1995 exploration of Cather's environmental imagination, for example, demonstrates that Cather's interest in the natural and agricultural sciences informed her carefully rendered Nebraska settings, which feature, for example, native plants of the prairies as well as species introduced by farmers ("Ecology of Place" 39–40). These botanical details are emblematic of the ways in which Cather's settings are "predicated on the uniqueness of place" (42). In a similar vein, Janis Stout describes Cather's accurate descriptions of nature as a defining aspect of her art: Cather's focus on selected details against an undefined background creates a feeling of "visual acuity" in her writing (128). Cather's closely observed settings have also played an important role in her reception as a regional writer, an image Cather herself promoted. As Cather explained to Elizabeth Shepley Sergeant in a 1913 letter, the physical geography of the landscape in which *O Pioneers!* is set (its lack of "rocks and ridges" and its "fluid black soil," for example) "influences the mood in which one writes of it—and so the very structure of the story" (*Selected Letters* 177). Here Cather suggests that the writing of *O Pioneers!* was made possible through her connection to that part of the country.

In a review of ecocritical interpretations of Cather's work, Cheryll Glotfelty observes that environmental scenes like those that take place in gardens "are crucial to the signifying system of Cather's writing" (34). One way in which nature scenes signify is as a marker of character, and scholars have shown that *O Pioneers!* and *My Ántonia* validate the characters who closely observe and carefully utilize the landscape. Rosowski, for example, argues convincingly that Cather maps out an evolving region in *O Pioneers!* that has as its center Alexandra's placement in and knowledge of the Divide "in all its particularity" ("Ecology of Place" 43). Providing another example, Patrick Dooley argues that an ethical form of stewardship emerges in *O Pioneers!* and *My Ántonia* in which the land flourishes under human caretaking. What redeems this type of land use from mere economic exploitation, in Dooley's view, is that the characters Alexandra in *O Pioneers!* and Ántonia in *My Ántonia* work the land for the benefit of future generations (73–75). The larger colonial context is often acknowledged in these discussions, but sustained attention to the ways in which settler colonial spatialities inform characters' observations and interactions with the landscape in Cather's fiction is warranted. Taking a close view of the land is part of the process whereby the settler comes to feel at home in a formerly strange and unwelcoming environment. These careful observations make the land legible to the newly arrived. With an ability to read the environment comes affinity for the place. Thus, establishing a character's rightful place within the landscape is an imperative of settler colonial fiction, as Alex Calder explains in his exploration of Cather's later fiction ("Beyond Possession").[4] Calder theorizes that literature concerned with settlement often features the story of a character who attains a deep and authentic relationship to land, appearing to occupy the place naturally. Framed in this way, Rosowski's compelling interpretation of Alexandra's "becoming native to a place" ("Ecology of Place" 42) signals the text's commitment to a story of settler belonging, and Dooley's reading of Alexandra's and Ántonia's careful shepherding of land for the next generation signals the texts' commitment to ensuring settler futurity through the inheritance of land.[5]

In her discussion of *O Pioneers!*, literary critic Karen E. Ramirez constructs a useful schema for thinking through the characters' relationship to land. She distinguishes between what she calls a "place-based" and a "space-based" attitude toward the land. In an ecologically minded, intimate, place-based relationship, as Ramirez describes it, the human connects with nature, believing it to have intrinsic value, and Ramirez demonstrates that Alexandra develops such a place-based relationship (110). Extending Ramirez's idea to *My Ántonia*, narrator Jim Burden also comes to enjoy a place-based relationship to the land, as in the famous scene when he is ensconced in the prairie garden and remarks, "I was entirely happy" (18). In both cases, the characters come to feel at home in the landscape, a marker of their integrity.

In contrast to this connected form of being, Ramirez proposes a "space-based" relationship, which is dependent upon an understanding of the land as empty, waiting for humans to capitalize on it: "The land remains imagined as a blank canvas alienated from the human markings imposed upon it" (98). Ramirez shows that this emptying of space is achieved through the cadastral system of mapping described above. Examining *O Pioneers!* through this schema, Ramirez concludes that, through Alexandra's characterization as someone who has both a commercial interest in land and a love for it, Cather calls into question the domination of the land. The coexistence within the novel of these different approaches to land, in Ramirez's reading, potentially destabilizes the text (113). In a settler colonial system, however, appreciation for the land, like that demonstrated by Alexandra and Jim, plays an important role in place-making, as I show in more detail below. Cather's novels suggest that colonialization and commercialization of the land are not necessarily antithetical to loving it. For example, as explained in the introduction to *My Ántonia*, Jim's attachment to land is part of what makes him successful: "He loves with a personal passion the great country through which his railway runs and branches. His faith in it and his knowledge of it have played an important part in its development" (xi). It becomes hard to disentangle these characters' attachment to the land from their roles in capitalizing on it.

I argue, therefore, that the processes of settlement inform the depictions of the landscape in these two novels. As I discuss in more detail below, these depictions help naturalize settler colonial reorderings of geography that were achieved through mechanisms like the survey and the grid. In settler colonialism, "the settlers come to stay, to seek out lives and identities grounded in the colony and for whom Indigenous people, their rights to land and resources, are obstacles that must be eliminated" (Kelm and Smith 2). This grounding of identity in the landscape is portrayed in the characterizations of Alexandra and Jim. Their relationships to the land follow a similar pattern, from alienation to connection, suggesting Cather's own experience in Nebraska.

O Pioneers! illustrates how Alexandra becomes at home in the Divide through her careful observations of and heightened appreciation for the land, plants, and animals. Early in the text her father, John Bergson, recognizes the skills that make her the appropriate family member to take over the farm after his death: her keen sense of observation and her willingness to learn about the place they are farming. She studies the stock market, observes her neighbors' failures, and pays careful attention to their cattle and pigs (28). Later on, her father's confidence in her is confirmed; Alexandra recognizes that the land on the Divide, rather than the lower land along the river, is better suited for farming at a profit. During a visit with her brother Emil to these lower-lying farms, she takes special note of what other farmers are doing, knowledge that she will later implement to high reward (63). Her first significant epiphany about the land occurs after this visit. The narrator explains her feelings: "For the first time, perhaps, since that land emerged from the waters of geologic ages, a human face was set toward it with love and yearning. It seemed beautiful to her, rich and strong and glorious. Her eyes drank in the breadth of it, until her tears blinded her" (64). This passage emphasizes Alexandra's literal vision, her ability to take in the vastness of the land without being alienated by it. Alexandra is learning to read the landscape. Here the sweeping view of the land, as she appreciates "the breadth of it," reveals the control she is beginning to exercise over the landscape. Her vision as a farmer is thus closely aligned to the depth of her feelings for and knowledge of the Divide, and this connection is spatialized in this scene through the act of looking.

Shortly thereafter, Alexandra fully identifies with the land, appreciating both the expanse of nature and its smallest inhabitants. Despite her brothers' belief that they should give up farming the high lands of the Divide, Alexandra has arrived at a point of emotional and physical connection from which she can successfully develop this farmland. The narrator describes her looking skyward:

> She always loved to watch them [the stars], to think of their vastness and distance, and of their ordered march. It fortified her to reflect upon the great operations of nature, and when she thought of the law that lay behind them, she felt a sense of personal security. That night she had a new consciousness of the country, felt almost a new relation to it. Even her talk with the boys [her brothers] had not taken away the feeling that had overwhelmed her when she drove back to the Divide that afternoon. She had never known before how much the country meant to her. The chirping of the insects down in the long grass had been like the sweetest music. She had felt as if her heart were hiding down there, somewhere, with the quail and the plover and all the little wild things that crooned or buzzed in the sun. (68–69)

In this scene Alexandra's view takes in nature and leaves her feeling secure. The operations of natural law are knowable to her. Alexandra is no longer alienated from the Divide. Heavily emphasized in this scene, these feelings of security and happy emplacement mark her as settled, and she apprehends this connection in part through the act of looking at nature.

At the end of the novel, the final description of Alexandra imagines her as literally part of the soil out of which the U.S. nation is built: "Fortunate country, that is one day to receive hearts like Alexandra's into its bosom, to give them out again in the yellow wheat, in the rustling corn, in the shining eyes of youth!" (274). In *Settler Common Sense* (2014), an analysis of literary works from the American Renaissance, Mark Rifkin examines the everyday ways in which settler colonialism operates to make settlers feel like they belong to the land and that the land belongs to them. These feelings of belonging are not a critique of settler ways of organizing space, of legal and political practices, but a reflection of it; Rifkin explains that "quotidian affective formations among nonnatives [like a sense of belonging] can be understood as normalizing settler presence, privilege, and power, taking up the terms and technologies of settler governance as ... the animating context for nonnatives' engagement with the social environment" (xv). These emotional responses to the landscape come about through settler colonial structures, not in spite of them.

The movement from feeling alienated to feeling at home, as a manifestation of settler sentiment, is integral to *My Ántonia* as well. When Jim first arrives in Nebraska, he is not able to locate himself in relation to the topography and feels overwhelmed: "There was nothing but land: not a country at all, but the material out of which countries are made. No, there was nothing but land. [...] I had the feeling that the world was left behind, that we had got over the edge of it, and were outside man's jurisdiction. I had never before looked up at the sky when there was not a familiar mountain ridge against it. [...] Between that earth and that sky I felt erased, blotted out" (7–8). Jim emphasizes how he feels disoriented by what he sees and does not see. His feeling of not belonging is spatialized as a lack of grounding in the landscape. He cannot get his bearings because he has no map yet through which to orient himself, no detailed understanding of the features of the environment. He is like the uninitiated observer, "the casual eye" that perceives no variety in the state's landscape in Cather's 1923 article "Nebraska: The End of the First Cycle" (236). Aileen Moreton-Robinson (Goenpul, Quandamooka First Nation) explains that, in colonial narratives, this sense of alienation from the landscape serves to legitimize settler claims by valorizing the effort it takes to build a place in the new environment (29).

Cather felt a similar lack of orientation when she first arrived in Nebraska as a child. She recounts in a 1913 interview that her feeling of alienation was closely tied to her perception of a landscape without divisions or markers: "The land was open range and there was almost no fencing. As we drove further and further out into the country, I felt a good deal as if we had come to the end of everything—it was a kind of erasure of personality" (*Willa Cather in Person* 10). Cather had left the familiar countryside of Virginia, tossed "into a country as bare as a piece of sheet iron" (10). From this initial disorientation, Cather developed a keen naturalist's eye, as Rosowski and Stout have suggested, in part by carefully studying the ecology and botany of the prairies. Cather's own grounding in place is suggested by her 1923 article, noted above, which opens with a geography lesson explaining the topography and climate of the state ("Nebraska" 236).

In *My Ántonia*, as the narrative progresses, Jim recalls experiences that connected him to the land as a child. Riding about on his pony during his first autumn in Nebraska, for example, Jim begins to know the land and feel less threatened by the lack of familiar landmarks: "The new country lay open before me: there were no fences in those days, and I could choose my own way over the grass uplands, trusting the pony to get me home again" (27). He recounts his close observations of the natural world: "I used to love to drift along the pale yellow cornfields, looking for the damp spots one sometimes found at their edges, where the smartweed soon turned a rich copper color and the narrow brown leaves hung curled like cocoons about the swollen joints of the stem" (28). Exploring on horseback, observing the local flora, and learning some history of the area allows Jim to map out the space and become attached to it. As in the scenes describing Alexandra's growing attachment, Jim's vision and emotional response to nature are emphasized.

Yet Jim's fullest appreciation for the land and deepest sense of being rightfully in place come as an adult, after he returns to the prairies from the East Coast. The introduction to the novel suggests that Jim feels disconnected from his life in New York City, but returning to Nebraska, he feels an authentic connection, heightened by a visit to Ántonia's farm. After this visit, toward the close of the narrative, Jim leaves Black Hawk, the town of his youth, behind:

> I took a long walk north of the town, out into the pastures
> where the land was so rough that it had never been ploughed

up, and the long red grass of early times still grew shaggy over
the draws and hillocks. Out there I felt at home again. Over-
head the sky was that indescribable blue of autumn; bright
and shadowless, hard as enamel. To the south I could see the
dun-shaded river bluffs that used to look so big to me, and
all about stretched drying cornfields, of the pale-gold color
I remembered so well. Russian thistles were blowing across
the uplands and piling against the wire fences like barricades.
Along the cattle paths the plumes of goldenrod were already
fading into sun-warmed velvet, gray with gold threads in it. (358)

As with Alexandra, Jim's feeling of belonging is enhanced through
this close observation of the landscape. He knows this landscape,
names its constituent parts, and feels an aesthetic appreciation for
it. The wild grass is now a memorial to a previous time, domesticated, and not a sign of humans' inability to make their mark upon
the prairies. His eye takes possession of the landscape, the distant
bluffs no longer appearing as large as they had when he was younger.
He then sheds his adult identity, reconnecting to his younger self
in finding the road upon which he and Ántonia had first arrived
in Nebraska: "I had the sense of coming home to myself. [. . .] For
Ántonia and for me, this had been the road of Destiny; had taken us
to those early accidents of fortune which predetermined for us all
that we can ever be" (360). His use of "destiny" and "predetermined"
underscores the rightness he feels in being there and gestures to
the inevitability of settler occupancy. Jim experiences belonging as
a feeling of homecoming. These passages, which come at the end
of the novel, signal the landscape's complete transformation into
a known entity—closely observed, aesthetically appreciated, and
connected to personal stories and memories for Jim. In telling his
story, Jim indigenizes his settler identity, rooting it in a known and
beloved landscape.

In addition to these characterizations of a settler's sense of belonging that derives from close observation and an intimate relationship
with the land, Cather reproduces the spatial ideologies of U.S. settler

Plate 1.—Republican Valley, Mouth of Elm Creek, Near Red Cloud, Neb.

Fig. 8.2. This illustration of Nebraska cropland and pasture is reminiscent of Cather's descriptions of the landscape that emphasize the surveyor's point of view and the demarcation of the land into grids. Digital object identifier 27955. History Nebraska.

colonial society by mapping out the improvement of unproductive wild lands into productive agricultural spaces in *O Pioneers!* and *My Ántonia*. In the scenes I examine below, I attend to three elements that invoke abstract space: the emphasis on a surveyor's point of view; the demarcation of land into grids; and the suggestion that the economic potential of the land is a product of the disciplining grid.

O Pioneers! maps the colonial organization of land and bodies that Mishuana Goeman lays out, and thus I concur with Melissa Ryan's reading that the enclosure and domestication of the land and people in the interest of nation-building animates this novel. Part I of *O Pioneers!* advances an emerging settler spatiality. Alexandra's father, John Bergson, is not yet at home on the Divide, and his view of the landscape underscores this lack of connection. He feels he has not made a definitive mark upon the land:

In eleven long years John Bergson had made but little impression upon the wild land he had come to tame. It was still a wild thing that had its ugly moods. [...] Its Genius was unfriendly to man. The sick man was feeling this as he lay looking out of the window, after the doctor had left him. [...] There it lay outside his door, the same land, the same lead-colored miles. He knew every ridge and draw and gully between him and the horizon. To the south, his plowed fields; to the east, the sod stables, the cattle corral, the pond,—and then the grass. (26)

His view out the window suggests the incomplete mastery of the landscape, which has not yet been fully defined by the grid. He has some knowledge of the landscape, but the grass marks the limit of his ability to farm the land. The grass resists the imposition of order implied in the plowed fields and farm buildings. Gazing out the window, John Bergson acknowledges that the transformation of the land is incomplete, the land remaining an "enigma" to him (27). The emphasis in this scene on his vision underscores how settler colonialism is a project grounded in the transformation of land and the assertion of a new geographical order.

John Bergson dies before he is able to transform the land, and it then becomes Alexandra's job to continue what her father began. Alexandra, as explained previously, feels at home on the Divide, and consequently, unlike her father who felt alienated, she views the land with love and learns to farm it effectively. The success of Alexandra's project and that of other Nebraska settlers is conveyed at the beginning of part II of *O Pioneers!* through an image of the transformed landscape. The narrator explains what has transpired since the passing of John Bergson: "The shaggy coat of the prairie [...] has vanished forever. From the Norwegian graveyard one looks out over a vast checker-board, marked off in squares of wheat and corn; light and dark, dark and light" (73). The narrative's vantage point from above, imagining the resurrected body of John Bergson looking out over the cultivated land, allows the human eye to dominate the landscape and registers the visual transformation of land that has occurred since Bergson's death. In place of the organic image of the prairie as a "shaggy" animal is that of the land regimented by the grid into geometric forms. The vanishing of the prairie thus attests to what historians Roger J. P. Kain and Elizabeth Baigent describe as "the imposition of a new economic and spatial order" (qtd. in Blomley 128). The narrator's catalog of securely established settler structures conveys the success of this new spatial order. The farmhouses are "gayly painted," the "gilded weather-vanes on the big red barns wink at each other," and the windmills "vibrate in the wind" but remain steadfast (73). The novel's opening images of impermanence—of a town "trying not to be blown away," of houses "set about haphazard on the tough prairie sod," and a single "deeply rutted road" (11)—have been replaced by images of physical and economic security. A landscape once lacking order and seemingly empty, as when Alexandra was young, has been replaced by one featuring well-orchestrated roads, a dense population, and fertile, highly productive land (73–74). The settlers are emplaced; the happiness and fruitfulness of this scene suggest the rightness of their occupancy.

Later in part II, Alexandra's childhood friend Carl Linstrum confirms this vision of an improved landscape: "He turned and looked back at the wide, map-like prospect of field and hedge and pasture. 'I would never have believed it could be done. I'm disappointed in my own eye, in my imagination'" (101). Carl's lamentation about his short-sightedness suggests the fundamental role spatial arrangements play in settler colonialism. Settler colonialism, with its basis in a regime of private property, maps out the land to facilitate ownership and economic development. Because Carl has been away from Hanover, he is able to appreciate the physical changes Alexandra has wrought on the land, changes that indicate the economic development Alexandra has orchestrated.

Two descriptions in *My Ántonia* of the changes to the Nebraska plains echo Carl's language. Toward the end of book I, Jim is reflecting on the death of Mr. Shimerda, Ántonia's father, who had died by suicide. Jim describes how, "[y]ears afterward, when the open-grazing days were over, and the red grass had been ploughed under

and under until it had almost disappeared from the prairie; when all
the fields were under fence, and the roads no longer ran about like
wild things, but followed the surveyed section-lines, Mr. Shimerda's
grave was still there" (114). His description conveys how the survey
lines and fences act to regulate the space, acknowledging the imposition of a settler spatial order. But this scene is also full of sadness
for what has been lost: Mr. Shimerda himself, who embodied for
Jim the best qualities of the first pioneers, and the natural scenes
that have disappeared through development. Looking at the crossroads near where Mr. Shimerda is buried, Jim describes how the
grave stands in contrast to the regimented landscape of survey lines:
"The road from the north curved a little to the east just there, and
the road from the west swung out a little to the south; so that the
grave, with its tall red grass that was never mowed, was like a little
island; and at twilight, under a new moon or the clear evening star,
the dusty roads used to look like soft gray rivers flowing past it. I
never came upon the place without emotion, and in all that country
it was the spot most dear to me" (114). Here, what is valorized is not
the domesticated space of the grid but the untouched red grass, a
sign of a previous era on the plains. The roads are described using
the language of nature, as gentle rivers washing by, in effect soften-
ing the impact of humans on the landscape and suggesting a desire
for a prairie untouched by settlers.

In connecting *My Ántonia* to contemporary debates over the
importance of preserving land as national parks, Joseph Urgo rightly
argues that this scene suggests Jim's desire to preserve the landscape
for personal and aesthetic reasons. The landscape both inspires Jim's
memories and contains them, becoming for Urgo a sign of Cather's commitment to preserving land, and he likens the grave to "an
attenuated national park" (52). Thinking of the grave as a national
park suggests how it functions as settler colonial space. In his book-
length treatment of settler colonial fiction from New Zealand, Alex
Calder examines moments in which settler characters try to erase
signs of human impact on the land by going back in time, arguing
that such intense nostalgia "is an expression of the misgivings that

accompany the transformation of new-world environments, of reservations that have as their literal monument those islands out of time we call national parks" (137).[6] Despite suggesting some misgivings, this nostalgia does not call into question the larger settler colonial project, according to Calder (138). Jim's nostalgia here acts similarly. Although Jim may have some misgivings about the transformation of the landscape, he continues to play a role in such change as a lawyer for a major railroad. The Shimerda gravesite becomes a kind of touchstone for Jim, a place outside of time, that connects him to that region and to the pioneer virtues that Mr. Shimerda represents. One thinks of Cather's description of the graveyards in her 1923 article about Nebraska. Looking at the graves of men she knew, Cather invokes this previous generation's strength of character: "When I stop at one of the graveyards in my own country, and see on the headstones the names of fine old men I used to know ..., I have always the hope that something went into the ground with those pioneers that will one day come out again. Something that will come out not only in sturdy traits of character, but in elasticity of mind, in an honest attitude toward the realities of life, in certain qualities of feeling and imagination" ("Nebraska" 237). Thus, rather than calling settler colonialism into question, these grave scenes confirm the qualities of those who came first and, in Jim's case, deepen his connection to the region and his feeling of belonging.

A few chapters later, another scene suggests the novel's validation of the spatial transformation underway. As part of Jim's explanation as to why corn grows so well in Nebraska and Kansas, he states, "The cornfields were far apart in those times, with miles of wild grazing land between. It took a clear, meditative eye like my grandfather's to foresee that they would enlarge and multiply until they would be [...] the world's cornfields; that their yield would be one of the great economic facts [...] which underlie all the activities of men, in peace or war" (132). This scene emphasizes the visual transformation of the landscape and ties it to the creation of a new economic order. This connection is spatialized through the act of looking; Jim's grandfather is able to visualize the agricultural means through which to build a nation and a global power, a vision that escaped John Bergson in *O Pioneers!* but was recognized by Alexandra, who "felt the future stirring" once she connected fully to the land (69). Jim establishes the inevitability of this reordering of space through the use of the literary device prolepsis. In his book, Calder theorizes prolepsis, in which a future development is presented as already existing, to be an important element in the settler's plot. In this scene in *My Ántonia*, Jim is explaining what happens out of chronological sequence. At this point in his story, Jim is living on the farm with his grandparents, and the settler transformation of the land is still in an early stage. By mentioning the partitioned, developed landscape at the end of book I before it happens, Jim suggests the inevitability of what is to come.[7] Thus, this prolepsis creates what Barnd calls "a predestined American geography" (128). In Jim's figuration, the land exists as an abstract entity, the engine that powers U.S. national development, and its transformation is the telos of Nebraska's settler history.

Susan J. Rosowski describes a visual dynamic in Cather's early fiction—one that is especially notable in *O Pioneers!*—in which the narrative moves "between the inclusive and the particular"; from wide views of the landscape, the field of vision narrows to describe intimate experiences in nature ("Ecology of Place" 47). I have argued that in appreciating and learning the details of their environments, the characters Alexandra and Jim have come to be at home in Nebraska. These characters' feelings of belonging are not a critique of settler ways of organizing and utilizing space but come about through settler colonial structures. As Mark Rifkin explains, there is a larger, often unacknowledged political and legal context within which these types of "settler sentiments take shape" (1). In *O Pioneers!*, John Bergson's possession of 640 acres indicates such a context (27). As stated in the explanatory notes to the scholarly edition, this figure includes land Bergson obtained through the Homestead Act of 1862 (Stouck 331). Along with other major pieces of legislation in 1862 (the Morrill Act and the Pacific Railroad Acts), the Homestead Act redistributed land taken from Indigenous peoples and was instrumental in furthering the United States' new spatial and economic order. As Mike Fischer explains in his discussion of *My Ántonia*, this act was "intended to consolidate control of these [western] lands" (39). The first recorded homestead claim was in Nebraska, and residents of Nebraska and the Dakota Territories filed the most claims under this act (Birk). John Bergson's 640 acres generate Alexandra's story; they tie her to the Divide and are the foundation of her success as a farmer. The land's division into half sections represents a new way of organizing space, which the novel validates through its descriptions of the order and harmony of Alexandra's farm. Alexandra's feeling of belonging, which is experienced and expressed as an intensely personal emotion, is engendered by this legal act; the acreage her father obtained under the Homestead Act is the structural foundation upon which Alexandra's feelings of belonging rest. In *My Ántonia*, although the source of Jim's grandparents' land is not acknowledged, the reader can assume that they also obtained their land through the Homestead Act. As Fischer notes, Jim "has engineered a cleaned up version of Nebraska's past" (38), one in which the legal acts propelling settler colonial acquisition and management of land are obscured, even as the profits from the commodified land are calculated by various characters.

Ultimately, *O Pioneers!* and *My Ántonia* can be regarded as "drama[s] of emplacement," to borrow Alex Calder's terminology, in which the territory for the newly arrived is mapped out and settler spatiality asserted (*Settler's Plot* 8). Of course, emplacement implies displacement; Aileen Moreton-Robinson convincingly argues that the "fiction of *terra nullius*"—the colonizer's belief that no one owned the land and that it was available for inhabitance—authorizes Indigenous dispossession (18). As critics Mike Fischer, Michael Gorman, Melissa Ryan, and Karen Ramirez have shown, to produce the prairie lands as empty space awaiting settler inhabitance, Cather's two novels erase Indigenous presence—but always partially. These traces, for instance, can be found in *My Ántonia*'s place-names, like Black Hawk, which Fischer connects to the Sauk leader Chief Black Hawk and the Black Hawk War of 1831–32 (34–35), and Omaha, Nebraska, which represents, as Gorman explains, the nineteenth-century U.S.

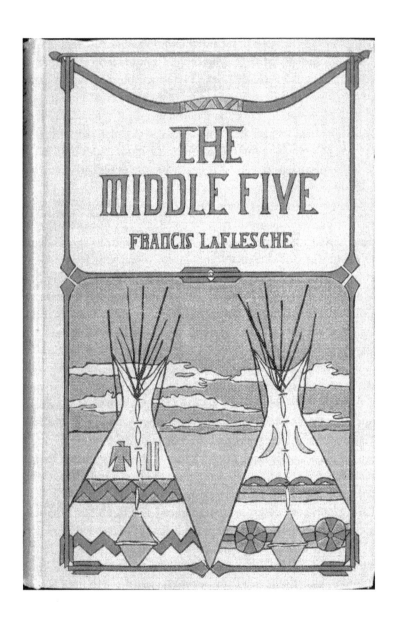

Fig. 8.3. The front cover of Francis La Flesche's *The Middle Five* (1900).
#nby_49697. Newberry Library, Chicago.

place-naming practice that memorialized the supposedly vanquished American Indians while "celebrating European territorial suprem- acy" (41). The scene in *My Ántonia* in which Jim observes "a great circle where the Indians used to ride" (60) indicates another partial erasure, the vague term "Indian" eliminating any reference to spe- cific tribal peoples and their land claims, as Gorman demonstrates (41–42). In a similar vein, I read Jim's description as an indication of Indigenous geographies that settler narratives seek to map over but which remain in place.

Challenges to settler spatialities, or "alternative modes of map- ping and geographic understandings" (Goeman 2), existed at the time Cather was writing. La Flesche's *The Middle Five* (1900), with its portrait of daily life in an on-reservation boarding school, pres- ents such an alternative. Countering the production of Nebraska as a settled space, the memoir portrays the Omaha Nation as an enduring entity that pre-dates the state of Nebraska. In my analysis, I distinguish the memoir's preface, which discusses the reasons La Flesche wrote the memoir, from the body of the text, which covers events from his childhood in the 1860s when he was a student at the Presbyterian mission school. The preface connects the Omaha nation of La Flesche's youth with the Omaha nation of his adult- hood. La Flesche composed and published this memoir while in Washington DC, maintaining his connection with home through regular visits, correspondence with his family, and work on Omaha materials. In the preface to his memoir, La Flesche calls the Omaha territory "our home, the scene of our history, . . . our country" (xx). Using the preface (with its unambiguous assertion of Omaha sov- ereignty over a homeland) to frame the childhood events recorded in his memoir, La Flesche (re)maps Nebraska as Omaha space, "a native space—dense with meanings, stories, and tenurial relations" (Blomley 129). La Flesche's critique of the transformation of Native territories into U.S. property and national space showcases the Oma- has as a self-determining people.

In the preface, La Flesche maps the Omaha reservation as it was in the 1860s, asserting Omaha sovereignty. He begins with a geography lesson: "Most of the country now known as the State of Nebraska (the Omaha name of the river Platt [*sic*], descriptive of its shallowness, width, and low banks) had for many generations been held and claimed by our people as their own, but when they ceded the greater part of this territory to the United States government, they reserved only a certain tract for their own use and home" (xix). La Flesche offers a brief history of the ownership of the land in question while drawing the reader's attention to the politics of place naming. He uses the phrase "now known as" to make visible the settler colonial project of geographic transformation, in which Indigenous lands are made into settler space, in part by marking the territory with new names. As noted above, Cather's novels participate in this process by mapping out a region through the use of actual and fictionalized place-names, some of which invoke Indigenous people and history even as the novels celebrate settler territorial expansion and inhabitance. By inserting the Omaha meaning of the word *Nebraska* into his narrative, La Flesche disrupts the appropriation of that term to designate settled colonial space. The Omaha word for the river, with its attention to the river's specific attributes, expresses knowledge that is not conveyed through the use of the term *Nebraska* to designate the state. Presenting the Omaha people's intimate knowledge of the terrain, La Flesche underscores his community's long tenure in this territory and shows how the settler colonial project of unmaking Native space involves a process in which Indigenous "toponymic knowledge is uprooted" (Cogos, Roué, and Roturier 49). La Flesche points out that the name *Nebraska* has been taken out of its sociolinguistic context, losing its original referent. The meaning has been altered to represent a new geographical configuration, the thirty-seventh U.S. state. In this way, place-names register the displacement, subordination, and loss of control over land experienced by many tribal nations. In noting the change in meaning of *Nebraska*, La Flesche calls attention to the process "in which the existing mode of representing space is replaced by that of the colonizer and adapted to the needs of the new economic, political, and social order" (Herman 80). Cather's two novels narrativize this process in showing the productivity of the land under the care of settlers, who, like Alexandra Bergson, have gained intimate knowledge of the terrain. La Flesche challenges that process, while also claiming the space as Omaha.

La Flesche also makes visible settler colonial practices of spatial control, pointing out how an Indigenous people like the Omaha were confined in increasingly smaller spaces through the signing of treaties and the creation of reservations. As Mishuana Goeman and Nicholas Blomley have shown, the new property-based land systems inaugurated by settler colonial powers were highly regulative, defining where Indigenous peoples were allowed (or not allowed) to go and how they should use the land. Yet it is important to note that La Flesche gives the Omaha people some agency in this process, choosing to use the active verbs "ceded" and "reserved" rather than passive verbs; as La Flesche explains, "[W]hen they [the Omahas] ceded the greater part of this territory to the United States government, they reserved only a certain tract for their own use and home" (xix). He reminds the reader that the U.S. government entered into a treaty with the Omahas, a sovereign nation, not a dependent people. Treaties, suggests La Flesche, are not single transactions but commitments to ongoing relationships that entail responsibilities. The Omahas were familiar with Washington's slowness in fulfilling its lawful obligations. As historian Norma Kidd Green describes, commodities promised as part of the 1854 treaty did not arrive, funds were slow to be dispersed, and agreed-upon buildings were slow to be built (17–27). The Omahas had to travel to Washington in 1861 to ask that the 1854 treaty be fully honored (28). In fact, in the opening chapter of the memoir La Flesche underscores that many of the buildings on the reservation, like "the Government saw and grist mills," exemplify treaty obligations: "All of these buildings stood for the fulfillment of the solemn promises made by the 'Great Father' at Washington to his 'Red Children,' and as part of the price paid for thousands and thousands of acres of fine land" (8). Utilizing quotation marks, La Flesche ironizes contemporary allotment discourse that suggested that Indigenous peoples were like children, dependent upon their fathers for guidance and sustenance, rather than independent, self-governing nations with which the U.S. government had made treaties. He also points to the ways in which land was being transformed through the treaty process. The lengthy descriptions of the mission school and other reservation buildings that precede this comment map out this altered space, and even as La Flesche acknowledges an agreement between nations, his ironic tone raises questions about the fairness of this exchange of "thousands and thousands of acres of fine land" for a collection of buildings, however important they might be to the sustenance of the Omaha people (8).

After La Flesche has established in his preface that the area now known as Nebraska had been, and continues to be, the homeland of the Omaha people, he describes the specific setting of his memoir:

> It is upon the eastern part of this reservation that the scene of these sketches is laid and at the time when the Omahas were living near the Missouri River in three villages, some four or five miles apart. The one farthest south was known as Ton'-won-ga-hae's village. [...] The middle one was Ish'-ka-da-be's village. [...] The one to the north and nearest the Mission school was E-sta'-ma-za's village. [...] Furniture, such as beds, chairs, tables, bureaus, etc., were not used in any of these villages, except in a few instances, while in all of them the Indian costume, language, and social customs remained as yet unmodified. (xix–xx)

This is the first physical description of the Omaha reservation the reader is offered. Although the boundaries of the reservation itself suggest the surveyor's grid that helped facilitate Omaha deterritorialization, the arrangement in villages, which La Flesche maps out via cardinal directions, pushes back against the regimentation of space that settler colonialism enacted. As historian Donald L. Fixico (Shawnee, Sac and Fox, Muscogee Creek, and Seminole) explains, "Originally Native people lived in communities, either sedentary or nomadic. These communities were also called towns, villages, bands, or camps" (474). These communities, either individually or collectively, constituted the tribal nation (476). Thus, in mapping the villages, La Flesche suggests a different way of occupying space, one that reflects a community-based arrangement rather than one based on private property ownership. In Cather's fiction, although there is an emphasis on farmers helping each other and other forms of community caretaking, private property ownership anchors most characters' relationship to land, evident in Alexandra's "squeezing and borrowing" to increase the size of her farm in *O Pioneers!* (108) and the success of immigrant Anton Cuzak, Ántonia's husband, in improving the value of their land from twenty dollars an acre to one hundred in *My Ántonia* (354).[8]

La Flesche also suggests the diversity within the Omaha community. Each of these villages has its own identity, which La Flesche conveys by translating their Omaha names: in Ton'-won-ga-hae's village, the reader is told, "the people were called 'wood eaters,' because they cut and sold wood to the settlers who lived near them" (xix); in Ish'-ka-da-be's village, inhabitants were called "'those who dwell in earth lodges'" due to "having adhered to the original aboriginal form of dwelling when they built their village" (xx); and in E-sta'-ma-za's village, the village led by La Flesche's father, "the people were known as the 'make-believe white-men,' because they built their houses after the fashion of the white settlers" (xx). In all three cases, although the inhabitants differ in certain aspects, they are united in their Omaha-ness, what La Flesche calls their "Indian costume, language, and social customs," which remained intact despite the larger forces being exerted upon them (xx). Anthropologist Mark J. Swetland speculates that the organization of these villages reflects political divisions among the Omaha people over how best to interact with settlers (205, 230). Yet La Flesche's preface makes no mention of these political differences; instead, in his mapping of the reservation as "home" (xix), La Flesche focuses on what unites the people, how they occupy and utilize the land.

The preface concludes with a paragraph that rejects the U.S. settler colonial view of land as empty space, a view made possible through the surveying and mapping processes discussed earlier and naturalized through Cather's narratives. In its entirety, the final paragraph reads, "The white people speak of the country at this period as 'a wilderness,' as though it was an empty tract without human interest or history. To us Indians it was as clearly defined then as it is to-day; we knew the boundaries of tribal lands, those of our friends and those of our foes; we were familiar with every stream, the contour of every hill, and each peculiar feature of the landscape had its tradition. It was our home, the scene of our history, and we loved it as our country" (xx). La Flesche emphasizes the continuity of Omaha land tenure over time, that the nation was "as clearly defined then," in the 1860s, "as it is to-day," at the time of the memoir's composition and publication, circa 1898–1900. Ending the preface with this unambiguous assertion of Omaha land rights strongly suggests that part of La Flesche's purpose in writing is to contest dominant spatial imaginings, like those that govern the production of Nebraska as settled space in Cather's novels. La Flesche refuses the erasure of Indigenous peoples necessary to produce this inhabited place as uninhabited "wilderness" (xx).

The memoir reconnects the land to the Omaha Nation to counter the violence of deterritorialization that sought to sever Indigenous peoples from their emplaced social, political, and cultural relationships. It peoples the territory, (re)mapping it as enduring Indigenous space. Three scenes from the body of the memoir exemplify this assertion of Native space. Although many of the memoir's scenes take place within the mission school itself, others involve locations across the reservation. As a means of pushing back against the physical restraints imposed by the settler colonial state, La Flesche focuses on movement, in particular the movement of Omaha students and their kin across the landscape. In the second chapter of the memoir, for example, La Flesche relates a story about an experience he had during a walk home from school: "Instead of taking the well-beaten path to the village, we all turned off into one that led directly to my father's house, and that passed by the burial-place on the bluffs" (16). Walking along, La Flesche or Frank, as he is called in the book, and his school friend Brush observe two white boys eating the traditional offering of pemmican from a bowl that was at the Omaha gravesite. Rushing home, they tell Frank's mother of "the dreadful things the white boys had done" and receive in return a lesson about Omaha cultural practices: "We listened with respectful attention as my mother explained to us this custom which arose from the tender longing that prompted the mourner to place on the little mound [of the grave] the food that might have been the share of the loved one who lay under the sod" (17). The relatives place the food there, not for the spirit to eat, explains Frank's mother, but because "people love their dead relatives; they remember them and long for their presence at the family gathering" (17). This scene suggests ways in which the Omaha people use the land in both quotidian ways (as in the "well-beaten path to the village") and for religious functions such as burial and memorial (16). Frank's mother is teaching the boys about customs that tie them to their community; the mother's explanation offers them a different way to map the world, one in which Frank is connected to the land through stories and rituals.

The description of the summer buffalo hunt, the subject of chapter 10 of *The Middle Five*, also demonstrates Omaha connection to place through cultural practices. La Flesche presents the hunt as a communal activity, one that causes great excitement among the schoolboys. He also contextualizes the hunt as an activity with severe consequences, as indicated by a later reference to the death of Omaha warriors in defense of their hunting grounds (143–44). La Flesche himself actively participated in buffalo hunts before it became impossible to do so (Green 50–52; Swetland 208). The Omaha people's access to buffalo had been under assault since at least the 1840s, with the scarcity of game being one of the reasons they entered into treaties with the United States (Green 7–9, 27). In the memoir, La Flesche chooses not to suggest the various forces at work to stop the buffalo hunt as a traditional practice. Instead, he articulates an Omaha geography, focusing on the hunt's importance as a collective event connected to a specific landscape. Frank tells the reader that "immediately after breakfast," with a "spy-glass" in hand, "we [Frank and some schoolmates who were staying behind] went to a high point whence we could watch the movements of the people in the village nearest the school" as they got ready to leave for the hunt (84). La Flesche engages the surveyor's view as he looks down from above and afar, but this view does not reveal land in the abstract, as it did in Cather. Frank explains the visual impact of the departing villagers: "It was a wonderful sight to us, the long procession on the winding trail, like a great serpent of varied and brilliant colors. At last I saw my father mount a horse and move forward, the rest of the family followed him, and I watched them until they finally disappeared beyond the green hills. It was nearly noon when the end of the line went out of sight" (84). His descriptions center the bond between the people and the place, as well as his bond with his family and village. The organicism of the "great serpent" image, in which the people move as one, emphasizes their collectivity. Moreover, the villagers move freely, neither their bodies nor the land seemingly subjected to the disciplining forces of settler colonial spatializations like the grid. The buffalo hunt involves an Indigenous formulation of geography, as Barnd has explained in relation to the Kiowa. One way to open up the land to settlers, therefore, was to eliminate the buffalo. Barnd elucidates this idea: "Without traditional subsistence practices [being able to take place], Native space could be effectively unmade, and remade as non-Native or settler space" (94). La Flesche counters by asserting the beauty and purposefulness with which Omaha people collectively use the land in the buffalo hunt.

The third example of (re)mapping involves a farming scene toward the end of the memoir. La Flesche tells the reader about an afternoon spent playing with bows and arrows with his "village playmates"— Omaha children who were not attending the mission school (142). He describes the course of their play: "Our shooting [of arrows] from mark to mark, from one prominent object to another, brought us to a high hill overlooking the ripe fields of corn on the wide bottom below, along the gray Missouri. Here and there among the patches of maize arose little curls of blue smoke, while men and women moved about in their gayly-colored costumes among the broad green leaves of the corn; some, bending under great loads on their backs, were plodding their way laboriously to the fires whence arose the pretty wreaths of smoke" (142).

In contrast to Cather's image of the Nebraska cornfields as the engine of economic progress and U.S. national development, La Flesche portrays the cornfields here on a smaller, more intimate scale. In place of the survey lines and grid patterns that define the agricultural landscapes of *O Pioneers!* and *My Ántonia*, La Flesche describes "patches" of corn and "curls" and "wreaths of smoke," organic, soft-edged images rather than sharply delineated geometric shapes. In Cather's depictions of agriculture discussed earlier, no people are visible. In La Flesche's portrait, the labor of the people working the land is presented. Although Frank is surveying the scene from above, as he did in the hunting scene, he does not present himself as disconnected from the scene. He portrays himself as part of the community, playing with the village boys and enjoying the realization that the smoke signifies a treat: "'They are making sweet corn,'" one of the boys shouts (142). La Flesche depicts the community as self-sustaining.

In this scene La Flesche utilizes two terms for the crop, calling it both "corn" and "maize" (142). The word *maize* calls attention to corn's indigenous roots and to traditional Omaha agricultural practices. At least since 1714, when the Omaha people came to reside near the Missouri River, they had been raising locally available types of maize (Swetland 203). This scene establishes agriculture as an ongoing Omaha method of food production and disrupts the teleology of colonial land usage—that Indigenous peoples did not improve the land and were therefore not entitled to it. This teleology informs Cather's representation of the flourishing of the former plains once they had been subjected to agricultural improvements. La Flesche alludes to a cross-cultural reality: that Indigenous peoples have been cultivating corn and using it ceremonially in the region now called the Americas for thousands of years (Dunbar-Ortiz 16). In a chapter titled "Follow the Corn," Roxanne Dunbar-Ortiz establishes the migration of corn as a crop throughout the Americas prior to Columbus's arrival, observing that "Indigenous American agriculture was based on corn" (16). Given La Flesche's work as an ethnographer recording aspects of various Indigenous cultures and his later founding membership in the Society of American Indians (SAI), the term *maize* signals a pan-Indigenous perspective.

In fact, La Flesche (re)maps Nebraska not only as Omaha space but also more broadly as Indigenous space. In the chapters "The Ponka Boys" and "A Rebuke," La Flesche introduces members of two other tribal nations: the Ponca and the Winnebago.[9] Although "The Ponka Boys" details a humorous incident in which Frank and his friends wrestle their sleds back from the boys who had taken them, La Flesche alludes to a more serious history. The memoir's line that "[t]he Ponkas made a determined resistance" (110) fits the narrative because the boys do not want to give up the sleds, but it also suggests the Ponca people's resistance against their forced removal to Indian Territory in 1877. Chief Standing Bear led this resistance, returning to Ponca homelands in 1879 to bury his son, whereupon he was arrested. Standing Bear's successful legal defense resulted in his remaining in Nebraska. La Flesche and his sister Susette accompanied Chief Standing Bear on his lecture tour of the East Coast in 1879–80 to make a case for Ponca land rights (Liberty 52).[10]

La Flesche also alludes to a history of dispossession and resistance in the chapter "A Rebuke," which centers on the mistreatment of a Winnebago boy. In that chapter, Frank's father and mother, disappointed that Frank did not defend the Winnebago boy, instruct him about ethical and charitable behavior (127–29). The Winnebago people sought refuge with the Omaha Nation after their forced removal from Minnesota to South Dakota in 1863. The Omahas eventually sold some of their land to form the Winnebago reservation. By alluding to these histories, which feature Indigenous refusals to comply with settler colonial geographies, La Flesche suggests the density and diversity of Indigenous spaces that endured despite the violence being exerted upon them. Thus, La Flesche moves beyond the assertion of Omaha land rights to a pan-Indigenous view. His (re)mapping expands his vision of Omaha space to include kinships and histories with other tribal nations.

Considering as typical the scenes I have examined, such as those relating to burial and mourning customs or subsistence practices, one might interpret the memoir as salvage anthropology. As explained by Michelle H. Raheja, "Salvage anthropology stressed that Indigenous people were destined to disappear off the face of the earth in a matter of years; therefore, great pains should be taken to preserve any Indigenous material or linguistic artifact" (285). Arguably, La Flesche conducted "[t]his anxiety-driven form of anthropology" (Raheja 285). Historian and anthropologist Margot Liberty speculates that, especially in his later work documenting Osage culture, "a sense of almost unbearable urgency may have affected La Flesche" (62). However, *The Middle Five* was written in a different genre than the ethnographic pieces he produced, and at the time of the memoir's composition La Flesche had turned from science to explore a "career 'in letters,'" as it was referred to in discussions and letters between La Flesche and his mentor, Alice Fletcher (Mark 273–77). Most important, the preface to the memoir makes clear his purpose to disrupt the misconceptions his settler audience had and to produce, as I demonstrate above, alternative geographical imaginings. In his memoir, La Flesche restores the land as part of a complex set of social relationships.

It is also important to recognize that La Flesche played a role in the Omaha allotment of 1883–84 as an assistant to Alice Fletcher, which might seem to contradict the assertions of Omaha land rights that I argue La Flesche advances in *The Middle Five*. Allotment, which was a means to further reduce the land base of Indigenous peoples, exemplified the use of the survey system to convert communally held lands into private property. Allotment thus seems antithetical to the stance La Flesche adopts in his memoir. Yet, as the Ponca and Winnebago stories in his memoir suggest, Indigenous rights to land at the time were precarious. The Omaha people experienced the constant threat of removal, diminishing food sources, and encroaching white settlements (Mark 69–71; Swetland 229–30). Having secure title to their land through allotment seemed to some, like La Flesche's father, to be the only way to guarantee that their people could stay in their homelands. As a counter to the ongoing precariousness of Omaha land rights stands La Flesche's opening statement that this place was "home" (xx).

My analysis has uncovered certain commonalities between the works of Willa Cather and Francis La Flesche. In both writers' works, relationships between the characters and the landscape are spatialized through the act of looking. In addition, emphasis is placed on the emotional response characters have to the landscape. In Cather's two novels, Alexandra and Jim establish an attachment to the Nebraska plains and eventually come to ground their identity in that place. In *The Middle Five*, La Flesche demonstrates the ongoing relationship he and his classmates have with Omaha lands as they move about the reservation, enjoying children's games and participating in communal tribal experiences. Moreover, in the works of both authors, a deep knowledge of the landscape is integral to a sense of belonging. In Cather's novels, Alexandra and Jim gain intimate knowledge of the prairie lands as part of their growing attachment to the region. La Flesche suggests a particular, enduring knowledge of place in his descriptions, knowledge passed down through generations. For both authors, places serve important functions, such as memorializing the dead. Thus, each writer maps out a region rich in stories and meanings.

Despite such commonalities, Cather's and La Flesche's maps fundamentally diverge. Cather portrays the settlement of Nebraska and the resulting transformation of the landscape as inevitable, even desirable. La Flesche asserts Omaha land tenure, pushing back against the U.S. settler colonial idea of the land as an empty wilderness. This notion of empty, abstract space, which was facilitated by land surveys and helped transform Indigenous land into private property, structures Cather's vision of the landscape. In Cather's novels, the emptied land becomes the setting for Alexandra's and Jim's stories of settler belonging in which improvement to land is the telos of their interaction with it. Cather's novels establish that the landscape is alien to the newly arrived; in contrast, La Flesche establishes the Omaha Nation as home from the start of his reminiscences. Moreover, La Flesche (re)maps the land to include other tribal nations, poignantly incorporating the story of the Winnebago boy, who has been displaced by colonial reorderings of space. Thus, relationships to place as depicted in these works serve divergent purposes: Cather's dramas of emplacement erase Indigenous presence and celebrate settler occupancy as right and natural, whereas La Flesche seeks to disrupt the naturalness of settler occupancy by describing the continued tenure and deep love of the Omaha people for their country. La Flesche's narrative signals a refusal to comply with settler colonial geographies.

Reading Cather, a settler writer, in the context of an Indigenous contemporary like La Flesche, denaturalizes her depictions of the landscape, revealing some assumptions about geography and belonging that I have explored here. In comparing La Flesche's Omaha memoir with Cather's two novels (both with autobiographical dimensions), I have become more aware of how, as a settler scholar, my own interpretive practices can be limited by assumptions I have, and I acknowledge with gratitude the scholars whose work I have utilized here to deepen my own thinking. Reading Cather and La Flesche together in the context of these vibrant, ever-growing bodies of interdisciplinary scholarship about settler colonialism, Indigeneity, and literature suggests further rich possibilities for expanding our understanding of Willa Cather as an American writer.

NOTES

1. The original subtitle of *The Middle Five: Indian Boys at School* was altered when it was reprinted in 1963, as reflected in the title of the edition included here in the list of works cited.

2. Given the connection I establish here between Cather and La Flesche and given that settler colonial geographies in the United States rely on Indigenous lands, I wish to acknowledge the recent research by Robert Lee showing that the University of Nebraska, as a land grant university under the Morrill Act of 1862, was partially endowed through Omaha lands ceded under the Treaty of 16 March 1854 (Lee). Robert Lee and Tristan Ahtone offer an overview of their findings in "Land-Grab Universities"

(2020), an article for *High Country News*. The database Lee has compiled shows parcels of Omaha land being distributed to multiple universities ("Morrill Act").

3. See *Willa Cather's Ecological Imagination*, edited by Susan Rosowski, for diverse treatments of the ways in which place functions, as I draw on only a few texts from that collection in my discussion. For a biographical treatment, see Sharon O'Brien's exploration of the significance of landscapes to Cather (*Willa Cather* 59–76). For a nuanced discussion of Cather as a regional writer, rather than solely a Nebraska writer, see the work of Guy Reynolds.

4. I thank Joseph C. Murphy for bringing this work to my attention.

5. Both Mark Rifkin and Tony Hughes-d'Aeth examine the role of legal disputes over land in settler fiction. Hughes-d'Aeth posits that in *O Pioneers!* questions about Native title to land "moved out of the text's overt events and into its political unconscious" (15). But alive in the text are questions of inheritance among Alexandra and her brothers, suggesting the importance of securing the succession of land in the generations that come after that of the initial pioneers.

6. Scholars have shown that national parks are an important part of settler colonial ways of reengineering the landscape. National parks function as a compromise; without undoing the changes wrought by development, land can be preserved (Calder, *Settler's Plot*). With no empty landscapes out of which to forge national parks in the United States, Indigenous nations had to be removed to create the image of an empty wilderness, and the customary uses of the land by these nations had to be blocked. See Mark David Spence's *Dispossessing the Wilderness*.

7. In the gravesite scene discussed previously, Jim, rather than looking forward, looks back in time. Calder calls this movement "prolepsis in reverse" (137), a desire for uncultivated nature that laments the changes wrought to the land without rejecting the process that necessitated these changes.

8. It's tempting to read Cather characters who abuse the property system, like Wick Cutter in *My Ántonia*, as troubling the commodification of land. Instead, we might think of these characters as scapegoats whose mishandling or profiteering from the land stands in contrast to the ethical land use of more sympathetic characters. According to Calder, in settler fiction the scapegoat's experiences provide a lesson about proper land management without undercutting the legitimacy of economic progress (*Settler's Plot* 136).

9. I will follow La Flesche's nomenclature for these two nations when discussing scenes from the memoir. When discussing the historical record, I will use the current spelling of "Ponca."

10. In 2019 Chief Standing Bear was commemorated in the U.S. Capitol's National Statuary Hall as one of two representatives of the state of Nebraska. Willa Cather was designated the other representative, and her statue was installed in 2023. Nebraska legislators voted to replace the previous statues (of Julius Sterling Morton and William Jennings Bryan) in 2018.

WORKS CITED

Barnd, Natchee Blu. *Native Space: Geographic Strategies to Unsettle Settler Colonialism*. Oregon State UP, 2017.

Birk, Megan. "Homestead Act." *Encyclopedia of Immigration and Migration in the American West*, edited by Gordon Morris Bakken and Alexandra Kindell. Ebook, Sage Publications, 2006.

Blomley, Nicholas. "Law, Property, and the Geography of Violence: The Frontier, the Survey, and the Grid." *Annals of the Association of American Geographers*, vol. 93, no. 1, 2003, pp. 121–41.

Calder, Alex. "Beyond Possession: Animals and Gifts in Willa Cather's Settler Colonial Fictions." *Western American Literature*, vol. 52, no. 1, 2017, pp. 55–74.

———. *The Settler's Plot: How Stories Take Place in New Zealand*. Auckland UP, 2011.

Cather, Willa. *My Ántonia*. 1918. Willa Cather Scholarly Edition, historical essay and explanatory notes by James Woodress, editing by Charles Mignon with Kari Ronning, U of Nebraska P, 1994.

———. "Nebraska: The End of the First Cycle." *The Nation*, 5 September 1923, pp. 236–38.

———. *O Pioneers!* 1913. Willa Cather Scholarly Edition, historical essay and explanatory notes by David Stouck, editing by Susan J. Rosowski and Charles W. Mignon with Kathleen Danker, U of Nebraska P, 1992.

———. *The Selected Letters of Willa Cather*, edited by Andrew Jewell and Janis P. Stout, Knopf, 2013.

———. *Willa Cather in Person: Interviews, Speeches, and Letters*, edited by L. Brent Bohlke, U of Nebraska P, 1986.

Cogos, Sarah, Marie Roué, and Samuel Roturier. "Sami Place Names and Maps: Transmitting Knowledge of a Cultural Landscape in Contemporary Contexts." *Arctic, Antarctic, and Alpine Research*, vol. 49, no. 1, 2017, pp. 43–51.

Dooley, Patrick K. "Biocentric, Homocentric, and Theocentric Environmentalism in *O Pioneers!*, *My Ántonia*, and *Death Comes for the Archbishop*." Rosowski, *Willa Cather's Ecological Imagination*, pp. 64–76.

Dunbar-Ortiz, Roxanne. *An Indigenous Peoples' History of the United States.* Beacon P, 2014.

Fischer, Mike. "Pastoralism and Its Discontents: Willa Cather and the Burden of Imperialism." *Mosaic: An Interdisciplinary Critical Journal*, vol. 23, no. 1, 1990, pp. 31–44.

Fixico, Donald. "From Tribal to Indian: American Indian Identity in the Twentieth Century." *Native Diasporas: Indigenous Identities and Settler Colonialism in the Americas*, edited by Gregory D. Smithers and Brooke N. Newman, U of Nebraska P, 2014, pp. 473–95.

Foster, Tol. "Of One Blood: An Argument for Relations and Regionality in Native American Literary Studies." *Reasoning Together: The Native Critics Collective*, by Janice Acoose et al., edited by Craig S. Womack, Daniel Heath Justice, and Christopher B. Teuton, U of Oklahoma P, 2008, pp. 265–302.

Glotfelty, Cheryll. "A Guided Tour of Ecocriticism, with Excursions to Catherland." Rosowski, *Willa Cather's Ecological Imagination*, pp. 28–43.

Goeman, Mishuana. *Mark My Words: Native Women Mapping Our Nations.* U of Minnesota P, 2013.

Gorman, Michael. "Jim Burden and the White Man's Burden: *My Ántonia* and Empire." *History, Memory, and War*, edited by Steven Trout, Cather Studies 6, U of Nebraska P, 2006, pp. 28–57.

Green, Norma Kidd. *Iron Eye's Family: The Children of Joseph La Flesche.* Johnsen Publishing for the Nebraska State Historical Society, 1969.

Herman, RDK. "The Aloha State: Place Names and the Anti-Conquest of Hawai'i." *Annals of the Association of American Geographers*, vol. 89, no. 1, 1999, pp. 76–102.

Hughes-d'Aeth, Tony. "Cooper, Cather, Prichard, 'Pioneer': The Chronotope of Settler Colonialism." *Australian Literary Studies*, vol. 31, no. 3, 2016, pp. 1–26.

Kelm, Mary-Ellen, and Keith D. Smith. *Talking Back to the Indian Act: Critical Readings in Settler Colonial Histories.* U of Toronto P, 2018.

La Flesche, Francis. *The Middle Five: Indian Schoolboys of the Omaha Tribe.* 1900. U of Nebraska P, 1978.

Lee, Robert. "Morrill Act of 1862 Indigenous Land Parcels Database." *High Country News*, 30 March 2020, github.com/HCN-Digital-Projects/landgrabu-data. Accessed 7 June 2021.

Lee, Robert, and Tristan Ahtone. "Land-Grab Universities: Expropriated Indigenous Land Is the Foundation of the Land-Grant University System." *High Country News*, 30 March 2020, hcn.org/issues/52.4/indigenous-affairs-education-land-grab-universities. Accessed 7 June 2021.

Liberty, Margot. "Francis La Flesche, Omaha, 1857–1932." *American Indian Intellectuals of the Nineteenth and Early Twentieth Centuries*, edited by Margot Liberty, U of Nebraska P, 2002, pp. 51–69.

Mark, Joan T. *A Stranger in Her Native Land: Alice Fletcher and the American Indians*. U of Nebraska P, 1988.

Moreton-Robinson, Aileen. *The White Possessive: Property, Power, and Indigenous Sovereignty*. U of Minnesota P, 2015.

O'Brien, Sharon. *Willa Cather: The Emerging Voice*. Harvard UP, 1997.

Raheja, Michelle H. *Reservation Reelism: Redfacing, Visual Sovereignty, and Representations of Native Americans in Film*. U of Nebraska P, 2010.

Ramirez, Karen E. "Narrative Mappings of the Land as Space and Place in Willa Cather's *O Pioneers!*" *Great Plains Quarterly*, vol. 30, no. 2, 2010, pp. 97–115.

Reynolds, Guy. "Willa Cather's Case: Region and Reputation." *Regionalism and the Humanities*, edited by Timothy R. Mahoney and Wendy J. Katz, U of Nebraska P, 2009, pp. 79–94.

Rifkin, Mark. *Settler Common Sense: Queerness and Everyday Colonialism in the American Renaissance*. U of Minnesota P, 2014.

Rosowski, Susan J, editor. *Willa Cather's Ecological Imagination*. Cather Studies 5, U of Nebraska P, 2003.

———. "Willa Cather's Ecology of Place." *Western American Literature*, vol. 30, no. 1, 1995, pp. 37–51.

Ryan, Melissa. "The Enclosure of America: Civilization and Confinement in Willa Cather's *O Pioneers!*" *American Literature*, vol. 75, no. 2, 2003, pp. 275–303.

Siegert, Bernhard. "(Not) in Place: The Grid, or, Cultural Techniques of Ruling Spaces." *Cultural Techniques: Grids, Filters, Doors, and Other Articulations of the Real*, translated by Geoffrey Winthrop-Young, Fordham UP, 2015, pp. 97–120.

Spence, Mark David. *Dispossessing the Wilderness: Indian Removal and the Making of the National Parks*. Oxford UP, 1999.

Stouck, David. Historical essay and explanatory notes. Cather, *O Pioneers!*

Stout, Janis P. "The Observant Eye, the Art of Illustration, and Willa Cather's *My Ántonia*." Rosowski, *Willa Cather's Ecological Imagination*, pp. 128–52.

Swetland, Mark J. "'Make-Believe White-Men' and the Omaha Land Allotments of 1871–1900." *Great Plains Research*, vol. 4, no. 2, 1994, pp. 201–36.

Urgo, Joseph. "*My Ántonia* and the National Parks Movement." Rosowski, *Willa Cather's Ecological Imagination*, pp. 44–63.

9 Willa Cather and Mari Sandoz

The Muse and the Story Catcher
in the Capital City

SALLIE KETCHAM

For generations of ambitious young Nebraskans, all roads led to Lincoln. The capitol's skyscraping golden dome, crowned with *The Sower* and visible for miles was—and remains—a range light for academics, scientists, artists, lawyers, entrepreneurs, and anyone fleeing the farm. Willa Cather (1873–1947) and Mari Sandoz (1896–1966) arrived before the dome's completion, but it was in Lincoln, the capital city, that these two iconic Nebraska writers pursued higher education, encountered resistance, navigated the town's matriarchal "blackball" caste system, and began to mold memory, the raw material of their art.

How did the small village of Lancaster, founded on a salt marsh two years after the Kansas-Nebraska Act, then rechristened "Lincoln" in 1867 (over the howling protests of Confederate sympathizers), influence Cather in fact and in fiction? Lincoln, self-proclaimed "Athens of the Plains," was an early but formative dislocation for Cather. By 1890 she was far from breezy Red Cloud; Lincoln had a brand-new Old Guard that valued property, propriety, family-of-origin, and cash. Social inclusion, club membership, participation in the arts, writing credits—these objectives were attainable by invitation only. Intellectually sophisticated, uncommonly cosmopolitan, and outspoken, Cather ultimately succeeded at treading the fine line between authentic self-expression and the established social conventions of Lincoln's university, Near South, and O Street elites. As the gifted, classically trained daughter of a respectable Virginia family, Cather passed. Her friends—Mary Letitia Jones, Katherine Weston, Mariel Gere, Louise Pound, Dorothy Canfield, and, in time, Edith Lewis—all passed.

Mari Sandoz did not pass. Malnourished, snow blind in one eye, running from an abusive marriage, Sandoz crash-landed in Lincoln with little more than an eighth-grade education and a Sandhills teaching certificate. Regardless, she was determined to tell her own gritty version of northwestern Nebraska history, which she did in books like *Old Jules*, *Slogum House*, *Crazy Horse*, and *Cheyenne Autumn*. In her explosive 1939 novel *Capital City*, Sandoz declared the city of Lincoln (dubbed Franklin in the book) "Buffalo Bill's prostitute," compared smug Lincolnites to "a cluster of lice along the vein of a yellowing leaf," and viciously lampooned its Depression-era civic leaders as fascists (1–7, 257). In one memorable scene, Sandoz gleefully killed off a thinly veiled knight of Ak-Sar-Ben in the men's room—as she put it, with his "feet sticking out from under the door of the can" (21).[1] *Capital City* was banned or restricted in several Nebraska communities, including rival Omaha. In 1948 Sandoz's name appeared on a list of communist and subversive writers compiled by the California legislature's Fact-Finding Committee on Un-American Activities (Stauffer 198). The backlash over *Capital City* resulted in death threats that drove Sandoz out of Lincoln for good.

And yet, despite their wildly differing aesthetic sensibilities, Cather and Sandoz led remarkably parallel lives. Cather was a generation older than Sandoz, but both writers lived through the final stages of Nebraska's frontier history: Cather in Red Cloud, Sandoz in the rugged Sandhills. Each was the eldest of several siblings, born to fathers who were well-known Nebraska boosters and pioneers. Their crowded childhood homes were managed by distracted mothers and long-suffering maternal grandmothers who moved in to help keep house. As writers, both women dedicated their lives to crafting stories of the mythic West; they both loved and brooded over the plains. They both mined complicated and conflicted memories of youth and childhood to produce bittersweet, authentic stories of life on the American borderlands. In the end, they both quit Nebraska, moved east, and died in Manhattan.

In Lincoln, both women experienced critical turning points in their development as writers, but their reception and recognition in the capital—as daughters, as university students, and as emerging writers—could hardly have been more different. Their formative years in Lincoln and at the University of Nebraska helped determine the trajectory of their careers, launching Cather toward national and international prominence while consigning Sandoz to regional writer status. Sandoz's work is still largely overlooked today. "The grandmothers of the town won't have Mollie," Sandoz wrote in *Capital City*, using yet another variant of her own name, "not those three old women who run it. [. . .] They won't have an outsider, a newcomer. The honors have to go to what they call the good old families, at least two generations old" (12).

When Cather's family of genteel, dislocated Virginians rolled into Catherton and Red Cloud, three generations strong, the shades of Willow Shade came with them. Cather's colonial ancestors held their land grant from Lord Fairfax; they were among the first European settlers in the lush Shenandoah Valley. Cather's maternal grandfather, William Lee Boak, and her great-grandfather, James Cather, had served simultaneously in the Virginia General Assembly. Of her comfortable and privileged childhood in Virginia, Cather would later drily comment that "people in good families were born good" (qtd. in Lee 26). Cather's courtly father, Charles Fectigue Cather, and her strong-willed, patrician mother, Mary Virginia ("Jennie") Boak Cather, had been "born good," and Nebraska knew it. Like Lincoln, Red Cloud was located south of the Platte River, Nebraska's ersatz Mason-Dixon Line. Although few enslaved persons were ever transported into the disputed Nebraska Territory, raw land in the southern half of the state attracted a distinct minority of settlers (often vocal Democrats) from Virginia, Missouri, and southern Ohio, particularly along the Kansas state line. Half of Nebraska's territorial governors were natives of Kentucky or South Carolina. In the fall of 1883, Cather was a student at the sod schoolhouse in "New Virginia," just south of Catherton. Meanwhile, in the booming capital, as Bernice Slote has noted, women with family backgrounds much like that of Cather's mother "moved in, took out their white kid gloves, subscribed to *Century*, shipped in oysters frozen in blocks of ice, and tried to keep life very much as it had been in Ohio, New York, Illinois, or Virginia" (7).

According to historian Frederick Luebke, Lincoln was considered "more Protestant, Anglo-Saxon, clean and moral," than immigrant-magnet Omaha and communities north and west (218). Although Omaha, the original territorial capital, ultimately lost a heated battle for the statehouse to "South Platters" in 1867, it remained the state's commercial hub. Compared to Lincoln, Omaha was a cow town, plain and simple. It boasted stockyards, meatpackers, the Livestock Exchange, Missouri River landings, and the Union Pacific Railroad (Olson 118, 209–10). However, in Nebraska, unlike virtually every other state, Lincolnites consolidated power and influence by taking all the rest that was of importance—the capitol building, the prestigious land-grant university, the lucrative courts, government offices and agencies, the state hospital, and the penitentiary (Barrett 60). They even took the Nebraska State Historical Society and the Home for the Friendless. Silas Garber, founder of Red Cloud and the model for Captain Forrester in *A Lost Lady*, was elected governor in 1874, then reelected in 1876. Lawyers, bankers, investors, land brokers, and insurance agents, many of whom were friends or business associates of Cather's affable father Charles, quickly set up shop. Eager to replicate the familiar pattern of civic life and leadership in their new western homes, prominent citizens and boosters quickly chartered business and fraternal organizations, women's clubs, philanthropic institutions, lodges, secret societies, and academic groups.

In Red Cloud, Charles Cather was repeatedly elected to leadership positions in city, county, and fraternal affairs. In 1888 he was elected venerable consul, manager, and delegate to Head Camp of the Modern Woodmen of America, forerunner of Omaha's insurance giant, Woodmen of the World ("Modern Woodmen" 1). Charles Cather may not have been as rich or as driven as his Lincoln peers, but as a refined Virginian and one of Nebraska's Old Settlers, he associated with a select set, as did his daughter. "She [Willa] came of a good cultured family," one of Cather's classmates noted, "and chose her friends of the cultured type" (Shively 141).

As in many (mid)western boomtowns and capitals, society in Lincoln stratified rapidly. The new brick-and-limestone "commercial blocks" of O Street represented the city's best business address. Lincoln's "O Street Gang," as the city's clannish first families, business leaders, and political power brokers eventually came to be known, jealously guarded access to the city for over half a century. Cather was clearly aware of their influence because she won their support and moved among them freely. To a 1918 Nebraska reader of *My Ántonia*, Jim Burden unmistakably confirms Lena Lingard's impressive rise from barefoot hired girl to society dressmaker in one brief exchange: "You are quite comfortable here, aren't you?" Lena says, looking around his room. "I live in Lincoln now, too, Jim. I'm in business for myself. I have a dressmaking shop in the Raleigh Block, out on O Street. I've made a real good start" (218). Cather did just that in the 1890s, when she quickly became the startling young arbiter of Lincoln's bustling university, O Street, and theatrical scenes.

Timothy R. Mahoney's groundbreaking spatial narrative, *Gilded Age Plains City: The Great Sheedy Murder Trial and the Booster Ethos of Lincoln, Nebraska*, provides unusual insight into the dynamic city of Lincoln (population fifty-five thousand) in 1891.[2] This was the year after Cather moved to Lincoln to attend the university's preparatory Latin School and the same year the sensational John Sheedy murder trial electrified Nebraska. According to Mahoney, the social, moral, and political issues raised at the trial caused "profound worries about the integrity of the class, gender, and racial systems that had sustained

208

SALLIE KETCHAM

Lincoln society for a generation" and "raised deep fears that other 'poseurs' and 'charlatans' might be living among them." Mari Sandoz's father, Old Jules, branded "the notorious Frenchman" by the *Omaha Daily Bee* on October 9, 1891, was just the sort of character many Lincolnites shunned on sight.

Mahoney's spatial narrative explores the trial, the booster ethos of Lincoln in the 1890s, and its principal players "at the micro historical level of lived experience in a specific time and place," contending that "space and the built environment of a city are not mere backdrops, backgrounds, or contexts in which events occurred. They play a central role in understanding the development of social and political order." The spatial narrative contains a vast and deeply documented research base of primary materials, biographical narratives, and images that reflect the politics, culture, economy, and society of Cather's Lincoln. It deconstructs relationships between Lincoln's established business and university elites and members of the middle or working classes. Gilded Age Lincoln was a tumultuous town. In 1888, from his position with a bird's-eye view atop a new five-story building on O Street, Thomas H. Hyde, president of the Lincoln News Company, described the chaotic street scene he saw below, where "the swelling, hurrying flood of animation, mingling with a world of commerce on wheels, crowded street cars, omnibuses, coaches and cabs, moves on," he reported. In Lincoln, Hyde continued, "youth jostles age, poverty on foot stares Croesus in his carriage" (qtd. in Mahoney intro). It is interesting to note that Cather, when walking from her boardinghouse at Tenth and L Streets to the university, or from the university to dinner at the elegant Queen Anne or Painted Lady homes of her friends, had to cross through the heart of P Street's "demimonde," a ramshackle district of bars, brothels, and billiard halls. Traces of the demimonde may survive in Cather's pool-shooting, cocktail-mixing heroine in "Tommy, the Unsentimental." In the boisterous capital, high and low moved shoulder to shoulder: separate, unequal, and crossing paths but maintaining their own appointed spheres. Like Tommy, Cather was notable for friends who "were her father's old business friends, elderly men who had seen a good deal of the world, and who were very proud and fond of Tommy" (6). When Cather and her mother traveled to Lincoln to select Cather's boardinghouse residence, they stayed at the home of Robert Emmett Moore (Woodress 69), former mayor of Lincoln and future lieutenant governor of Nebraska. Jennie Cather, Willa's formidable mother, must have been determined to secure safe and suitable living quarters for her teenage daughter. It's also possible that she initiated social calls and introductions at this time.

University tuition was free in 1891, but the cost of sending a daughter to live in Lincoln and attend the university (for those families who would even entertain the idea) was significant. The estimated expense of $350 per year or $175 per semester (Manley 114) was the equivalent of $11,833 in 2023 dollars.[3] The price was prohibitive for most Nebraskans. It also sparked criticism. In 1889 one legislator declared that the university "was maintained by the poorest people of the state for the purpose of giving the rich man's son a free education" (qtd. in Manley 109). Many of Cather's female classmates were the daughters of prominent and well-educated Lincoln judges, legislators, businessmen, or bankers. There were no dormitories, so these young women walked to class and lived at home. Including her preparatory year at Latin School, Cather would spend five years living and boarding in Lincoln on her own.

In 1919, nearly twenty-five years after Cather's graduation, the official *Semi-Centennial Anniversary Book of the University of Nebraska, 1869–1919* made explicit the general expectations, both personal and professional, for the young women who had attended the University of Nebraska:

> What should be said about the thousands of women graduates of the University of Nebraska? Their highest contribution is that of home-builder. They are the mothers of many of the sons and daughters who have come and will come to the Alma Mater of their parents. As the wives of alumni, their contributions are interwoven with those of their husbands. They have followed their husbands into the missionary fields of China and Japan.

They have worked side by side with them in their research and their publications; while those who have not trained their own sons and daughters have helped to train others. (*Semi-Centennial* 68)

Willa Cather had other ideas. In March 1891, while she was still a prep student, her impressive first essay was published by the *Nebraska State Journal*. In the fall of 1892, she became an associate editor of the *Hesperian*, the university's leading student publication. The *Hesperian* would publish her earliest short stories. By the following year she had become managing editor. A fellow staff member recalled that "the *Hesperian* was Willa practically" (qtd. in Slote 12). On 5 November 1893 her pithy column on literature, local life, and traveling theater productions began to appear in the Sunday *Journal*. For this, for her "meat-axe" theater reviews, and for her later *Courier* articles, Cather was paid—usually one dollar per column (Woodress 84). Against long odds, she had turned semiprofessional. During the last two years of her college career, Cather was writing at a furious pace for pleasure and for profit. She was gaining remarkable skills, but it is unlikely that she was able to cover her living expenses without supplemental assistance from her family in Red Cloud. Soon after her graduation, Cather returned home, where she could live for free as she struggled to create a viable path to personal and financial independence. Although she continued traveling to Lincoln to write and to review theater, Cather quickly turned her attention to obtaining a university teaching position.

Cather's university years seem more intriguing, collegial, and financially secure than she portrays them in her later writings and fiction. In 1891 the appearance of Willa Cather's provocative alter ego, William Cather Jr. (would-be MD), on campus, sporting chopped hair and masculine-style clothing, should have triggered every wrought-iron lock on every Victorian door from Greek Row to O Street. But in Cather's case it didn't. Instead, Cather socialized as an equal with the sons and daughters of the wealthiest, best-known, and most politically connected families in the state: the Pounds, Geres, Westons,

Fig. 9.1. Willa Cather at the time she entered the University of Nebraska as a first-year student. Archives and Special Collections, University of Nebraska–Lincoln Libraries.

Moores, Harrises, Canfields, and others. Despite her unconventional and sometimes deliberately provocative appearance, from the time Cather arrived on campus she was received in the paneled libraries and Eastlake parlors of Lincoln's "best" families like the prodigal daughter. She was one of theirs, and they were willing to protect, promote, advise, or defend her. "Willa always followed her own inclinations, anyway," Mariel Gere told a reporter in 1924. "[S]he didn't care much what other folks said or thought. She was always a little eccentric, but as she grew and went on through school, her notions seemed to change, and she became more like the other girls" (qtd. in Wyman 6). As late as 1950—six decades after Cather first arrived in Lincoln—Mariel Gere was still defending her friend against accusations of arrogance ("thinking so well of herself," a cardinal sin in Nebraska), friendlessness, and cross-dressing (Hoover and Bohlke 10).

Mariel Gere would know; her mother played the decisive role in Cather's grudging transformation. It is possible that Cather's mannish appearance was tacitly accepted so long as she pursued her interest in the male-only fields of science and medicine. According to Dr. Julius Tyndale, an early mentor, Cather told him "she had always wanted to be a boy," but she didn't break "the last straw" until she wore boys' clothing to a party at a private home, at which point Tyndale told her point-blank she had to be less conspicuous (Wyman 6).

In 1883 fifty-two young men were enrolled in the university's new and controversial College of Medicine. Many professors and university administrators considered medical school "technical training" and thus incompatible with, and unworthy of, the university's mission of classical education. Admittedly, the incoming medical students did little to endear themselves to the administration. After several Lincoln physicians declined to teach in campus classrooms and anatomy lessons were canceled due to a lack of cadavers, a few disappointed but enterprising medical students climbed on top of University Hall and scrawled CASH FOR STIFFS across the roof in lead paint. They then proceeded to outrage church-going Lincolnites by organizing body-snatching expeditions to rural cemeteries (Manley 95–98). In May 1887 the regents shut down the College of Medicine with a sigh of relief, but Cather would have known about the rowdy department and its well-publicized exploits; it may even have piqued her adolescent interest in vivisection, dissection, and rabble-rousing. As a child, Mari Sandoz also dreamed of becoming a doctor. A sympathetic former teacher recalled how Sandoz carried a little roll of rag bandages, needles, thread, and antiseptic with her everywhere. Regrettably, "she often had occasion to use them" (Cass).

Although Cather's large family was not wealthy by Lincoln standards, it is unlikely that the cost of her education required serious financial sacrifices at home, at least not until 1893. In 1890 the *Red Cloud Republican* failed (taking Charles Cather's investment with it), and he likely borrowed money to send Willa to Lincoln's Latin School—where she promptly moved into the city's best boarding-house.[4] Cather could not live like a male student on campus, cutting costs by living in a cheap, overcrowded rooming house or "batching" it, as Will Owen Jones, Cather's friend and editor, later reminisced about his college days (*Semi-Centennial* 42). Had she done so, her family would have lost face and she would have lost her reputation.

Classmate Edward Elliot remembered Willa Cather as "one of those more fortunate students" who did not have to work and therefore "had the benefit of time to give to extra-curricular matters" (Shively 124). Even the financial Panic of 1893 and the unprecedented drought of 1894—events that ruined thousands of families statewide—did not derail her studies. By 1895 Charles Cather was employed by Robert Emmett Moore, president of Lincoln's Security Investment Company. After serving three terms in the state senate, Moore had just been elected lieutenant governor. His brother and business partner, John Huntington Moore, a former Red Cloud banker, was a close friend of the Cather family. Willa was a frequent visitor at Robert Moore's turreted mansion on E Street. In 1921 Moore left an estate worth $2.5 million. Unlike Lincoln, in small-town Nebraska wealth and status might be respected, resented, or quietly acknowledged, but they were rarely on display; among other objections, flaunting was considered bad for business. "Father is a very modest man and he wants me to be modest," Cather noted (qtd. in Bennett 27). Common courtesy was obligatory, but lifestyle differences could be enormous, especially in the privacy of the home.[5] In *My Ántonia*, Widow Steavens remarks that Ambrosch's wedding gift to Ántonia, a set of plated silver, was "good enough for her station" (309), but for the Cathers of Webster County, weddings were an Old

Dominion affair, subject to a very different set of expectations and etiquette. In 1896, when Cather took charge of her cousin's wedding breakfast in Red Cloud—the Province of Siberia, as she liked to call it—she had fresh strawberries, tomatoes, and watercress shipped in from Chicago, in the dead of winter (*Complete Letters* #0022).

Although Cather may have preferred rumpled menswear, the many formal portraits of her from the period show her well dressed and crisply tailored. Fashion (like association) is a reliable indicator of social status and respectability in the 1880s and 1890s. Even in unceremonious Red Cloud, Willa Cather's mother, Jennie, was fastidious in her dress, carrying parasols that matched her expensive ensembles. Compared to Judge Stephen and Laura Biddlecombe Pound's family, however, the Cathers were barely keeping up appearances. In Cather's well-known 16 June 1892 letter to Louise Pound— the letter in which Cather, utterly infatuated with Louise, admires her at a party—there is mention of Louise wearing her new "Worth Costume" (*Complete Letters* #0010). That's not Woolworth's; it can only be House of Worth, founded by Charles Worth, the most celebrated French couturier of the Gilded Age. Worth designs and bespoke copies were available in America at the time. They were coveted by high-ranking socialites, opera singers, and celebrated actresses in society bastions like Newport, New York, and Washington; they were works of art. Louise Pound, soon to pursue her doctorate degree at the University of Heidelberg, was turned out like Sarah Bernhardt or Consuelo Vanderbilt in her parents' Nebraska home.

Cather could be imperious, but she was no snob. Her *Hesperian* fiction betrays uncomfortable ambivalence toward Lincoln society and her place in it. From the shallow, social-climbing sorority girls Cather mocked in "Daily Dialogues or, Cloakroom Conversation as Overheard by the Tired Listener" to her parody of Grand Tour Americans demanding pumpkin pie in Rome, Cather frequently skewered the behavior of her peers (Shively 93–108). In early short stories like "Peter," "Lou, the Prophet," and "The Clemency of the Court," Cather's sympathetic protagonists are loners, struggling farmers, or mistreated laborers. As Kelsey Squire demonstrates in "Legacy and Conflict: Willa Cather and the Spirit of the Western University," Cather drew continually on her social and pedagogical experiences at the University of Nebraska in her later work, particularly *My Ántonia*, *One of Ours*, and *The Professor's House*. Squire notes that Cather disparages "strategic social moves" like Jim Burden's society marriage or Harris Maxey's "feverish pursuit of social advantages and useful acquaintances" at university, as well as the commercialization of Tom Outland's scientific legacy (250).

In her junior year, Cather turned her "meat-axe" on Roscoe Pound, declaring Louise's brother a pretentious has-been, bore, and bully in her *Hesperian* column "Pastels in Prose." It was too much; the backlash was public and likely coordinated. Classmate Ernest C. Ames, "fed up" with Cather's "cruel, cynical, unjust and prejudiced criticism of everyone on the campus, students and profs," sent a front-page retort to the *Daily Nebraskan* titled "Postals in Paste" (Shively 135). In the piece, published in the spring of 1894, he compared Cather to Louis XIV proclaiming "Moi, le Roi," and suggested Cather wanted all her benighted classmates sent down with "Bohunkus" to ignominious Doane College (Ames 1). Reigning clubwoman Laura Biddlecombe Pound also retaliated. She closed her doors to Willa Cather; Cather was not to be received. Uncharacteristically, other Lincoln matriarchs, including Mariel Clapham Gere and Flavia Canfield, did not follow suit but apparently sought to mend Cather's costly breach of manners (Krohn 74). Willa Cather held her own. Mari Sandoz would not be so fortunate.

The Geres proved particularly influential in Cather's university life and budding career. Charles H. Gere, publisher of the *Nebraska State Journal*, had served as a state senator in the first legislature, as private secretary to Governor David Butler, as chairman of the State Republican Committee, and as president of the University of Nebraska Board of Regents. In a heartfelt 1912 letter to Mariel Gere, Cather recalled her first invitation to dine at the Geres' welcoming home, soon after her arrival in Lincoln. This type of invitation was rarely spontaneous; "good families" offered hospitality to their peers after receiving personal requests or letters of introduction. Willa

216

SALLIE KETCHAM

Cather was duly vetted and approved; in fact, she captivated the
Yankee Geres. In a 24 April 1912 letter to Mariel Gere, she recalled
that Charles Gere had told her she looked like "Sadie Harris" (*Complete Letters* #0223). ("Sadie" was Sarah Butler Harris, the outspoken
social page editor and suffragist who held court from her Italianate
home on K Street; in 1895 she hired Cather as associate editor of
the *Courier*.) In the same letter, Cather memorialized the kindness,
persuasiveness, and gentle humor of Mrs. Gere. No one else, Cather
claimed, could have convinced her to grow out her hair, and she
particularly appreciated the fact Mrs. Gere did not scold young people (presumably a reference to Cather's own mother). Evidently,
Cather felt constant pressure over her unwillingness to conform. In
a 23 February 1913 letter to her aunt Frances Smith Cather, Cather
expressed her relief at finally overcoming her childhood shyness
and, in a phrase that flies off the page, her "queer fears" around her
family. As a child, she says, she felt that all of them, even her father,
wanted to change her, to make her over, and she most emphatically
did not want to be made over (*Complete Letters* #0245).

Cather's appearance changed dramatically over the course of five
years in the capital. As she entered Lincoln society and took the
university by storm, the vestiges (even the proud signature) of William Cather Jr. slowly but inevitably disappeared. By graduation day,
Cather seems to have made a new personal and social calculus, based
on hard reality. Biographer Hermione Lee detects something potentially "camp" in Cather's well-known graduation portrait (44), the
photograph depicting Cather in full debutante array (ivory net over
ivory satin ballgown, leg-o'-mutton sleeves, and white kid gloves), her
titian hair piled on her head, her gaze intense and inscrutable. Lee
may be correct. But Cather is also the very image of high society's
unattainable and independent Gibson Girl, the New Woman who
has seen the future and decided (despite the odds) that it is female.[6]
This is a socialite's photo for public consumption. Significantly, in
March 1895, during her expensive week of grand opera in Chicago,
Cather slipped away to have two entirely different graduation portraits made at William McKenzie Morrison's studio: one in severe

Fig. 9.2. Willa Cather's university graduation portrait, 1895. Archives and Special Collections, University of Nebraska–Lincoln Libraries.

black cap and gown, the other in her fur-lined opera cloak. Morrison was the leading theatrical photographer of his day, specializing in cabinet cards of celebrated actors and opera singers.

For Cather, the risks, the stakes, and the rewards of social acceptance were sky high. In Lincoln, Cather was not an outsider trying to write her way in. She was an insider trying to write her way out:

"For I shall be the first, *if I live*, to bring the Muse into my country" (*My Ántonia* 264, emphasis added). Just as Jim Burden ponders Virgil's line in *My Ántonia*, countless Cather readers have reflected on the line's significance to Cather and to her work. Cather seems well aware that she could not live to achieve her full potential as an artist in Nebraska. She needed and longed for a wider world. Yet to many readers, Cather did not *bring* the muse; Cather *is the muse*. She turned the prairie into living art. She lives in her work, she is virtually embodied there, and that body of work remains both an object of beauty and desire and a source of inspiration. Clearly, writing for the *Hesperian* and the Lincoln newspapers had ignited her imagination and ambition. She had acquired readers and a byline. Ultimately, Cather cannot "bring the Muse" without the support and approbation of the lifelong friends and advocates she had acquired in Lincoln. Upon graduation, Cather faced the same three options as nearly all her other female classmates: she could marry and take her place in society, she could live with her family and teach, or she could close her eyes and pray for a miracle.

Cather's "miraculous" leap from Red Cloud to Pittsburgh in 1896 was the combined result of her precocious talent, hard work, and her powerful Lincoln connections. James Axtell could have hired any established East Coast writer to edit his new magazine, *Home Monthly*. Instead, he bet on the brilliant Nebraskan. She must have been recommended by friends Charles Gere and *Nebraska State Journal* editor Will Owen Jones. In addition, she had a growing reputation for excellence among other Nebraska journalists. A columnist for the *Omaha World-Herald* wrote, "If there is a woman in Nebraska who is destined to win a reputation for herself, that woman is Willa Cather." The *Beatrice Weekly Express* described her as "a young woman who is rapidly achieving a western reputation, and who will soon have a national reputation. She is one of the ablest writers and critics in the country, and she is improving every week" (qtd. in Slote 27).

When she arrived in Pittsburgh, Cather spent several weeks living in the Axtells' home, as an equal, as a guest. James Axtell's wife, Nellie Minor Axtell, had lifelong family connections in Lincoln, where she was a frequent visitor. She was the niece of Nebraska land magnate Rolla O. Phillips, whom Cather also knew. Phillips's Richardsonian Romanesque mansion, "The Castle," with its enormous carriage house, fifteen fireplaces, and third-floor ballroom, is a Lincoln landmark. Writing from Pittsburgh on 13 July 1896, Cather told Mariel Clapham Gere she intended to ask "Captain Phillips" for a personal favor (*Complete Letters* #0026). Cather needed a photo of Mary Baird Bryan for her article "Two Women the World Is Watching." She got it, too, "[f]or," as Cather deadpanned in the article itself, "there is such a thing as society, even in Nebraska" (4–5).

By the time Cather left Red Cloud for Pittsburgh, for France, for New York, for Grand Manan, her experiences had made her far more self-protective, self-possessed, and intellectually fiery than virtually all her hometown friends and readers. Cather feared few things, but as she later confided to Elizabeth Shepley Sergeant, she feared dying in a Nebraska cornfield, under a windmill, where there was no place to hide (Sergeant 49). And yet, in Lincoln, as her *Hesperian* fiction suggests, it appears that Cather was already casting that long look back over her shoulder. She was beginning to render her past. These were heady—but wistful—years for Cather, a time of intense and inescapable social contrasts. It was a time when nostalgia quickened and, in the words of Jim Burden, "I suddenly found myself thinking of the places and people of my own infinitesimal past. They stood out strengthened and simplified now, like the image of the plough against the sun" (*My Ántonia* 262).

In the years to come, Cather would continue to think—and sometimes to write—about her Nebraska home. In 1913 *O Pioneers!*, the book she considered her "real" first novel (actually her second, preceded by *Alexander's Bridge*), was published. Writing the book had engaged her tremendously, "because it had to do with a kind of country I loved" and was "about old neighbors, once very dear." As she wrote the book, she knew that "the novel of the soil" was unfashionable. Remembering a New York critic's comment that "I simply don't give a damn about what happens in Nebraska," she expected that the novel would never be published ("My First Novels" 964).

But it was, to enthusiastic reviews. The *Boston Evening Transcript*, for example, reported "that with *O Pioneers!* Cather introduced a new kind of story and a new part of the country into American fiction, commending especially Cather's disclosure of the splendid resources of the immigrant population and the changing face of the country" (qtd. in Stouck 295–96). Five years later, when *My Ántonia* appeared, reviews were even more enthusiastic, but they did not emphasize the newness of the novel's Nebraska country and characters. Clearly, Cather had already established the muse in her Nebraska home country. According to David Stouck, Cather "had achieved what Virgil wrote of in those lines that she quoted in *My Ántonia*. . . . *O Pioneers!* was certainly the novel in which she first brought the muse into her country" (302). And "her country" included not only the rural, small-town world of Red Cloud and Webster County but also Lincoln and its university, which figure so importantly in *My Ántonia* and *One of Ours*.

Mari Sandoz, Cather's closest literary counterpart, didn't bring the muse to Hay Springs, Nebraska, but what she lacked in sheer artistry she made up for in incendiary bomb–throwing. Her graphic portraits of homesteading in the Nebraska Sandhills exposed the dark cartoons hidden beneath Cather's epic pastoral landscapes. "The underprivileged child," Sandoz later explained, "if he becomes a writer, becomes a writer who is interested in social justice, and destruction of discrimination between economic levels, between nationalist levels, between color levels and so on" (Stauffer, *Mari Sandoz* 5).

Marie Susette Sandoz ("Mari" approximated her family's French pronunciation, MAHR-ree) was born by the Running Water of the Niobrara River to Swiss immigrant Jules Ami Sandoz and his desperately unhappy fourth wife, Mary Fehr Sandoz, both of whom worked their eldest daughter like the hired girl's hired girl from an early age. The head manuscript reader at *McClure's Magazine* once told Edith Lewis that if Willa Cather had been a scrubwoman, she would have scrubbed much harder than all the other scrubwomen (Lewis 30); Mari Sandoz *was* a scrubwoman. She scrubbed floors, sweat-drenched work shirts, greasy iron pots, and a long line of babies. Northwestern Nebraska was arid cattle country, the last region of the state to develop. In 1910 the living conditions in the Panhandle were far more primitive and isolating than Cather's Divide in 1880. At the age of eleven, Mari served as her mother's midwife and helped deliver her sister Flora.

Old Jules Sandoz was a legend among the Kinkaid homesteaders of western Nebraska. Intelligent, foul-tempered, and fearless, Old Jules considered the settlement and development of the Sandhills country his life's mission. Utilizing an early form of chain migration, he was the region's principal land locator, scouting homesteads for late-arriving immigrants. He was the Sandhills' greatest booster and a crack rifleman, famous for taking potshots at his neighbors. When Old Jules served as postmaster, his tumbledown frame house—Mari called it "hot as an iron bucket in the sun"—was the community's central meeting place (*Sandhill Sundays* 8). Old Jules beat all four of his wives, all six of his children, and most of his horses. He was also a master horticulturalist whose vineyards and orchards made the Sandhills bloom. Unlike most of his neighbors, Jules Sandoz had made good friends and hunting partners on the Pine Ridge and Rosebud Reservations. Mari interacted with tribe members from an early age, along with ranchers, farmers, magical water dowsers, traveling musicians, and the state penitentiary parolee her father boarded for cheap labor, despite his prior conviction for "criminal intercourse with a little girl three years old" (*Old Jules* 271).

After supper and dish duty, Old Jules's hungry daughter spent her evenings crouched on a crate behind the woodstove, "story-catching," in her words, her father's tales of range wars, the dispossession of the Cheyenne and the Lakota peoples, and the early settlement of western Nebraska. "In my childhood," she later wrote, "old trappers and Indian traders or their breed descendants still came to visit around our fire on the Niobrara River. . . . The old-timers talked long and late hours about those days and the earlier years" (*Cheyenne Autumn* xi). The oral tradition would figure strongly in all her work. (Interestingly, Cather is said to have hidden under a quilting frame at Willow Shade, listening to her elders and absorbing the material she would later transform into *Sapphira and the Slave Girl* [Lewis 10].)

Mari spoke French and German with her parents until she was finally allowed to attend school at the age of eight. When she was ten, the *Omaha Daily News* published a story she had secretly submitted for its children's page. Her outraged father responded by locking her in the pitch-black cellar with the bull snakes and the mice (Stauffer, *Letters* 135). Mari would prove as indomitable as Old Jules. As she learned to read, Sandoz (like Cather) sought out sympathetic neighbors who were willing to lend her books. She developed a particular fondness for Thomas Hardy. In Hardy, she claimed, she found life as she saw it about her. So life was like that everywhere, she decided, and that was best to know (*Old Jules* 340). "Hardy and [Joseph] Conrad fit the sandhills better than any other writers I know," she later explained. "There is in their work always an overshadowing sense of the futility in life. This is revealed in their novels as it was revealed in the tragic, desperate lives of the settlers whom my father brought to Nebraska" (qtd. in Holtz 41). Sandoz was still in her teens when she began teaching in rural schools, married a local rancher to escape her father's house, and began to write in earnest.

When Mari Sandoz Macumber finally fled the Sandhills for Lincoln in 1919, not long after the publication of Cather's *My Ántonia*, she had no money, no husband (her divorce from Wray Macumber for "extreme mental cruelty" was socially stigmatizing), no introductions, and no connections. Her "drab, mismatched, and often threadbare clothing" immediately signaled her status as an impoverished girl from the outstate (Switzer 111). Worse, her father's reputation for eccentricity, lawsuits, gun violence, and pro-German, antiestablishment, anti-everything statements preceded her. "You know I consider writers and artists the maggots of society," Old Jules informed his daughter in 1926 (qtd. in Stauffer, *Letters* 81). In Lincoln, Sandoz cleaned houses, trained as a stenographer, worked at a local drug company stuffing pill capsules at the rate of twenty-five cents per thousand, took business classes by day, and wrote by night. She was probably exaggerating only slightly when she explained how

Fig. 9.3. Mari Sandoz's parents, Old Jules and Mary Fehr Sandoz. Nebraska State Historical Society Photograph Collections.

she finally enrolled in the university's Teachers College as an "Adult Special": "I came to Lincoln, sat around in the anterooms of various deans for two weeks between conferences with advisors who insisted that I must go to high school. Finally bushy-haired Dean Sealock got tired of me and said, 'Well, you can't do any more than fail—' and registered me" (*Sandhill Sundays* 156).

After Sandoz gate-crashed the university, she quickly excelled. As one of "Lowry Wimberly's Boys," she was in the vanguard of New Regionalism in American literature. Her short story "The Vine" appeared in Wimberly's first issue of *Prairie Schooner*. Louise Pound, by this time one of the nation's most distinguished professors of linguistics and folklore, also recognized Sandoz's intelligence and mentored her raw talent. It was Pound who urged Sandoz not to compromise her authentic western dialect and idioms to suit New York editors. Sandoz's "authenticity," however, did little to advance her career in Lincoln. According to Mari's sister Caroline Sandoz Pifer, Louise Pound introduced Mari "to many fine homes and . . . defend[ed] her right to expression in her own way" (Pifer 62). It didn't work, and the feeling was mutual. "Lincoln treated Mari like a cowgirl in their china shop," Lincoln friend Sally Johnson Ketcham recalled in an interview. "They didn't like her style or her subjects; she was decades ahead of her time."[7]

Influential reporter Eleanor Hinman, to whom Willa Cather granted a rare and lengthy interview in 1921, was a close friend of and advocate for Sandoz. Hinman and Sandoz traveled together frequently, researching Native history, collecting documents, and interviewing tribe members on the Pine Ridge and Rosebud Reservations. Sandoz also attracted the attention of H. L. Mencken, who shared her scorn of the "booboisie," but as the Great Depression deepened and national editorial rejections kept rolling in, Sandoz returned to the Sandhills in despair. Sandoz could be as irascible as Cather. She vented her frustration and bitterness in a 1933 letter to Hinman:

My dear Eleanor:

Will you please go to Hell?

If I'm tired and disgusted and want to lay down with my face in the sand, please remember that sand is plentiful and the face is, after all, mine. . . . I have made no secret of my opinion that Lincoln is the last word in decadent, middle class towns, sterile, deadening. Only by a conscious defensiveness did I exist there at all. While the sandhillers are equally antagonistic to

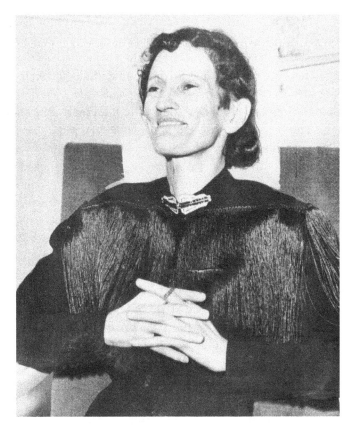

Fig. 9.4. Mari Sandoz as a young writer in Lincoln. Nebraska State Historical Society Photograph Collections.

the creative mind they at least are not superior or patronizing about it; do not set themselves up as beings of supreme culture. They openly consider me an amusing fool but assume no responsibility for my reformation, which, incidentally, is something. (Stauffer, *Letters* 59)

It wasn't long before Sandoz tired of the antagonistic Sandhillers and returned to the antagonistic Lincolnites, determined to write history. Ever the dutiful child, Sandoz wrote *Old Jules*, her breakout biography, only because it was her father's deathbed request. Just before the book's acceptance, but after fourteen rejections, she hauled another seventy manuscripts into the backyard of her fifteen-dollar-a-month Lincoln apartment, dumped them in a washtub, and set them on fire, literally cremating youth (Stauffer, *Sandoz, Story Catcher* 88).

Old Jules was a sensation. "Wouldn't Old Jules snort if he knew that his story won the $5,000 Atlantic Monthly Press prize?" Sandoz wrote to her mother incredulously (Stauffer, *Letters* 84). However, no amount of critical acclaim could persuade many Nebraskans to embrace Sandoz's unpopular, unromantic, and increasingly political stories of pioneer life as she herself had lived it. One sly reviewer of Sandoz's second novel, *Slogum House*, summarized the general objections: "Instead of the usual pious portrait of god-fearing Methodists who voted the Republican ticket straight, and who spent their days plowing the virgin soil and killing grasshoppers, or baking cornbread and rocking the cradle in a glow of self-sacrificial ardor for making the state safe for democracy, Mari Sandoz has given us a family of roaring, bawdy cut-throats whose passionate desire for personal gain, and unscrupulous means of getting it, are only [the] exaggerated overflowing of the uncontrolled red blood that must have run in the veins of many of the men who made our state" (Kauffman). *Slogum House* was censored by the mayor of Omaha, who labeled it "unnecessarily lewd" and "revealingly vulgar" (Woerner). Sandoz's next novel, *Capital City*, exposed O Street corruption, homegrown fascism, back-alley abortion, drug deals, and unjustified police raids on boys who "wore silk panties" (*Capital City* 149). Horrified Lincolnites read it (often correctly) as a roman à clef. Sociologist Michael R. Hill studied and taught the allegorical novel as "a sociologically-grounded thought experiment" (38).

Today Sandoz's astonishing body of work, as meticulously researched as Cather's but with its emphasis on land use, water rights, Native dispossession, women's history, ethnic and minority communities, and the legacy of conquest, reads like some radical precursor of modern New Western historians like Glenda Riley and Patricia Nelson Limerick. Historian Betsy Downey explores this topic in depth in "'She Does Not Write Like a Historian': Mari Sandoz and the Old and New Western History": "When Mari Sandoz's *The Cattlemen* was published in 1958 a reviewer for *The Christian Science Monitor* commented that Sandoz 'does not write like a woman.' He admitted that his observation was 'not all compliment.' Reviewer Horace Reynolds might well have said 'Sandoz does not write like a historian.' Such re-phrasing, with its implications of both compliment and criticism, is a good place to begin examining Sandoz as historian" (9).

Sandoz never fit comfortably into the arena of western writers or western historians. Her writing style was an idiosyncratic hybrid: too florid for history, too staccato for literature. Sandoz's authentic and distinctive western voice set her apart, as did her exhaustive primary research and her attempts to reconstruct Native dialogue and figures of speech. Vine Deloria Jr., author of *Custer Died for Your Sins* and a well-known activist and preeminent member of the Standing Rock Sioux, held Sandoz in the highest regard. Deloria read Sandoz's works after her death, but of *Crazy Horse* he wrote,

> [At first] I was a little offended that a non-Sioux had written a biography of one of the legendary personalities of my tribe. Surely, I thought, she would know little of the nuances of meaning that characterize Indian communities . . . [but] Mari Sandoz had presented a masterful and wholly authentic account of the struggle for the northern plains. . . . I was stunned at the wealth of detail contained in each line of text—material that must have come from her conversations over time with a large number of elders, filed then in some great and efficient memory bank, and later skillfully woven into a chronicle of the times that overflows with authenticity. (Deloria, introduction vi)

Cather and Sandoz never met. In 1931 Sandoz sent a letter to Cather praising *Shadows on the Rock*. "*Shadows on the Rock* becomes a part of the life the reader lives, not for the short span of the reading but for his always. May I thank you for the rare experience?" (Stauffer, *Letters* 27). Cather replied with her standard one-line acknowledgment of the letter's receipt. In 1944 Jean Speiser of *Life* magazine wrote to Cather proposing a joint photo essay based on *My Ántonia* and Red Cloud. Appalled, Cather suggested substituting Sandoz's *Old Jules* and western Nebraska instead. Cather told Carrie Miner Sherwood in November 1944 that the switch would save her embarrassment and would likely please Sandoz who, Cather had heard, was not averse to any amount of personal publicity (*Complete Letters* #1678). Cather's comment wasn't really fair or true. Sandoz was proud, generous, and easily hurt. She wanted what Cather wanted; she wanted recognition.

Although Sandoz considered *Sapphira and the Slave Girl* surprisingly "thin" (Stauffer, *Letters* 180), she revered Cather and her prairie novels, describing Cather's luminous prose as like "sunlight on a swale" (*Love Song* 227). In 1959 Sandoz traveled to Red Cloud, where she met with Mildred Bennett and discussed Bennett's early work on the Willa Cather Pioneer Memorial, calling it "so much more important than anyone but you can see now" (Stauffer, *Letters* 346). Sandoz spent several years working at the Nebraska State Historical Society, preserving and adding research materials to history files ranging from "Bohemians in Nebraska" to the 1819 military post Fort Atkinson.

For Sandoz, recognition arrived with an honorary doctorate from the University of Nebraska in 1950. She went on to win a John Newbery Honor Medal in 1958 and the Western Writers of America's Spur Award in 1963. In 1954 she received the Distinguished Achievement Award of the Native Sons and Daughters of Nebraska. The Mari Sandoz High Plains Heritage Center in Chadron is dedicated to her legacy, and with the publication of the first volume of the Sandoz Studies series (from the University of Nebraska Press, in July 2019), an important reevaluation of her work is underway.

After the publication of *Old Jules*, Sandoz responded to one disoriented reader's question: "Have there been two strikingly different pioneer Nebraskas?" In her response, Sandoz differentiated between the comparatively settled environments of Willa Cather's lyrical prairie novels and the make-or-break frontier farm- and ranchsteads depicted in *Old Jules*. According to one scholar, "The problem [for

Fig. 9.5. Mari Sandoz frequently returned to Lincoln to conduct research at the Nebraska State Historical Society (shown in background). Nebraska State Historical Society Photograph Collections.

pioneers] was what one finds so superbly portrayed in *My Ántonia* and *O Pioneers!*—the problem of adjustment rather than one of staying at all at any price" (Holtz 42). The contrast was particularly stark for those who, like Sandoz and her family, could not afford to leave or were too stubborn to go.

Sandoz's comment still resonates. In *Becoming Willa Cather*, Daryl Palmer considers the importance of Sandy Point, Cather's make-believe town, in the development of her creative and territorial imaginations (20–23). Sandy Point, a place Cather often returned to in her mind, was a tidy, well-ordered country town. It boasted a wide Main Street lined with homes, offices, and shops. Cather served as mayor and news editor. In effect, it was her own personal parish. When Sandoz stood in the doorway of her father's house as a child and surveyed the world beyond the bleak cattle fence, she said she saw Jötunheim, the land of capricious gods and giants: "Out of this almost mythical land, so apparently monotonous, so passionless, came wondrous and fearful tales" (*Sandhill Sundays* 24). To read the works of Cather and Sandoz side by side, especially *My Ántonia* and *Old Jules*, two books that draw on such similar material, is to engage in a tale of two conflicting and conflicted Nebraskas. Each informs and explicates the other. Together they provide human dimension and historical context for Cather's and Sandoz's pivotal years as young, evolving writers, for the Lincoln of their past, and for their strangely parallel yet nonintersecting worlds.

NOTES

1. Ak-Sar-Ben or Aksarben (Nebraska spelled backward), established in 1895 after the devastating economic Panic of 1893, remains one of the state's leading charitable foundations. The organization's annual ball and the crowning of its "royal court" constituted the highlight of the social season.

2. The fifty-five thousand figure is an 1890 U.S. Census estimate.

3. "$350 in 1890 → 2023 | Inflation Calculator," Official Inflation Data, Alioth Finance, 23 November 2023, officialdata.org/us/inflation/1890?amount =350.

4. The 1890 University of Nebraska catalog lists Latin School student Willa Cather's residence as 1618 Washington Street. The new rooming house at that address was home to John Huntington Moore in 1891 and to the Rev. DeWitt Clinton Huntington, future chancellor of Nebraska Wesleyan University, in 1893.

5. In the 1900 U.S. federal census, Jefferson Burns Weston, father of Cather's friend Katherine Weston, employed a full-time domestic servant and a coachman.

6. See Sharon O'Brien's *Willa Cather: The Emerging Voice* for additional context regarding Pound, Cather, and the New Woman movement.

7. Sally Johnson Ketcham, curator of history at the Nebraska State Historical Society (1951–60) and Sandoz were friends and fellow researchers. Along with Louise Pound and Elsie Cather, Ketcham was also a member of

Pound's private professional women's club, the Wooden Spoons, founded by Pound in 1919.

WORKS CITED

Ames, Ernest C. "Postals in Paste." *Daily Nebraskan*, 20 April 1894.

Barrett, Jay Amos. *Nebraska and the Nation*. Ainsworth & Company, 1906.

Bennett, Mildred R. *The World of Willa Cather*. U of Nebraska P, 1961.

Cass, Betty. "Madison Day by Day." *Wisconsin State Journal*, 6 February 1936.

Cather, Willa. *The Complete Letters of Willa Cather*, edited by the Willa Cather Archive team, *Willa Cather Archive*, cather.unl.edu/writings/letters. Accessed December 13, 2020.

———. *My Ántonia*. 1918. Dover Publications, 1994.

———. "My First Novels (There Were Two)." *Willa Cather: Stories, Poems and Other Writings*, Library of America, 1992, pp. 963–65.

———. "Tommy, the Unsentimental." *Home Monthly*, vol. 6, August 1896, pp. 6–7.

———. "Two Women the World Is Watching." *Home Monthly*, vol. 6, September 1896, pp. 4–5.

Deloria, Vine, Jr. *Custer Died for Your Sins: An Indian Manifesto*. New preface, U of Oklahoma P, 1988.

———. Introduction to *Crazy Horse: The Strange Man of the Oglalas: A Biography*, by Mari Sandoz, 3rd ed., U of Nebraska P, 2008.

Downey, Betsy. "'She Does Not Write Like a Historian': Mari Sandoz and the Old and New Western History." *Great Plains Quarterly*, vol. 16, no. 1, Winter 1996, pp. 9–28, jstor.org/stable/23531730.

Hill, Michael R. "Novels, Thought Experiments, and Humanist Sociology in the Classroom: Mari Sandoz and 'Capital City.'" *Teaching Sociology*, vol. 15, no. 1, 1987, p. 38, doi.org/10.2307/1317816.

Holtz, Dan. "The Pioneer in Bess Streeter Aldrich, Willa Cather, and Mari Sandoz." *Heritage of the Great Plains*, vol. 45, nos. 1–2, 2012–13, pp. 38–47, esirc.emporia.edu.

Hoover, Sharon, and L. Brent Bohlke. *Willa Cather Remembered*. U of Nebraska P, 2003.

Kauffman, Bernice. "Browsing among the Books." *Daily Nebraskan*, 7 December 1937.

Ketcham, Sally Johnson. Personal interview. November 2020.

Krohn, Marie. *Louise Pound: The 19th Century Iconoclast Who Forever Changed America's Views about Women, Academics, and Sports*. American Legacy Historical Press, 2008.

Lee, Hermione. *Willa Cather: Double Lives*. Vintage, 2017.

Lewis, Edith. *Willa Cather Living*. Knopf, 1953.

Luebke, Frederick C. *Nebraska: An Illustrated History*. U of Nebraska P, 1995.

Mahoney, Timothy R. *Gilded Age Plains City: The Great Sheedy Murder Trial and the Booster Ethos of Lincoln, Nebraska*. U of Nebraska–Lincoln, 2007, gildedage.unl.edu/.

Manley, Robert N. *Centennial History of the University of Nebraska*. U of Nebraska P, 1969.

"The Modern Woodmen." *Red Cloud Chief*, 18 May 1888, p. 1.

O'Brien, Sharon. *Willa Cather: The Emerging Voice*. Oxford UP, 1987.

Olson, James C. *History of Nebraska*. U of Nebraska P, 1955.

Palmer, Daryl W. *Becoming Willa Cather: Creation and Career*. U of Nevada P, 2019.

Pifer, Caroline Sandoz. *Making of an Author*. Gordon Journal, 1972.

Sandoz, Mari. *Capital City*. 1939. U of Nebraska P, 2007.

———. *Cheyenne Autumn*. 1953. Introduced by Alan Boye, U of Nebraska P, 2005.

———. *Love Song to the Plains*. 1961. U of Nebraska P, 1967.

———. *Old Jules*. U of Nebraska P, 1935.

———. *Sandhill Sundays and Other Recollections*. U of Nebraska P, 1966.

Semi-Centennial Anniversary Book, 1869–1919. U of Nebraska, 1919.

Sergeant, Elizabeth Shepley. *Willa Cather: A Memoir*. J. B. Lippincott, 1953.

Shively, James R. *Writings from Willa Cather's Campus Years*. U of Nebraska P, 1950.

Slote, Bernice. *The Kingdom of Art: Willa Cather's First Principles and Critical Statements, 1893–1896*. U of Nebraska P, 1967.

Squire, Kelsey. "Legacy and Conflict: Willa Cather and the Spirit of the Western University." *Great Plains Quarterly*, vol. 34, no. 3, 2014, pp. 239–56, doi.org/10.1353/gpq.2014.0058.

Stauffer, Helen Winter, editor. *Letters of Mari Sandoz*. U of Nebraska P, 1992.

———. *Mari Sandoz*. Boise State U, 1984.

———. *Mari Sandoz, Story Catcher of the Plains*. U of Nebraska P, 1982.

Stouck, David. Historical essay to *O Pioneers!* by Willa Cather. Willa Cather Scholarly Edition, edited by Susan J. Rosowski and Charles W. Mignon with Kathleen Danker, U of Nebraska P, 1992, pp. 183–303.

Switzer, Dorothy Nott. "Mari Sandoz's Lincoln Years: A Personal Reflection." *Prairie Schooner*, vol. 45, no. 2, Summer 1971, pp. 107–15.

Woerner, Otto. "Browsing among the Books." *Daily Nebraskan*, 4 February 1938, p. 2.

Woodress, James. *Willa Cather: A Literary Life*. U of Nebraska P, 1987.

Wyman, Marjorie. "Willa Cather, Novelist, Was Modern Flapper at Nebraska U, 30 Years Ago." *Lincoln Sunday Star*, 29 June 1924.

10 "Blue Sky, Blue Eyes"
Unsettling Multilingualism in *My Ántonia*

ANDREW P. WU

Language was like clothes; it could be a help to one, or it could give one away.

—Willa Cather, *The Song of the Lark*

Multilingualism emerges as a robust and vibrant theme from the very beginning of *My Ántonia* (1918): the highly visible and eye-catching diacritical-capped *Á* of the title; the Latin epigraph from Virgil's *Georgics* that precedes the novel's introduction ("*Optima dies ... prima fugit*" [iii]); the authorial footnote in the first line of the first chapter, preempting unfamiliarity and intervening to govern the pronunciation of "Ań-ton-ee-ah"(3). Jim Burden's first memory of his journey from Virginia to Nebraska involves a conductor with "cuff-buttons engraved with hieroglyphics" and who is "more inscribed than an Egyptian obelisk" (4). The first line of direct speech Jim recounts is a comment on multilingualism: the conductor tells Jim that "[t]hey can't any of them speak English, except one little girl [Ántonia], and all she can say is 'We go Black Hawk, Nebraska'" (4). From the reader's very first encounters with the novel, we find ourselves in a material and narrative environment permeated by language diversity.

The first sample of speech Jim provides is especially illuminating. To the young Jim at the beginning of his journey west, this worldly and sophisticated conductor, traversing the separate train cars that segregate recent European immigrants from native-born and assimilated Americans, is an observer and arbiter of language. The passage affirms (American) English as the norming linguistic standard from the beginning of Jim and Ántonia's shared journey, showcases Jim's (and Cather's) precise and subtle ear for dialect, and implicitly demonstrates how using and deciphering language simultaneously reveals and indexes social identities. After all, while pronouncing the immigrants' English as lacking—"They can't any of them speak English" (4)—the conductor also inadvertently reveals that his own variety of spoken English might also be considered dialectal and nonstandard.

Multilingualism—as a construct itself—resists any simple or flat definitions. Epistemological problems for language and human diversity per se notwithstanding, the processes involved with recognizing and categorizing named languages have always been fraught with problems concerning language standardization and intralingual, interpersonal complexity. And yet, observations, opinions, and experiences of language diversity are prevalent in almost all social groups, communities, and societies. As individuals, we are deftly attuned to recognize and adjust to differences in linguistic codes, interactional norms, discursive abilities, and communicative styles. We learn and adapt quickly according to our circumstances. We inherit and develop ideas, assumptions, and interpretations toward others' communicative practices as part and parcel of our social life. As such, any specific observations about multilingualism necessarily depend upon dynamic analytical frameworks—whether academic or not, codified or not—that delimit our views and experiences of language, culture, and society.

Like her narrator Jim Burden, Cather was dislocated from Virginia and subsequently grew up in a cosmopolitan, multilingual Nebraska.

In a 1913 interview with the *Philadelphia Record*, she recounts her early years: "We had very few American neighbors—they were mostly Swedes and Danes, Norwegians and Bohemians.... Even when they spoke very little English, the old women somehow managed to tell me a great many stories about the old country" (F.H.). Situations where different named languages and dialects coexist in a shared context permeate Cather's work and life: Thea Kronborg masters the languages of Western opera, Archbishop Jean Marie Latour experiences and contemplates Native American languages of the Southwest, and Cather herself, like Jim Burden, studied Latin and Greek. Cather also taught high school Latin and was well read in French. And yet, Cather's multilingualism is much more complex than a cluster of named languages. As the opening passages of *My Ántonia* demonstrate, Cather had a keen ear for language diversity and wove it into her fiction in numerous ways. In this chapter I use the word *multilingualism* in broad senses: multilingualism can be observed within individual characters, such as in Ántonia's Bohemian language and American English or Jim's learning of Latin and Greek; it can be observed between characters in discourse, such as when the Burdens visit the Shimerdas or when Mr. Shimerda, Ántonia, and Jim visit the Russians; it exists as a material fact within the manuscript, such as the juxtapositions of the Latin Virgilian epigraph against English and other languages; it is presented through characters' eye-dialect (deliberate nonstandard spellings or usage to emphasize phonological, syntactic, or social difference), such as in the direct speech of Ántonia, "Blind d'Arnault," or even the train conductor. Finally, encapsulating these senses above, multilingualism might also be extended and interpreted in Bakhtinian *heteroglossia* terms, such as how Jim Burden's narrative voice and Cather's authorial voice are inherently merged from the novel's onset, how Ántonia adopts momentarily, for her narrative purposes, specific characteristics of the suicidal tramp's speech, or how Ántonia and Lena Lingard, though both immigrants, are presented differently in terms of their language proficiencies and developments. To this end, multilingualism can go beyond just the purely linguistic and extend to all aspects of the novel as discourse. Cather as author transfixes and deploys different forms and levels of multilingualism to engage her readership. Taking those together, I adopt for analytical purposes an ecological view of language and language diversity, treating multilingualism as a series of nested, interwoven, and interdependent levels of systems that are complex, adaptive, dynamic, and inseparable from the communities from which representations of multilingualism are configured.

First proposed by Einar Haugen in 1972, the concept of language ecologies adopts an extended metaphor from biology, treating languages as living species that live, grow, interact, change, evolve, and diminish, all through interactions among each other and with the environment. Analyzed as both psychological and sociological, language ecologies have become a useful approach in considering how languages are perceived and managed within a given context. One way to start is by identifying the named languages within a given context. The language ecology of *My Ántonia* in this view involves at least ten languages or dialects: (American) English, Bohemian, Russian, Norwegian, German, Black American Vernacular English (Ebonics), Italian, French, Latin, and Greek, as well as even Egyptian hieroglyphs and Hebrew. Also, within and between these language varieties, a conceptual framework that can be used to interpret language ecologies is Nancy Hornberger's Continua of Biliteracy. The full framework is often used to analyze language policies and is beyond the scope of this chapter, but an important tenet of the framework is to treat contact between language varieties as points on a series of intersecting continua along the domains of language contexts, development, contact, and media. Through juxtaposition and accumulating examples, we can glean attitudes and ideologies involving multilingualism more generally as well as the relationships between specific languages, ultimately drawing conclusions about the language ecology as experienced by members of the language user groups.

Returning to the novel's opening scene, we see that Jim tightly weaves the Shimerdas' lack of English with a common association between foreignness and suspicion or discrimination. Declining the conductor's suggestion to visit the immigrant train car, Jim retreats into his familiar *Life of Jesse James* (a quintessentially "American" dime novel likely written in colloquial American English), and his guardian Jake Marpole comments "approvingly" that "you were likely to get diseases from foreigners" (5). However, upon arrival in Nebraska, Jim is immediately drawn to the immigrant family's speech by a sense of novelty rather than fear: "I pricked up my ears, for it was positively the first time I had ever heard a foreign tongue" (6). As the narrative unfolds, it is clear that Jim's ears remain ever vigilant and attentive, and his prose reflects these perceptions, weaving together a rich tapestry of discursive interactions from his memories.

Before Jim recounts his first visit to the Shimerdas, he recalls an observation that suggests precisely how multilingualism is not just perceptions but has very tangible material consequences. On one hand, the Shimerdas must tolerate the mendacity of Peter Krajiek, a duplicitous fellow Bohemian immigrant who swindles them, simply because he is more proficient in English. On the other hand, however, Jim suggests that a possible remedy to this problem can also be solved through multilingualism: Austrian immigrant Otto Fuchs, who retains an "awkward" grasp of his native German (82), remarks that Mr. Shimerda knows some German and could potentially bypass Krajiek—but for the "natural distrust" Bohemians bear toward Austrians (19–20). Jim's observations underscore how multilingualism moves beyond the abstract, arbitrary, and prescriptive sets of rules by which learners are measured and "standard" native speakers are imagined. Multilingualism necessarily adapts to the social and interactional needs of the specific situation in context, and it evolves as moments unfold and accumulate toward more complex understandings of human interactions.

The first time Jim officially meets Ántonia and her family is a careful and considered example of multilingualism at work. Even with limited proficiency, Mrs. Shimerda's energetic speech manages to convey the desperation of her circumstances: "Very glad, very glad!" (21), "House no good, house no good!" (22), "Much good, much thank!" (22). Jim also observes how his grandmother, on her part, "always spoke in a very loud tone to foreigners, as if they were deaf" (22), highlighting again how foreignness is often instinctively perceived as Other and deficient. The first explicit act of interlingual translation occurs during this visit, when Mrs. Shimerda asks Krajiek to interpret for her in an attempt to quell any apprehensions about her disabled son Marek and to praise her older, favored boy Ambrosch (23). These interactions set the stage for a distinct contrast to Ántonia's first interaction with Jim. While Ántonia shares her mother's impulsiveness and voraciousness, she is unlike her mother in other important facets of temperament. Ántonia is joyous, intuitive, curious, and generous. She immediately starts to build interpersonal connections through a shared appreciation of nature, manifesting her eagerness to absorb the local language. As Jim recalls,

> Ántonia pointed up to the sky and questioned me with her glance. I gave her the word, but she was not satisfied and pointed to my eyes. I told her, and she repeated the word, making it sound like "ice." She pointed up to the sky, then to my eyes, then back to the sky, with movements so quick and impulsive that she distracted me, and I had no idea what she wanted. She got up on her knees and wrung her hands. She pointed to her own eyes and shook her head, then to mine and to the sky, nodding violently.
> "Oh," I exclaimed, "blue; blue sky."
> She clapped her hands and murmured, "Blue sky, blue eyes," as if it amused her. While we snuggled down there out of the wind she learned a score of words. She was quick, and very eager. (25–26)

This passage, delineating the start of Jim and Ántonia's lifelong friendship, illustrates an important insight into multilingualism: some named languages may be more dominant, but imbalances need not be barriers. Experience and meaning remain constantly negotiated and co-constructed through shared interaction. Ántonia instinctively focuses on nature to transcend linguistic barriers, highlighting her eagerness to engage with and integrate herself into her new country, and as such, by the end of this interaction, her English has already progressed far beyond the likely memorized chunk "We go Black Hawk, Nebraska" (4). Ántonia has already begun to demonstrate and develop her unique voice, co-creating with Jim the multilingual narratives of their lives. And although Mr. Shimerda inaugurates this process formally by handing Jim's grandmother a bilingual primer and pleading, "Te-e-ach, te-e-ach my Án-tonia!" (27), Ántonia's absorption of English seems to come about less through book-learning than through social practice in a community of multiple languages and dialects.

With help from Jim, Ántonia's English continues to develop. Her eagerness to communicate, buoyed by practical support, accelerates her learning. In a matter of a few short months, Ántonia has become capable of delivering substantial pieces of discourse, for example: "My papa find friends up north, with Russian mans. Last night he take me for see, and I can understand very much talk. Nice mans, Mrs. Burden. One is fat and all the time laugh. Everybody laugh. The first time I see my papa laugh in this kawn-tree. Oh, very nice!" (31–32). From a linguistic development perspective, Jim's/Cather's eye-dialect of an English learner is spot on: the overgeneralization of plural nouns, the not fully mastered subject-verb agreement and verb tenses, and the occasional pronunciation variation all reflect substantial, realistic progress. However, the effects of depicting Ántonia's language development move beyond the orthography of the eye-dialect; her singular, gregarious character continues to stand out, and the vivid details of her memory, her self-expression, and her care for her father continue to bridge the foreign and the familiar. Soon afterward, Ántonia is able to interpret for Jim, which in turn helps to build Jim's relationships with the Russians and Mr. Shimerda: "My *tatinek* say when you are big boy, he give you his gun," Ántonia interprets, as her father speaks to Jim with a "far-away look." "Very fine, from Bohemie. It was belong to a great man, very rich, like what you not got here; many fields, many forests, many big house. My papa play for his wedding, and he give my papa fine gun, and my papa give you" (40). In contrast to the more conventional use of eye-dialect in literature to encase characters in stereotype, Cather's depictions of Ántonia's evolving skills continue to showcase her unique character. Ántonia does not just assimilate into American society; she plays a vital role in how this community of multilingualism, formed in the New World, forges shared connections with the Old.

As the novel progresses, these connections are continuously changing and becoming more complex. As Jim and Ántonia's friendship deepens, they continue to explore the New World, but this does not mean that conflicting ideologies about language and identity disappear. A contentious moment emerges during the snake crisis, after a terrified Ántonia shouts at Jim in Bohemian, frightened by the rattler. Jim's accusatory "What did you jabber Bohunk for?" (44) underscores a realistic point: that their default languages, the ones they use by instinct, are still different. Jim's impulsive, annoyed reaction here calls attention to how English, the lingua franca, is favored and dominant in their relationship and how Ántonia's native Bohemian is still stereotyped negatively (the term *Bohunk* is derogatory), judged as Other and a stumbling block when communication breaks down.

Most of the time, though, multilingualism creates synergy, and one of the most prominent examples can be found in the story of Peter and Pavel. The horrific tale of the wedding party is unburdened by Pavel in a variety of Russian "not very different from Bohemian" (33), interpreted by Ántonia, and finally set onto the page by Jim. Moving away for a short while from direct speech and eye-dialect, Cather uses her text to demonstrate how, in America, diverse repertoires of language resources (Russian, Bohemian/Czech, English) are pooled together to reinterpret and co-construct meaning and memory in the standard English of her unfurnished style. By filtering the story through these multiple languages, Cather evokes the immigrants' history and experiences of the Old World as haunted and tragic, distant and fading. Jim concludes his retelling by fusing these received memories of the Old World with his own in the New: "At night, before I went to sleep, I often found myself in a sledge drawn by three horses, dashing through a country that looked something like Nebraska and something like Virginia" (59). These connections are achieved only through the shared multilingualism of Jim, Ántonia, and her fellow immigrants.

Thus far, Ántonia's English development has enabled Jim to connect with the Old World, but over time Ántonia becomes more and more capable, and Cather's eye-dialect demonstrates how Ántonia also becomes capable of reinterpreting her own experiences in America—in English. In about three years, by the time she is working for the Harlings, Ántonia's multilingualism is so versatile that she can overtake the narration, if only briefly. Jim/Cather uses Ántonia's own voice in full to retell the story of the tramp's suicide, quoted here in part:

> "He comes right up and begins to talk like he knows me already. He says: 'The ponds in this country is done got so low a man could n't drownd himself in one of 'em.'
>
> "I told him nobody wanted to drownd themselves, but if we did n't have rain soon we'd have to pump water for the cattle.
>
> "'Oh, cattle,' he says, 'you'll all take care of your cattle! Ain't you got no beer here?' I told him he'd have to go to the Bohemians for beer; the Norwegians did n't have none when they thrashed. 'My God!' he says, 'so it's Norwegians now, is it? I thought this was Americy.'" (172)

Even in this short excerpt, it is clear that Ántonia's English is now so proficient that she presents very few nonstandard markers of her own. What is even more impressive (and realistic) is how she is now able to perform the nonstandard linguistic features of others, in this case the tramp's. Her imitation of the tramp's use of "drownd" and "Americy" is not only perceptive and handsome storytelling, it unsettles commonly held expectations and stereotypes. Specifically, the tramp's comment about immigrants allows Ántonia's audience to read him as "American" (like the Burdens and Harlings), but simultaneously, by way of Ántonia's linguistic mimicry, it is the tramp, not Ántonia, who is presented as Other. This reversal highlights further not only Ántonia's linguistic and narrative skills but also her strong metalinguistic knowledge gleaned from experiences in her adopted country. This example of multilingualism draws a contrast to Jim's retelling of the Russians' story, which emerges from Ántonia's translations but relegates her narrative role to the background. Here Ántonia's first-person narration, delivered with full fluency, is jarring, immediate, and vital. As such, Cather demonstrates how multilingual development repositions, reshapes, and even transforms the nuances of social identities.

As Ántonia's English development reaches this pinnacle, Jim's narration gradually shifts in focus, and as Ántonia and Jim's lives begin to further diverge, the text also carves out a different pattern of individual multilingualism. Ántonia, an eastern European immigrant, is of the lower working class and cannot receive formal schooling, but she is compelled by her circumstances to move beyond her native Bohemian to develop English as a second language. Her progression exemplifies what sociolinguists sometimes term "folk bilingualism"; Jim, an American by birth, is of a higher social class and able to pursue formal and higher education, thus achieving literacy in English, Latin, and Greek. It is from here that the Virgil epigraph of the novel emerges. Jim's development is what is termed, by contrast, "elite bilingualism." Each of their paths is well traveled in U.S. history, and Cather's novel marshals both and juxtaposes them to depict a vision of a multilingual, transnational America.

After Jim leaves to start his university education, his depictions of multilingualism move away from eye-dialect and become more descriptive and literary. Jim recalls how he studies Latin with Gaston Cleric and works on his Greek—a period of personal intellectual enlightenment. Jim recounts several aspects of Cleric's erudition and temperament, including how they discuss Dante and Virgil, yet curiously, while Jim goes into considerable detail about the manner and style of Cleric's speech, Cleric barely has any direct speech in the novel. The multilingualism Jim shares with Cleric, as well as the reader's experience of multilingualism, are distinctly different here from what Jim shares and depicts with Ántonia. The two men meet on the page through literary languages, and it is here that Jim translates the Virgilian epigraph, that "the best days are the first to flee" (256). This newly developed repertoire allows Jim to more fully reinterpret the memories of his childhood. What Cather achieves here is a continuation of how she builds connections from the New World to the Old—in this case, through the inheritance of literary multilingualism, which simultaneously contrasts with the immigrants' lived experiences and lends mythical weight to them.

The one character who bridges these two types of multilingualism is Lena Lingard. Just as Ántonia's multilingualism helps Jim form connections with the Russians and the Shimerdas, Lena's multilingualism allows Jim to gain insight into Ole Benson, who is known generally for not conversing much but would speak in Norwegian to Lena (273–74). Like Ántonia, Lena comes from an immigrant farming family and arrives in town as a "hired girl" to work. She also arrived in America as a young girl and had to learn English. However, unlike Ántonia, Lena Lingard appears in the novel fully proficient in English. One might argue that perhaps this is due to Lena being slightly older than Ántonia or because she is set to work in a shop rather than a household (which would suggest that she interacts with many more people and is required to adapt faster), but from the day Lena arrives in town, her English is portrayed as indistinguishable from that of nonimmigrants. Furthermore, nearly all the other immigrant characters present eye-dialect features in their speech, even if they are proficient. Lena's direct speech never shows markers of eye-dialect, even in Jim's retrospective descriptions of their earlier years. This is also not because Cather never depicts a Scandinavian accent (she does for Mrs. Lee, Lou Bergson's mother-in-law in *O Pioneers!*, for example). It is perhaps a conscious narrative choice to idealize Lena in a different way from Ántonia. Lena is the childhood friend with whom Jim shares high culture; they go to the theater together, and Jim is affected by Lena's responses. Also, after Lena's visit to Jim's residence, he finds himself revisualizing Lena in one of his old erotic dreams, now reinterpreted and captioned with "the mournful line: *Optima dies . . . prima fugit*" (262). Experiences and memories of Lena prompt Jim to synthesize his childhood and young adult experiences.

Furthermore, while Lena's English never shows eye-dialect markers, Jim devotes an entire paragraph to parsing the appealing blend of foreignness and conventionality in her speech:

> Lena's talk always amused me. Ántonia had never talked like the people about her. Even after she learned to speak English readily, there was always something impulsive and foreign in her speech. But Lena had picked up all the conventional expressions she heard at Mrs. Thomas's dressmaking shop. Those formal phrases, the very flower of small-town proprieties, and the flat commonplaces, nearly all hypocritical in their origin, became very funny, very engaging, when they were uttered in Lena's soft voice, with her caressing intonation and arch naïveté. Nothing could be more diverting than to hear Lena, who was almost as candid as Nature, call a leg a "limb" or a house a "home." (272–73)

It is therefore precisely through comparative observations of Ántonia's and Lena's multilingual experiences that Jim appreciates both the diversity of his childhood community and both characters' unique characteristics. By thinking and writing in these heteroglossic ways, Cather (by way of Jim) continues to deepen and complexify a shared history, at once making the novel a unique achievement of (language) diversity in Nebraska as well as an emblem of American social life, an idealized nation-state that easily shifts between the rural and the urban, farming/working-class experiences and academic/high cultures, the New World and the Old.

My Ántonia celebrates nature, diversity, and change, which makes it an apt subject on which to apply the concept of language ecologies. As with any biological ecology, the lives and rhythms of a language ecology are neither static nor linear. Individuals' and groups' language use is constantly subject to change, and successive generations become part of the ecology by experiencing their own development and learning. Jim's memories of his first visit with Ántonia's family after being many years apart depict these changes with subtlety and beauty.

By the time Jim reunites with Ántonia two decades later, she is married to a Bohemian named Anton Cuzak and has a large family. Jim arrives at their home and hears, in a callback to the opening train station scene, the sounds of children speaking "in a language I had not heard for a long while" (319). The Cuzak family speaks Czech among themselves, but this time around, Jim's narration highlights familiarity, not strangeness. What is also different is how the English direct speech of all the Cuzak children is not in eye-dialect but standard—this is a new generation of children raised and going to school in America. The multilingualism here, if only briefly, appears to value both Czech and English equally. It is a picture of America that can be interpreted as more integrated and equal, or perhaps as a relic of a particular time and place that is quickly fading. In an emphasis of this latter interpretation, we encounter an older Ántonia at a further stage of her language development, such that even as the names of their shared past are revived, the English context of those names is gradually fading. Ántonia introduces her daughter to Jim:

> "She's Nina, after Nina Harling," Ántonia explained. "Ain't her eyes like Nina's? I declare, Jim, I loved you children almost as much as I love my own. These children know all about you and Charley and Sally, like as if they'd grown up with you. I can't think of what I want to say, you've got me so stirred up. And then, I've forgot my English so. I don't often talk it any more. I tell the children I used to speak real well." She said they always spoke Bohemian at home. The little ones could not speak English at all—didn't learn it until they went to school. (324)

The return of slightly nonstandard usage such as "I've forgot" and "I don't often talk it [English]," paired with Ántonia's own reflection on how her English has faded due to lack of use, highlights how multilingualism (from both individual and collective perspectives) is context dependent, dynamic, adaptive, and therefore nonlinear. Varieties gain or lose prominence; they grow, evolve, and diminish; they move along various continua. And yet, there is a shared history that has been shaped by what came before. Jim presents Ántonia and her family now not as othered, as when they were children, but as just as American as himself, to the point where he even claims shared heritage of the family's language and culture:

> "Show him the spiced plums, mother. Americans don't have those," said one of the older boys. "Mother uses them to make *kolaches*," he added.
> Leo, in a low voice, tossed off some scornful remark in Bohemian.
> I turned to him. "You think I don't know what *kolaches* are, eh? You're mistaken, young man. I've eaten your mother's *kolaches* long before that Easter day when you were born." (328)

According to the *Oxford English Dictionary* and the *Dictionary of American Regional English*, these direct, translingual uses of the word *kolaches* demarcate the introduction of the word *kolach* or *kolache* into the English language (Jewell 72–73). Earlier, in *O Pioneers!* (1913), Cather uses a more generalized description for the *kolaches*: Marie Shabata presents "a pan of delicate little rolls, stuffed with stewed apricots, and began to dust them over with powdered sugar" (175). Since Cather adopts the original Czech word, without explanation, in *My Ántonia*, we might say that the language ecologies of which Cather and her readers are a part have evolved as well. Cather implicitly advocates for a cosmopolitan, multicultural America in which multilingualism is commonplace—not a society in which everything becomes "Americanized."

Cather's multilingualism developed over time. Her first published work of fiction, "Peter" (1892), a prototype story for *My Ántonia*, opens with the conversation of a father-son immigrant duo. Cather chooses a register of English that evokes the style of the King James Bible to stand in for the foreign language, differentiating the code by suggesting that the immigrants' speech is "older": "No, Antone, I have told thee many times, no, thou shalt not sell [the old fiddle] until I am gone." Before Peter commits suicide, Cather's narration tells us that he "said brokenly all the Latin he had ever known, 'Pater noster, qui in coelum est.'" In "Peter," Cather does not yet present the subtle, mature forms of eye-dialect of *My Ántonia*, but her heightened register for foreign language and the Latin prayer quote, like her depictions in *My Ántonia*, already suggest the dignity and cultivation of American immigrants from the Old World.

In *The Song of the Lark* (1915), the novel directly preceding *My Ántonia*, Cather (while still not using much eye-dialect), presents language diversity by juxtaposing English with other languages in direct speech, as in the character of Professor Wunsch. According to the *Oxford English Dictionary*, the year 1916, during which Cather first wrote to her brother Roscoe about her idea for *My Ántonia*, was also the year when the word *multilingualism* first appeared in print. The historical context therefore aligns with Cather's developments in multilingualism in her fiction. In the midst of a world war, when foreign language education policies were a hot topic for national debate and anti-immigrant sentiments were on the rise, *My Ántonia*, with its eye-dialect and direct borrowing of *kolaches*, is Cather's multilingual argument for presence and diversity, an adamant rebuke of the contemporary "Americanization" debate.[1]

As Cather's career progressed, her uses of multilingualism continued to evolve. In "Neighbour Rosicky" (1930/1932), a work that can be read as a "sequel" to *My Ántonia*, Anton Rosicky emerges from the outset as someone fluent in English, but his speech is presented in eye-dialect throughout the story: "So? No, I guess my heart was always pretty good. I got a little asthma, maybe. Just a awful short breath when I was pitchin' hay last summer, dat's all" (7). The purpose of the eye-dialect is not to stereotype but to add depth and uniqueness to his character. Furthermore, presented with the same dignity and respect for the immigrant pioneers of the prairie as in *My Ántonia*, "Neighbour Rosicky" takes multilingualism in America further still. Rudolph, Anton's son, marries an "American girl," Polly, who does not speak the Czech family language. Despite Rosicky's best efforts to embrace and include Polly in family rituals (Cather's narration highlights how Rosicky actively chooses English over Czech in storytelling, for example), the conclusion of the novella leaves behind both grief and foreboding. Anton Rosicky, of the pioneer generation, does not live long enough to pass on the family language and culture to his unborn grandchild. His son Rudolph appears progressively distant from his inherited language and culture, with the lingering possibility of seeking a more modern, industrial, and urban (read, in part, "Americanized") future for his family—a transition of which Rosicky would disapprove. At this level of analysis, Cather's multilingualism changes from active to diminished presence. And though this image of American multiculturalism is still presented as poised, subtle, beautiful, and nostalgic, it evolves with time, from hopeful to apprehensive.

Multilingualism stays in Cather's work till the end of her life and career. Having mastered her particular brand of eye-dialect, Cather reaches further back into her childhood past and writes *Sapphira and the Slave Girl* (1940), her last novel, applying her keen dialectal ear once more to present unique voices and distinct registers in the Black American Vernacular English of late nineteenth-century Virginia. Unlike the mostly satirizing Mark Twain, the documentation-oriented William Dean Howells, or the more cryptic William Faulkner, Cather, under the judgment of Toni Morrison's *Playing in the Dark*, demonstrates "urgency and anxiety in [her] rendering of black characters" (14). In her problematizing of critical consensus surrounding *Sapphira and the Slave Girl*, Morrison concludes that "Cather returns to a very personal, indeed private experience. . . . [She] works out and toward the meaning of female betrayal as it faces the void of racism. She may not have arrived safely, like Nancy, but to her credit she did undertake the dangerous journey" (28). Part of why Morrison experiences Cather's "urgency" and gives her credit for her undertaking, I suspect, is Cather's mature and deft use of eye-dialect, her rendering of the subtleties in language diversity inherent in regional and Black American English.

In "The Novel Démeublé" (1922), Cather's treatise on fiction writing, she opens by claiming that "we take it for granted whoever can observe, and can write the English language, can write a novel. Often the latter qualification is considered unnecessary" (5). Farther down, she famously writes, "Whatever is felt upon the page without being specifically named there—that, it seems to me, is created. It is the inexplicable presence of the thing not named, of the overtone divined by the ear but not heard by it, the verbal mood, the emotional aura of the fact or the thing or the deed, that gives high quality to the novel or the drama, as well as to poetry itself" (6). The distinctly musical language and the extralinguistic descriptors Cather uses here are well suited to conclude this brief unsettling of her multilingualism. As Cather continued to adapt to a rapidly changing America and a world torn apart by war, she continuously expanded and refined her presentations of the diverse language ecologies that made up her world. The effects of these presentations of multilingualism, both as concretely named and depicted language varieties and as deftly rendered eye-dialect, can be "felt upon the page," as the "over-tone divined by the ear," creating "the verbal mood" and "the emotional aura" (6). These effects, like all effects of discourse, are not readily summarized but must be experienced through accumulation over time. As Cather reached further and further back into her own life, as she moved through a diversity of cultures and language variations in her life and career, she continued to marshal her own brand of multilingualism as a means to review, refine, and reimagine "the precious, the incommunicable past" (360).

NOTES

1. For an in-depth analysis, see the chapter on Americanization in Guy Reynolds's book *Willa Cather in Context*, pp. 73–98.

WORKS CITED

Cather, Willa. *My Ántonia*. 1918. Willa Cather Scholarly Edition, edited by Charles Mignon and Kari Ronning, historical essay and explanatory notes by James Woodress with Kari Ronning, Kathleen Danker, and Emily Levine, U of Nebraska P, 1994.

———. "Neighbour Rosicky." *Obscure Destinies*. 1932. Willa Cather Scholarly Edition, historical essay and explanatory notes by Kari A. Ronning, textual essay by Frederick M. Link with Kari A. Ronning and Mark Kamrath, U of Nebraska P, 1998, pp. 1–62.

———. "The Novel Démeublé." *New Republic*, 12 April 1922, *Willa Cather Archive*, cather.unl.edu/writings/nonfiction/nf012. Accessed 7 July 2021.

———. "Peter." *The Hesperian*, 24 November 1892, *Willa Cather Archive*, cather.unl.edu/writings/shortfiction/ss019. Accessed 7 July 2021.

———. *Sapphira and the Slave Girl*. 1940. Willa Cather Scholarly Edition, historical essay and explanatory notes by Ann Romines, textual essay and editing by Charles W. Mignon, Kari A. Ronning, and Frederick M. Link, U of Nebraska P, 2009.

———. *The Song of the Lark*. 1915. Willa Cather Scholarly Edition, historical essay and explanatory notes by Ann Moseley, textual essay and editing by Kari A. Ronning, U of Nebraska P, 2012.

F.H. "Willa Cather Talks of Work." *Philadelphia Record*, 10 August 1913, *Willa Cather Archive*, cather.unl.edu/writings/bohlke/interviews/bohlke.i.05. Accessed 7 July 2021.

Haugen, Einar. "The Ecology of Language." *The Ecology of Language: Essays*, edited by Anwar S. Dil, Stanford UP, 1972, pp. 325–39.

Hornberger, Nancy N. "Continua of Biliteracy." *Continua of Biliteracy: An Ecological Framework for Educational Policy, Research, and Practice in Multilingual Settings*, edited by Nancy H. Hornberger, Multilingual Matters, 2003, pp. 3–34.

Jewell, Andrew. "'A Crime Against Art': *My Ántonia*, Food, and Cather's Anti-Americanization Argument." *Willa Cather Newsletter and Review*, vol. 54, no. 2, 2010, pp. 72–76.

Morrison, Toni. *Playing in the Dark: Whiteness and the Literary Imagination*. Harvard UP, 1992.

"Multilingualism." *Oxford English Dictionary Online*, Oxford UP, 2021, oed.com/view/Entry/244233. Accessed 9 September 2021.

Reynolds, Guy. *Willa Cather in Context: Progress, Race, Empire*. Palgrave Macmillan, 1996.

11 Regionalism Démeublé

Reflective Nostalgia in Cather's *Death Comes for the Archbishop*

JACE GATZEMEYER

> Men travel faster now, but I do not know if they
> go to better things.
>
> —Willa Cather, *Death Comes for the Archbishop*

In early 1908, at the Boston home of Annie Fields, Willa Cather, thirty-four-year-old editor of *McClure's Magazine* and aspiring novelist, met veteran regionalist writer Sarah Orne Jewett.[1] The two women sensed an instant connection and kept up an active correspondence until Jewett's death sixteen months later. Jewett advised Cather, who was at a crossroads in her literary career, to take "time and quiet to perfect your work" by quitting her editorial job to become a full-time writer and "to be surer of your backgrounds" by relying more on the regional settings of Nebraska and Virginia (Cather, *Selected Letters* 117). This advice, Deborah Carlin writes, "cemented for all of Cather's biographers and the majority of her critics the centrality of this relationship as the crucial turning point in Cather's career" (172). Indeed, Cather scholarship has customarily assumed the enormous influence of Jewett as a literary model and mentor, and evidence certainly appears to support this reading. Cather herself stresses in particular Jewett's regionalist influence, to which critics often attribute her shift from the Jamesian realism of her first novel, *Alexander's Bridge* (1912), to the midwestern regionalism of her more successful subsequent novels, *O Pioneers!* (1913), *The Song of the Lark* (1915), and *My Ántonia* (1918). Highlighting this regionalist connection in a 1921 interview, Cather told the *Bookman*, "[Jewett] said to me that if my life had lain in a part of the world that was without a literature, and I couldn't tell about it truthfully in the form I most admired, I'd have to make a kind of writing that would tell it, no matter what I lost in the process" (qtd. in Bohlke 22). Cather even edited *The Best Stories of Sarah Orne Jewett* for Houghton Mifflin in 1925. Her preface to the two-volume collection lauds Jewett's stories as "almost flawless examples of literary art" and locates her as a central figure in the canon of American literature: "If I were asked to name three American books which have the possibility of a long, long life, I would say at once, 'The Scarlet Letter,' 'Huckleberry Finn,' and [Jewett's] 'The Country of the Pointed Firs'" (9).

But by 1936 Cather had completely reframed her relationship to Jewett. In *Not under Forty*, Cather pulled back markedly from the older author's influence and consigned her regionalist mode to a fading nineteenth-century tradition of "local color" writing. In "Miss Jewett," a revised and expanded version of her preface to *The Best Stories of Sarah Orne Jewett*, Cather subtly turned commendation into critique. Jewett, she said, "had never been one of those who 'live to write'" but one for whom writing was "one of many preoccupations," merely "a ladylike accomplishment" (*Not under Forty* 85–86). In a backhanded compliment suggesting the "limits" of Jewett's regional settings, Cather noted the "fine literary sense" that allowed the older author to revere "contemporary writers of much greater range than her own" (89–90). Whereas she had called *The Country of the Pointed Firs* a "masterpiece" in her preface, Cather now reduced the collection to mere "provincialism" by suggesting "[Jewett's] stories were but reflections" of "personal pleasure" derived from "the Maine country and seacoast" (*Not under Forty* 87). Excising the bold pronouncement that placed Jewett's fiction firmly in the canon of American literature alongside works by Hawthorne and Twain, Cather concluded, "Among those glittering novelties which have now become old-fashioned Miss Jewett's little volumes made a small showing. A taste for them must always remain a special taste" (92).

Why would Cather revise her attitude toward Jewett in this way? Why diminish the author she had previously considered a mentor and a model? While Sharon O'Brien has argued that Cather was simply reporting Jewett's altered standing among "a new class of unsympathetic readers," Carlin notes that this explanation "doesn't even attempt to address Cather's quite specific references to—and veiled critiques of—Jewett's work" (120). Carlin suggests instead that Cather intended to signal to reviewers critical of her own work that she, in contrast with Jewett, was "not burdened by nostalgia for an irretrievable past" (185). Carlin eloquently describes Cather's "unconscious strategy" as a process of internalization and sublimation that "arises not only out of cultural exigency but also out of maturation, self-actualization, and the changing self within the life cycle" (186). In other words, though she had at first encouraged comparisons between herself and Jewett in terms of regionalism, Cather sought in the 1930s to separate herself—in the public sphere, at least—from the burden of nostalgia in Jewett's regional writing. Judith Fetterley and Marjorie Pryse have argued as much in their influential reading of Cather's "Old Mrs. Harris" (1932), the story of a Southern family relocated to a small town in Colorado. Closing their anthology *American Women Regionalists* with "Old Mrs. Harris," Fetterley and Pryse argue that the story announces "the 'end' of regionalism as a viable mode" (595). In the intergenerational conflict of "Old Mrs. Harris," they write, the story "articulates Cather's need to separate from the writing tradition created by an earlier generation of women," such as Jewett, Mary Wilkins Freeman, and Kate Chopin (*Writing Out of Place* 56).[2] Like her revised "Miss Jewett" essay, Cather's "Old Mrs. Harris," in their words, "underscores the limitations of regionalism

for a modernizing culture committed to separating from its past"
(58). In "Old Mrs. Harris," they argue, regionalism becomes simply
a "comforting memory" (57).

But what others interpret in "Miss Jewett" and "Old Mrs. Harris"
as a closure I take as an opening. In distancing herself from Jewett
in the 1930s, Cather does not signal the end of regionalism as such
but rather the beginning of a new approach to regionalism, a modernist regionalism that abandons the reactionary nostalgia of "local
color" for more progressive nostalgia that looks longingly into the
past not as a rejection of or retreat from the modern present but in
order to reconsider, critique, and reimagine modernity. Cather's work
does indeed "underscore the limitations of regionalism," as Fetterley
and Pryse put it (58), but only the regionalism of a previous generation, a regionalism predicated on what Svetlana Boym calls "restorative nostalgia," which seeks to "return to the original stasis, to the
prelapsarian moment" (49). Cather's fiction, by contrast, reveals the
development of a modernist regionalism grounded in a "reflective
nostalgia," which offers a critical vantage point on modernity and,
in Boym's words, "opens up a multitude of potentialities, nonteleological possibilities" (50).

What did this new regionalist mode look like for Cather? Her masterpiece, *Death Comes for the Archbishop* (1927), provides an answer.
This regionalist novel constitutes a search for "authenticity" in an
imagined legendary past, but rather than, as she put it, "hold[ing]
the note" by forcing an explicit commentary into her narratives,
Cather instead sought "to touch and pass on," that is, to allow the
contradictions, conflicts, and complexities of modernity to arise from
its contrast with the past (*Cather on Writing* 9). Despite the fact that
critics in the 1930s would misread this nostalgic mode as regressive
and conservative, tagging Cather with the "escapist" reputation that
would follow her work for the next several decades, *Death Comes for
the Archbishop* reveals an *engagée* novelist committed to critical reflection on modernity by way of nostalgia for the regional past. Moving from the heartland prairies of her youth to nineteenth-century
New Mexico, Cather depicts a regional past that can subtly call

into question the norms, values, and beliefs of the modern present. This novel constitutes Cather's clearest articulation of a modernist regionalism, a narrative mode taking the regional space as the site of a "reflective nostalgia" with the power to critique modernity and imagine a better future.

The question of whether Cather can truly be considered a "modernist" remains unsettled. "To some," write Melissa J. Homestead and Guy Reynolds, "linking Willa Cather to 'the modern' or more narrowly to literary modernism still seems an eccentric proposition" (xi). Indeed, in its very title and theme, *Willa Cather at the Modernist Crux*, a 2017 volume in the Cather Studies series devoted to the question of Cather's modernism, suggests an author straddling the boundaries between two literary modes, at "an imaginative crossroads," as the volume's editors put it, not quite Victorian, not quite modernist (Moseley et al. xi). As Richard H. Millington points out, "One will look in vain for Cather's name in the index of most accounts, whether new or old, of the nature and history of Anglo-American modernism" ("Cather's American Modernism" 51). Addressing this "general blindness," Millington acknowledges the elusiveness of Cather's modernism, which, he writes, "is most powerful and most original when it has all but disappeared from sight" ("Cather's Two Modernisms" 56). In some ways, this neglect appears justified. Born into a late Victorian world, Cather was significantly older than canonical American modernist novelists like F. Scott Fitzgerald and Ernest Hemingway, and in many of her public statements and fictional motifs she appeared to spurn modernity. Moreover, her work was fundamentally shaped by her reception, marketing, and self-fashioning as a regionalist writer, granting her a reputation that seemed to exclude her from urban-centric modernism.[3] In fact, this may have been the decisive factor in her exclusion from the canon; as Jo Ann Middleton argues, "the designation of regional writer ... served to relegate Cather to a relatively minor role in the development of American literature" (20).

In the last few decades, however, as Cather's stock in the academy and the canon has continued to rise, many critics have made convincing cases for her work's modernism. On one hand, scholars have pointed to its modernist formal qualities. Janis P. Stout's *Cather among the Moderns*, for instance, positions Cather "against a crowded backdrop of her contemporaries ... [who] were recognized as moderns and modernists" (xii). Likewise, both Phyllis Rose and Jo Ann Middleton have argued for Cather's affinities with the aesthetic ideals of particular modern artists, such as D. H. Lawrence or Virginia Woolf. On the other hand, recent historicist readings have argued for Cather's modernism via emphasis on the historical resonances of particular themes or episodes, highlighting the way she attempts "to synchronize and bridge very different cultural eras" (Homestead and Reynolds xx). In *Willa Cather in Context: Progress, Race, Empire*, for example, Reynolds reads Cather's works as "bound up within the intellectual, political, and social debates of her age" (vi).[4] Similarly, Kelsey Squire argues for Cather's modernism on the grounds that her work is "complicated by twentieth-century economics, consumerism, and cosmopolitanism" (49). Millington artfully blends these approaches by acknowledging Cather's "two modernisms," one concerned with "questions of history" and the other with "choices of form" ("Cather's Two Modernisms" 41).

Yet, even as Cather has today been largely incorporated into the modernist canon, neither formalist nor historicist approaches have adequately addressed the heart of her original exclusion, namely, her regionalism.[5] The formalist approach goes no further than identifying regionalism as the source of Cather's deceptive simplicity of style, while the historicists too often rely on the vague assertion that, merely because Cather's content is "regional" and her context is "modern," the former must be somehow "complicated" by the latter. While recent historicist readings usefully remind us that Cather's work seeks to "recall and capture the past in order to understand the present and, perhaps, create a bridge to the future," they often neglect the crucial role of the spatial (Homestead and Reynolds xx). Incorporating formalist and historicist concerns, my reading of Cather also accounts for the critical regionalism at the heart of her aesthetic project. *Death Comes for the Archbishop* reveals her own conception of a modernist regionalism in practice, a *démeublé* regionalist method relying on a reflective nostalgia to suggest and engage with the failings and potentials of modernity.

REGIONALISM DÉMEUBLÉ, MODERNISM NOSTALGIC

Although Cather had enjoyed critical and popular acclaim and a firm position as a major writer throughout the 1920s, many prominent reviewers in the 1930s soured on her work, condemning her regionalist mode as "escapist" and "nostalgic." "As Cather seemed to retreat further and further into the past in search of an orderly and harmonious world," writes Sharon O'Brien, "travelling first to the nineteenth-century Southwest and then to seventeenth-century Quebec, the pages of left-wing journals like the *New Republic* and *The Nation* as well as those of the *New York Times Book Review* began to fill with criticism of Cather as a romantic, nostalgic writer who could not cope with the present" (115). Most notably, Granville Hicks's "The Case against Willa Cather," published in the *English Journal* in 1933, presented Cather as a writer who had "surrendered to the longing for the safe and romantic past" (710). On one hand, of course, Cather had turned toward the legendary past of the Southwest at just the wrong moment. As O'Brien writes, "Cather and her literary reputation were caught in the midst of a generational and ideological shift in American literary culture as a new cohort of critics began to apply different standards to determine literary merit" (116). The criteria by which works of literature were judged had shifted in the wake of the Great Depression, and critics now demanded clear social relevance. On the other hand, however, these critics' interpretation of Cather's work also relied on a foundational misreading not only of her most recent novels but also of her larger aesthetic project and goals. What they interpreted as an unwillingness to confront modernity or a desire to escape into the regional past was part of Cather's subtle pursuit of "the inexplicable presence of the thing not named," her attempt to subtly make manifest and reflect on the modern present without overt identification or explanation (*Not under Forty* 50).

Lionel Trilling's "Willa Cather," published in the *New Republic* in 1937, perfectly exemplifies this misinterpretation. Perhaps having recently come across *Not under Forty*, a collection of Cather's essays published the previous year, Trilling thought he had discovered just what constituted "the subtle failure of her admirable talent" (283). He identified "The Novel Démeublé," an essay originally published in 1922 and reprinted in *Not under Forty*, as "the rationale of a method which Miss Cather had partly anticipated in her early novels and which she fully developed a decade later" (283). In this essay, Trilling argued, Cather had "pleaded for a movement to throw the 'furniture' out of the novel—to get rid, that is, of all the social fact[s]" (283). For Trilling, the supposed "spirituality" of her latest novels "consists chiefly of an irritated exclusion of those elements of modern life with which she will not cope" (287).

Far from a proposal to exclude reality, "The Novel Démeublé" constitutes Cather's rebuttal of, as she put it, "the popular superstition that 'realism' asserts itself in the cataloguing of a great number of material objects, in explaining mechanical processes, the methods of operating manufactories and trades, and in minutely describing physical sensations" (*Not under Forty* 45). Trilling's misreading is instructive, however. In fact, he almost cuts to the heart of Cather's modernist regionalism. "We use the word 'escape' too lightly," he writes, but "we must realise that the return to a past way of thought or life may be the relevant criticism of the present" (287). Not all depictions of a previous era are "escapist," then, says Trilling; some can mount a "relevant" challenge to the conditions of the present. *Death Comes for the Archbishop* constitutes Cather's attempt to do just that, to subtly evoke and confront the conditions of the present through her depiction of a particular region's imagined legendary past, but perhaps because she never declares this purpose outright, Trilling assumes that Cather's turn to the past is defeatist, merely "the weary response to weariness" (287). In abandoning the "social facts," he writes, she loses "the objectivity that can draw strength from seeking the causes of things" (287). But Cather's *démeublé* method does *not* in fact mean abandoning material realities, only abandoning the "cataloguing" and "enumeration" practices of the novelist as "interior decorator" (47). Far from omitting material realities, Cather sought instead to omit explicit sermonizing about those realities. She sought to make modernity manifest and to provide a critical vantage point on it, yet avoid the tactless, heavy-handed lecturing that so often accompanied so-called "political" novels. Indeed, she had grown frustrated at the proliferation of writers seeking not art in their fiction but an excuse for political pontification. Hermione Lee characterizes Cather's position in the 1930s as a struggle to "detach fiction from polemics" (328). "At this particular time few writers care much about their medium except as a means for expressing ideas," Cather wrote in an essay on Katherine Mansfield (*Not under Forty* 134). By contrast, Mansfield's gift, she wrote, was her ability "to approach the major forces of life through comparatively trivial incidents," to create an "overtone" suggesting that which "lie[s] hidden under our everyday behavior" (135). Far from "an irritated exclusion of those elements of modern life with which she will not cope," as Trilling put it, Cather aimed to refine and perfect the method she detected in Mansfield, to "approach the major forces of life," yet to make those conditions "felt upon the page without being specifically named there" (50).

To be sure, critics like Hicks and Trilling had good reason to be skeptical of the political implications of regionalist writing. After all, as Richard H. Brodhead and Amy Kaplan have shown, the nostalgic longing central to the "local color" fiction of the late nineteenth century often served as a subtle ideological tool, a way for readers unsatisfied with the industrial present to project images of their desire for a simpler time onto the past as represented in regionalist fiction. Rather than engaging with unsatisfactory social conditions, readers escaped these conditions in the nostalgic mode of regionalism, which described for them an imagined space and time removed from the concerns of industrial urban life and characterized instead by unchanging values and authentic traditions. But Cather had recognized the failings of "local color" writing's reactionary nostalgia. In fact, Cather had by 1927 reimagined the modernist possibilities of regionalist writing. In *Death Comes for the Archbishop* Cather had developed a "modernist regionalism" grounded in a kind of nostalgic longing that would elicit not disengagement with modernity in favor of a prelapsarian place and time but rather a critical awareness of modernity's potentials and pitfalls. Far from the regressive, reactionary nostalgia identified by her critics in the 1930s, the nostalgia evoked by Cather in this novel was a more decidedly "modern nostalgia."

Modernist scholars have recently recovered nostalgia, traditionally considered antithetical to modernism, as a key feature of much modernist aesthetic production.[6] Stephen Spender, an early theorist of this notion, asserted that in some ways "nostalgia has been one of the most productive and even progressive forces in modern literature" (212). In contrast with Victorian expressions of "Golden-age nostalgia," Spender argued, the "elaborate irony" of the modern era "put nostalgia itself into perspective, by making it appear not just as hatred of the present and yearning for the past, but as a modern state of mind, a symptom of the decline that was also modern" (213). Likewise, Tammy Clewell, in her introduction to *Modernism and Nostalgia*, notes that many modernist writers discovered in nostalgia "the potential for a productive dialogue where the past is brought into conversation with the present" (1). Such a dialogue, she writes, "might nurture regressive fantasies of returning to the preindustrial or prelapsarian, but it also might lead to creative visions for self-fashioning, culture, and artistic practice" (1). A decidedly modernist use of nostalgia, then, need not be understood as a mere fixation on an idealized past. Rather, modernist nostalgia might serve as a safeguard against unexamined conformity to the conditions of the present, a critical perspective on the existing order, and creative source for imagining the future.

More specifically, the modernist nostalgia Cather develops through her regionalist mode in *Death Comes for the Archbishop* can be understood as roughly parallel to what Svetlana Boym has

262

JACE GATZEMEYER

labeled "reflective nostalgia." In *The Future of Nostalgia*, Boym argues that nostalgia can be divided into two types, "the restorative and the reflective" (xviii). As opposed to "restorative nostalgia," she writes, which "stresses *nostos* and attempts a transhistorical reconstruction of the lost home," reflective nostalgia "consists in the exploration of other potentialities and unfulfilled promises of modern happiness" (xviii, 342). Whereas restorative nostalgia "protects the absolute truth," according to Boym, reflective nostalgia "calls it into doubt" (xiii). Rather than seeking to restore the past as established in a particular place, then, reflective nostalgia can provide a critical vantage point on the present, so that "the past opens up a multitude of potentialities, nonteleological possibilities of historic development" (50). Thus, if restorative nostalgia depends on a chronological notion of corrupting progress, reflective nostalgia, by contrast, "opens up" the past not as sequential but as synchronous and alive within the present. Indeed, drawing on Henri Bergson's notion that the past, as he put it, "will act by inserting itself into a present sensation from which it borrows the vitality," Boym argues that reflective nostalgia "tends to be *prospective* rather than *retrospective*, a kind of future perfect with a twist" (168). In this sense, she writes, reflective nostalgia "is not a nostalgia for the ideal past, but only for its many potentialities that have not been realized" (168). In *Death Comes for the Archbishop* Cather uses reflective nostalgia for the imagined past of a particular regional space to evoke—without moralizing upon—the shortcomings of modernity and to suggest a better way forward.

DEATH COMES FOR THE ARCHBISHOP

"It seems inevitable in retrospect," writes James Woodress, "that some day [Cather] would write a novel about the Southwest" (391). The region had fascinated her since childhood and had especially provoked her imagination after a formative first visit in 1912.[7] Since then, she had continued to revisit the Southwest both in person and in her fiction, situating sections of *The Song of the Lark* and *The Professor's House* there. Not until *Death Comes for the*

Archbishop, however, which she finished in the fall of 1926, had she attempted a novel in which the Southwest served as the central setting. After all, much of her previous fiction had drawn on her extensive memories of the people and places of the Midwest, and she had relatively little experience in the Southwest. But in the summer of 1925 Cather found her southwestern subject in an obscure book, William Howlett's *The Life of the Right Reverend Joseph P. Machebeuf* (1908). Having long admired the bronze statue of Archbishop Jean-Baptiste Lamy, the first bishop of New Mexico, in Santa Fe, Cather explained that Lamy "had become a sort of invisible personal friend," and Machebeuf, the subject of Howlett's biography, had been Lamy's longtime friend and vicar-general in New Mexico. Howlett's book thus provided the background she needed to create their tale: "At last I found out what I wanted to know about how the country and the people of New Mexico seemed to those first missionary priests from France" (*Cather on Writing* 8). Opening in the aftermath of the Mexican-American War, *Archbishop* tells the story of these two priests, Father Jean Marie Latour (Lamy) and Father Joseph Vaillant (Machebeuf), sent by the Roman Catholic leadership to minister to the Indians, Mexicans, and encroaching Americans occupying the newly annexed New Mexico territory. Through nine books, the essentially episodic novel narrates the gradual organization of the new territory's vast diocese. Although it is based on historical records and features historical persons, Cather's novel is by no means a conventional historical novel. Woodress calls it "the most innovative of all Cather's experiments with the novel form" (398). Reynolds has argued that *Archbishop*, far from historical romance, "eschews the dramatic foreground of history" in favor of "the hinterland of history … the quotidian background, the everyday ministrations of Fathers Latour and Vaillant as they reform and strengthen their Church" (*Cather in Context* 150–51).[8] Even contemporary reviewers noted this reversal of the historical novel form. In 1927 Henry Longan Stuart defined Cather's novel "not so much as an historical novel, as a superimposition of the novel upon history" (32).

In this sense, then, *Archbishop* not only constituted a marked change in setting and subject matter for Cather but also a distinct shift in narrative method. As she explained the genesis and method of the novel in a letter to *Commonweal* in late 1927, "I had all my life wanted to do something in the style of legend, which is absolutely the reverse of dramatic treatment" (*Cather on Writing* 9). In hagiography, particularly the medieval *Golden Legend* and the nineteenth-century frescoes of Pierre Puvis de Chavannes, Cather found the model for this reversal, an episodic flatness with regard to the past that eschewed the grandly melodramatic and instead infused the everyday with deep significance. In these works, she wrote, "the martyrdoms of the saints are no more dwelt upon than are the trivial incidents of their lives" (9). Disdainful of the contemporary emphasis on "situation," the "tendency to force things up" with sensationalism and suspense, Cather sought, as she put it, "something without accent, with none of the artificial elements of composition" (9). Through this method, downplaying the dramatic foreground and focusing on the "hinterland of history," she could *e*voke modernity without *in*voking it. Indeed, much like her pursuit of "the inexplicable presence of the thing unnamed," Cather explains in her commentary on *Archbishop* that "the essence of such writing is not to hold the note, not to use an incident for all there is in it—but to touch and pass on" (9). Rather than "hold[ing] the note," using a story to make a point or as an excuse to pontificate, she seeks "to touch and pass on," allowing the complexities and contradictions of modernity to emerge spontaneously. In an analogy with New Mexico churches, she illustrates this method, her notion of simply allowing stories to signify "without accent": "I used to wish there were some written account of the old times when those churches were built, but I soon felt that no record of them could be as real as they are themselves. They are their own story, and it is foolish convention that we must have everything interpreted for us in written language. There are other ways of telling what one feels, and the people who built and decorated those many, many little churches found their way and left their message" (5–6). Rather than relying on artificial "situation" or external explanations, these churches to Cather "seemed a direct expression of some very real and lively human feeling" (5). Likewise, she thought, her novel need not give an "account of the old time," explaining the past in terms of the present, but only, like the little churches of New Mexico, be its "own story" (5–6).

As Edith Lewis, Cather's domestic partner for almost forty years, wrote, "[Cather] could make the modern age almost disappear, fade away and become ghostlike, so completely was she able to invoke her vision of the past and recreate its reality" (120). Millington, too, notes this ethereal quality in his assertion that Cather's modernism is most apparent "when it has all but disappeared from sight" ("Cather's Two Modernisms" 56). Indeed, in *Archbishop* the modern age almost disappears—almost. Modernity becomes "ghostlike," haunting the narrative like an unarticulated specter. Although the novel is "all in the direction of suggestiveness and evocation, away from propaganda and orthodoxy," writes Lee, yet there is the presence of "something ferocious and unreconciled . . . placed at arm's length" (267, 260). Even as it pines for the imagined regional past of Fathers Latour and Vaillant, *Archbishop* develops a reflective nostalgia that opens up critical perspectives on the modern present. Far from advocating the restoration of nineteenth-century New Mexico, Cather's nostalgic longing evokes the promises and pitfalls of the regional past—the promise of cultural pluralism represented by Catholicism, for instance, and the pitfall of imperialist expansion represented by Americanization. Even in its narrative method, which eschews linear time for synchronicity, the novel undermines the notion of inevitable progress so central to modernity and instead imagines the past as a series of nonteleological possibilities. In his final moments, Father Latour himself even enacts this reflective nostalgia, treating his memories not as ideals but as objects "for reflection, for recalling the past and planning the future" (229).

Yet *Archbishop* also reveals the limits of Cather's reflective nostalgia. In her attempts to avoid the explicitly political, to "touch and pass on," Cather leaves largely unexamined the question of Native American and Mexican exploitation, past and present. Despite her close ties to a southwestern community of modernist artists and intellectuals strongly committed to Native American rights, Cather's interests were, as Stout has shown, "aesthetic and historical ... centering primarily on landscape" (112). Indeed, Molly H. Mullin argues that "Cather's interest in Indians never developed much beyond their usefulness as material for her fiction; at least she never took much interest in living Indians and the political struggles to which her friend [Elizabeth] Sergeant became so committed" (44). In attempting to allow her stories to signify "without accent," in other words, Cather's narrative method may in fact ultimately *de*-accent some of the profound political injustices experienced by the marginalized communities represented in her narrative. Even as it exposes the problematics of modernity, then, *Archbishop* nonetheless largely occludes the "pressures" of the Mexican and Indigenous past.

Archbishop suggests Catholicism as a contrast against the homogenizing force of encroaching modernity and American empire. For Cather, Reynolds has argued, Catholicism "was not the monolithic autocracy caricatured by American nativists; it was instead a repository of European culture, endlessly adapting itself to alien environments" (*Cather in Context* 157). Much like the midwestern immigrant cultures of her early novels, then, the Catholicism of Cather's Southwest represents, in Reynolds's words, "an enriching cultural pluralism" (157). This Catholic diversity finds its clearest illustration in the moment when Father Latour first hears the Angelus bell ringing in Santa Fe. As he explains to Father Vaillant, "I am trying to account for the fact that when I heard it this morning it struck me at once as something oriental. A learned Scotch Jesuit in Montreal told me that our first bells, and the introduction of the bell in the service all over Europe, originally came from the East. He said the Templars brought the Angelus back from the Crusades, and it is really an adaptation of a Moslem custom" (48). The Angelus bell suggests a cosmopolitan mixture, a European tradition with roots in the East. Speculating further on the bell's origin, Latour notes that "the Spaniards handed on their skill to the Mexicans, and the Mexicans have taught the Navajos to work silver; but it all came from the Moors"

(48). Likewise, the novel's prologue, depicting a meeting of several Catholic leaders, stresses this diversity. In this prologue, an Italian cardinal from Venice, a French cardinal from Normandy, a Spanish cardinal with English ancestry, and an Irish bishop with French ancestry meet to appoint Latour as bishop of the New Mexico territory: "The Italian and French Cardinals spoke of it as *Le Mexique*, and the Spanish host referred to it as 'New Spain'" (5). Even Catholic doctrine seems to allow for diversity and hybridization, as in the early "Hidden Water" scene. When Father Latour loses his way on a journey to Durango, he happens upon a Mexican settlement named Agua Secreto in which the inhabitants have combined elements of local Indigenous beliefs with the Catholicism brought to them generations ago by the Spanish. In this village full of "old men trying to remember their catechism to teach to their grandchildren," the bishop is surprised to find on a mantelpiece "a little equestrian figure, a saint wearing the costume of a Mexican *ranchero*" (29). A local boy identifies this wooden figure as Santiago, "the saint of horses," asking, "Isn't he that in your country?" (29). "No," replies the bishop, "I know nothing about that" (29). The boy explains, "He blesses the mares and makes them fruitful. Even the Indians believe that" (29). Catholicism in *Archbishop* thus stands for enriching diversity and cultural pluralism, while the figure of the American, by contrast, evokes a mood of encroaching modernity and imperialism.

The novel's Americans "are almost always unpleasant," as Lee puts it, while "all other cultures are carefully celebrated" (279). One of the first Americans encountered in the narrative, Buck Scales, serves to establish the theme. On the road to Mora, the church fathers seek shelter in a humble house: "a man came out, bareheaded, and they saw to their surprise that he was not a Mexican, but an American of a very unprepossessing type" (70). The man, Buck Scales, speaks "in some drawling dialect they could scarcely understand" and seems "evil-looking," as well as "not more than half human" and "malignant" (71). Luckily, the man's Mexican wife, Magdalena, warns them of danger, and they are able to escape. Magdalena had known her husband "for a dog and a degenerate—but to Mexican girls, marriage with an American meant coming up in the world" (76). Not only are the novel's Americans figured as rude interlopers then, but they also appear to be representative of the powerful developmental force of modernity, a way for marginalized groups to Americanize themselves in order to "come up in the world." Likewise, the inhabitants of Agua Secreto feel this pressure: "They had no papers for their land and were afraid the Americans might take it away from them" (26). When Latour explains that Americans are not "infidels," one young man asserts, "They destroyed our churches when they were fighting us, and stabled their horses in them. And now they will take our religion away from us. We want our own ways and our own religion" (27).

Even Kit Carson, the famous frontiersman, who at first seems to exemplify the less "unpleasant" features of the American type, is ultimately tied to encroaching modernity and American imperialism. "The great country of desert and mountain ranges between Santa Fe and the Pacific coast was not yet mapped or charted," the *Archbishop* narrator explains, informing readers that "the most reliable map of it was in Kit Carson's brain" (82). While the local Indigenous people imbue the landscape with symbolic and ritualistic meaning, taking it as essential to their identities, Carson reduces the landscape to mere political representation, the conceptual space of a map. But Carson's "world-renowned explorations" take an even more nefarious turn by the end of the novel. Latour remembers from his deathbed "his own misguided friend, Kit Carson, who finally subdued the last unconquered remnant of [the Navajo tribe]; who followed them into the Canyon de Chelly, wither they had fled from their grazing plains and pine forests to make their last stand" (308). Serving as an agent of the U.S. government, Carson had led American troops into the canyon to destroy and take possession of the Navajo people's ancestral lands: "Carson followed them down into the hidden world between those towering walls of red sandstone, spoiled their stores, destroyed their deep-sheltered corn-fields, cut down the terraced peach orchards so dear to them. When they saw all that was sacred to them laid waste, the Navajos lost heart" (308–9). With "subtle pressures" in moments like these between Catholic diversity and

American imperialism emerging throughout the narrative, Cather conjures a sense of encroaching modernity and its devastating effects even without explicit commentary on the latter.

Yet the reflective nostalgia of *Archbishop* also evokes and critiques the forces of modernity in its narrative method, which destabilizes modern notions of progress and linear time. The narrative moves fitfully and episodically through the regional past, with events connected thematically rather than chronologically. Crucial events like the conquering of the Navajo people are passed over without being emphasized or rendered dramatically. Likewise, narrative suspense is spurned. When Father Vaillant leaves for Denver, for instance, anticipation is preempted with Father Latour's thoughts: "he seemed to know, as if it had been revealed to him, that this was a final break; that their lives would part here, and that they would never work together again" (263). As Lee puts it, "'Memorable occasions,' such as the building of the new cathedral, are anticipated or recalled, but not enacted. Dates are withheld, and sometimes work backwards" (271). The novel's final section, for instance, opens with the discovery of a letter from Latour dated 1888, then recalls the arrival of his assistant in 1885, shows his move into Santa Fe in 1888, then moves backward to the building of the cathedral in 1880, and finally to his journey to Navajo country in 1875. Like her hagiographic models, then, Cather presents not a continuous narrative but a series of related panels, a set of loosely related images from key moments in the lives of Fathers Latour and Vaillant. Her reflective nostalgia deliberately subverts the notion of sequential time so central to modernity in favor of a sort of synchronicity, a concurrence of timeless moments rather than a chronological development.

In rejecting sequentiality, Cather forgoes what Boym calls "restorative nostalgia," which relies on a notion of chronological progress in its desire to restore some idealized antediluvian moment. Rather than reactionary longing for paradise, the reflective nostalgia that permeates *Archbishop* imagines the past as nonteleological, full of hidden potentialities, and permeating the present. In Father Latour's attitude toward miracles Cather suggests precisely this reflective attitude toward the past, an understanding of the past as a force that "acts," in Bergson's words, from within the present. Hearing of the miraculous shrine of Our Lady of Guadalupe, Father Vaillant is stirred, saying to Latour, "Doctrine is well enough for the wise, Jean; but the miracle is something we can hold in our hands and love" (53). As opposed to the discursive immateriality of "doctrine," Vaillant seems to say, miracles are embodiments of God, idols to be held and worshipped. On the contrary, replies Latour, the miraculous is not static but surrounds us at all times. The miraculous, he says, requires only the right kind of awareness to discern: "The Miracles of the Church seem to me to rest not so much upon faces or voices or healing power coming suddenly near to us from afar off, but upon our perceptions being made finer, so that for a moment our eyes can see and our ears can hear what is there about us always" (54). Rather than a shrine to be worshipped or a situation to be brought "near to us from afar off," Cather suggests here, the past exists within and acts upon the present—all one needs is fine "perceptions" to see and hear "what is there about us always."

In the novel's final section, as Latour's health begins to fail, his consciousness seems almost to coalesce into the reflective nostalgic mode of *Archbishop* itself. As he drifts deeper and deeper into his own past, Latour imagines not a chronological development but a set of collected moments, which he calls "the great picture of his life" (305). Searching through his own past for hints of its failings and potentials, Latour begins to see his own life as *Archbishop* does, without "perspective," as synchronous:

> He observed also that there was no longer any perspective in his memories. He remembered his winters with his cousins on the Mediterranean when he was a little boy, his student days in the Holy City, as clearly as he remembered the arrival of M. Molny and the building of his Cathedral. He was soon to have done with calendared time, and it had already ceased to count for him. He sat in the middle of his own consciousness; none

of his former states of mind were lost or outgrown. They were all within reach of his hand, and all comprehensible. (305)

Outside of "calendared time" Latour sees all the moments of his life at once, "all within reach of his hand," which allows him what he calls "a period of reflection." "Now," says the narrator, "when he was an old man and ill, scenes from those bygone times, dark and bright, flashed back to the Bishop" (313). In these final death-bed thoughts, Latour himself suggests the defects and potentials of modernity by juxtaposing discordant moments in the regional past of his memories.

When Latour compares the Santa Fe of 1851 to that of the present day, he finds the latter in need of a proper sense of "setting," of harmony between people and their place. As he recalls, "The old town was better to look at in those days. [...] In the old days it had an individuality, a style of its own; a tawny adobe town with a few green trees, set in a half-circle of carnelian-coloured hills; that and no more" (282). The modern era had warped Santa Fe, he thinks, made it "incongruous" with its surroundings: "the year 1880 had begun a period of incongruous American building. Now, half the plaza square was still adobe, and half was flimsy wooden buildings with double porches, scroll-work and jack-straw posts and banisters painted white" (282). Rather than retreating into the past, however, Latour's nostalgia draws into question the shortcomings of modernity symbolized by these "flimsy wooden buildings" and imagines instead a structure that would encompass the best of both worlds, past and present, Old World and New, and reflect its regional setting—namely, his cathedral. The capstone of his career, his cathedral, with its Midi Romanesque style and its gold rock, "seemed to start directly out of those rose-coloured hills—with purpose so strong that it was like action" (283). Like *Archbishop* itself, Latour rejects notions of teleological development for a reflective nostalgia that calls the supposedly self-evident values of the modern present into doubt and imagines the potentials of the past inherent in the present, culminating in the construction of his grand cathedral. Indeed, in one telling moment from this final section, Latour hears precisely this blending of the past and the present: "As the darkness faded into the grey of a winter morning, he listened for the church bells,—and for another sound, that always amused him here; the whistle of a locomotive. Yes, he had come with the buffalo, and he had lived to see railway trains running into Santa Fe. He had accomplished an historic period" (285). Modernity has left the world with blemishes, to be sure, but the future looks bright to Latour: "It was the Past he was leaving. The Future would take care of itself" (304).

"The world broke in two in 1922 or thereabouts," Cather famously wrote in her "prefatory note" to *Not under Forty*, "and the person and prejudices recalled in these sketches slid back into yesterday's seven thousand years" (v). Laying the groundwork for decades of "escapist" accusations, the critics of the 1930s found in statements like these and in Cather's fiction not only resentment for the avant-garde but also a certain "smugness." Comparing Cather to T. S. Eliot, who in 1927 had converted to Anglicanism, Louis Kronenberger found in this prefatory note "an odd feeling of guilt, of a deep feeling of regret for the past and a self-righteous loyalty in going to the past's defense" (qtd. in Woodress 473). Even as Cather has been recuperated since the 1990s, scholars still have generally understood this preface as expressing Cather's "grumpily disaffected" attitude with regard for her own era (Lee 328). Such a reading is appealingly simple. But a renewed understanding of *Archbishop* that incorporates formalist and historicist concerns while also attending closely to the regionalism at the core of Cather's aesthetic project helps us reframe this ostensibly exclusionary statement and her understanding of the gap between the modern present and the imagined past. Rereading the reflective nostalgia of *Archbishop* reveals Cather as firmly engaged with the conditions of the cosmopolitan present by way of the local past. The tale of Fathers Latour and Vaillant does not call us to recreate the world of nineteenth-century New Mexico but rather to reconsider the modern present and the bits of the regional past that might still be embedded within it—as Woodress puts it, "their lives renew faith in human possibilities" (405). Indeed, *Archbishop* exemplifies the ways modernism and regionalism, though they have been customarily been taken as antagonistic, ultimately coalesce around a set of shared methods and concerns. Cather suggests as much in her prefatory note to *Not under Forty*. "Thomas Mann," she writes, "to be sure, belongs immensely to the forward-goers, and they are concerned only with his forwardness. But he also goes back a long way, and his backwardness is more gratifying to the backward" (v). To one of "the backward," like Cather, modernism's regional "backwardness" was just as crucial as its global "forwardness," the potential of the past just as important as the need to "make it new."

NOTES

1. James Woodress offers details on this meeting between Cather and Jewett (197).

2. Critics have at times insisted on sharp distinctions between "local color" and "regionalism." Judith Fetterley and Marjorie Pryse, for instance, characterize the former as "a destructive form of cultural entertainment that reifies not only the subordinate status of regions but the hierarchical structures of gender, race, class, and nation" and the latter as a discursive strategy that "uncovers the ideology of local color and reintroduces an awareness of ideology into discussions of regionalist politics" (*Writing Out of Place* 6). I do not make such an acute distinction between "regionalism" and "local color," which I merely take as a periodizing term denoting a particular kind of regionalist mode practiced in the late nineteenth century.

3. On the genesis and effects of Cather's reputation as a regionalist, see Guy Reynolds's essay "Willa Cather's Case."

4. Another example of this historicist approach is Joseph R. Urgo's *Willa Cather and the Myth of American Migration*.

5. Cather's regionalism tends to be treated as totally separate from her modernism. One of the best readings of Cather's regionalist writing, Robert Thacker's insightful essay "Willa Cather's Glittering Regions," for instance, does not mention modernism at all. Thacker argues that, in Cather's fiction, "landscape is where representation begins and so roots characters in their imagined regions" (522).

6. See, for instance, Robert Hemmings's *Modern Nostalgia: Siegfried Sassoon, Trauma, and the Second World War*, Greg Forter's *Gender, Race, and*

Mourning in American Modernism, and *Modernism and Nostalgia: Bodies, Locations, Aesthetics*, edited by Tammy Clewell.

7. On the influential first visit Cather made to the Southwest in 1912, see Woodress (3–11).

8. In "Willa Cather's Rewriting of the Historical Novel in *Death Comes for the Archbishop*," Enrique Lima has made a similar argument about the novel's reversal of the traditional historical novel genre, arguing that "Cather portrays elements of Jean Marie's quotidian life as embodying the long past that define a culture" (181).

WORKS CITED

Bohlke, L. Brent, editor. *Willa Cather in Person: Interviews, Speeches, and Letters.* U of Nebraska P, 1986.

Boym, Svetlana. *The Future of Nostalgia.* Basic Books, 2001.

Brodhead, Richard H. *Cultures of Letters.* U of Chicago P, 1993.

Carlin, Deborah. "Cather's Jewett: Relationship, Influence, and Representation." *Willa Cather and the Nineteenth Century*, edited by Anne L. Kaufman and Richard H. Millington, Cather Studies 10, U of Nebraska P, 2015, pp. 169–88.

Cather, Willa. *Death Comes for the Archbishop.* 1927. Willa Cather Scholarly Edition, edited by John J. Murphy, Charles W. Mignon, Frederick M. Link, and Kari A. Ronning, U of Nebraska P, 1990.

———. *Not under Forty.* Knopf, 1936.

———. Preface. *"The Country of the Pointed Firs" and Other Stories*, by Sarah Orne Jewett, Doubleday Anchor, 1956. Originally published as *The Best Stories of Sarah Orne Jewett*, Houghton Mifflin, 1925.

———. *Selected Letters of Willa Cather*, edited by Andrew Jewell and Janis Stout, Penguin, 2014.

———. *Willa Cather on Writing: Critical Studies on Writing as an Art.* U of Nebraska P, 1988.

Clewell, Tammy. "Introduction: Past 'Perfect' and Present 'Tense': The Abuses and Uses of Modernist Nostalgia." Clewell, *Modernism and Nostalgia*, pp. 1–22.

———, editor. *Modernism and Nostalgia: Bodies, Locations, Aesthetics.* Palgrave Macmillan, 2013.

Fetterley, Judith, and Marjorie Pryse, editors. *American Women Regionalists, 1850–1910.* Norton, 1992.

————. *Writing Out of Place: Regionalism, Women, and American Literary Culture*. U of Illinois P, 2003.

Forter, Greg. *Gender, Race, and Mourning in American Modernism*. Palgrave Macmillan, 2011.

Hemmings, Robert. *Modern Nostalgia: Siegfried Sassoon, Trauma, and the Second World War*. Cambridge UP, 2008.

Hicks, Granville. "The Case against Willa Cather." *English Journal*, vol. 22, no. 9, 1933, pp. 703–10.

Homestead, Melissa J., and Guy Reynolds, editors. *Willa Cather and Modern Cultures*, Cather Studies 9, U of Nebraska P, 2011.

Kaplan, Amy. "Nation, Region, Empire." *The Columbia History of the American Novel*, edited by Emory Elliot, Columbia UP, 1991, pp. 240–66.

Lee, Hermione. *Willa Cather: Double Lives*. Vintage, 1989.

Lewis, Edith. *Willa Cather Living*. U of Nebraska P, 1976.

Lima, Enrique. "Willa Cather's Rewriting of the Historical Novel in *Death Comes for the Archbishop*." *Novel*, vol. 46, no. 2, 2013, pp. 179–92.

Middleton, Jo Ann. *Willa Cather's Modernism: A Study of Style and Technique*. Fairleigh Dickinson UP, 1990.

Millington, Richard H. "Willa Cather's American Modernism." *The Cambridge Companion to Willa Cather*, edited by Marilee Lindemann, Cambridge UP, 2005, pp. 51–66.

————. "Willa Cather's Two Modernisms." *Letterature d'America*, vol. 33, no. 144, 2013, pp. 41–56.

Moseley, Ann, John J. Murphy, and Robert Thacker, editors. *Willa Cather at the Modernist Crux*, Cather Studies 11, U of Nebraska P, 2017.

Mullin, Molly H. *Culture in the Marketplace: Gender, Art, and Value in the American Southwest*. Duke UP, 2001.

O'Brien, Sharon. "Becoming Noncanonical: The Case against Willa Cather." *American Quarterly*, vol. 40, no. 1, 1988, pp. 110–26.

Reynolds, Guy. *Willa Cather in Context: Progress, Race, Empire*. St. Martin's Press, 1996.

————. "Willa Cather's Case: Region and Reputation." *Regionalism and the Humanities*, edited by Timothy R. Mahoney and Wendy J. Katz, U of Nebraska P, 2009, pp. 79–94.

Rose, Phyllis. "Modernism: The Case of Willa Cather." *Modernism Reconsidered*, edited by Robert Kiely, Harvard UP, 1983, pp. 123–45.

Spender, Stephen. *The Struggle of the Modern*. U of California P, 1963.

Squire, Kelsey. "Jazz Age Places: Modern Regionalism in Willa Cather's *The Professor's House*." Homestead and Reynolds, *Willa Cather and Modern Cultures*, pp. 46–66.

Stout, Janis P. *Cather among the Moderns*. U of Alabama P, 2019.

Stuart, Henry Longan. "Death Comes for the Archbishop." 1927. *Willa Cather: Critical Assessments, Volume 2*, edited by Guy Reynolds, Helm Information, 2003.

Thacker, Robert. "Willa Cather's Glittering Regions." *A Companion to the Regional Literatures of America*, Wiley-Blackwell, 2003, pp. 513–31.

Trilling, Lionel. "Willa Cather." 1937. *Willa Cather: Critical Assessments, Volume 1*, edited by Guy Reynolds, Helm Information, 2003, pp. 283–88.

Urgo, Joseph R. *Willa Cather and the Myth of American Migration*. U of Illinois P, 1995.

Woodress, James. *Willa Cather: A Literary Life*. U of Nebraska P, 1987.

12 The Neuroscience of Epiphany in *Lucy Gayheart*

JOSHUA DOLEŽAL

Lucy Gayheart, of Willa Cather's eponymous 1935 novel, has disappointed many readers. Cather claimed she tired of Lucy's character before finishing the book, and she wrote to E. K. Brown on 7 October 1946 that she felt the story "picks up after all the Gayhearts are safe in the family burial lot" (*Selected Letters* 667). Hermione Lee finds Lucy's aspirations "fragile and escapist" (338), Janis P. Stout laments Lucy's "abject hero worship" and "failure to be an artist in her own right" (271), and Susan J. Rosowski frames the narrative elements in *Lucy Gayheart* as "silly" and "too conventional," emphasizing Lucy's "blindness and dependency" on womb-like enclosures, which smother her imagination and cause her to retreat from, rather than reach toward, potential moments of illumination and expansion ("Cather's Female Landscapes" 240). David Porter similarly positions Lucy Gayheart at the end of an arc that rose with Cather's early heroines, who mirrored her own irrepressible talent, and sank with the frustrated artists of her later years, who "reflected the cruel diminishments Cather was experiencing in her own life" ("From *Song of the Lark*" 165). And Joseph Urgo concludes that "Cather makes it impossible to read anything less than disappointment out of the character. By all standards Lucy Gayheart is a limited young woman, not the stuff into which inspiration is embodied" (125).

How could it be that so many of Cather's musical friends, including the discerning Hambourgs, regarded *Lucy Gayheart* as Cather's finest work (*Complete Letters* #1281), when literary scholars have so overwhelmingly concluded the opposite? Even more generous views of the novel seem to cede Urgo's point that Lucy is constitutionally incapable of experiencing creative awakening. Although David Stouck lauds the book for its philosophical depth, he emphasizes mortality as a universal condition that Clement Sebastian, Lucy Gayheart, and Harry Gordon all struggle against. Just as the story is driven by "images of life's irreversible flow," he suggests, the narrative works against Cather's more common motif of the exceptional individual: the creative genius or savant (Stouck 221). Clement Sebastian is such a figure, but he is less defined by success than he is by sorrow, grief, and middle age. Even his performances, Stouck writes, are those of "a man at journey's end, from [whose] perspective all of life's movement is seen as a hurrying forward to death" (219). Stouck anticipates Richard Millington's critique of the "hieratic view of the artist" that has steered many scholars toward "a rhetoric of diminishment" as they lament Lucy's failures (30). Millington explains that because Lucy never pretends to aspire to greatness as a performer, only to the rich experience of art known to the listener, viewer, or reader, *Lucy Gayheart* is less "a book about creativity" than it is "a book about responsiveness" (30).

Although my own view of *Lucy Gayheart* aligns more squarely with Stouck's and Millington's, I mean to challenge Urgo's claim that Lucy just isn't built for real inspiration. Epiphany is the hallmark of the great artist in Cather's other works, the chief quality that readers have found wanting in Lucy's character. Yet Lucy's struggle against her own flawed perception reveals one of Cather's most nuanced portrayals of creative thought. In the end Lucy does experience epiphany, but her cognitive setbacks are just as instructive: not as signs of deficiency in Lucy's creative faculties but as necessary impasses without which illumination might not break through.

I remain mindful in examining Lucy's struggle of the distinctions between empirical science and literary fiction. Even so, Cather's precision in animating her characters' inner lives makes her work not only amenable to scientific analysis but potentially predictive of future discoveries about the creative mind. Approached in this way, literature is a close companion of cognitive science: an artistic simulation of established neuroscience and a source of testable hypotheses about imagination and reasoning that might also guide future research.

EPIPHANY OR PSEUDO-INSIGHT?

Epiphany might seem to mark an impassable boundary between literature and science, but much depends on how that apex of creative thought is defined. The proverbial "Aha!" moment could accompany a range of subjective experiences that each individual interprets differently. Neuroscientists John Kounios and Mark Beeman, coauthors of *The Eureka Factor: Aha Moments, Creative Insight, and the Brain*, suggest that the mere strangeness of an idea can make it seem more novel than it really is: "Perhaps the feeling of suddenness is an illusion, a misinterpretation of the emotion that accompanies an unforeseen result. If an unexpected idea comes to mind, it might feel sudden not because the idea entered awareness abruptly, but because the idea wasn't what you bargained for" (57).[1] Kounios and Beeman prefer the phrases "creative insight" or "sudden insight" to epiphany, perhaps to distinguish their inquiry from religious experience and also to emphasize that the cognitive breakthroughs they recognize are objectively reliable: solutions to a problem rather than mere bursts of feeling. Even so, I intend to use epiphany and sudden insight interchangeably. Lucy's breakthrough near the novel's end might not be objectively measurable in the way brain scans are, but Cather presents Lucy's epiphany as the solution to a cognitive problem, a sudden realization that permanently transforms her under-

Sudden insight = Kegan's seeing one's immunity to change + Big Assumption

standing. In that sense, Lucy's arc as a character is a faithful enough representation of Kounios and Beeman's work in neuroscience to warrant examination of Lucy's awakening as deeply analogous to, if not wholly interchangeable with, the cognitive event that they describe as sudden insight.

While some neuroscientists regard epiphany as "pseudo-insight" or "analytic thinking garnished with emotion" (61), Kounios and Beeman claim to have proven that insight can be reached instantaneously, "in a single bound" (62), rather than by piecemeal analysis. In one study of remote associates problems, Kounios and Beeman surveyed participants about which of their answers came from analysis or creative insight. Remote associates problems present a cluster of three words that can each form a compound or familiar phrase with a fourth word. For instance, "pine, tree, and crab" can all be paired with "apple." This answer can be found through analytical elimination or by sudden insight, and nearly all of the participants in the study had solved some problems by analysis and others by spontaneous insight (67–68). By measuring brain activity throughout the experiment with functional magnetic resonance imaging (fMRI) and electroencephalograms (EEG), Kounios and Beeman discovered that both methods revealed dramatically different brain behavior at the moment of epiphany from when an analytical solution was reached. Epiphany manifested in the EEG as "a sudden burst of high-frequency EEG activity known as 'gamma waves'" and in the fMRI as "a corresponding increase in blood flow ... in a part of the brain's right temporal lobe called the 'anterior superior temporal gyrus,' an area that is involved in making connections between distantly related ideas, as in jokes and metaphors" (70). As a result, Kounios and Beeman claim to have discovered the "neural signature of the aha moment: a burst of activity in the brain's right hemisphere," which they characterize as the literal "spark of insight" (71).

While Kounios and Beeman might be the first neuroscientists to capture the physical moment of epiphany, their work dovetails with older models of creativity. For instance, as early as 1926, in *The Art of Thought*, Graham Wallas proposed four stages of creative thought:

preparation, incubation, illumination, and verification. However, Anna Abraham notes that four of Wallas's stages describe conscious thought, whereas cognitive science now shows that "most aspects of information processing are unconscious insofar as we have no voluntary access to or awareness of the workings of these operations" (63). Furthermore, none of Wallas's stages of creative awakening has been empirically verified (63). A more recent heuristic for cognitive creativity is the Geneplore model, proposed by Ronald A. Finke, Thomas B. Ward, and Steven M. Smith in 1992. The Geneplore model proposes three creative phases, which Abraham describes as follows:

> The first phase is a generative one in which "preinventive" or internal precursor structures are produced. These preinventive ideas can be generated either in an open-ended exploratory manner or triggered by goal-directed inquiry. Depending on the task context and requirements, they can be simple or complex, conceptually focused or relatively ambiguous. This generative phase is followed by an explorative phase where the generated structures are evaluated in terms of their usefulness and feasibility. The generate-and-explore cycle repeats until a satisfying solution is reached in the form of a creative idea, which needs to be optimal given the product constraints on hand. (65)

Just as Wallas's stages are difficult to test empirically, so the Geneplore phases resist tangible measurement. Abraham concludes that both models ignore the "essentially spontaneous nature of creative thinking where the generation of an idea is rapidly, immediately, and involuntarily accompanied by the evaluation of the idea" (67).

In contrast to the Wallas and Geneplore models, Kounios and Beeman propose a theory of cognitive awakening that is grounded in empirical data. They chart a mental path to epiphany from *immersion* in a conceptual problem to a cognitive *impasse*, which requires *diversion* to yield *insight*. This heuristic was inspired, in part, by their ostensible discovery of an "alpha brain blink," a slower frequency of brain waves that they liken to a car idling in park, which occurs immediately before creative insight (84). One hallmark of this brain blink is a brief reduction in visual stimulus, which "allows one's attention to find the new idea and jolt it into consciousness" (86). Our bodies seem to instinctively understand this process, since we often look away from a person or the thing we are contemplating, or close our eyes, when we are trying to think. Just as the brain can automatically diminish visual activity to make room for creative thought, we can consciously restrict sensory perception to increase the likelihood of creative insights. Kounios and Beeman explain that epiphanies in the shower could be the result of "white noise" from the water, which mutes other sounds. Warm water can also diminish the sense of touch by blurring distinctions between internal and external temperature, and visual impressions might be blurry, if one's eyes are open at all. Fading our awareness of sound, touch, and sight can "cut off the environment, focus … thoughts inwardly, and [yield] an insight" (87). While extreme measures for inducing epiphany, such as Jonathan Franzen's rumored method of writing "in the dark while wearing earplugs, earmuffs, and a blindfold" (Kounios and Beeman 88), are not necessarily more effective, some dulling of the senses seems to push creative ideation forward. As I will show presently, the causal link between diminished sensory stimulus and epiphany offers a novel explanation of Lucy's delayed response to an opera performance while grieving the death of her artistic mentor and emotional paramour, Clement Sebastian.

Kounios and Beeman argue that the single second separating the alpha blink from epiphany is not enough time for the brain to generate the idea *de nouveau*, hence "the solution must already be ready and waiting—unconsciously—when the blink enables you to find it" (87). What distinguishes Kounios and Beeman from their precursors, in addition to their rigorous empirical testing, is their sense of struggle as a necessary precursor to spontaneous discovery. Even if the "Aha!" moment feels involuntary, its suddenness is the result of a cognitive roadblock, which requires turning away from the problem for a time and either consciously or accidentally reducing external stimuli so the idea, which has been "lurking just below the threshold of awareness, ready to emerge," can finally burst into consciousness (131). Urgo's claim that Lucy Gayheart lacks the constitution for real inspiration suggests that she also lacks the ability to struggle purposefully toward insight. David Porter says it more directly: "Lucy comes across as compliant, complacent, and even a bit spineless" ("From *Song of the Lark*" 158). A closer reading of *Lucy Gayheart* shows that Lucy's immersion in the conceptual problem that her epiphany resolves was lifelong, intensified by Sebastian's death but not wholly defined by her relationship to him.

As much potential as Kounios and Beeman's work offers for a fresh understanding of *Lucy Gayheart*, I remain mindful of nuances that their framework cannot wholly explain. For instance, they recognize that thought and feeling are intertwined; this is why the experience of sudden insight is joyful (27), but it can also mean that too positive or negative a mood might distort one's perception of meaning (148). While Kounios and Beeman feel that they understand the ideal conditions under which epiphany might occur, they recognize that sudden insight requires a constellation of coordinated thoughts, feelings, memories, and behaviors, which are all highly individualized and necessarily mysterious (102, 150). What scholars have previously found more satisfying in the creative awakenings of Cather's other artistic characters, compared to Lucy Gayheart's more muddled development, is the very wholeness and simplicity that make the Wallas and Geneplore models unreliable explanations of creativity. Epiphany, as Kounios and Beeman understand it, requires a prolonged period of frustration, even failure, to produce sudden insight. According to this view, Cather may reveal more about creative awakening through the distractions and indirections that delay Lucy's epiphany than she does in other characters' more straightforward and ostensibly inevitable breakthroughs.

While many scholars have defined Lucy Gayheart by her failures, some have noted how her struggles parallel more triumphant characters, such as Thea Kronborg in *The Song of the Lark*. For instance, David Porter acknowledges frustration as fundamental to Thea's emergence as an artist, noting that her "compound of persistence and vision" allows her to outlast her professional and existential set-backs ("From *Song of the Lark*" 150–51). Likewise, Porter notes how Thea experiences "sudden revelation" in her craft as a performer after prolonged feelings of futility (151). Porter even tracks similar language in Cather's descriptions of Thea's epiphany about art in Panther Canyon and Lucy's epiphany about her future after hearing *The Bohemian Girl*, noting that in each case Cather describes the idea as "flashing" into her young character's mind (161). However, like many others, Porter consistently presents Lucy's very nature, not just her story, as the opposite of Thea's, suggesting that *Lucy Gayheart* serves to "highlight qualities that Thea possesses—and that Lucy lacks" (160). While my purpose here is less to contrast *The Song of the Lark* with *Lucy Gayheart* than to examine Lucy's cognitive arc on its own merits, I see Thea's and Lucy's cognitive struggles as more similar than different. Cather's own physical and mental decline in the years separating the two novels might well have influenced her emphasis on struggle in Lucy's character, but the design of *Lucy Gayheart* also suggests a more mature understanding of the creative mind. That is, ideas emerge from recursive experience in *Lucy Gayheart* rather than developing along linear timelines. Lucy does not need a change in scenery to break through her creative frustrations so much as a subtle shift in her attention and her physical disposition. To ignore these nuances risks not only misreading Cather's narrative but misrepresenting the human mind.

FAILED EPIPHANY OR COGNITIVE IMPASSE?

Many studies of *Lucy Gayheart* cite Lucy's failed epiphany in the second chapter of book I, after she has been skating with Harry Gordon, as evidence that she lacks the creative intelligence of a real artist. The moment, which I will hereafter describe as the star scene, initially seems to have all of the hallmarks of awakening. Lucy feels "drowsy and dreamy" beneath Harry's robes and "glad to be warm" on the sleigh ride home (13). Lucy's indolent state and expansive sur-roundings are the very conditions that predispose Thea Kronborg to her iconic epiphany in *The Song of the Lark*. Thea spends much of a summer resting in Panther Canyon, where she discovers the ruins of an Anasazi village and imagines a kinship between herself and the women who carried water in earthen jars from the river to their cliffside dwellings. One morning while bathing, Thea is surprised by a vision of art as a vessel for life; just as the Anasazi women caught the rushing water in their jars, so she hopes as a singer to catch the elusive stream of life in her throat (*Song* 334–35). For a moment, Cather's scene in *Lucy Gayheart* seems to move toward the same kind of creative insight:

> The sleigh was such a tiny moving spot on that still white country settling into shadow and silence. Suddenly Lucy started and struggled under the tight blankets. In the darkening sky she had seen the first star come out; it brought her heart into her throat. That point of silver light spoke to her like a signal, released another kind of life and feeling which did not belong here. It overpowered her. With a mere thought she had reached that star and it had answered, recognition had flashed between. Something knew, then, in the unknowing waste: something had always known, forever! That joy of saluting what is far above one was an eternal thing, not merely something that had happened to her ignorance and her foolish heart. (13)

Not only is Lucy's momentary vision vague (defined by three "somethings" in the space of two sentences), it is also undercut by doubt; the intensity of thought seems uncharacteristic of her, the unlikely fruit of "ignorance" and a "foolish heart." Soon enough, Lucy's insight falters: "The flash of understanding lasted but a moment. Then everything was confused again. Lucy shut her eyes and leaned on Harry's shoulder to escape from what she had gone so far to snatch. It was too bright and too sharp. It hurt, and made one feel small and lost" (14).

Epiphany is characterized by suddenness, but the lack of focus and staying power in Lucy's vision also seem to mark this scene as a cognitive failure. For a moment she feels reassured by the star, and just as quickly the idea leaves her feeling diminished. For Merrill Maguire Skaggs, Lucy's retreat from the star ensures "that [she] will come to no good end" (156). Susan Rosowski contrasts the scenes from *The Song of the Lark* and *Lucy Gayheart* to highlight Lucy's defects of character. Whereas Thea participates in a "creative union" in Panther Canyon, straining toward the ideas that emerge out of the landscape, Rosowski sees Lucy withdrawing from her vision and "den[ying] the active receptivity necessary for art" ("Cather's Female Landscapes" 236, 240). In another comparative study of Thea and Lucy, Isabel Caruso rehearses Cather's putative view that "the true artist [Thea] possesses the will and desire first hand, . . . and this desire must be present in sufficient intensity to withstand any challenge to the creation and bringing forth of an artist" (8). David Porter's conclusion that "Lucy Gayheart falls short of the heights and depths of both artistic ambition and human passion" (*On the Divide* 272) similarly hinges on Lucy's inability to seize what she thought she saw in the evening star. In fact, the "fugitive gleam" of a "briefly brilliant sunset sky" is, by Porter's lights, the defining motif in Lucy's story ("From *The Song of the Lark*" 163). Whatever insight might flare up in Lucy is, by these measures, destined to fade.

The Kounios/Beeman model for creative insight suggests that many readers of the star scene mistake a cognitive impasse for artistic failure. Even though the second chapter of book I gives us our first direct glimpse of Lucy, as she is skating with Harry Gordon and then riding home with him, Cather's introduction of her character is misleading because it omits so much context. That is, Lucy occupies a transitional cognitive stage when she imagines the star signaling to her. Just three months have passed since she first heard Clement Sebastian perform in Chicago, the most profound experience that she had ever known. Lucy has not yet become Sebastian's accompanist or fallen in love with him when we see her in chapter 2; by all measures, she is still immersed in her conceptual problem, perhaps still trying to define it. Lucy's failure to experience a sustained epiphany is unsurprising at this stage, not evidence of creative deficiency.

Lucy herself seems to understand that she is in the midst of transformation during the star scene. Restored to her Chicago apartment soon after, Lucy muses: "Out there in Haverford she had scarcely been herself at all; she had been trying to feel and behave like someone she no longer was; as children go on playing the old games to please their elders, after they have ceased to be children at heart" (29–30). Lucy implies that she is maturing, even if Haverford is not yet ready to see her as an adult, but Rosowski reads these changes in a sinister light, characterizing Sebastian as a predatory figure who entrances Lucy (*Voyage Perilous* 225). Lee similarly sees Sebastian exerting psychic control over Lucy by having "penetrated and taken her over" (343). According to such reasoning, Lucy loses autonomy over even her innermost thoughts and must be deluding herself if she thinks Sebastian is contributing to her personal growth. In fact, Deborah Carlin describes Lucy's development as an "elaborate and even ironic … self-deception" (132). If this is so, we must also distrust Lucy's awakening near the novel's end, when she renews her pursuit of beauty and delight. However, if we dispute that Lucy wholly surrenders her faculties to Sebastian's influence and instead accepts her self-awareness as emerging (but still only partially realized), the stages that Kounios and Beeman outline as precursors to insight offer a more affirming view of Lucy's development.

LUCY'S PATH TO EPIPHANY

The beginning of Lucy's path to insight is not revealed until the very moment of her awakening near the novel's end, so I must work against Cather's narrative structure to trace Lucy's cognitive arc. An unusual moment embedded in Lucy's epiphany undercuts much of what the story has led us to believe about Lucy's fundamental nature and carries us back in time, long before she had heard Sebastian sing, long before she had even had any thought of leaving Haverford. After a performance of *The Bohemian Girl* leaves Lucy trembling with inspiration, she recognizes the feeling as familiar: "Every nerve was quivering with a long-forgotten restlessness. How often she had run out on a spring morning, into the orchard, down the street, in pursuit of something she could not see, but knew! It was there, in the breeze, in the sun; it hid behind the blooming apple boughs, raced before her through the neighbours' gardens, but she could never catch up with it" (194). No one else in the novel seems to understand this about Lucy, that she has always been pursuing a real idea rather than simply flitting about. The collective voice of Haverford in the first chapter compares Lucy to "a bird flying home" (5) and mistakes her energy for an "irrepressible light-heartedness" (6). But Lucy understands her younger self to have been seeking the source of her desire, not fleeing from it. Lucy's "long-forgotten restlessness" marks the immersion stage that Kounios and Beeman identify as the beginning of creative thought. Lucy knows that her sensory knowledge of wind, sun, and apple blossoms is not enough; this physical beauty contains meaning that she cannot yet grasp but that she passionately hopes to understand.

So much is contained in this moment: Lucy's earliest conception of herself, the conceptual problem she understood herself to be grappling with from a young age, and the memory of Sebastian's temporary resolution of that problem for her. As her awakening unfolds, Lucy recalls that Sebastian "had made the fugitive gleam an actual possession. With him she had learned that those flashes of promise could come true, that they could be the important things in one's life. He [. . .] was, in his own person, the door and the way to that knowledge" (194). This was true at the recital where Lucy first heard Sebastian perform, when "[t]he dark beauty of the songs seemed to her a quality in the voice itself, as kindness can be in the touch of a hand. It was as simple as that—like light changing on the water" (32). From that first encounter, Lucy understood Sebastian as part of her awakening, a stepping stone to enlightenment rather than an obstacle to it.

Whereas Lucy's initial reaction to Sebastian's singing bears resemblance to the helplessness that Rosowski describes, Lucy herself does not recall Sebastian's influence as suffocating or enervating during her own awakening. Her first encounter with Sebastian left Lucy "struggling with something she had never felt before. A new conception of art? It came closer than that. A new kind of personality? But it was much more. It was a discovery about life, a revelation of love as a tragic force, not a melting mood, of passion that drowns like black water" (33). Much has been made of this passage as ominous foreshadowing of Sebastian's drowning, as well as of Lucy's own eventual death by drowning, presumably fated by her association with him. But it is also possible to read Lucy's reflection here as limited to the German songs Sebastian sang, when the performance conjured powerful aesthetic and emotional responses that dissolved the barriers between symbols and the things themselves. At the end of *Der Doppelgänger*, Sebastian left Lucy (and presumably many others in the audience) with the lingering perception of "moonlight, intense and calm, sleeping on old human houses; and somewhere a lonely black cloud in the night sky" (32). Such a spellbinding effect is what great performers seek, and feeling Schubert's angst in the music is quite different from literally despairing of life.

Notably, Lucy's prevailing attitude toward Sebastian during her own awakening is gratitude for introducing her to art as a consuming experience; "flowers and music and enchantment and love" are "all the things she had first known with [him]" (195). Participating in Sebastian's conception of art gives Lucy the very confidence she lacked when she could not sustain her vision of the evening star, an early "flash of promise" that she was not yet ready to seize. Here I must quarrel gently with Janis Stout's false dichotomy between Lucy "fixating on the star performer ... and return[ing] her vision to the distant star of art" (267). Lucy's independent awakening is an outgrowth of Sebastian's influence, not a liberation from it, which is to say that her memories are of a piece with her epiphany.

If Lucy's original struggle was grasping meaning in the world (that incomprehensible energy racing before her in sun and wind and blooming trees), and if Sebastian brought that knowledge to her for a time, he was, while living, the best answer to her conceptual problem. For instance, Lucy found such fulfillment in Sebastian's presence that she rendered the entire city of Chicago according to her feelings for him: "Lucy carried in her mind a very individual map of Chicago: a blur of smoke and wind and noise, with flashes of blue water, and certain clear outlines rising from the confusion; a high building on Michigan Avenue where Sebastian had his studio—the stretch of park where he sometimes walked in the afternoon—the Cathedral door out of which she had seen him come one morning—the concert hall where she first heard him sing" (27). Lucy's Chicago is a "city of feeling [that] rose out of the city of fact like a definite composition,—beautiful because the rest was blotted out" (27). Sebastian's death then intensifies Lucy's original search for the "fugitive gleam" with the existential question of how to find meaning in her life without Sebastian in it: whether life is worth living without the knowledge she had possessed and then lost. Cather writes, "To have one's heart frozen and one's world destroyed in a moment—that was what it had meant. She could not draw a long breath or make a free movement in the world that was left. She could breathe only in the world she brought back through memory" (164). But this is a different problem from grieving a sweetheart: her impasse represents a mortal question for Lucy.

While Lucy's months in Haverford after Sebastian's death seem like a rudderless time, Kounios and Beeman explain that diversion from an impasse enables insight. Lucy feels "alien" in her own house, "tense" in her own bed, "on her guard against something that was trying to snatch away her beautiful memories, to make her believe they were illusions and had never been anything else" (164). She finds diversion primarily in the family apple orchard, the only place where "the hard place in her breast [would] grow soft" (166), perhaps because it is also a place that she remembers had sparked her creative desire long ago. The orchard is crucial for Lucy's cognitive development because it is an optimal environment for defocused attention, which Anna Abraham identifies as a salient quality of highly creative people (57). Among the unpruned trees, Lucy has no task or obligation other than to "remember and think, and try to realize what had happened to her" (Cather, *Lucy Gayheart* 163).

Lucy also experiences diversion when she reluctantly accompanies her father to the performance of *The Bohemian Girl* mentioned earlier. She expects nothing from the opera and approaches it in a thoroughly defocused state, the ideal frame of mind for enabling insight. Kounios and Beeman explain why seemingly purposeless activities are crucial in cognitive diversion: "[F]ailing to solve a problem sensitizes you to things in the environment that may subsequently trigger an insight. . . . Exposing yourself to a variety of experiences or thoughts—especially unusual ones—during a break will help you to dismiss these unproductive thoughts and increase your chances of encountering an insight trigger" (109). The opera is not one Lucy would have chosen to attend in Chicago; she recognizes it as old-fashioned, far afield of the music she rehearsed with Sebastian. Yet these very qualities prime Lucy for surprise and discovery.

Just as she was swept into Sebastian's personality through his voice, Lucy is taken by a "sympathy, a tolerant understanding" for the soprano in the opera, despite the singer's age and flaws as a vocalist. The woman's voice "gave freshness to the foolish old words" of "'I dreamt that I dwelt in marble halls'" (191), prodding Lucy to contemplate the contrast between what the diva had lost—"youth, good looks, position, the high notes of her voice"—and the sweetness with which she sang (191–92). The singer rekindles the most vital part of Lucy's nature, her "long-forgotten restlessness." Whereas her earlier meditation on the evening star left Lucy feeling muddled and lost after a brief flash of emotion, the awakening sparked by *The Bohemian Girl* has more staying power: "A wild kind of excitement flared up in her. She felt she must run away tonight, by any train, back to a world that strove after excellence—the world out of which this woman must have fallen" (192).

As Kounios and Beeman caution, a surge of feeling does not qualify as insight. The crucial difference between bare ecstasy and joyful awakening is understanding the reason for one's abrupt shift in mood (145). Lucy knows very well that she is homing in on an answer to her problem, even if it takes most of the next day to apprehend it fully: "The wandering singer had struck something in her that went on vibrating; something that was like a purpose forming, and she could not stop it. When she awoke in the morning, it was still there, beating like another heart" (192). After a busy morning of Christmas Eve errands, Pauline asks Lucy to rest before dinner. This respite from work, conversation, and other cognitive noise enables a lull akin to the brain blink that precedes insight. Lucy's excitement is piqued, but her external influences have all slowed down: "[She] did not feel tired, she was throbbing with excitement, and with the feeling of wonder in the air" (194). Lucy raises the blinds, opens her window, and watches the snow, which simplifies the visual scene even as "[t]he daylight in her room grew greyer and darker" (194). Cather's language describes the literal conditions under which insight is more likely to occur. Kounios and Beeman stress that "expansive surroundings" enhance creative thinking by encouraging remote association, whereas tight spaces constrict thought. Dimly lit spaces diminish visual detail, which encourages "generality, abstraction, and broad attention" (204–5). As her external sensations simplify, the vibrating idea Lucy has been living with since hearing the opera has space to assert itself.

In an instant, Lucy recalls the stages that have led her to the threshold of epiphany: her unsatisfied restlessness and the pursuit of meaning that she believed Sebastian had fulfilled with his presence and taken back with his death. These memories, combined with her recent excitement, allow her to see beyond her grief: "Tonight, through the soft twilight, everything in her was reaching outward, straining forward. She could think of nothing but crowded streets with life streaming up and down, windows full of roses and gardenias and violets—she wanted to hold them all in her hands, to bury her face in them" (195). Then comes Lucy's epiphany:

> Suddenly something flashed into her mind, so clear that it must have come from without, from the breathless quiet. What if—what if Life itself were the sweetheart? It was like a lover waiting for her in distant cities—across the sea; drawing her, enticing her, weaving a spell over her. [...] Oh, now she knew! She must have it, she couldn't run away from it. She must go back into the world and get all she could of everything that had made

him what he was. Those splendours were still on earth, to be sought after and fought for. (195)

Lucy's breakthrough vindicates the sense of meaning she found, then lost, in the evening star. If she approaches the world as a sweetheart, rather than an "unknowing waste," it will reciprocate, love her back. While David Porter sees Lucy's fate as sealed by her association with fading sunsets, he affirms her awakening to the "evanescent sweetness of life and the need to seize life at once" ("From *The Song of the Lark*" 161). Yet this is no fleeting insight. Lucy discovers that the shift in her perspective is also the answer to her existential struggle to find meaning in a world without Sebastian in it. Instead of Chicago becoming the touchstone for Sebastian in her private landscape of the city, the love and perception Lucy knew through Sebastian become her touchstone for the world. Sebastian might linger as a metaphor, but Lucy is well positioned to fully realize her own desire as the thing itself. She has her answer.

Lucy's untimely death soon after her awakening is perhaps her most disappointing act as a character. Deborah Carlin implies that Lucy's drowning reflects Cather's flawed vision for the novel: "*Lucy Gayheart* remains . . . a failed attempt to revise what Cather complained was the chief failure of awakening novels, that is, the debilitating limitations of their female protagonists. Cather's text does revise the kind of awakening its heroine will have, and then it blithely marches her off to a version of the suicide with which these novels end" (139). Skaggs more harshly concludes that, "as the subject of a morality play, [Lucy] exists to deserve her fate. The primary moral she conveys is the crucial importance of a woman's self-consciously and energetically choosing the direction of her own life and then [being] willing to make her chosen life happen" (157). Others point to Lucy's reaction to *Der Doppelgänger* as evidence of Sebastian's sinister power over her. Lucy imagines that the song will "have some effect upon her own life" and feels that it haunts her "like an evil omen" (35). Her response prompts the narrator to reflect that Lucy is one of those people for whom "fate is what hap-

294

JOSHUA DOLEŽAL

pens to their feelings and their thoughts—that and nothing more"
(35). David Porter develops a compelling argument for the subtler
overtones of fatalism in Schubert's *Die Winterreise*, which Sebastian
performs in the second concert that Lucy attends. The winter setting
of the song cycle conjures a "barren, frozen world of loneliness, tragic
memories, and failed hopes" ("From *The Song of the Lark*" 160), and
one of the closing titles of the cycle is "Täuschung," or "Delusion"
(163). Such nuances, coupled with the narrator's later observation
that Lucy had been "lost by a song" (189), seem to foreshadow both
Sebastian's and Lucy's deaths by drowning.

However, Cather's conclusion offers a more unsettling suggestion,
which is that by the novel's end Lucy has effectively overcome the fate
implied by those foreboding feelings and musical allusions or by the
tropes of female awakening that precede *Lucy Gayheart*. The narrator
suggests that Lucy was "very nearly saved" by *The Bohemian Girl* (189),
which is not to say that the vision the opera left her with was insuf-
ficiently redemptive, only that Lucy's time to live out her new vision
was cut short. Fate is what happens to Lucy's feelings in the final
scene, when she returns to the river with her skates and the frozen
ground and bitter wind persuade her to turn back. She hears Harry
Gordon's sleigh and hopes he will give her a lift. When he drives cal-
lously by, "[s]uch a storm of pain and anger boiled up in her that she
felt strong enough to walk into the next county. Her blood was racing, and she was no longer conscious of the cold" (209). Lucy thinks
skating will assert her independence, keep her from suffering Harry's
slights again, but her anger blinds her to the dangers: "She was not
looking about her, she saw nothing—she would get away from this
frozen country and these frozen people, go back to light and freedom
such as they could never know" (209). Lucy's death is tragic because
she is finally on the outward path, resolved to pursue the things that
give her life meaning: the love of art that her father also lived for and
determined that she would have a chance at claiming. It happens to
be winter. The river happens to have changed its banks. Harry happens to stoke Lucy's anger at the very moment she has decided against
going skating. None of these accidents discredits Lucy's existential

triumph, which I hope to have demonstrated as being a reliable representation of epiphany by both literary and scientific measures.

If Lucy's death is an accident, rather than the result of what Stout sees as a "fatal deficiency" in her nature (270), then her epiphany retains its integrity. Lucy's discovery not only solves her own conceptual problem, it makes her personal awakening universal: empowering to anyone caught in the throes of depression or grief, as well as instructive to anyone seeking insight into the creative mind. Embracing life itself as a lover—it is still a good vision to live by.

NOTES

1. John Kounios is a professor of psychology and director of the PhD program in applied cognitive and brain sciences at Drexel University. Mark Beeman is a professor and chair of psychology at Northwestern University and a fellow of the National Academy of Sciences and the Association for Psychological Science.

WORKS CITED

Abraham, Anna. *The Neuroscience of Creativity*. Cambridge UP, 2018.
Carlin, Deborah. *Cather, Canon, and the Politics of Reading*. U of Massachusetts P, 1992.
Caruso, Isabella. "The Impure and the Pure in Cather's Female Artists." *Willa Cather Pioneer Memorial Newsletter and Review*, vol. 43, no. 1, 1999, pp. 5–9.
Cather, Willa. *The Complete Letters of Willa Cather*, edited by the Willa Cather Archive team, *Willa Cather Archive*, cather.unl.edu/writings/letters. Accessed 15 May 2019.
———. *Lucy Gayheart*. 1935. Willa Cather Scholarly Edition, historical essay by David Porter, explanatory notes by Kari A. Ronning and David Porter, textual essay and editing by Frederick M. Link and Kari A. Ronning, U of Nebraska P, 2015.
———. *The Selected Letters of Willa Cather*, edited by Andrew Jewell and Janis Stout, Knopf, 2013.
———. *The Song of the Lark*. 1915. Willa Cather Scholarly Edition, historical essay and explanatory notes by Ann Moseley, textual essay and editing by Kari A. Ronning, U of Nebraska P, 2012.

Finke, Ronald A., Thomas B. Ward, and Steven M. Smith. *Creative Cognition: Theory, Research, and Applications*. MIT P, 1992.

Kounios, John, and Mark Beeman. *The Eureka Factor: Aha Moments, Creative Insight, and the Brain*. Random House, 2015.

Lee, Hermione. *Willa Cather: Double Lives*. Pantheon, 1989.

Millington, Richard H. "An Elegy for the Reader: Europe and the Narrative of Self-Formation in *Lucy Gayheart*." *Willa Cather Newsletter and Review*, vol. 58, no. 2, 2015, pp. 29–34.

Porter, David. "From *The Song of the Lark* to *Lucy Gayheart*, and *Die Walküre* to *Die Winterreise*." *Willa Cather at the Modernist Crux Studies*, edited by Ann Moseley, John J. Murphy, and Robert Thacker, Cather Studies 11, U of Nebraska P, 2017, pp. 149–69.

———. *On the Divide: The Many Lives of Willa Cather*. U of Nebraska P, 2008.

Rosowski, Susan J. *The Voyage Perilous: Willa Cather's Romanticism*. U of Nebraska P, 1986.

———. "Willa Cather's Female Landscapes: *The Song of the Lark* and *Lucy Gayheart*." *Women's Studies*, vol. 11, no. 3, 1984, pp. 233–46.

Skaggs, Merrill Maguire. *After the World Broke in Two: The Later Novels of Willa Cather*. UP of Virginia, 1990.

Stouck, David. *Willa Cather's Imagination*. U of Nebraska P, 1975.

Stout, Janis P. *Willa Cather: The Writer and Her World*. UP of Virginia, 2000.

Urgo, Joseph. *Willa Cather and the Myth of American Migration*. U of Illinois P, 1995.

Wallas, George. *The Art of Thought*. Harcourt, Brace, 1926.

13 Unsettling Accompaniment
Disability as Critique of Aesthetic Power in Willa Cather's *Lucy Gayheart*

ELIZABETH WELLS

my poem on
Gay man's
performance

In "Willa Cather and the Performing Arts," Janis Stout defines Cather's concept of aesthetic power in terms of ability and strength. According to Stout, the power of an artistic performance for Cather consisted of an "artist's enormous personal vigor, his intense investment in his art" (113), and "a force or intensity ... which engaged her response and lifted her out of herself into another dimension of reality" (107). The "transformation of life" at the center of Cather's aesthetics, Stout argues, derives from her representation of artists as forcibly compelling, as able to hoist audiences above their disappointments and propel them toward transcendent beauty (113). More recently, Susan Meyer has echoed Stout's argument while extending it further to argue that Cather's "adulation of the vitality of the artist has an amoral quality" (98). In her article on *The Song of the Lark*, Meyer argues that protagonist Thea Kronborg repeatedly encounters threats to her body's strength in the form of "shadowy bodies, ill bodies, unfortunate bodies, dying bodies," and that the novel cruelly celebrates Thea's unlikely triumph of her own robust-

297

ness while revealing her "bodily precariousness," her vulnerability to the "dark undercurrent" of illness, weakness, and disability that modernity's conditions pose (112). Meyer concludes that Cather's fiction regularly privileges aesthetics over ethics in a way that is "at odds with familiar moral standards, at odds with self-denial and sympathy with the weak and suffering" (111).

The strong aesthetic ascribed to Cather in these readings carries serious implications for the signification of less powerful characters in her texts, those "shadowy bodies" that Meyer mentions. In particular, it immediately complicates the presence of artists with disabilities in Cather's texts, characters who are surprisingly numerous. In *The Song of the Lark* there is the concert pianist Andor Harsanyi, who has a glass eye, and in *My Ántonia* there are three performers with disabilities: Blind d'Arnault, the lame actress in *Camille*, and the singer Maria Vasak, who breaks her leg in the Alps.[1] When her performers themselves are not disabled, Cather also represents disability in accompanists and assistants: in "Paul's Case," Paul, whose teachers describe him as wrong-headed, strange, and "a bad case," is the Carnegie theater usher and the unofficial dresser for the actor Charley Edwards (*Youth* 219); Miletus Poppas, who has chronic facial neuralgia, is the accompanist to Cressida Garnet in "The Diamond Mine"; and James Mockford, who limps from a bad hip, is the piano accompanist for Clement Sebastian in *Lucy Gayheart*. If what Meyer argues is true and Cather defines her aesthetics in opposition to illness and disability, then what are we to make of Cather's interest in representing so many of her artists and accompanists as disabled?

Perhaps the perfect text for rethinking Cather's aesthetic power is *Lucy Gayheart*, a novel that showcases not only an accompanist with a disability, James Mockford, but also a protagonist who is anything but robust. Slight in body and easily fatigued, Lucy also shuns powerful connections, identifying more easily with the immigrants and tramps in Chicago than with her hometown hero. Lucy is diminutive not only in body but also in stage presence, for unlike Thea Kronborg, she is not a diva but a lowly accompanist, a title denoting that she is at once necessary to the performance but also less significant. In his historical essay for the novel's scholarly edition, David Porter has described Cather's turn from Thea to the weaker Lucy as a pessimistic variation on the theme of artistic development, arguing that while *The Song of the Lark* delivers a fully formed artist, *Lucy Gayheart* aborts its artists and accompanists wholesale, representing a "darkening of [Cather's] imaginative palette" in an "erosion of her vision of transcendent musical success" during her later years (277–79). But Cather's move from Thea to Lucy need not be pessimistic, for it may merely indicate her perspectival shift away from artistic formation and toward artistic production and accompaniment. Emphasizing the rift between ethics and aesthetics, accompanists draw attention to the offstage labors necessary for an aesthetic triumph like Thea's, one that demands accompaniment to compensate for what is lacking in the artist's performance.

Lucy Gayheart is a work that grapples with accompaniment as a theme at the heart of artistic production, and it does so distinctively through its representation of disability. Accordingly, it engages deeply with narrative prosthesis, what disability theorists David Mitchell and Sharon Snyder have described as art's unappreciative reliance upon abnormal bodies. As Mitchell and Snyder have argued, characters with disability often symbolize narrative possibility; acting as points of departure, their alterity pulls stories out of the stasis of convention and into a "search for the strange": "What calls stories into being, and what does disability have to do with this most basic preoccupation of narrative? Narrative prosthesis (or the dependency of literary narratives upon disability) forwards the notion that all narratives operate out of a desire to compensate for a limitation or to rein in excess. . . . A narrative is inaugurated 'by the search for the strange, which is presumed different from the place assigned it in the beginning by the discourse of the culture' from which it originates" (53). In *Lucy Gayheart* the theme of prosthesis unfolds in a number of complex layers, beginning with the onstage appearance of the central narrative prosthesis, James Mockford. Through its strangeness, Mockford's disability creates the opportunity for the narrative to occur at all, pulling Lucy from her humdrum experiences of teach-

ELIZABETH WELLS

ing music in Haverford toward becoming a satellite in Sebastian's artistic orbit. Mockford also brings narrative possibility to Sebastian, who gains years of success through the influence and support of his accompanist. Beyond plot, Mockford's appearance onstage initiates the novel's own search for the strange: limping across the stage as "a rag walking" (Cather, *Lucy Gayheart* 41), Mockford is a metonym for disability in narrative motion, a prosthesis made of print.

Despite its importance to narrative movement, however, Mockford's role is complicated by his disability and his supposed unsuitability for the stage. Indeed, this combination of narrative significance and undesirability is a hallmark of narrative prosthesis. According to Mitchell and Snyder, although authors often need disability, as they rely on it to create meaning, they also demand that it be removed in order to cleanse the narrative; having performed the service of artistic prosthesis, characters with disabilities are then let go. Sebastian's move to cut ties with Mockford in order to avoid giving him his rights fits well with how narrative prosthesis often works by relying on disability but then disposing of it once it has served its purpose. Understanding Mockford's removal—both from Sebastian's service and from the narrative—helps to make visible the deeper theme of prosthesis in the form of the novel's multiple cruel reliances and breakups masquerading as friendships. Nearly all of the friendships in the book are defined by compensatory service and terminations: failing as props for his artistic career, Sebastian's relationships repeatedly end when his friends disagree with him. Despite describing friends as beloved, Sebastian drops each of them whenever they begin to demand a relationship of more equivalence, one open to critique and disagreement. The same pattern of behavior holds true for Harry Gordon, who also employs his relationship with Lucy to compensate for the missing artistic pursuits in his life without endangering his reputation. Unable to abide threats to their power, both Sebastian and Harry abandon friendships whenever asked for more critical relationships. Cather thus portrays narrative prosthesis as both necessary and undesirable to both Sebastian and Harry, for both look to their accompanists to compensate for their inadequacies while also disdaining the presence of discord in their ventures.

Reading *Lucy Gayheart* through the theory of narrative prosthesis reveals how disability signifies imbalance in aesthetic compensation; however, it does not explain why this problem is so difficult to perceive. Lucy, our eyes and ears for most of the novel, never once suspects or doubts Sebastian, and even though she is an accompanist herself, she transfers her distrust entirely onto Mockford. Rivalries spring up everywhere in the plot, making it often difficult to know whose perspective to trust: besides the dispute center stage between Sebastian and his would-be "assisting artist," the novel also takes us to a backstage consumed by infighting, where assistants are eyeing each other suspiciously as they vie for positions. To understand why Cather creates such an environment of mistrust, I turn to disability scholar Rosemarie Garland-Thomson and her theory of the normate. Analyzing the confusion that occurs in encounters with disability, Garland-Thomson argues that the nondisabled react with disgust and fear as they scramble toward a haven of normalcy—what Garland-Thomson names the normate perspective. Garland-Thomson's theory helps to explain multiple moments in Cather's fiction, including Aaron Dunlap's discomfort and fascination with Virginia Gilbert in "The Profile," Thea Kronborg's abhorrence of Mary the Hungarian maid, Jim Burden's initial fear of Marek, and of course Lucy's aversion toward Mockford. In addition to its explanation of these visceral responses, the normate concept also clarifies the themes of jealousy and competitive "insinuation" in this text, revealing that Lucy's revulsion stems from her fear of losing her attachment to Sebastian and the norms he represents. Despite her confusion and prejudice, Lucy never realizes that her reading of Mockford is misguided; uncritically loyal to Sebastian, she cannot see that *he* is the one who is untrustworthy. Indeed, in Sebastian's repeated action of gaslighting—of portraying his past relationships as broken and abnormal to his new prospects—he embodies the perspective of the normate, that which defines its own normalcy only by slandering the validity of the other. Pitting his new accompanists against ᴜⅼe old, he convinces them to see themselves as normal against the mental and physical instabilities of his previous accompanists. As with his interest in his valet Giuseppe, Sebastian's interest in Lucy Gayheart is in someone who will be eternally loyal without ever turning on him, without ever having a claim to a voice within their relationship—a quality that would make her instantly undesirable.

The disability theories of narrative prosthesis and the normate perspective thus illuminate the ways in which *Lucy Gayheart* establishes an arduous leading role for disability while also revealing how poorly its performance will be received. This dramatic dilemma is apparent from the initial appearance of Mockford onstage and Lucy's subsequent disgust; despite disability being allowed onstage to take its bow, its presence nevertheless unsettles, causing viewers to experience repulsion, fear, or envy in efforts to avoid abnormality. Through her complex exploration of the politics and psychology of narrative accompaniment, Cather creates an original disability aesthetic that critiques the artistic practices of avoiding abnormality. In contrast to the arguments of Stout and Meyer, this new aesthetic does not lift the artist above disability but pulls the artist down by disrupting the processes of both creation and interpretation.

Unsettling readers instead of transporting them to a transcendent realm, Cather opposes an aesthetic that only appreciates strength by demonstrating the essential work of disability's accompaniment while also revealing why this accompanist is forced to remain backstage to meet the expectations of the normate. The novel's three endings bring this weight to bear on those in the narrative who have refused it; in Sebastian's drowning by Mockford, in Lucy's drowning death, and in Harry Gordon's lifelong guilt, described as "a wooden leg" (233), Cather constructs permutations of the union of the unsettling accompanist with the artist. By dragging down and unsettling the viewer, Cather's symbolic endings critique an aesthetic that encourages strength at all costs, particularly at the cost of the well-being of accompanists who have given their energies to sustain art.

TARNISHING AND VANISHING: MUSICAL
ACCOMPANIMENT AS NARRATIVE PROSTHESIS

On the night that Lucy sees Clement Sebastian perform,
she is impressed by how perfectly he suits the look of a great artist. Large and heavy, he "took up a great deal of space and filled it
solidly." His torso has a pleasantly round shape, "unquestionably
oval," and he is dressed with tailored perfection, "sheathed in black
broadcloth and a white waistcoat" (31). Offstage, Sebastian is no
different; whether buttoning up his dinner jacket, putting on an
overcoat, turning up his collar, or winding a scarf around his neck,
Sebastian is usually binding up his dress and appearance to maintain its shape. As Susan Rosowski has argued in *The Voyage Perilous*,
Cather suggests vampiric qualities in Sebastian's formal dress and in
his preying on young things: besides Mockford, whom he took on
years ago, and now Lucy, there is also his adopted child, Marius (223–
25). But another way of reading these gothic elements in Sebastian
is in terms of his insistence on an appearance that is unblemished,
tightly contained, and whole.

As with his articles of clothing, Sebastian seeks accompanists who
will round out his performances. We learn from Mockford that
Sebastian has been searching eagerly over the years for replacement
accompanists—"he rather fancies breaking in a new person"—but
that he is almost never satisfied with replacements because they are
not "personally sympathetic to him" (61). The criterion for that personal sympathy becomes clear only when Lucy tries out for him.
Despairing aloud that she has been too timid in execution, Sebastian reassures her that the only important thing in accompaniment
is an absence of ugliness. "The point is," he says to her, "you do not
make ugly sounds; that puts me out more than anything" (38). After
returning to her own apartment, Lucy thinks admiringly about the
orderliness of Sebastian's apartment, unconsciously summarizing
Sebastian's aesthetic in a single phrase: "Evidently nothing ever came
near Sebastian to tarnish his personal elegance" (48).

Ugliness is what Sebastian cannot tolerate in his presence, and so it makes sense that he is hard at work finding a replacement for James Mockford, whose disability threatens to disrupt Sebastian's performances. Through Lucy, we witness this firsthand: during Sebastian's first performance, Lucy enters a trance so deep that she does not even notice Sebastian's exit. However, her trance is broken abruptly by Mockford's appearance: "The moon was gone, and the silent street.—And Sebastian was gone, though Lucy had not been aware of his exit. The black cloud that had passed over the moon and the song had obliterated him, too. There was nobody left before the grey velvet curtain but the red-haired accompanist, a lame boy, who dragged one foot as he went across the stage" (32–33). The sound and sight of Mockford's dragging foot breaks the spell of Sebastian's performance, upsetting its ambience. When Lucy sees a second performance, she focuses even more upon Mockford's unpleasant effects, as she says to herself that his walk across the stage bothers her: "His lameness gave him a weak, undulating walk" (41). Mockford's limping gait clashes with Sebastian's elegance, taking away from its power by rendering it weak and ruffling its smoothness with its undulations, its irregularities.

Mockford's ugliness is not only problematic onstage but also off, as Sebastian and Lucy struggle repeatedly with his intrusions upon their tête-à-têtes. Mockford interrupts them when he comes to Sebastian's apartment requesting a favor several times—train tickets, a cab ride, a place to store his chair before their tour—and even though these requests might not appear unusual from a long-term friend, Sebastian nevertheless calls Mockford's manner "brassy" and impertinent (97). Mockford strikes Lucy and Giuseppe in the same way. Lucy describes his fingers as "insinuating" and thinks of him as "selfish and vain" (41, 64), and Giuseppe complains of Mockford's request to keep his large lounge chair in the apartment, calling it an "ugly chair" that belongs in a secondhand shop (130); it is the chair Mockford uses to stretch out his bad leg. As furniture pieces, lounge chairs have the power to evoke high art through their association with painting studios, the *chaises longues* that elongate the

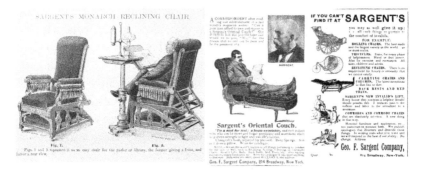

Fig. 13.1. Mockford's "ugly chair" straddles the line between high-art furniture, like an artist studio's *chaise longue*, and functional patent furniture, like chairs and recliners. Advertisements for adjustable lounge chairs from New York patent and "invalid furniture" maker Geo. F. Sargent Company: (*left*) the Monarch recliner (Van Dyk); (*center*) the Oriental Couch (*McClure's*); (*right*) a general advertisement for "invalid furniture" from Geo. F. Sargent that shows a range of their available products in the *Century Illustrated Monthly*, vol. 49, 1894.

figures of the most beautiful painting subjects in the world. However, as so-called invalid furniture, Mockford's lounge chair brings to mind only illness and shabbiness, his body's imperfections. Like his limping gait, Mockford's chair mars Sebastian's beautiful canvas.

In contrast to Mockford, with his "brassy" manners and "ugly chair," Giuseppe and Lucy both aspire to make no ugly sounds, indeed, to make no sounds at all. After Sebastian changes into formal dress, Giuseppe compliments his beautiful appearance, "'*Ecco una cosa molto bella*!' [. . .] before he vanished through the entry hall" (52). Small and unassuming, Giuseppe is desirable as a servant to Sebastian precisely because he serves then disappears without leaving a trace. "I haven't a friend in the world who would do for me what that little man would," Sebastian tells Lucy, for Giuseppe serves without brassiness (47). Like Giuseppe, Lucy is small and unobtrusive, appealing to Sebastian because she vanishes so easily: he first spots Lucy literally hiding behind a pillar (43). It does not take Lucy long to surmise that it is her absence of substance that makes her appealing to Sebastian: "She felt that he liked her being young and ignorant and not too clever. It was an accidental relationship, between someone who had everything and someone who had nothing at all; and it concerned nobody else" (64). Although Lucy recognizes the imbalance of roles in her relationship with Sebastian, she believes she is dependent upon him and owes him gratitude. Much like Giuseppe, she erases her own importance whenever Sebastian is near, and this erasure is what Sebastian seeks in assistants—to prevent ruffles in his perfect appearance.

However, these two vanishing assistants do not believe that they are invisible—quite the opposite, since they regard their meaningfulness to Sebastian as their entire raison d'être. When Sebastian glosses the meaning of Giuseppe's appearance to Lucy, she is in awe and expresses a great desire to become a sign just as meaningful as Giuseppe:

> "I've never had better service. Think of it, he has got all those lines on his forehead worrying about other people's coats and boots and breakfasts." [...]
> Something in the way he said this made Lucy feel a trifle downcast. She almost wished she were Giuseppe. After all, it was people like that who counted with artists—more than their admirers. (47)

Envying the furrows in Giuseppe's forehead that signify his long service to Sebastian's artistic endeavors, Lucy wants nothing more than to gain meaning by also becoming a legible signal. Indeed, Cather presents Lucy's escape from Haverford as a hermeneutic search, with Lucy desiring to become a signifier to bring meaning to her world, and she believes she can become one through her service to Sebastian. What Lucy does not notice, however, is the toll of fatigue in that service; both Mockford and Giuseppe, for instance, are presented physically (as composites of fresh youth and worn age) Cather suggests that the process of escaping conventional life and becoming a sign in another's firmament is also wearying and destructive: "it hurt and made one feel small and lost" (14). Initially smothered by the absence of meaning in her small town, Lucy tries to become meaningful in the city but instead dissolves into another smothering embrace.

Having worn out his own meaningfulness, Mockford no longer suits Sebastian, who plans to dismiss him and train Lucy toward the same end. In his plans to eliminate Mockford, Sebastian hopes to replace his disabled accompanist, a man whose impertinence tarnishes the great artist's desired image, with milder accompanists. According to the terms of Mitchell and Snyder's theory of narrative prosthesis, Lucy and Giuseppe represent the "cures" needed to eliminate disability's presence and repair the disruption it has caused. Just as Sebastian is constantly binding up his body with coats, scarves, and ribbons, so he attempts to stitch up the snags that Mockford has left as a prosthesis. This patch job, however, is only part of the story of how prosthesis works. Mitchell and Snyder explain that to understand why the narrative needs to cure itself by eliminating disability, we must first understand why disability was ever invited into the narrative in the first place. Narratives, they explain, cannot come into existence without the aid of deviation, and in the case of representations of disability, that deviation comes in the form of an abnormal body that not only challenges expectations for normalcy but also builds motion into the story, pushing it forward from its complacency. Analyzing the classic tale *The Steadfast Tin Soldier*, they explain how the soldier's missing leg acts as the impetus for the entire story's plot and significance:

> The anonymity of normalcy is no story at all. Deviance serves as the basis and common denominator of all narrative. In this sense, the missing leg presents the aberrant soldier as the story's focus, for his physical difference exiles him from the rank and file of the uniform and physically undifferentiated troop. Whereas a sociality might reject, isolate, institutionalize, reprimand, or obliterate this liability of a single leg, narrative embraces the opportunity that such a "lack" provides—in fact, wills it into existence—as the impetus that calls a story into

being. Such a paradox underscores the ironic promise of disability to all narrative. (54–55)

Because they diverge from social order, characters with disability
have the unique ability to build narrative meaning. The "ironic
promise" that disability as narrative prosthesis provides is that it
offers to compensate for a lack in narrative—its absence of deviation—by destroying that normalcy.

Such is the case with Mockford, who besides disturbing Sebastian's perfection also acts as a narrative source, an origin point for
the story's arc and significance. Indeed, it is Mockford's disability
that gives Lucy her opportunity to become Sebastian's accompanist,
and although Lucy herself admits this debt to Mockford's disability,
she does little to understand the implications of this admission since
she is too repulsed by his disability: "It was contemptible to hold a
man's infirmity against him; besides, if this young man weren't lame,
she would not be going to Sebastian's studio tomorrow,—she would
never have met him at all. How strange it was that James Mockford's
bad hip should bring about the most important thing that had ever
happened to her" (41). Later she learns that it is this "queer, talented,
tricky boy" who teaches Sebastian so much about the German Lieder
and who brings him so many years of success through his accompaniment (97). In his notes to the scholarly edition, David Porter
rightly points out that it is not unusual for Mockford to demand
some recognition for his accompaniment: "Mockford's wish is to
be acknowledged as what any great lieder accompanist must be: a
collaborator, not just an accompanist. Sebastian has earlier acknowledged how much he relies on Mockford ('I've got a great many
hints from him' [59]), but here he rejects Mockford's wish to be
more than 'second fiddle'" (376–77). As Porter suggests, Mockford's
request to be billed as "assisting artist" rather than accompanist is
warranted since interpreting the Lieder requires creative ability. And
while Sebastian does not deny the fact that he has benefited greatly
from Mockford's talents, even calling him a "little genius," he refuses
to give him that recognition (59).

When we connect disability to the origins of Sebastian's art, we can better interpret why Cather attributes to Mockford such a strangely artificial appearance throughout the text. Critics have tended to read his ghastly whiteness as a symbolic association with death.[2] However, his appearance is more directly tied to the artifice of the stage and works of art. "He couldn't help looking theatrical," Lucy says about him, for "he was made so, and she couldn't tell whether or not he liked being unusual" (62). Lucy describes Mockford as having curls and dress that make him appear like a statue—"she thought she remembered plaster casts in the Art Museum with just such curls"—and she repeatedly observes that his face is as white as flour, plaster, or paint, a whiteness that disturbs her throughout the novel (41). Mockford's whiteness appalls not necessarily as a reminder of death but as the whiteness of the page, a place where a work of art comes into being. His whiteness represents artistic fascination and becoming; Lucy cannot stop thinking about it, wishing that "she could get his white face out of her mind" (64). But it also frightens with its otherness, its threat to the story. His white face resembles Stéphane Mallarmé's *abîme blanchi*, the whitened abyss of the page that threatens to swallow up the artist's idealized but unrealized materials (460), for Mockford's whiteness appalls with its artistic promises and disappointments.

Mockford's whiteness also acts as a foil to the blackness and shadow that pervade Sebastian and Lucy's moments together. "The black cloud that had passed over the moon and the song had obliterated him, too," Lucy says in a trance after seeing Sebastian perform, emphasizing the perfection and desirability of the stage's emptiness (32). When Lucy becomes Sebastian's accompanist, she describes her time with him as an event of utter solitude that blots out the representation of a world: "For two hours, five days of the week, she was alone with Sebastian, shut away from the rest of the world. It was as if they were on the lonely spur of a mountain, enveloped by mist. They saw no one but Giuseppe, heard no one; the city below was blotted out" (80). When Lucy is not alone with Sebastian, she is often alone, savoring her memories of Sebastian, and in her thoughts during these moments Lucy often indicates a desire for indistinction, for a dark and shadowy pleasure:

> Her memories did not stand out separately; they were blended and pervasive. They made the room seem larger than it was, quieter and more guarded; gave it a slight austerity. [...] She put on her dressing-gown, turned out the gas light, and lay down to reflect. (30)

> Lucy often spent the long hot evenings in Sebastian's music room, lying on the sofa, with the big windows open and the lights turned out. [...] When she couldn't sit still any longer, there was nothing to do but to hurry along the sidewalks again; diving into black tents of shadow under the motionless, thick-foliaged maple trees, then out into the white moonshine. And always one had to elude people. (143)

Hinting at onanistic pleasure in these passages, Cather repeatedly emphasizes the absence of creativity in Lucy's solitary reflections upon Sebastian by demonstrating the absence of differentiation in her memories: they are dark, blended together, and exist only for her. When Sebastian and Lucy embrace for the last time before his tour departure, Cather describes their union as sublimely pleasurable but having a "blackness above them [that] was soft and velvety" (135). While Mockford's tarnishing accompaniment contributes to the making of art, Lucy's and Giuseppe's accompaniments blot out all representation of a world of difference in efforts to be fully subsumed, to vanish into Sebastian's undifferentiated solidity.

The dispute between Mockford and Sebastian thus plays out an allegory of narrative prosthesis in which disability's artistic power is first appropriated to build a work of art by compensating for its absence of abnormality and is then thrown out to erase its presence and return the text to normalcy. Mitchell and Snyder argue that the act of eradicating characters with disability is a punishment that results from the author's action of attempting to restore normalcy in a text: "Disability inaugurates narrative, but narrative inevitably punishes its own prurient interests by overseeing the extermination of the object of its fascination" (56–57). Indeed, in *Sebastian*, Cather represents an artist who intentionally "throw[s] over" one of his oldest friends in order to build a more fitting collaboration with a new accompanist (Cather, *Lucy Gayheart* 104). But Cather also suggests that these efforts at erasing disability's presence fail, for the story ends when Mockford is thrown away: when Mockford drowns, so, too, does Sebastian. And there is no encore, no collaborative performance of Sebastian with his vanishing accompanist.

PERSPECTIVAL GASLIGHTING: "SECOND FIDDLE" LOYALTY AND THE NORMATE

Perhaps the most challenging part of reading *Lucy Gayheart* is interpreting the action from the often unreliable perspective of Lucy. Lucy believes to the end, for instance, that Mockford was responsible for Sebastian's death and that she should have alerted Sebastian "to beware of Mockford, that he was cowardly, envious, treacherous, and she knew it!" (166). Even though she never admits her suspicions to Sebastian, she certainly makes clear her own dislike for Mockford after every encounter with him, describing him as vain, insinuating, and untrustworthy. Critics have tended to adopt Lucy's distrust for Mockford, viewing him as a negative character, particularly one who symbolizes death and self-destruction. James Woodress has read Mockford as a "sinister homosexual" and jealous "rival for Sebastian's affections," arguing that he ultimately triumphs in his duel against Lucy (451). David Stouck has read Mockford as a theatrical personification of Death whose limp represents the creeping resolution of mortality (219–20). Likewise, Susan Rosowski has argued that, with his ghastly whiteness, Mockford represents death and a vampiric rapacity for youth and beauty. Reading his death as a metaphor for Sebastian's clinging to Lucy and draining her of vitality, Rosowski also trusts Lucy's interpretation of Mockford as a harbinger of death and destruction ("Cather's Female Landscapes" 242).

ELIZABETH WELLS

However, there are a number of reasons not to fully trust Lucy's observations on Mockford. From her first sight of him onstage, Lucy emphasizes how Mockford makes her extremely uncomfortable. When she meets him for the first time face-to-face, she tries to understand the confusing effects of his manner upon her: "His manner was a baffling mixture of timidity and cheek. One thing was clear; he was uncomfortable in her company, and certainly she was in his" (62–63). For a moment she wonders if it is jealousy that is causing her dislike, but she waves that idea off; she certainly does not, however, dismiss the idea that Mockford himself is motivated by jealousy. In her nightmare, she imagines Mockford as consumed with murderous jealousy, his "green eyes [. . .] full of terror and greed" (166).

With her theory of the normate, Rosemarie Garland-Thomson offers clues for understanding Lucy's reactions to Mockford, both onstage and off. Garland-Thomson argues that reactions to the disabled when they are onstage differ from real-life encounters because of the psychological and physical stressors that occur to the nondisabled in their efforts to adhere to the boundaries of normalcy: "The interaction is usually strained because the nondisabled person may feel fear, pity, fascination, repulsion, or merely surprise, none of which is expressible according to social protocol," while a "nondisabled person often does not know how to act toward a disabled person: how or whether to offer assistance; whether to acknowledge the disability. . . . Perhaps most destructive to the potential for continuing relations is the normate's frequent assumption that a disability cancels out other qualities, reducing the complex person to a single attribute" (12). Indeed, before Lucy has met Mockford, she already has reduced him to his impairment, to a limp rag walking, even scolding herself subsequently for doing so: "It was contemptible to hold a man's infirmity against him" (41). After the performance, she does not meet Mockford for some weeks, and she expresses great relief that he "never dropped in upon them" (59); however, to her disappointment, Lucy accidentally meets him face-to-face when he answers the door of Sebastian's apartment: "It was Mockford who opened the door for her and asked her to come in. She drew back and would have run away if she could" (59–60). Despite Lucy's fear, Mockford politely greets her and invites her in, takes her coat, and brings her a chair, all while walking slowly and with difficulty. The two of them exchange long "searching look[s]" before Mockford reluctantly opens up and shares with Lucy his frustrations about his impending surgery and about having to miss the upcoming season (60). While he talks, Lucy says very little but stares at him throughout, at his eyes, his dress, and his hands, fixating on their strangeness, wondering whether he is wearing a wig or "whether or not he liked being unusual" (62). After Mockford recounts some of Sebastian's dissatisfactions with touring and his positive review of her accompaniment, Lucy is soon so flustered that she leaves the building abruptly, brooding over her disappointments:

> Lucy went down in the elevator, wondering whether she would ever go up in it again. She had dreaded meeting Mockford, but she couldn't have imagined that such a meeting would break her courage and hurt her feelings. She fiercely resented his having any opinions about her or her connection with Sebastian. This was the first time a third person had in any way come upon their little scene, and she hated it. [. . .] She felt that this strange man who was neither young nor old, who was picturesque and a little repelling, was not altogether trustworthy. (63–64)

In her extreme skittishness, her paralysis, and in her staring throughout their encounter, Lucy demonstrates what Garland-Thomson describes as the confusion and frustration of the nondisabled when failing to sort out proper social behaviors. Moreover, her "fierce resent[ment]" against Mockford for sharing Sebastian's favorable opinion about her reveals Lucy's immense insecurities (63). Besides offering insight into Lucy's psychology, Garland-Thomson's theory also helps to explain how Lucy's misreading of Mockford as repulsive, fascinating, and above all threatening emerges from an underlying ideological problem of trust in the novel. Garland-Thomson argues that in encounters with disability the nondisabled

Trump's
henchman

unconsciously construct the normate position in opposition to the disabled in order to validate their normalcy: "The term *normate* usefully designates the social figure through which people can represent themselves as definitive human beings. Normate . . . is the constructed identity of those who, by way of the bodily configurations and cultural capital they assume, can step into a position of authority and wield the power it grants them" (8). Although Lucy is hired only as a temporary replacement for Mockford, she nonetheless despises the idea that Mockford be included in any discourse that involves Sebastian. In her association with Sebastian, she clings to their union as a relationship that excludes Mockford, whose otherness stretches too far the "little scene" that she and Sebastian occupy (63). Identifying herself with Sebastian and against Mockford, Lucy seeks to inhabit the position of the normate; loyal only to Sebastian, she regards Mockford as an interloper who cannot be trusted.

Lucy's unshakable loyalty to Sebastian prevents her from perceiving the patterns of mistrustful behavior in all of Sebastian's relationships. At a moment when the narrative shifts to Sebastian's perspective, he admits to himself that he has no knowledge of what true companionship is—"[w]ell, he had missed it, whatever it was" (83)—and that his life is a series of failed relationships. Of his best friend, Larry MacGowan, who dies early in the novel, Sebastian laments that their friendship ended long before Larry's death because of a fight that the two had when Larry visited him years earlier. When Lucy asks about it, Sebastian gives her this account: "I had looked forward to Larry's visit, but it didn't turn out well. He didn't like our house or our servants or our friends, or anything else. He showed it plainly, and I was disappointed and piqued. Our parting was cold. I think he must have been breaking up even then. He was difficult about everything, and he made criticisms that hurt one's feelings" (88–89). Rather than regret his own action of cutting the friendship off, Sebastian rationalizes ending the friendship by describing Larry's behavior as pathological—"he must have been breaking up even then"—attributing it to his much later mental illness. Soon after, Sebastian tells Lucy that he plans to fire Mockford because of a dispute, again labeling as unwell a friend who disagrees with him: "He's all right at bottom, but he's not well. That makes him peevish. Just now he's fighting with me; for his rights, he says. Some of his cronies have put it into his head that he ought to be printed on my programs as 'assisting artist' instead of accompanist. I won't have it, and he's sulky" (97). Mockford has asked Sebastian to bill him as a bigger part of the act, and rather than cooperate, Sebastian decides to reward Mockford's long and loyal service to him—indeed, Mockford is "one of the few friends who have lasted through time and change" (56)—with a pink slip. In his explanation of their dispute, Sebastian performs the same kind of manipulation with Mockford that he does with Larry, calling him unwell and "sulky" because of his disability and calling his request to be seen as a more equal part of the act an unfortunate result of "peevishness" attributable to his disability.

Although critics have trusted Sebastian in his villainizing of Mockford, it is important to consider the possibility that this characterization fits a pattern of gaslighting, of deceptively painting his friends as abnormal whenever they criticize him.[3] When Lucy is put off by Mockford, Sebastian laughs at her reaction, chiding her for not having "much skill in dissimulation" (97), suggesting in subtext that *he* certainly does. He has no problem, for instance, telling Mockford that he will give him what he has requested—his billing as assisting artist—when in actuality he tells Lucy that he plans to let him go. From everything that Sebastian has told her, Lucy is encouraged to see Mockford as untrustworthy, and when she directly asks Sebastian if he is indeed disloyal, Sebastian laughs off the question: "Loyal? As loyal as anyone who plays second fiddle ever is. We mustn't expect too much!" (97). To Sebastian, all relationships are pairings of master and accompanist wherein the "second fiddle" will eventually demand a greater piece of the pie. No wonder, then, that he seeks out the vanishing accompanists, Lucy and Giuseppe, and loves them for being wholly loyal, for never seeking any "claim" upon him. "He wants someone young and teachable, not somebody who will try to teach him," says Lucy's teacher, Paul Auerbach, about the kind of replacement Sebastian has requested (36). Fed up with being taught by others, with taking criticism and hints from his accompanists and friends, Sebastian seeks out relationships with others—people who will never clash with him and will stand behind him when he abandons older friends. His deceptive actions perform well the work of the normate, of defining himself as master in opposition to accompanists who, in their abnormality, pose a threat to his position of power. Moreover, the intense loyalties of Giuseppe and Lucy to Sebastian's normate perspective destabilize their own opinions and reactions, revealing them to be contributors to the ideological shoring up of normalcy.

Sebastian dies shortly after divulging to Lucy his plan to fire Mockford, who clings to Sebastian in a final embrace. While Lucy blames Mockford for Sebastian's death, seeing him as a hideous "white thing" that drowned him, her interpretation fails to recognize the truth in Mockford's claims versus the dissimulation of Sebastian (166). As the "white thing" that drags Sebastian down, Mockford becomes a nemesis figure. His deadly hold on his partner and friend dramatizes the accompanist's refusal to be ignored and cast off as dross, as nothing more than "second fiddle" (97).

EMBRACING THE MOCKING WORLD ON A WOODEN LEG: RESOLUTIONS THROUGH DISABILITY

Following the deaths of Sebastian and Mockford, Lucy's story comes to a halt. After returning to Haverford, she refuses to teach or even to communicate with others about her despair. It is not until the night of the stage performance of *The Bohemian Girl* that Lucy's story begins to move forward again, and once again this change emerges from an encounter with an abnormal body. When Lucy goes with her father and sister to see the opera, she is stunned at how moved she is by the performance of an aging soprano miscast in the role of a young girl. Consequently, she finds herself compelled to assist in the performance: "Why was it worth her while,

Fig. 13.2. The prosthetic wooden leg found at Cather's childhood home, Willow Shade, in a hidden compartment during late twentieth-century renovations. The leg is thought to have belonged to a family member, Alfreda, who lost her leg in the 1860s from tuberculosis. Willow Shade owner Sandy Pumphrey is pictured. *Winchester Star*/Jeff Taylor.

Lucy wondered. Singing this humdrum music to humdrum people, why was it worth while? This poor little singer had lost everything: youth, good looks, position, the high notes of her voice. And yet she sang so well! Lucy wanted to be up there on the stage with her, helping her do it" (191–92). While Lucy was initially drawn to Sebastian by his perfection and grandeur, here she is instead attracted to the absence of perfection in this soprano's presence. It is through the singer's imperfections that Lucy recognizes her quality, an artistic goodness that draws Lucy in as an accompanist, though this time she describes the work very differently. Rather than feeling a soft and velvety blackness, Lucy describes her choice to return to music as an impending scandal that she will face head on: "Let it come! Let it all come back to her again! Let it betray her and mock her and break her heart, she must have it!" (195). Embracing the storm of life, Lucy communicates her epiphanic comprehension of a new kind of aesthetic economy, one that welcomes the vicissitudes of a "mocking" world upon her own bodily form rather than forcing one to wear out the life of an accompanist. Although Lucy never sympathizes overtly with Mockford, her desire to join the soprano onstage and her subsequent decision to teach music—rather than continue as an accompanist—suggest that Lucy ultimately resolves the problem of cyclic consumption that she witnessed in the artistic pair of Sebastian and Mockford. Moreover, Lucy's decision to accept the "mocking" world by becoming a music teacher also suggests that she no longer views her small town as a place that is necessarily meaningless. In the few days that remain before her death, she turns toward Harry and the other parts of Haverford in an effort to stop viewing them as limitations that prevent her from having a significant experience of the world. Instead, Cather suggests that Lucy becomes more like the aging soprano, whose imperfections become agents that draw others toward a more meaningful shared experience.[4]

Despite her final artistic epiphany, however, Lucy still dies in a reprise of Sebastian's and Mockford's drowning deaths. Critics have tended to see Lucy's death as a singular choice of Cather rather than as an organic part of the novel's action. Merrill Maguire Skaggs, for instance, argues that Lucy is tragically destined to be "dispatched" from the text because she lacks ambition and narrative interest as a character (156–61); indeed, Cather herself complained in a letter about "los[ing] patience" with her heroine's silliness (*Selected Letters* 488–89). James Woodress reads Lucy's death as a natural consequence of "the darkening vision" of "an aging novelist" (449). More recently, David Porter has similarly argued that in Lucy's death Cather represents her own frustrations with seeing "the brightest of futures prove a fugitive gleam" ("From *Song of the Lark*" 165). In addition to his biographical reading, Porter also views Lucy's death as Cather's representation of the inescapable punishment of the universe, a part of what Cather once described as the "seeming original injustice that creatures so splendidly aspiring should be inexorably doomed to fail" ("From *Song of the Lark*" 167–68). However, I would argue that

Lucy's death is neither a narrative nor cosmic punishment but rather the tragic and unjust result of Harry's refusal to help her. It is thus in Harry's story line that Cather most fully resolves the problem of disability as narrative accompaniment.

Much like Sebastian with Mockford, Harry has always wanted Lucy to act as an accompanist for him. He recognizes that Lucy has "a gift of nature [...] to go wildly happy over trifling things" and that when he is with her, he can "catch it from [her] for a moment, feeling it flash by his ear. [...] His own body grew marvellously free and light, and there was a snapping sparkle in his blood that made him set his teeth" (234–35). However, he only likes to experience this gift through *her*. Like Sebastian, Harry has an eminent presence, and he is often concerned with dressing well and looking important; however, he believes that he cannot maintain his reputation if he allows himself to take pleasure in "trifling things," in art and nature. With Lucy, he attempts to sublimate these passions so that he does not have to let them disrupt his life. In fact, in reflections upon his desire to marry Lucy, he thinks of using Lucy as his lifelong "excuse" for experiencing feelings that would normally appear unsuitable in a businessman: "He was full of his own plans, and the future looked bright to him. There was a part of himself that Harry was ashamed to live out in the open (he hated a sentimental man), but he could live it through Lucy. She would be his excuse for doing a great many pleasant things he wouldn't do on his own account" (114). Like Mockford's queerness and disability, Lucy's sensibility offers Harry the chance to live a fine and meaningful life without detracting from his prestige. Harry desires to make of Lucy a prosthesis that will accomplish the wholeness of his own career, appropriating her gifts while also distancing himself from any vulnerability to ensure his ongoing success.

However, once Harry is married, Lucy can no longer be that accompanist for him; consequently, when he sees her, he cannot help being unmoored by the feelings that he has for her and his desire for fineness and grace in his life. In this way, his rejection of Lucy mirrors Sebastian's rejection of Mockford: the threat of her relationship becoming one of equals, one that will not force her to carry the burden of sentiment, is too much for him and he pushes her away. Like Mockford, Lucy becomes indignant and impertinent toward Harry in the last moments of her life, screaming to him to recognize the injustice of his actions to her. Much later, Harry thinks about this claim in terms of the surprising authority he heard in her voice: "Many a time, going home on winter nights, he had heard again that last cry on the wind—'Harry!' Indignation, amazement, authority, as if she wouldn't allow him to do anything so shameful" (232). David Porter has described Lucy's final shout as witheringly futile compared to the strong voice of Thea Kronborg ("From *Song of the Lark*" 152); however, I read her angry call as being extremely powerful. It echoes her exasperated shout at him during their fight in the restaurant in Chicago: "Can't you understand *anything*?" (118). Each time they argue, Lucy feels that Harry does not hear her, that he fails to listen. But Lucy has long desired a different kind of relationship with Harry, one where she is allowed to critique him or disagree with him without him turning against her. When she tries to renew ties with him after returning to Haverford, she thinks of their communication as the most important part of their friendship: "If she could only get a message to him, Lucy was thinking as she walked away. She wanted little more than a friendly look when he passed her on the street, the sort of look he used to give her, careless and jolly" (158). Her need for transmitting a message to Harry is brought to a tragic end when she drowns only because she did not know that the river's bed had shifted. Right before her death she plans to reach out to Harry to ask him about the "new habit the light had taken on" since she had moved away:

> Did that pink flush use to come there, in the days when she was running up and down these sidewalks, or was it a new habit the light had taken on? If there was anyone in Haverford who could tell her, it would be Harry Gordon. He was the only man here who noticed such things, and he was deeply, though unwillingly, moved by them. [...] Harry kept that side of himself well

hidden. He could feel things without betraying himself, because he was so strong. If only she could have that strength behind her instead of against her! (199)

Lucy's question, never heeded by Harry, not only requests information that would save her life—we may infer that the light has changed because of the altered landscape and sunken trees resulting from the river's shifted course—but also asks for a change in their relationship that would place them on more equal footing. Moreover, Lucy requests that Harry recognize his own gifts and hide them less so that the two of them might support each other in their mutual efforts.

But Harry refuses to listen to Lucy's messages, even when she shouts at him in fury. In his rejection of a plea from his friend who is asking him for a new kind of relationship not defined by accompaniment, Harry resembles Sebastian. However, unlike Sebastian, Harry's shameful rejection of his accompanist does not result in his own death. Instead, he survives with "a life sentence," as he calls it, a burden of memory that Cather describes as being like a wooden leg: "'Well, it's a life sentence.' That was the way he used to think about it. Lucy had suffered for a few hours, a few weeks at most. But with him it was there to stay. [...] As time dragged on he had got used to that dark place in his mind, as people get used to going through the world on a wooden leg" (232–33). Representing his accountability to Lucy's memory as a prosthetic leg, Cather again presents disability as narrative accompaniment and prosthesis; however, while Sebastian treated his disabled accompanist as someone to use up and then cut loose, Harry Gordon does neither with the "wooden leg" of his past. Stopping the cycle of feeding upon the energies of one's accompanist, Harry incorporates his prosthesis into himself; as Linda Chown describes in her reading of Harry Gordon as the most significant narrator in the novel, Harry "achieves finally an accommodation to his inner self" alone (134). But this accommodation is one that reminds him constantly of his own failure to welcome Lucy when she no longer served him on his own terms. Her footsteps cemented in the sidewalk—a repetition of Mockford's unsettling gait—are the "white things" that cling to him, pulling him away from an aesthetic that consumes its accompanists.

CONCLUSION: UNSETTLING ACCOMPANIMENT AND DISABILITY AESTHETICS

Nearly twenty years before writing *Lucy Gayheart*, Cather was likely beginning to work out some of her earliest thoughts on musical accompaniment and artistic prosthesis, specifically in "The Diamond Mine." In this story, a Greek Jew named Miletus Poppas is the accompanist to the opera sensation Cressida Garnet. Although Poppas does not have a disability as apparent as Mockford's, he does have facial neuralgia that makes him suffer in cold, humid air— which explains why he moves to a warm, dry destination in Asia at the story's end.[5] Poppas differs markedly from Mockford in that his employer is kind and loyal to him, leaving him a fair share of her inheritance; however, like Mockford, he is portrayed as envious and potentially untrustworthy. Cather focuses less on his disability to create these qualities and more on his race, engaging in antisemitic portraiture to call him "a vulture of the vulture race" (*Youth* 84).[6] Nevertheless, in Poppas we can see an early sketch of Cather's theorizing of accompaniment and disability, particularly in this passage, where the narrator describes the relationship between Garnet and her accompanist:

> Poppas was indispensable to her. He was like a book in which she had written down more about herself than she could possibly remember—and it was information that she might need at any moment. He was the one person who knew her absolutely and who saw into the bottom of her grief. An artist's saddest secrets are those that have to do with his artistry. Poppas knew all the simple things that were so desperately hard for Cressida, all the difficult things in which she could count on herself; her stupidities and inconsistencies, the chiaroscuro of the voice

itself and what could be expected from the mind somewhat mismated with it. He knew where she was sound and where she was mended. With him she could share the depressing knowledge of what a wretchedly faulty thing any productive faculty is. (*Youth* 98)

Here Cather characterizes Poppas as a receptacle for the parts of Garnet's artistry that must remain hidden but are also essential to her art. Specifically, Poppas represents a narrative container, a book that records the history of Garnet's artistry as a series of failures and losses.

Acting as a metaphor for the narrative importance of disability-as-imperfection, Poppas prefigures the characters of Mockford and the aging soprano in *Lucy Gayheart*. However, this theme is only lightly touched upon in "The Diamond Mine," as Poppas remains mostly a minor character with narrow symbolic significance. In their theorization of narrative prosthesis, Mitchell and Snyder warn of the unethical problem of employing disability in this way to symbolize artistic imperfection, explaining that the reality and personhood of characters with disability is often overshadowed by symbolic burden: "While stories rely upon the potency of disability as a symbolic figure, they rarely take up disability as an experience of social or political dimensions" (48). Such is perhaps the case with Cather's portrayal of Miletus Poppas as an accompanist with a disability who is not only racially slandered as a "vulture of a vulture race" but whose disability also acts primarily as a vessel for the theme of imperfection as both necessary and unpleasant to behold.

Lucy Gayheart, however, is considerably more developed in its consideration of ethics. Although the novel does charge James Mockford with prosthetic symbolism, it also draws attention to this action as problematic and harmful to those burdened with this task. Moreover, in the way it represents the deception and jealousy that cloud perception of this harmful process, the novel acts as a metatext for the relationship between narrative prosthesis and the normate, revealing how appreciation for the labor of prosthesis is often made impossible

by the perspective of the normate, a viewpoint that projects deception and villainy upon its prosthetic supports in order to validate its
power. Denying friendship and courtesy to their accompanists, the
examples of Sebastian and Harry deliver a moral of artistic accountability, of imagining ways to embrace the presence of disability in
the text rather than expunge it.

One of the ways that Cather imagines this incorporation of disability is through aesthetics, for, in addition to its ethical insights,
Lucy Gayheart also offers trenchant aesthetic reflections on the representation of disability as narrative accompaniment. Expressing
dissatisfaction with art forms that abandon disparity and heteroge-
neity, Cather's novel condemns the practices of conventional aesthetics, emphasizing the continuing need for artists to "embrace
the mocking world," to hone an aesthetic that is open to criticism
and maturation.

In his book *Concerto for the Left Hand*, disability studies author
Michael Davidson argues that artistic prosthesis, despite posing the
ethical dangers that Mitchell and Snyder decry, can sometimes be
executed in such a way that challenges and innovates artistic form.
Davidson examines the example of Maurice Ravel's *Concerto for
the Left Hand*, a piece that Ravel wrote specifically for concert pianist Paul Wittgenstein—brother to Austrian philosopher Ludwig
Wittgenstein—who lost his right arm in World War I. Davidson
argues that the concerto *can* be read as an unethical artistic prosthesis, a compensatory piece that attempts to normalize and fix
Wittgenstein's impairment; however, he argues that Ravel instead
discovers new approaches to musical form by imagining the limits
of playing with one hand: "[B]y enabling Wittgenstein, Ravel dis-
ables Ravel, imposing formal demands upon composition that he
might not have imagined had he not had to think through limits
imposed by writing for one hand. Indeed, the *Concerto for the Left
Hand* is a considerably leaner, less bombastic work than most of
Ravel's orchestral music. In this regard, Ravel's concerto could be
linked to the work of artists whose disability, far from limiting pos-

Fig. 13.3. Austrian pianist Paul Wittgenstein (brother of philosopher Ludwig), who lost his right arm in World War I but continued to play and commission pieces of music written for one hand. Photographer unknown. Wikimedia Commons.

sibilities of design or performance, liberates and changes the terms for composition" (2–3).

Borrowing a term from theorist Tobin Siebers, Davidson calls this adaptive innovation to aesthetics "disability aesthetics." He goes on to argue that disability aesthetics often critiques Kantian standards of disinterest by revealing how they ignore the social and bodily origins of aesthetic judgments:

[D]isinterestedness in Kant can only be validated when it appears to elicit a reciprocal response in others. . . . Here, the specter of social consensus haunts the aesthetic—as though to say, "My appreciation of that which exceeds my body depends on other bodies for confirmation. The body I escape in my endistanced appreciation is reconstituted in my feeling that others must feel the same way." It is this spectral body of the other that disability brings to the fore, reminding us of the contingent, interdependent nature of bodies and their situated relationship to physical ideals. Disability aesthetics foregrounds the extent to which the body becomes thinkable when its totality can no longer be taken for granted, when the social meanings attached to sensory and cognitive values cannot be assumed. (3–4)

Davidson eloquently summarizes the ways in which disability aesthetics emphasizes the importance of challenging disinterestedness by reminding the artist that the body is a site not of escape but of destination. The "spectral body of the other" that is conjured through disability's representation critiques aesthetics that attempt to eliminate the body's limitations by moving beyond them, demanding instead a "reconstitution" of aesthetic ideals within the disabled body. Artistic appreciation is, then, grounded in relationships of physical and social difference, in the "contingent, interdependent nature of bodies and their situated relationship to physical ideals."

In *Lucy Gayheart*, Cather summons just such a "spectral body" to critique artistic disinterestedness as a practice that ignores and dismantles the relevance of corporeal accompaniment. We can see this spectral body literally in the figure of Mockford, whose white form startles Lucy from her aesthetic detachment. Symbolically, the novel contains multiple iterations of spectral bodies and their chilling effects: there is Mockford's dead body, which clings to Sebastian and reappears in Lucy's nightmares; Lucy's frozen corpse, ensnared in a tree submerged in the icy river; and last, Lucy's ghostly footprints in the cement that Harry preserves. With her death, the novel makes of Lucy herself a spectral body, one that disgraces Harry for failing to recognize the importance of corporeal accompaniment. Like Lucy and like Harry, we are invited to be haunted by the spectral bodies of the accompanists in this novel, to be stirred by their indignant demands to register what is lost when aesthetics become complacent, placid, and self-serving.

Returning, then, to the initial inquiry into Cather's aesthetics and the role of strength, one may posit that if *Lucy Gayheart* represents at all artistic triumph over the ill and disabled, it does so in order to critique that kind of art. By contrast, Cather embraces in this novel an aesthetic that opposes bodily perfection and strength by immersing artist and viewer in the undercurrents of corporal uncertainty. The novel's pageant of spectral bodies works to unsettle the aesthetic acts of construction, reception, and interpretation by recalling the hidden work of disability's accompaniment. Indeed, *Lucy Gayheart* enlists its spectral bodies to act as accompanists to the reader's interpretation, asking the reader to remain open to unsteadiness and incompletion rather than cling to fulfillment. In its demand that disability accompany and unsettle the act of interpretation, *Lucy Gayheart* recalls what Joseph Urgo has described in his reading of *Sapphira and the Slave Girl* as planting "dock burs in yo' pants": "[T]he Catherian dock bur is a narrative road sign; something that arrests . . . to push the reader past pleasure toward transcendence by means of a temporary roughness, or discomfort" (28, 37). But while the hermeneutic image of "dock burs in yo' pants" is comedic and playful, the ghostly images of Mockford's grasp and Lucy's cemented footprints are gothic and funereal. *Lucy Gayheart* may suggest more than temporary discomfort, instead narrating a parable that exposes the damage that comfortable aesthetics and interpretation can, and often do, cause. Like *My Ántonia* and *The Song of the Lark*, *Lucy Gayheart* narrates the artist's quest for achieving wholeness; however, like *Sapphira and the Slave Girl*, it showcases the prosthetic bodies indispensable to this quest and the system of deception required to maintain power over them. Giving audience to these prosthetic figures, *Lucy Gayheart* involves us in a gripping, virtuoso performance of disability aesthetics, awakening us to the underhanded practices of an aesthetic that seeks to disentangle itself from its mortal accompaniment.

NOTES

1. For more on the relevance of representations of disability in *My Ántonia*, see Wells.

2. Stouck (463) and Rosowski ("Cather's Female Landscapes" 242) have argued that Mockford represents death rather than his own interests as an artistic character.

3. Skaggs touches briefly upon this side of Sebastian's personality, saying, "At the very least, Sebastian seems a narcissistic man of weak attachments. At the most, he is careless of others and a sexual tease" (161). She suggests that Sebastian and Mockford are lovers and that Mockford "refuses to be played with and discarded" (161) by Sebastian, so he avenges himself upon Sebastian by clinging to him and forcing them both to drown.

4. See also Porter's historical essay in the *Lucy Gayheart* scholarly edition, where he reads Lucy's identification with the soprano as a recognition and acceptance of her limitations as an artist (303); and the essay by Linda Chown, who connects Lucy's learning "from the aging soprano a genuine respect for honest human sentimentality even when filtered through limited talent" to Harry's self-acceptance (132).

5. In the scholarly edition of Cather's *Youth and the Bright Medusa*, which includes the story "The Diamond Mine," Mark Madigan notes Poppas's condition, connecting it to the diagnosis of trigeminal neuralgia (tic douloureux) and confirming the likelihood of environmental triggers like cold air (398).

6. See the essay by Donald Pizer (61–64) for an analysis of antisemitic portraiture in the characters of Miletus Poppas in "The Diamond Mine" and Louis Marcellus from *The Professor's House*.

WORKS CITED

Cather, Willa. *Lucy Gayheart*. 1935. Willa Cather Scholarly Edition, historical essay by David Porter, explanatory notes by Kari A. Ronning and David Porter, textual essay and editing by Frederick M. Link and Kari A. Ronning, U of Nebraska P, 2015.

———. *My Ántonia*. 1918. Willa Cather Scholarly Edition, edited by Charles Mignon with Kari A. Ronning, historical essay by James Woodress, contributions by Kari Ronning, Kathleen Danker, and Emily Levine, U of Nebraska P, 1995.

———. "The Profile." *McClure's Magazine*, vol. 29, June 1907, pp. 135–41, *Willa Cather Archive*, cather.unl.edu/writings/shortfiction/ss002. Accessed 24 July 2021.

———. *The Selected Letters of Willa Cather*, edited by Andrew Jewell and Janis Stout, Knopf, 2013.

———. *The Song of the Lark*. 1915. Willa Cather Scholarly Edition, historical essay and explanatory notes by Ann Moseley, textual essay and editing by Kari A. Ronning, U of Nebraska P, 2012.

———. *Youth and the Bright Medusa*. 1920. Willa Cather Scholarly Edition, historical essay and explanatory notes by Mark J. Madigan, textual essay and editing by Frederick M. Link, Charles W. Mignon, Judith Boss, and Kari A. Ronning, U of Nebraska P, 2009.

Chown, Linda. "'It Came Closer Than That': Willa Cather's *Lucy Gayheart*." *Cather Studies, Volume 2*, edited by Susan J. Rosowski, U of Nebraska P, 1993, pp. 118–39.

Davidson, Michael. *Concerto for the Left Hand: Disability and the Defamiliar Body*. U of Michigan P, 2008.

Garland-Thomson, Rosemarie. *Extraordinary Bodies: Figuring Physical Disability in American Culture and Literature*. Columbia UP, 1997.

Madigan, Mark J. Historical essay and explanatory notes. Cather, *Youth and the Bright Medusa*.

Mallarmé, Stéphane. "Un coup de dés." *Mallarmé: Oeuvres complètes*, Bibliothèque de la Pléiade, Gallimard, 1945, pp. 455–77.

Meyer, Susan. "Contamination, Modernity, Health, and Art in Edith Wharton and Willa Cather." *Willa Cather and the Nineteenth Century*, edited by Anne L. Kaufman and Richard H. Millington, Cather Studies 10, U of Nebraska P, 2015, pp. 97–115.

Mitchell, David T., and Sharon L. Snyder. *Narrative Prosthesis: Disability and the Dependencies of Discourse*. U of Michigan P, 2014.

Pizer, Donald. "Edith Wharton and Willa Cather." *American Naturalism and the Jews: Garland, Norris, Dreiser, Wharton, and Cather*, U of Illinois P, 2008, pp. 50–64.

Porter, David. "From *The Song of the Lark* to *Lucy Gayheart*, and *Die Walküre* to *Die Winterreise*." *Willa Cather at the Modernist Crux*, edited by Ann

Moseley, John J. Murphy, and Robert Thacker, Cather Studies 11, U of Nebraska P, 2017, pp. 149–69.

Porter, David, and Kari A. Ronning. Historical essay and explanatory notes. Cather, *Lucy Gayheart*.

Rosowski, Susan. *The Voyage Perilous: Willa Cather's Romanticism*. U of Nebraska P, 1986.

———. "Willa Cather's Female Landscapes: *The Song of the Lark* and *Lucy Gayheart*." *Women's Studies*, vol. 11, no. 3, December 1984, pp. 233–46.

Skaggs, Merrill Maguire. *After the World Broke in Two: The Later Novels of Willa Cather*. UP of Virginia, 1990.

Stouck, David. *Willa Cather's Imagination*. U of Nebraska P, 1975.

Stout, Janis P. "Willa Cather and the Performing Arts." *The Cambridge Companion to Willa Cather*, edited by Marilee Lindemann, Cambridge UP, 2005, pp. 101–15.

Urgo, Joseph. "'Dock Burs in Yo' Pants': Reading Cather through *Sapphira and the Slave Girl*." *Willa Cather's Southern Connections*, edited by Ann Romines, UP of Virginia, 2000, pp. 24–37.

Van Dyk, Stephen. "Mobility, Comfort and Style—Designing for the Disabled in Victorian America." Unbound Series, Smithsonian Libraries and Archives, blog.library.si.edu/blog/2019/10/03/mobility-comfort-and-style-designing-for-the-disabled-in-victorian-america/. Accessed 12 June 2024.

Wells, Elizabeth. "Something Deficient and Great: Disability Aesthetics and Narrative Prosthesis in Willa Cather's *My Ántonia*." *Modern Fiction Studies*, vol. 67, no. 3, Fall 2021, pp. 487–516.

Woodress, James. *Willa Cather: A Literary Life*. U of Nebraska P, 1987.

CONTRIBUTORS

SARAH CLERE, an independent scholar, is on the editorial board of the *Willa Cather Review*. Her research on Willa Cather has appeared in *Willa Cather and Modern Cultures* (Cather Studies 9), *Studies in the Novel*, and the *Willa Cather Review*.

JOSHUA DOLEŽAL is professor of English emeritus at Central College and a book coach and developmental editor. He is the author of a memoir, *Down from the Mountaintop: From Belief to Belonging*, a Substack newsletter called the *Recovering Academic*, and many essays in venues as varied as the *Chronicle of Higher Education*, *Literature and Medicine*, and the *Kenyon Review*.

LISBETH STRIMPLE FUISZ teaches American literature and writing at Georgetown University. She received a Nebraska Cather Collaborative Grant in 2022 to do archival research on the Cather family's relationship to place. She has published two articles in the *Willa Cather Review* and contributed an essay to the collection *Willa Cather: Critical Insights* (2012).

GENEVA M. GANO is a professor of English at Texas State University. She is the author of *The Little Art Colony and U.S. Modernism: Carmel, Provincetown, Taos* (2020) and a number of essays on hemispheric American literatures, modernism, and multiethnic women's writing. She is completing a manuscript on the impact of the Mexican Revolution on U.S. writing in the early twentieth century.

332

Contributors

JACE GATZEMEYER is an independent scholar from Bancroft, Nebraska. After receiving his PhD in English from Pennsylvania State University in 2019, Jace returned to his home state, teaching writing at numerous Nebraska colleges and universities before settling into a career in grant writing and grants management. He is grants portfolio lead coordinator at the Nebraska Department of Health and Human Services, Division of Public Health, as well as founder and principal consultant at GrantCraft Consulting, LLC.

BARRY HUDEK is a senior lecturer in the English Department at the University of Illinois Urbana-Champaign. He mostly teaches first-year writing classes but has also taught classes on contemporary Black literature as well as introductory literature classes. His dissertation at the University of Mississippi focused on biblical allusions in Faulkner, Cather, and Hurston, with other work on Cather appearing in the *Willa Cather Review*.

SALLIE KETCHAM is the author of *Laura Ingalls Wilder: American Writer on the Prairie* (2014) and several essays on Wilder and her globetrotting daughter, the writer Rose Wilder Lane. She is a former instructor at the Loft Literary Center in Minneapolis. Her work has appeared in the *Willa Cather Review* and *South Dakota History*, among others, and her third children's book is forthcoming from South Dakota Historical Society Press.

MARILEE LINDEMANN is an associate professor of English and executive director of College Park Scholars at the University of Maryland. She is the author of *Willa Cather: Queering America* (1999) and editor of *The Cambridge Companion to Willa Cather* (2005). She edited *Alexander's Bridge* (1997) and *O Pioneers!* (1999) for Oxford University Press and has published numerous articles, chapters in books, review essays, and blogs. She co-directed the Seventeenth International Willa Cather Seminar, held in 2019.

MOLLY METHERD is a professor of English and women's and gender studies and is currently serving as associate dean of the School of Liberal Arts at Saint Mary's College of California. She teaches nineteenth- and twentieth-century American literature and U.S. Latino literature. She has published on transnational and Latino literatures. Her essay on Willa Cather's *Death Comes for the Archbishop* was published in *Western American Literature* (Winter 2021).

ANN ROMINES, professor emerita of English at George Washington University, is a member of the Board of Governors of the National Willa Cather Center, a coeditor of the *Willa Cather Review*, and formerly co-director of two International Cather Seminars in Virginia. She is the author or editor of many essays and books about American women's writing and cultures, including *The Home Plot: Women, Writing, and Domestic Ritual* and the scholarly edition of *Sapphira and the Slave Girl*. She has also joined the board of a new nonprofit, Willa Cather's Virginia, which has purchased and will soon restore Willa Cather's Virginia birthplace.

STEVEN B. SHIVELY is associate professor of English emeritus at Utah State University. He has been an editor of the *Willa Cather Review* and *Teaching Cather* and coeditor of *Teaching the Works of Willa Cather*. His Cather scholarship has focused on the topics of religion, popular culture, and pedagogy, and he has also published essays on the folklorist Benjamin Botkin, Nella Larsen, Harper Lee, and several Nebraska writers. He served for twenty-one years on the Board of Governors of the Willa Cather Foundation.

ELIZABETH WELLS teaches composition and literature courses as an adjunct lecturer at SUNY Cortland. She earned her PhD in English at Louisiana State University in 2018 and has since received multiple honors and fellowships for her research on disability representation. She has published articles on Willa Cather in *Modern Fiction Studies*, the *Willa Cather Review*, and in the forthcoming volume 15 of the Cather Studies series, and she is currently at work on a book titled *Unfit: Disability in Willa Cather's Works*.

HANNAH J. D. WELLS is a PhD candidate in English at Baylor University, where she studies American literature. She is currently writing a dissertation on Delia Bacon's place in the nineteenth-century American literary landscape. Her research has appeared in the *Eudora Welty Review* and the volume *Critical Insights: The Adventures of Tom Sawyer*. She serves as the assistant editor of the *Mark Twain Journal*.

TRACYANN F. WILLIAMS is assistant dean for student support and success at Fordham College at Lincoln Center. Prior to Fordham, she worked for over twenty years as a senior administrator and faculty member at The New School. Her research focuses on mixed-race women in modern fictions. She has received numerous awards and recognition for her research and teaching, including a Helena Rubinstein Foundation fellowship and the Distinguished University Teaching Award from The New School, and she recently served as a fellow in the inaugural Leadership for a New Academy, sponsored by the American Council for Learned Societies.

ANDREW P. WU is completing a dual PhD in educational linguistics and anthropology at the University of Pennsylvania. His research focuses on language diversity and canonical issues in language education, with a focus on language/education policy in East Asia. He studied clinical psychology and English literature at Fu Jen Catholic University (Taiwan) and the University of Bayreuth (Germany), where he completed his master's thesis on Cather's *The Song of the Lark* and the Wagnerian sublime.

masters, 9–10, 52–53, 54, 55–56, 65n8, 73; resistance and agency of, 23, 26, 29, 30, 32, 36, 40, 43n11, 78, 80, 83–84. *See also* Blacks; workers

Slogum House (Sandoz), 204, 226

Slote, Bernice, 70, 106, 206

Smith, Keith D., 166

Smith, Steven M., 281

Snyder, Sharon, xv, 299, 300, 307, 310, 323

social class: in Cather novels, 86, 87; indicators of, 2–3, 5, 6, 235, 243, 245; in Lincoln, 203–4, 206, 207–9, 214, 215–16, 217, 218–19; of Mari Sandoz, 220; in *My Ántonia*, 149, 152; in *Sapphira*, x, 2, 8, 14, 46–47, 48, 81–83; in *Song of the Lark*, 119; upward mobility in, 4; of Willa Cather, ix, 204, 207, 210–11, 213, 215, 216, 217

social norms: defiance of, 119; language and, 238–39, 240, 241–42, 243; in *Song of the Lark*, 127, 130

Society of American Indians (SAI), 195

Soderball, Tiny, 149, 150, 152, 159

"Song of the Lark" (Breton), 161n7

The Song of the Lark (Cather): artistic power in, 297; artists with disabilities in, 298; autobiographical elements in, 113–14; comparison of, with *Lucy Gayheart*, xv, 283–84, 285, 286, 299, 327; feminine heroism in, xii, 119, 136; language diversity in, 248; marriage plot in, 161n2; public reception of, 116, 130, 134,

253; setting of, 128, 139n7, 262; west to east progression in, 120

"Songs of the Slave" (Brown), 72

"A Son of the Celestial" (Cather), 111n4

South, American: Blacks in antebellum, 25, 26; Blacks in postbellum, 87; gender relations in, 48; material culture of, 9; slaves' living conditions in, 29, 31, 35; socioeconomic hierarchy in, 8; songs and music of, 70, 72–73, 86, 87; Willa Cather's memories of, 70

South Carolina, 206

South Dakota, 195

Southern, Eileen, 74

Southwest, American, 125, 236, 258, 262–63

Spanish Johnny, 123, 125, 126, 138n5

Spanish people and culture, 123, 125, 127, 138, 266, 267

spatiality, definition of, 166

Speiser, Jean, 228

Spender, Stephen, 261

Squire, Kelsey, 214–15, 257

"Squirl, He Tote a Bushy Tail," 85

Standing Bear, Chief, 195, 200n10

Standing Rock Sioux, 227

Stansell, Christine, 145

The Steadfast Tin Soldier (Andersen), 307–8

Steavens, Widow, 160, 213

Stouck, David, 101, 220, 277, 278, 311, 328n2

Stout, Janis P.: on aesthetic power, 297, 302; on concept of place, 176; on cultural differences in *Song of the Lark*, 127, 138n6; on

WAS it as it was for Forester in Maurice
to have being endured & live often coming to an
awareness of history. Disagree w essays here - so much
of book is affirmation & Sebastian is enduring figure
She claims authorial mind, more being

Note her own quest as a writer + the Westward shift in early 1900s when the avante guard, surrealist, cubists, + counter cultural movements became / rose to prominace.

The collection of essay covers the whole range of Cather's writing. Included are her 4 masterpieces along with two lesser known, but equally important novels that reveal her ideas about race and disabilities.

At core in these studies is the issue of gender + how Cather spoke created a range of female protagonists. Some Although some are oppressive a reflect the conventional role of women as nineteenth century house keepers, many explore the divergent understanding of women who were the authors of their love life + professional aspirations. Most intriguing were the essays that turn what seems to be minor, or secondary characters into major characters. For instance, Miss Antonia in the eponymist novel is who is developed + romanticism in in the novel My Antonia Jimmy Burden, become comes across a someone a figure The main male character who lived, although heroically, a conventional life. Her friend may l become the more interesting + daring female character, carving out her own career + deciding who her lover would be + how they should act.